Genealogical & Local History Books in Print

5th Edition

General Reference & World Resources Volume

GENEALOGICAL *&* LOCAL HISTORY BOOKS IN PRINT

5th Edition

General Reference *&* World Resources Volume

Compiled and Edited by
Marian Hoffman

G&LHBIP

Published by Genealogical Publishing Co., Inc.
1001 N. Calvert St., Baltimore, MD 21202
Library of Congress Catalogue Card Number 97-70715
International Standard Book Number 0-8063-1538-5
Made in the United States of America

Contents

Introduction

The *General Reference & World Resources Volume*, the second volume of the new 5th edition of *Genealogical & Local History Books in Print*, contains (1) a list of genealogical books that are not linked to a specific geographical location and (2) a list of books dealing with particular countries (other than the U.S.) and their people. Divided into two sections—General Reference and World Resources—this volume lists several thousand books that were available and in print at the time of this book's publication.

Typically, each entry gives the full title of the work, the author or sponsoring institution, date of publication, whether indexed or illustrated, in cloth or paper, number of pages, selling price, and vendor number (publisher, bookseller, etc.). Sometimes the same work is available from more than one source. Any inconsistencies and/or omissions in the listed information reflect what was provided to us by the vendor. Vendors are listed separately in the front of the book, both numerically and alphabetically, with addresses and special ordering information given to enable you to place orders. In addition, for maximum convenience in your research, this book contains both an index of authors and an index of titles.

To order any of the listed publications, locate the vendor number at the bottom right of each listing. The names and addresses of these vendors are listed in the front of the book. Send your order to the vendor and include the proper fee. Be sure to mention that you saw their work advertised in *Genealogical & Local History Books in Print*. Unless otherwise stated next to the price or in the special ordering information included in the List of Vendors on page xi, the prices given in this volume include shipping and handling costs. They do not, however, include sales tax. *You must pay the state sales tax required by the government of the state in which you reside if you order books from vendors operating in your state.*

The aim of this volume is to include as many books that fit into the categories of general reference or world resources as possible. Some books that are printed on demand or do not remain in print for any length of time have not been included. Compilation of the next edition of the *General Reference & World Resources Volume* will begin almost as soon as this volume is published; all authors or publishers are invited to list their publications. Write for information to Genealogical & Local History Books in Print, 1001 N. Calvert Street, Baltimore, MD 21202. Authors and publishers are also encouraged to send in listings for the *Family History Volume* and the *U.S. Sources & Resources Volume* of *Genealogical & Local History Books in Print*.

List of Vendors
(organized numerically)

G0006 Madrue Chavers-Wright, 2410 Barker Avenue, Suite 14-G, Bronx, New York 10467-7634; tel. 718-654-9445

G0010 Genealogical Publishing Co., Inc., 1001 N. Calvert Street, Baltimore, MD 21202-3879; tel. 410-837-8271; Fax: 410-752-8492
Shipping & handling: On orders over $10.00: one book $3.50, each additional book $1.25; on orders totaling $10.00 or less: $1.50. When ordering sets: First volume $3.50, each additional volume, $1.25. Maryland residents add 5% sales tax; Michigan residents add 6%.

G0011 Clearfield Company, 1001 N. Calvert Street, Baltimore, MD 21202; tel. 410-625-9004; Fax: 410-752-8492
Shipping & handling: One item $3.50; each additional item $1.25. MD residents add 5% sales tax, MI residents add 6%.

G0026 Donald Underwood, 12001 Prospect Hill Drive, Gold River, CA 95670

G0028 Susan R. Alexander, PO Box 460614, Houston, TX 77056-8614

G0050 Sandra Johnson, Marketing Manager, University of Nebraska Press 312 N. 14th Street, Lincoln, NE 68588-0484; tel. 402-472-5937; Fax: 402-472-0308

G0061 Family Publications—Rose Caudle Terry, 5628 60th Drive, NE, Marysville, WA 98270-9509; e-mail: cxwp57a@prodigy.com

G0064 Arkansas Research, PO Box 303, Conway, AR 72033; Fax: 501-470-1120

G0069 Gloucester County Historical Society, 17 Hunter Street, Woodbury, NJ 08096-4605

G0070 Remsen-Steuben Historical Society, PO Box 284, Remsen, NY 13438

G0074 Joan W. Peters, PO Box 144, Broad Run, VA 22014

G0081 Genealogical Books in Print, 6818 Lois Drive, Springfield, VA 22150
Shipping & handling: $1.75 for first $10.00; 35¢ for each additional $10.00.

G0082 Picton Press, PO Box 250, Rockport, ME 04856; tel. 207-236-6565, (sales) 800-742-8667; Fax: 207-236-6713; e-mail: Picton@midcoast.com
Shipping & handling: $4.00 for first book, $2.00 for each additional book.

G0093 Heart of the Lakes Publishing, PO Box 299, Interlaken, NY 14847-0299; tel. 800-782-9687; Fax: 607-532-4684; e-mail: HLP Books@AOL.com
Visa & MasterCard accepted. Shipping additional: $4.00 for first book; $1.00 for each additional book; most shipping via UPS—provide appropriate delivery address.

G0109 Indiana Historical Society, 315 W. Ohio Street, Indianapolis, IN 46202; tel. 317-232-1882
Shipping & handling: $2.75 for first book, $1.00 for each additional book.

G0112 W. E. Morrison & Co., Ovid, NY 14521; tel. 607-869-2561

G0117 John T. Humphrey, PO Box 15190, Washington, DC 20003; tel. 202-544-4142

G0118 Scholarly Resources, 104 Greenhill Avenue, Wilmington, DE 19805-1897; tel. 800-772-8937

G0130 South Carolina Department of Archives and History, PO Box 11669, Columbia, SC 29211; tel. 803-734-8590
   Make checks payable to "Archives and History."

G0134 Elder's Book Store, 2115 Elliston Place, Nashville, TN 37203

G0135 Kenneth Luttner, Ohio Genealogy Center, PO Box 395, St. Peter, MN 56082; tel. 507-388-7158

G0140 Family Line Publications, Rear 63 E Main Street, Westminster, MD 21157; tel. 800-876-6103
   Shipping & handling: First item $2.00, each additional item $.50.

G0145 Mildred S. Wright, 140 Briggs, Beaumont, TX 77707-2329; tel. 409-832-2308

G0148 Archive Publishing/Microform Books, 4 Mayfair Circle, Oxford, MA 01540-2722; tel. 508-987-0881

G0150 Lancaster Mennonite Historical Society, 2215 Millstream Road, Lancaster, PA 17602-1499; tel. 717-393-9745

G0153 Mary Dudley-Higham, c/o Genesis Publications, 5272 Williams Road, Suisun, CA 94585

G0160 Hope Farm Press & Bookshop (publishers & distributors), 1708 Route 212, Saugerties, NY 12477; tel. 914-679-6809 (inquiries; 1-6 p.m. eastern time), 800-883-5778 (orders); e-mail: hopefarm@hopefarm.com; website: http://www.hopefarm.com
   Shipping & handling: $3.95 for first book ordered, $1.00 for each additional one. NY residents must pay sales tax.

G0174 Colorado Genealogical Society Inc, Pub. Dir., PO Box 9218, Denver, CO 80209

G0179 Tuttle Antiquarian Books, Inc., 28 South Main Street, Rutland, VT 05701; tel. 802-773-8229; Fax: 802-773-1493; e-mail: Tuttbook@interloc.com

G0183 Tennessee Valley Publishing, PO Box 52527, Knoxville, TN 37950-2527; tel. 800-762-7079; Fax: 423-584-0113; e-mail: tvp1@ix.netcom.com

G0192 Dr. Larry D. Crummer, 2649 Mission Greens Drive, San Jose, CA 95148-2568; tel. 408-270-4113

G0193 German Genealogy Digest, Inc., 245 N Vine #106, Salt Lake City, UT 84103

G0195 Origins, 4327 Milton Avenue, Janesville, WI 53546; tel. 608-757-2777

G0197 Ernest Thode, RR 7, Box 306GB, Kern Road, Marietta, OH 45750-9437

G0198 Carl Boyer, 3rd, PO Box 220333, Santa Clarita, CA 91322-0333

G0203 Family History Educators, PO Box 510606, Salt Lake City, UT 84151-0606; tel. 801-359-7391; Fax: 801-359-7391

G0204 Blount County Genealogical & Historical Society, PO Box 4986, Maryville, TN 37802-4986

G0245 Rosamond Houghton Van Noy, 4700 Hwy. K East, Conover, WI 54519; tel. 715-479-5044

G0256 Arthur Louis Finnell Books, 9033 Lyndale Avenue S., Suite 108, Bloomington, MN 55420-3535

G0259 Higginson Book Company, Publishers and reprinters of genealogy and local history, 148-BP Washington Street, PO Box 778, Salem MA 01970; tel. 508-745-7170; Fax: 508-745-8025.
   Complete catalogs are available free with your order, or $4.00 separately. To order: We accept checks or money orders, or MC/VISA. Please add $3.50 for

the first book and $1.00 for each additional book. We bind our books to order; please allow six to eight weeks for delivery, plus two additional weeks for hardcover books.

G0287 Larry G. Shuck, 164 Julep Lane, Cincinnati, OH 45218-1206

G0322 Rhoda J. Morley, 3215 Hwy. 441-N., Okeechobee, FL 34972-1854; tel. 941-467-2482

G0333 Oscar H. Stroh, Ph.D., 1531 Fishing Creek Valley Road, Harrisburg, PA 17112-9240; tel. 717-599-5117
  Add $3.00 for packing and mailing regardless of number of books ordered.

G0372 Robert Haydon, 12 Fenchley Court, Little Rock, AR 72212; tel. 501-224-1313; Fax: 501-224-7081

G0406 New England Historic Genealogical Society Sales Dept., 160 N. Washington Street, 4th floor, Boston, MA 02114-2120; tel. 617-536-5740; Fax: 617-624-0325; e-mail: nehgs@nehgs.org

G0448 Dr. Lawrence Kent, 608 South Conway Road, Suite G, Orlando, FL 32807-104408

G0450 Kinship, 60 Cedar Heights Road, Rhinebeck, NY 12572; tel. 914-876-4592; e-mail: 71045.1516@compuserve.com
  Shipping & handling: $1.50 per book. NY residents must add sales tax. 10% discount if 4 or more books are ordered.

G0455 Irish Genealogical Foundation, PO Box 7575, Kansas City, MO 64116; tel. 816-454-2410; Fax: 816-454-2410; e-mail: 71334.3034@compuserve.com

G0457 American Association for State and Local History, 530 Church Street, #600, Nashville, TN 37219-2325

G0458 AKB Publications—Annette K. Burgert, 691 Weavertown Road, Myerstown, PA 17067-2642

G0460 Janice L. Jones, 4839 Towne Centre Drive, St. Louis, MO 63128-2816

G0465 Jaussi Publications, 284 East 400 South, Orem, Utah 84058-6312; tel. 801-225-7384

G0467 Judy A. Deeter, 4 Altezza Drive, Mission Viejo, CA 92692-5107

G0473 Antonia S. Mattheou/GFHC, 75-21 177 Street, Flushing, NY 11366; Fax: 718-591-9342

G0474 Rose Family Association, 1474 Montelegre Drive, San Jose, CA 95120; tel. 408-268-2137

G0475 Mrs. Sigrid R. Maldonado—AS WAS Publishing, PO Box 40075, Fort Wayne, IN 46804-0075
  Indiana residents add sales tax of $1.20 each. Shipping and handling in the U.S.: $3.00 for each book. Contact vendor for shipping and handling to locations outside the U.S.

G0478 Ancestor Publishers, 6166 Janice Way, Dept. GBIP96, Arvada, CO 80004-5160; tel. 800-373-0816: Fax: 303-425-9709; e-mail: ancestor@net1comm.com

G0481 Leo Baca, 1707 Woodcreek, Richardson, TX 75082

G0485 ACPL Foundation—PERSI Project, PO Box 2270, Ft. Wayne, IN 46801; tel. 219-424-7241, ext. 2227; Fax: 219-422-9688; e-mail: mclegg@everest.acpl.lib.in.us

G0488 Illinois State Genealogical Society, PO Box 10195, Springfield, IL 62791-0195; tel. 217-789-1968

G0490 Santa Monica Press, PO Box 1076, Dept. 321, Santa Monica, CA 90406; tel. 310-395-4658; Fax: 310-395-6394

G0491 Westland Publications, PO Box 117, McNeal, AZ 85617; e-mail: worldrt@primenet.com

G0492 Marietta Publishing Company, 2115 North Denair Avenue, Turlock, CA 95382; tel. 209-634-9473
California residents add 7.375% sales tax.

G0496 TCI Genealogical Resources, PO Box 15839, San Luis Obispo, CA 93406; tel. 805-739-1145

G0501 Illinois State Historical Society, 1 Old State Capitol Plaza, Springfield, IL 62701-1507; tel. 217-782-4286; Fax: 217-524-8042

G0502 JWC Low Company, PO Box 472012, San Francisco, CA 94147

G0504 Family History World, PO Box 22045, Salt Lake City, UT 84122-1045, Publication Division, The Genealogical Institute; tel. 800-377-6058

G0513 Vicki Renfroe, PO Box 872, Alvin, TX 77512

G0515 Round Tower Books, PO Box 12407, Fort Wayne, IN 46863-2407

G0516 Les Tucker, 1116 NW 197th Street, Edmond, OK 73003

G0518 Hearthside Press, 5735-A Telegraph Road, Alexandria, VA 22303; tel. 703-960-0086; Fax: 703-960-0087; e-mail: info@hearthstonebooks.com; website: www.hearthstonebooks.com

G0521 Jean S. Morris, PO Box 8530, Pittsburgh, PA 15220-0530

G0523 Iron Gate Publishing, PO Box 999, Niwot, CO 80544; tel. 303-530-2551; e-mail: FNC|Z92C@prodigy.com

G0525 Richard H. Taylor, 1211 Seneca Road, Benton Harbor, MI 49022; tel. 616-925-9813

G0531 The Bookmark, PO Box 90, Knightstown, IN 46148; tel. 800-876-5133, ext. 170; Fax: 1-800-695-8153
Indiana residents must add 5% sales tax.

G0536 Closson Press, 1935 Sampson Drive, Apollo, PA 15613-9209; Fax: 412-337-9484; e-mail: rclosson@nauticom.net
Shipping and handling in the Continental U.S.A. is $4.00 for any size order except for special order books where additional shipping/handling is requested.

G0546 Family Historian Books, 404 Tule Lake Road, Tacoma, WA 98444; tel. 800-535-0118; 206-535-0108

G0548 Howard L. Porter III, PO Box 7533, Winter Haven, FL 33883

G0549 Mountain Press, PO Box 400, Signal Mountain, TN 37377-0400; tel. 423-886-6369; Fax: 423-886-5312

G0552 AGLL, PO Box 329, Bountiful, UT 84011-0329; tel. 801-298-5446
Contact vendor for shipping and handling rates.

G0553 The Library Shop, The Library of Virginia, 800 E. Broad Street, Richmond, VA 23219-1905; 804-692-3524; Fax: 804-692-3528
Add $4.50 shipping & handling for first book, $.50 each additional book. VA residents add 4.5% tax.

G0554 Pennsylvania Historical & Museum Commission, Publications Sales Program, PO Box 11466, Harrisburg, PA 17108-1466; tel. 717-783-2618; Fax: 717-787-8312

G0555 Aberdeen & North East Scotland Family History Society, 164 King Street, Aberdeen, Scotland, UK AB24 5BD; Fax: 011 441 224 639096

G0556 Scottish Genealogy Association, 15 Victoria Terrace, Edinburgh, Scotland, UK EH1 2JL; Fax: 011 441 312 203677

G0557 Society of Genealogists, 14 Charterhouse Buildings, Goswell Road, London, England, UK Ec1M 7BA; tel. 011 441 71 251 8799

G0558 Public Record Office, The Bookshop, Ruskin Avenue, Kew Surrey, England, UK TW9 4DU; tel. 011 441 81 392-5271; Fax: 011 441 81 392 5266; e-mail: enterprises.pro.kew@gtnet.gov.uk

G0559 Avotaynu, Inc., PO Box 900, Teaneck, NJ 07666; tel. 201-387-7200; Fax: 201-387-2855; e-mail info@avotaynu.com; web: www.avotaynu.com
S&h in U.S.: Up to $25, $2.50; $25.01 to $35, $3.50; $35.01 to $75, $4.50; $75.01 to $130, $6.50; $130 and above, $8.50. NJ residents add 6% sales tax.

G0560 Gale Research, PO Box 33477, Detroit, MI 48232-5477; Fax: 1-800-414-5043; e-mail: galeord@gale.com or 72203.1552@compuserve.com
Sales tax applicable in CA, CO, CT, FL, GA, KY, MA, MD, NJ, NY, OH, PA, TN, TX, VA; and Canada.

G0561 Hunterdon House, 38 Swan Street, Lambertville, NJ 08530; tel. 609-397-2523

G0562 Bookshop, Institute of Heraldic and Genealogical Studies, 72-82 Northgate, Canterbury, Kent CT2 1BA, England; tel. 011 441 227 768664; Fax: 011 441 227 765617

G0563 Society of Australian Genealogists, Richmond Villa, 120 Kent Street, Sydney NSW Australia 2000; Fax: 61-2-241-4872

G0564 Ulster Historical Foundation, Balmoral Buildings, 12 College Square East, Belfast, Ireland

G0565 National Archives and Records Administration, NWPS Dept. 735, PO Box 100793, Atlanta, GA 30384; tel. 800-234-8861 (credit card orders)
Make all checks payable to National Archives Trust Fund. Shipping & handling: Up to $50.00, $3.00; $50.01 to $100.00, $5.00; over $100, add 5% of merchandise total.

G0566 The Library of Congress, Humanities and Social Sciences Division, Washington, DC 20540

G0568 The Ontario Genealogical Society, 40 Orchard View Boulevard, Suite 102, Toronto, Canada M4R 1B9; tel. 416-489-0734; Fax: 416-489-9803; Website: http://www.interlog.com/~dreed/ogs_home.htm

G0569 Dr. George K. Schweitzer, 407 Ascot Court, Knoxville, TN 37923-5807

G0570 Ancestry, Inc., PO Box 476, Salt Lake City, UT 84110-0476; Fax: 801-531-1798
Call for shipping & handling costs. Utah residents add 6.13% sales tax.

G0574 Ye Olde Genealogie Shoppe, 9605 Vandergriff Road, PO Box 39128, Indianapolis, IN 46239; tel. 317-862-3330; Fax: 317-862-2599
Shipping & handling: $4.00 per order. IL, IN, MI, MN, OH, & WI residents add sales tax.

G0575 Donna Przecha, 10576 Rancho Carmel Drive, San Diego, CA 92128

G0576 Sutton Publishing Ltd., U.S.: c/o Books International, PO Box 605, Herndon, VA 20172-0605; tel. 703-435-7064: Fax: 703-689-0660. UK address: Phoenix Mill, Far Thrupp, Stroud, Gloucestershire GL5 2BU, England
Shipping & handling: $5.00 for first book, $1.00 ea. additional book.

G0579 Phillimore & Co. Ltd., Shopwyke Manor Barn, Chichester, West Sussex PO20 6BG, England; tel. 011 441 243 787636: Fax: 011 441 243 787639
Add 15% for overseas shipping and handling. Overseas customers are asked to pay by G.B. pounds sterling bank draft or credit card.

G0580 Betterway Books, 1507 Dana Avenue, Cincinnati, OH 45207; tel. 800-289-0963
 Shipping & handling: $3.50 for first book, $1.00 for each additional book. OH residents add 5.5% sales tax.

G0581 Henry Z Jones, Jr., F.A.S.G., PO Box 261388, San Diego, CA 92196-1388
 California residents pay 6% sales tax.

G0583 Park Genealogical Books, PO Box 130968, Roseville, MN 55113-0968; tel. 612-488-4416; Fax: 612-488-2653; e-mail: mbakeman@parkbooks.com

G0584 General Register Office, Joyce House, 8-11 Lombard Street East, Dublin 2, Ireland

G0586 North Carolina Division of Archives and History, Historical Publications Section Department of Cultural Resources, 109 East Jones Street, Raleigh, NC 27601-2807; tel. 919-733-7442; Fax: 919-733-1439
 Shipping & handling: $2.00 for orders of $1.00-$5.00; $3.00 for orders of $6.00-$12.00; $3.00 for orders over $12.00. NC residents add 6% sales tax.

G0587 New York State Archives and Records Administration, 10D45 Cultural Education Center, Albany, NY 12230
 Make check payable to New York State Archives.

G0588 Federation of Family History Societies, FFHS Publications, 2-4 Killer Street, Ramsbottom, Bury, Lancs BL0 9BZ, England
 Payment should be made out to FFHS Publications. Sterling money orders are preferable to bankers checks for overseas orders. Check for shipping costs.

G0589 General Register Office for Scotland, New Register House, Edinburgh EH1 3YT, Scotland; tel. 011-441-31-334-0380; Fax: 011-441-31-314-4400

G0590 Broadfoot Publishing Company, 1907 Buena Vista Circle, Wilmington, NC 28405; tel. 910-686-4816; Fax: 910-686-4379
 Shipping & handling: $4.00 for the first volume, $1.75 for each additional volume. NC residents add 6% sales tax (before adding shipping).

G0591 The National Library of Wales, Aberystwyth, Dyfed SY23 3BU, Wales

G0601 Texas State Archives, Texas State Library, PO Box 12927, Austin, TX 78711-1276
 Texas residents add 8% sales tax. Add $1.00 to total amount for shipping & handling on all orders. Make checks or money orders payable to the Texas State Library.

G0602 Brent H. Holcomb, PO Box 21766, Columbia, South Carolina 29221
 Mailing charges: $3.00 for first book, $1.00 for each additional book to the same address.

G0604 The Genealogy Centre, 4-22 Butcher Street, Derry BT48 6HL, Northern Ireland; Fax: 011 441 504 374818
 Shipping & handling for overseas (surface mail): Up to £10, £3.00; £10 to £25, £6.00; over £5.00, £9.00.

G0608 The Publishing Post, 3406 Middleton Way, Colleyville, TX 76034; e-mail: JGRP@aol.com

G0609 T.L.C. Genealogy, PO Box 403369, Miami Beach, FL 33140-1369; tel. 800-858-8558; e-mail: staff@tlc-gen.com; website: http://www.tlc-gen.com/
 All prices are postpaid. Florida residents add 6.5% sales tax.

G0610 Southern Historical Press. Inc., PO Box 1267, 275 West Broad Street, Greenville, SC 29602-1267; tel. 864-233-2346
 Shipping & handling: $3.50 for first book, $1.50 for each additional book. SC residents add 5% sales tax.

G0611 Frontier Press (publishers and distributors), PO Box 3715, Suite 3, Galveston, TX 77552; tel. (order line) 800-772-7559; Fax: 409-740-7988; e-mail: kgfrontier@aol.com
Shipping & handling: $3.50 for the first book; $1.00 for each additional book. Phone for shipping rates to international and Canadian addresses.

G0614 Alberta Genealogical Society, Box 12015, Edmonton, Alberta T5J 3L2, Canada
Prices include mailing cost within Canada. Write for price when mailing outside of Canada. When ordering, add 7% GST (tax).

G0615 Western Pennsylvania Genealogical Society, 4400 Forbes Avenue, Pittsburgh, PA 15213-4080
Add $2.50 shipping & handling for first item, then $1.00 for each addiitonal item. PA residents must pay tax on items & handling.

G0616 Heraldry Today, Parliament Piece, Ramsbury, Marlborough, Wiltshire, SN8 2QH, England 01672 52617; Fax: 011 441 672 520183; e-mail: heraldry@cccp.net Contact vendor for cost of postage.

G0617 Maryland Historical Society, 201 West Monument Street, Baltimore, MD 21201
Non-member and book trade orders to: Alan C. Hood and Co., Inc., PO Box 775, Chambersburg, PA 17201. Add $3.50 shipping & handling; MD residents add 5% sales tax; PA residents add 6%.

G0618 The Everton Publishers, Inc., PO Box 368, Logan, UT 84323-0368; tel. 800-443-6325; Fax: 801-752-0425
Add $1.50 shipping & handling for first book, $.50 for each additional book.

G0619 Flyleaf Press, 4 Spencer Villas, Glenageary, Co. Dublin, Ireland

G0620 General Society of Mayflower Descendants, c/o Mayflower Families PO Box 3297, Plymouth, MA 02361
Shipping & handling (in US): $3.00 for orders under $12.00, $4.00 for orders over $13.00. MA residents add 5% sales tax.

G0627 National Genealogical Society, 4517 17th Street N., Arlington, VA 22207-2399; e-mail: 76702.2417@compuserve.com

G0628 California Genealogical Society, 300 Brannon Street, Suite 409, PO Box 77105, San Francisco, CA 94107-0105; tel. 415-777-9936
Shipping & handling: $2 for each book. CA residents add 8.5% sales tax.

G0629 Family History Library, Salt Lake City Distribution Center, 1999 West 1700 South, Salt Lake City, UT 84104-4233; Fax: 801-240-3685

G0632 Iberian Publishing Company (publishers and distributors), 548 Cedar Creek Drive, Athens, GA 30605-3408; tel. (orders) 800-394-8634; e-mail: iberian@ix.netcom.com; website: http://www.netcom.com/~iberian/

G0637 D. R. Barnes Associates, Box 5755, Rockville, MD 20855-0755

G0638 University Press of Mississippi, 3825 Ridgewood Road, Jackson, MS 39211

G0639 University of Minnesota Press, 2037 University Avenue Southeast, Minneapolis, MN 55414

G0640 Dundurn Group, University of Toronto Press, 250 Sonwil Drive, Buffalo, NY 14225 800-565-9523; Fax: 800-221-9985
Shipping & handling: $4.00 per book.

G0641 David Dobson, 46 Lawmill Gardens, St. Andrews, Fife, Scotland KY168QS

G0642 Frances McDonnell, 46 Lawmill Gardens, St. Andrews, Fife, Scotland KY168QS

G0643 Federation of Genealogical Societies, PO Box 830220, Richardson, TX 75083-0220

G0660 McClain Printing Company, PO Box 403, 212 Main Street, Parson, West Virginia 26287; Fax: 304-478-4658

G0661 Southwest Oklahoma Genealogical Society, PO Box 148, Lawton, OK 73502-0148
  Shipping & handling: Add $2.50 for first book, $.50 for each additional book.

G0663 Diane Snyder Ptak, 12 Tice Road, Albany, NY 12203

G0669 Willow Bend Books, Route 1, Box 15A, Lovettsville, VA 22080-9703

G0671 Gloryann Hawkins Young, Route 2, Box 55, Wister, OK 74966

G0710 Bryan County Heritage Association, PO Box 153, Calera, OK 74730-0153
  Shipping & handling: $2.50 for first book; $1.00 for each additional book.

G0723 Illiana Genealogical & Historical Society Box 207, Danville, IL 61834-0207

G0726 Judith Allison Walters, PO Box 129, Bothell, WA 98041

G0729 Oklahoma Genealogical Society, Special Publications Chairman, PO Box 12986, Oklahoma City, OK 73157
  Shipping & handling: $2.50 for 1st book; $.50 each additional book. OK residents add 8.375% sales tax.

G0731 H. V. Roberts, Gullivers, Main Street, Tugby, Leicestershire, LE7 9WD England

G0732 Joyce Schneider Oshrin, Panther Valley, 72 Bald Eagle Drive, Hackettstown, NJ 07840

G0735 Welton Chamberlain, PO Box 246, Pinckney, MI 48169

G0742 Chicago Genealogical Society, PO Box 1160, Chicago, IL 60690
  Shipping & handling: $2.50 for first book; $.50 each additional book.

G0768 Omnigraphics, Inc., Penobscot Building, Detroit, Michigan 48226

G0769 Eriksson Enterprises, 850 E. 1050 N. Bountiful, UT 84010

G0770 Masthof Press, Route 1, Box 20, Morgantown, PA 19543-9701

G0771 Linda Croupe, E.E., 210 Allan Drive, Bolton, Ontario, Canada L7E 1Y7

G0772 Random House, Inc., Attn: Order Entry Department, 400 Hahn Road, Westminster, MD 21157

G0775 Professor Robert Rice, 14466 Sunrise Drive, NE, Bainbridge Island, WA 98110

G0776 Oryx Press, 4041 North Central Avenue, Suite 700, Phoenix, AZ 85012-3397
  Add 10% for shipping. Arizona and Canadian residents add sales tax.

G0777 F-AMI-LEE Publishing Company, 37070–82nd Avenue, Decatur, MI 49045

G0779 Association of Professional Genealogists, 3421 M Street Northwest, Suite 236, Washington, DC 20007-3552

G0780 Scriptorium Family History Centre, 386 Ferrars Atreet, Albert Park, Australia; Fax: (03) 696 2382

G0781 American Library Association, 50 E. Huron Street, Chicago, IL 60611; Fax: 312-944-8741

G0782 Jan Jennings, 3324 Crail Way, Glendale, CA 91206

G0784 Lower Delmarva Genealogical Society, PO Box 3602, Salisbury, Maryland 21802-3602
  MD residents add $1.75 sales tax.

List of Vendors
(organized alphabetically)

Aberdeen & North East Scotland Family History Society, Vendor G0555
ACPL Foundation—PERSI Project, Vendor G0485
AGLL, Vendor G0552
AKB Publications, Vendor G0458
Alberta Genealogical Society, Vendor G0614
Alexander, Susan R., Vendor G0028
American Association for State and Local History, Vendor G0457
American Library Association, Vendor G0781
Ancestor Publishers, Vendor G0478
Ancestry, Inc., Vendor G0570
Archive Publishing/Microform Books, Vendor G0148
Arkansas Research, Vendor G0064
Association of Professional Genealogists, Vendor G0779
Avotaynu, Inc., Vendor G0559
Baca, Leo, Vendor G0481
Barnes, D. R., Associates, Vendor G0637
Betterway Books, Vendor G0580
Blount County Genealogical & Historical Society, Vendor G0204
Bookmark, The, Vendor G0531
Boyer, Carl, 3rd, Vendor G0198
Broadfoot Publishing Company, Vendor G0590
Bryan County Heritage Association, Vendor G0710
Burgert, Annette K., Vendor G0458
California Genealogical Society, Vendor G0628
Chamberlain, Welton, Vendor G0735
Chavers-Wright, Madrue, Vendor G0006
Chicago Genealogical Society, Vendor G0742
Clearfield Company, Vendor G0011
Closson Press, Vendor G0536
Colorado Genealogical Society Inc., Vendor G0174
Croupe, Linda, Vendor G0771
Crummer, Dr. Larry D., Vendor G0192
Deeter, Judy A., Vendor G0467
Dobson, David, Vendor G0641
Dudley-Higham, Mary, Genesis Publications, Vendor G0153
Dundurn Group, Vendor G0640
Elder's Book Store, Vendor G0134
Eriksson Enterprises, Vendor G0769
Everton Publishers, Inc., The, Vendor G0618
F-AMI-LEE Publishing Company, Vendor G0777
Family Publications—Rose Caudle Terry, Vendor G0061
Family Historian Books, Vendor G0546
Family History Educators, Vendor G0203
Family History World, Vendor G0504

Family Line Publications, Vendor G0140
Family History Library, Vendor G0629
Federation of Family History Societies, Vendor G0588
Federation of Genealogical Societies, Vendor G0643
Finnell, Arthur Louis, Books, Vendor G0256
Flyleaf Press, Vendor G0619
Frontier Press, Vendor G0611
Gale Research, Vendor G0560
Genealogical Books in Print, Vendor G0081
Genealogical Publishing Co., Inc., Vendor G0010
Genealogy Centre, The, Vendor G0604
General Register Office (Ireland), Vendor G0584
General Society of Mayflower Descendants, Vendor G0620
General Register Office for Scotland, Vendor G0589
German Genealogy Digest, Inc., Vendor G0193
Gloucester County Historical Society, Vendor G0069
Haydon, Robert, Vendor G0372
Heart of the Lakes Publishing, Vendor G0093
Hearthside Press, Vendor G0518
Heraldry Today, Vendor G0615
Higginson Book Co., Vendor G0259
Holcomb, Brent H., Vendor G0602
Hope Farm Press & Bookshop, Vendor G0160
Humphrey, John T., Vendor G0117
Hunterdon House, Vendor G0561
Iberian Publishing Company, Vendor G0632
Illiana Genealogical & Historical Society, Vendor G0723
Illinois State Genealogical Society, Vendor G0488
Illinois State Historical Society, Vendor G0501
Indiana Historical Society, Vendor G0109
Institute of Heraldic and Genealogical Studies, Vendor G0562
Irish Genealogical Foundation, Vendor G0455
Iron Gate Publishing, Vendor G0523
Jaussi Publications, Vendor G0465
Jennings, Jan, Vendor G0782
Jones, Henry Z, Jr., F.A.S.G., Vendor G0581
Jones, Janice L., Vendor G0460
JWC Low Company, Vendor G0502
Kent, Dr. Lawrence, Vendor G0448
Kinship, Vendor G0450
Lancaster Mennonite Historical Society, Vendor G0150
Library of Congress, The, Vendor G0566
Library of Virginia, The, Vendor G0553
Lower Delmarva Genealogical Society, Vendor G0784
Maldonado, Mrs. Sigrid R., AS WAS Publishing, Vendor G0475
Marietta Publishing Company, Vendor G0492
Maryland Historical Society, Vendor G0617
Masthof Press, Vendor G0770
Mattheou, Antonia S./GFHC, Vendor G0473
McClain Printing Company, Vendor G0660
McDonnell, Frances, Vendor G0642
Morley, Rhoda J., Vendor G0322

Morris, Jean S., Vendor G0521
Morrison, W. E., & Co., Vendor G0112
Mountain Press, Vendor G0549
National Archives and Records Administration, Vendor G0565
National Library of Wales, The, Vendor G0591
National Genealogical Society, Vendor G0627
New England Historic Genealogical Society, Vendor G0406
New York State Archives and Records Administration, Vendor G0587
North Carolina Division of Archives and History, Vendor G0586
Ohio Genealogy Center, Kenneth Luttner, Vendor G0135
Oklahoma Genealogical Society, Vendor G0729
Omnigraphics, Inc., Vendor G0768
Ontario Genealogical Society, The, Vendor G0568
Origins, Vendor G0195
Oryx Press, Vendor G0776
Oshrin, Joyce Schneider, Vendor G0732
Park Genealogical Books, Vendor G0583
Pennsylvania Historical & Museum Commission, Vendor G0554
Peters, Joan W., Vendor G0074
Phillimore & Co. Ltd., Vendor G0579
Picton Press, Vendor G0082
Porter, Howard L., III, Vendor G0548
Przecha, Donna, Vendor G0575
Ptak, Diane Snyder, Vendor G0663
Public Record Office, Vendor G0558
Publishing Post, The, Vendor G0608
Random House, Inc., Vendor G0772
Remsen-Steuben Historical Society, Vendor G0070
Renfroe, Vicki, Vendor G0513
Rice, Professor Robert, Vendor G0775
Roberts, H. V., Vendor G0731
Rose Family Association, Vendor G0474
Round Tower Books, Vendor G0515
Santa Monica Press, Vendor G0490
Scholarly Resources, Vendor G0118
Schweitzer, Dr. George K., Vendor G0569
Scottish Genealogy Association, Vendor G0556
Scriptorium Family History Centre, Vendor G0780
Shuck, Larry G., Vendor G0287
Society of Australian Genealogists, Vendor G0563
Society of Genealogists, Vendor G0557
South Carolina Department of Archives and History, Vendor G0130
Southern Historical Press, Inc., Vendor G0610
Southwest Oklahoma Genealogical Society, Vendor G0661
Stroh, Oscar H., Ph.D., Vendor G0333
Sutton Publishing Ltd., Vendor G0576
Taylor, Richard H., Vendor G0525
TCI Genealogical Resources, Vendor G0496
Tennessee Valley Publishing, Vendor G0183
Texas State Archives, Vendor G0601
Thode, Ernest, Vendor G0197
T.L.C. Genealogy, Vendor G0609

Genealogical & Local History Books in Print

5th Edition

General Reference & World Resources Volume

SECTION I: GENERAL REFERENCE

Adoption, Orphans, and Heredity

Coble, Janet. **Children of Orphan Trains from NY to IL & Beyond**. 1994. Indexed. Paper. $10 members/$12.00 nonmembers. 122 pp. .... Vendor G0488

Holt, Marilyn Irvin. **The Orphan Train: Placing Out in America**. 1992. Indexed. Illus.
   The book sheds valuable new light on the phenomenon of a relocation system that attempted to find new homes in the West for urban poor children. It does so in the context of 19th-century ideals about childhood, welfare relief for the poor, western development, and rail expansion.
Cloth, $33.50. Paper, $13.45. x + 262 pp. .... Vendor G0050

Inskeep, Carolee. **The Children's Aid Society of New York:** An Index to the Federal, State, and Local Census Records of Its Lodging Houses (1855-1925). 1996.
   Includes the names of 5,000 children who lived in one of the dozen or so lodging houses of the Children's Aid Society long enough to be counted as a resident in one of the federal, state, or city enumerations conducted between 1855 and 1925.
Paper. $20.00. 166 pp. .... Vendor G0011

Inskeep, Carolee. **The New York Foundling Hospital:** An Index to the Federal, State, and Local Census Records [1870-1925]. 1995.
   Between 1853 and 1929, an estimated 200,000 poor, abandoned, and orphaned children were shipped from New York City orphanages to western families for adoption. The names in this volume represent 13,000 children who lived in the Roman Catholic New York Foundling Hospital between 1870 and 1925.
Paper. $27.50. 350 pp. .... Vendor G0011

King, Susan L. **History and Records of the Charleston Orphan House, 1790-1860**. 1984. Indexed.
   The Charleston Orphan House was the first municipal orphanage in the United States. Many of the orphans were children of Revolutionary soldiers. Contains the records of approximately 1,800 children.
Cloth. $25.00. 204 pp. .... Vendor G0610

Krause, Carol. **How Healthy is Your Family Tree: A Complete Guide to Tracing Your Family's Medical and Behavioral History**. 1995.
   This is a beginner's introduction to this subject, suitable for readers without a scientific background.
Paper. $12.00. 167 pp. .... Vendor G0611

McNabb, Luanne, Elizabeth Curtis, and Kathleen Bowley. **Family Health Trees: Genetics and Genealogy**. 1995.
    A practical guide for the layman who is interested in genetics and genealogy.
Paper. $14.00 (cdn), $15.50 (US). 64 pp. .... Vendor G0568

Milunsky. **Heredity and Your Family's Health**. 1992.
    Written from the perpective of family health, this book explains the complex science of genetics and describes numerous hereditary disorders. This is a scholarly work, which is not written with the genealogist in mind.
Paper. $18.95. 488 pp. .... Vendor G0611

Nelson-Anderson. **Genetic Connections: A Guide to Documenting Your Individual and Family Health History**. 1995.
    An intermediate level approach to this subject. Well illustrated and easy to follow. This is the book of choice for most interested in the subject.
Paper. $34.95. 301 pp. .... Vendor G0611

Pollen, Daniel A. **Hannah's Heirs: The Quest for the Genetic Origins of Alzheimer's Disease**. (1993) reprint 1996.
    Genetic genealogy in action! This book follows the genetic descent of Hannah's gene, known for leading to Alzheimer's disease, and the medical information being gathered. A well-written book.
Paper. $14.95. 310 pp. .... Vendor G0611

Your Family's Health History, An Introduction. NGS Quarterly, Special Issue, Vol. 82, No. 2, June 1994. 1994.
    A guide to becoming a family health historian.
Paper. $10.00. .... Vendor G0627

⚜ Bible Records ⚜

Lester, Memory Aldridge. **Old Southern Bible Records**. Transcriptions of Births, Deaths and Marriages from Family Bibles, Chiefly of the 18th and 19th Centuries. (1974) reprint 1996. Indexed.
Paper. $37.50. 378 pp. .... Vendor G0011

⚜ Bibliographies ⚜

Albaugh, Gaylord P. **History and Annotated Bibliography of American Religious Periodicals and Newspapers**. 2 vols. 1994.
    Gives locations and/or microform sources for thousands of religious periodicals and newspapers published in America from 1730-1830. Tremendous detail included. 8½" x 11".
Cloth. $125.00. 1,456 pp. .... Vendor G0611

Child, Sargent B., and Dorothy P. Holmes. **Check List of Historical Records Survey Publications**. Bibliography of Research Projects Reports. (1943) reprint 1996.

An important bibliography for genealogical research, this checklist encompasses all the publications of the several Historical Records Survey programs of the WPA and various related federal programs, most of which were issued between 1936 and 1943. Paper. $15.00. 110 pp. .... Vendor G0011

FFHS. **Current Publications by [FFHS] Member Societies**. 8th ed.
A British book published by the Federation of Family History Societies.
£6.00 (overseas surface). .... Vendor G0588

Filby, P. William. **American and British Genealogy and Heraldry: A Selected List of Books**. 1983.
Cloth. $18.50. 940 pp. .... Vendor G0406

Filby, P. William. **American and British Genealogy and Heraldry: 1982-1985 Supplement**. 1987.
Cloth. $6.00. 230 pp. .... Vendor G0406

Filby, P. William. **A Bibliography of American County Histories**. (1985) reprint 1987.
Cloth. $24.95. 449 pp. .... Vendor G0010

Hoffman, Marian, ed. **Genealogical & Local History Books in Print. 5th Edition**. Family History Volume. 1996. Indexed.
Paper. $25.00. 479 pp. .... Vendor G0010

Hoffman, Marian, ed. **Genealogical & Local History Books in Print. 5th Edition**. U.S. Sources & Resources Volume. 1997.
Contact vendor for information. .... Vendor G0010

Horowitz. **A Bibliography of Military Name Lists from Pre-1675 to 1900: A Guide to Genealogical Sources**. 1990.
Extremely useful guide to hundreds of little-known sources. This will expand your search.
Cloth. $99.50. 1,118 pp. .... Vendor G0611

Humphery-Smith, C. R. **A Genealogist's Bibliography**. 1977.
Paper. £11.95. 128 pp. .... Vendor G0562

Joel Munsell's Sons. **The American Genealogist,** Being a Catalogue of Family Histories . . . From 1771 to . . . (1900). 5th ed. (1900) reprint 1997.
Bibliography of family histories, pedigrees, and genealogies published as books, pamphlets, etc., between 1771 and 1900.
Paper. $36.50. 406 pp. .... Vendor G0011

Kaminkow, Jack, ed. **A Complement to Genealogies in The Library of Congress: A Bibliography**. 1981.
Cloth. $95.00. 1,118 pp. .... Vendor G0010

Kaminkow, Jack, ed. **United States Local Histories in The Library of Congress: A Bibliography**. 5 vols. 1976.
Cloth. $300.00. Over 5,000 pp. .... Vendor G0010

Library of Congress. **Guides to Genealogical Research:** A Selected List.
Compiled for the beginning genealogist, this selected list of references includes basic and general introductory books for United States genealogical research. The text of this is available on the Local History and Genealogy Reading Room's home page: http://lcweb.loc.gov/rr/genealogy.
Free. Contact vendor for information. 4 pp. .... Vendor G0566

Library of Congress. **Handbook for Foreign Genealogical Research: A Guide to Published Sources in English**. Compiled by Virginia Steele Wood.
The text of this is available on the Local History and Genealogy Reading Room's home page: http://lcweb.loc.gov/rr/genealogy.
Free. Contact vendor for information. 23 pp. .... Vendor G0566

Library of Congress. **Immigrant Arrivals:** A Guide to Published Sources. Compiled by Virginia Steele Wood.
The text of this is available on the Local History and Genealogy Reading Room's home page: http://lcweb.loc.gov/rr/genealogy.
Free. Contact vendor for information. 13 pp. .... Vendor G0566

Library of Congress. **LH&G News: Recent Acquisitions in the LH&G Reading Room**. Compiled by Judith P. Reid.
Free. Contact vendor for information. Approx. 11 pp. .... Vendor G0566

Library of Congress. **A Select Bibliography of Works at the Library of Congress on Norwegian-American Immigration and Local History**. Compiled by Lee V. Douglas.
The text of this is available on the Local History and Genealogy Reading Room's home page: http://lcweb.loc.gov/rr/genealogy.
Free. Contact vendor for information. 8 pp. .... Vendor G0566

Moule, Thomas. **Bibliotheca Heraldica Magnae Britanniae**.
Reprint of the only comprehensive bibliography of heraldry, genealogy, nobility, knighthood, and ceremonies, 1469-1821.
Cloth. £45.00. 692 pp. .... Vendor G0616

Nevins, Allan, James I. Robertson, and Bell I. Wiley. **Civil War Books: A Critical Bibliography**. 2 vols. in 1. Indexed.
Cloth. $75.00. 604 pp. .... Vendor G0590

Society of Genealogists. **Genealogy: A Basic Bibliography**. Rev. ed. 1994.
A British book published by the Society of Genealogists.
Leaflet. £0.20. .... Vendor G0557

Thomson, T. R. **A Catalogue of British Family Histories**. Third edition, with Addenda by G. Barrow. 1980.
Cloth. £12.00. 229 pp. .... Vendor G0616

Wright, John. **Compendium of the Confederacy: An Annotated Bibliography**. 2 vols. Indexed.
Cloth. $150.00. .... Vendor G0590

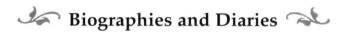

Biographies and Diaries

Alexander, Susan R., comp. **The Diaries of John M. Miller of Westwood/Cincinnati, Ohio: Excerpts from 1869-1870 and 1881-1894**. 1993. Indexed. Illus.
John M. Miller (1822-1894) was the son of Mary (Ludlow) and George Carter Miller. His wife was the former Huldah Woodhull Nicholas, daughter of Sarah (Woodhull) and Elias Nicholas. Huldah and John Miller had 13 children. John Miller's diaries reflect his busy life as a devoted family man, staunch Presbyterian, carriage-manufacturing company president, and involved citizen. His first-person account vividly evokes the horse-and-buggy days of late 19th-century Westwood (where he lived) and Cincinnati (where he worked). Other frequently mentioned surnames include Applegate, Bruce, Burnham, Davis, Drake, Ernst, Gamble, Gibson, Glasby, Hazen, Hedges, Hinsch, Kugler, Lawrence, Logan, McMicken, Moore, Mussey, Oehlman, Peterson, Powell, Ricketts, Rowland, Sanders, Sayre, Walker, Ward, Williams, Wilson, and Wise.
Besides the 34-page name index, supplementary material consists of pictures of people, carriages, and buildings; maps; family notes and charts; and a table of notable events and items.
Cloth. $54.95. 634 pp. .... Vendor G0028

Bakeless. **Daniel Boone: Master of the Wilderness**. (1939) reprint 1989.
A fully documented biography of this hero.
Paper. $13.95. 480 pp. .... Vendor G0611

Baker, Ruthe, ed. **The Diaries of Samuel Mickle, Woodbury, Gloucester County, New Jersey 1792-1829**. 2 vols. 1991. Indexed.
Thirty-seven years of local, state, and national events, including Revolution, War of 1812, 5,000 vital statistics of South Jersey.
Paper. $63.00. 834 pp. .... Vendor G0069

Brumgardt, ed. **Civil War Nurse: The Diary and Letters of Hannah Ropes**. 1993.
   Chief nurse of the Union Hospital in Washington, D.C., describes life and stress in
the hospital.
Paper. $10.95. 149 pp. .... Vendor G0611

Campbell, James Brown. **Across the Wide Missouri: The Diary of a Journey from
Virginia to Missouri in 1819 and Back Again in 1822**.
Paper. $19.95. .... Vendor G0632

Chamberlain, Welton, ed. **Marching to California on the Emigrant Trail 1852-
1853**. From a Journal Kept by Benjamin F. Chamberlain. 1995. Indexed. Illus.
   A diary kept by Benjamin F. Chamberlain while traveling the emigrant trail from
Dexter, Michigan to California.
Cloth. $14.95. 94 pp. .... Vendor G0735

Civil War Letter and Diary of Joshua Winters. 1975.
Paper. $10.00. .... Vendor G0660

Creswell, Stephen, ed. **We Will Know What War Is: The Civil War Diary of Sirene
Bunten**. 1993.
   The diary begins on the first day of 1863, spans the war years, and ends in the
1870s. In 1901 Sirene Bunten picked up her diary one last time and made a final entry.
In her diary we see what war was like for many West Virginians. The diary's postwar
entries show the rural life lived by a young West Virginia woman.
Paper. $8.00. .... Vendor G0660

Darlington, William M. **An Account of the Remarkable Occurrences in the Life &
Travels of Col. James Smith,** During His Captivity with the Indians, in the Years
1755-1759. (1870) reprint 1993.
Cloth, $29.00. Paper, $19.00. 190 pp. .... Vendor G0259

Diary of Joshua Hempstead 1711-1758. (1901) reprint 1985. Indexed. Illus.
   Book # 1432.
Cloth. $45.00. 766 pp. .... Vendor G0082

The Diary of Matthew Patten of Bedford, New Hampshire 1754-1788. (1903)
reprint 1993. Indexed. Illus.
   Book #1424.
Cloth. $49.50. 640 pp. .... Vendor G0082

Friel, Florence, ed. **The Diary of Job Whitall, Gloucester County, New Jersey
1775-1779**. 1992. Indexed.
   Description of everyday life in the midst of opposing armies—"The Battle of Red
Bank."
Paper. $16.50. 200 pp. .... Vendor G0069

Gale Research. **Abridged Biography and Genealogy Master Index**. 3 vols. 1995.
Cloth. $475.00/set. 4,511 pp. .... Vendor G0560

Gale Research. **Biography and Genealogy Master Index, 1991-1995 Cumulation**.
3 vols. 1995.
Cloth. $925.00/set. 4,533 pp. .... Vendor G0560

Gale Research. **Biography and Genealogy Master Index, 1996**.
Cloth. $315.00. 1,281 pp. .... Vendor G0560

Gilbert, Frank, and Wayne E. Morrison, Sr. **Jethro Wood, Inventor of the Modern Plow**. 1882. Illus.
Paper. $14.00. 52 pp. .... Vendor G0112

Haydon, Robert. **Thomas Haydon—England to Virginia—1657**. (1995) reprint 1996. Indexed. Illus.
The life and times of Thomas Haydon circa 1640 to 1717. The development of social structure of Virginia from 1657 to 1717.
Cloth. $39.00. 105 pp. .... Vendor G0372

Hendrick, Burton J. **The Lees of Virginia**. Biography of a Family. (1935) reprint 1996. Indexed. Illus.
Paper. $39.95. 455 pp. .... Vendor G0011

Herrick, Margaret. **A Civil War Soldier's Diary, Peter W. Funk, 150th NY Vol**. 1991. Indexed.
Diary of a foot soldier in the Union Army, 1862-1865; genealogical information and comment by Burton Coon.
Paper. $13.50. 54 pp. .... Vendor G0450

Hood, Margaret Scholl. **Margaret Scholl Hood Diary 1851-1861**. 1992. Indexed. Illus.
Book #1321.
Cloth. $25.00. 480 pp. .... Vendor G0082

Humphery-Smith, C. R. **Hugh Revel**. (1994) reprint 1994. Indexed. Illus.
Cloth. £19.70. 136 pp. .... Vendor G0562

Hyamson, Albert M. **A Dictionary of Universal Biography** of All Ages and of All Peoples. (1916) reprint 1995.
A guide to biographies of eminent or prominent men and women cited in more than fifty encyclopedic publications in existence at the time of the work's original appearance in 1916; 110,000 biographies in all.
Paper. $47.50. 744 pp. .... Vendor G0011

Lee, Eleanor Agnes. **Growing Up in the 1850's: The Journal of Agnes Lee**. 1984.
The journal of Eleanor Agnes Lee, Robert E. Lee's fifth child, from the age of twelve. Remarkable glimpse into a southern girl's life.
Paper. $9.95. 151 pp. .... Vendor G0611

The Life & Times of Rev. Samuel Patton. Reprint 1996.
$28.50 (perfect bound). .... Vendor G0549

Lofaro. **The Life and Adventures of Daniel Boone**. 1986.
A highly readable biography.
Cloth. $18.00. 150 pp. .... Vendor G0611

McDonald. **A Woman's Civil War: A Diary with Reminiscences of the War, from March 1862**. 1992.
The fascinating Civil War diary of Cornelia Peake McDonald, of Winchester, Virginia. A Southern woman's lonely struggle in the midst of chaos.
Paper. $14.95. 303 pp. .... Vendor G0611

Memoirs of Sam Williams.
$18.50 (perfect bound). .... Vendor G0549

Monk, William. **Theodore and Alice: A Love Story**. 1994.
The story of Theodore Roosevelt and his first wife, Alice Lee. Includes the genea-logical background of both families.
Cloth. $20.00. 80 pp. .... Vendor G0093

Morley, Rhoda J. **Between the Wild Blue Yonder and the Deep Blue Seas**. A Biog-raphy of Henry C. (Hank) Morley 1918-1983. 1990. Illus.
Cloth. $22.00. 108 pp. .... Vendor G0322

Naylor, Natalie A., Douglas Brinkley, and John Allen Gable, editors. **Theodore Roosevelt, Many-Sided American**. 1992. Indexed. Illus.
Forty-two essays on the many and diverse sides of the 26th president of the United States. Includes family genealogy.
Cloth. $55.00. 676 pp. .... Vendor G0093

Note-Book Kept by Thomas Lechford, Lawyer in Boston. (1885) reprint 1988. Indexed.
Book #1106.
Cloth. $49.50. 512 pp. .... Vendor G0082

Schlissel. **Women's Diaries of the Westward Journey**. 1992.
Pioneering was a family matter, and the westering experiences of American women are central to an accurate picture of what life was like on the frontier. First-hand accounts.
Paper. $14.00. 278 pp. .... Vendor G0611

Schwartz. **A Woman Doctor's Civil War: Esther Hill Hawks' Diary**. 1989.
Paper. $14.95. 289 pp. .... Vendor G0611

Turino, Kenneth C., ed. **The Civil War Diary of Lieut. J. E. Hodgkins 1862-1865**. Indexed. Illus.
Book #1523.
Cloth. $22.50. 224 pp. .... Vendor G0082

Ulrich. **A Midwife's Tale**. 1990.

Based on Martha Ballard's diary of her midwifery and her life from 1785-1812 in Hallowell, Maine. Many locals mentioned, but this book is especially interesting for the portrait of the medical practices, religious squabbles, and sexual mores of the time.

Paper. $13.00. 444 pp. .... Vendor G0611

Wallace, Paul A. W. **Daniel Boone in Pennsylvania**. Rev. ed. 1987.

Recounts the story of Daniel Boone's early life in Pennsylvania and his later activity in Kentucky, describing his Quaker family and the popular traditions that have survived the years.

Paper. $1.95. 21 pp. .... Vendor G0554

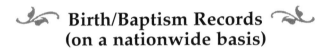

Birth/Baptism Records
(on a nationwide basis)

Humphrey, John T. **Understanding and Using Baptismal Records**. 1996. Indexed.

Paper. $20.95. 166 pp. .... Vendor G0117

Cemetery, Burial, and
Death Records

Gale Research. **Cemeteries of the United States**. 1994.

Cloth. $155.00. 1,607 pp. .... Vendor G0560

Heisey, John W. **Church and Tombstone Records**.

Paper. $10.00. 30 pp. .... Vendor G0574

Kot. **United States Cemetery Address Book**. 1994.

Over 25,000 U.S. cemeteries, their mailing addresses, and their locations are listed in this indispensable guide. Indexed by state, city, and county.

Cloth. $50.00. 896 pp. .... Vendor G0611

Stemmons, Jack, and Diane Stemmons. **Cemetery Record Compendium**.

Paper. $19.95. 270 pp. .... Vendor G0618

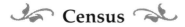 Census

A Century of Population Growth from the First Census of the United States to the Twelfth, 1790-1900. (1909) reprint 1989. Illus.
Cloth. $39.95. 303 pp. .... Vendor G0010

A Century of Population Growth: From the First Census of the United States to the Twelfth, 1790-1900. 1989. Indexed. Illus.
Relates the histories of censuses that were taken in the United States and Europe.
Cloth, $35.00. Paper, $22.50. 303 pp. .... Vendor G0552

Dollarhide, William. **The Census Research Kit**.
Paper, $9.95. Cardstock, $17.95. .... Vendor G0552

Dubester, Henry. **Annotated Bibliography of Censuses of Population Taken After Year 1790**. (1948) reprint 1990.
By states and territories.
Paper. $9.00. 73 pp. .... Vendor G0531

Family History Library. **A Key to the 1880 United States Federal Census**. Reprinted 1994.
Paper. $6.95. 85 pp. .... Vendor G0552

Lainhart, Ann S. **State Census Records**. (1992) reprint 1994.
Shows the researcher what is available in state census records, listed state by state, year by year, and often county by county and district by district.
Cloth. $17.95. 116 pp. .... Vendor G0010

National Archives. **The 1790-1890 Federal Population Censuses**. Catalog of National Archives Microfilm. (1979) reprint 1993.
Paper. $3.50. 128 pp. .... Vendor G0565

National Archives. **The 1900 Federal Population Census**. Catalog of National Archives Microfilm. (1978) reprint 1995.
Paper. $3.50. 84 pp. .... Vendor G0565

National Archives. **The 1910 Federal Population Census**. Catalog of National Archives Microfilm. 1982.
Paper. $3.50. 62 pp. .... Vendor G0565

National Archives. **The 1920 Federal Population Census**. Catalog of National Archives Microfilm. 1991.
Paper. $3.50. 96 pp. .... Vendor G0565

Parker, J. Carlyle. **City, County, Town and Township Index to the 1850 Federal Census Schedules**. (1979) reprint 1994.
Comprehensive index to all cities, etc. and wards in 1850.
Cloth, $32.45. Microfiche, $10.95. 215 pp. .... Vendor G0492

Precision Indexing. **Census Birth Year Reference Chart**. 1990. Illus.
Chart. $2.00. .... Vendor G0552

Saldaña, Richard. **A Practical Guide to the "Misteaks" Made in Census Indexes**. Indexed. Illus.

Includes examples of the types of errors that have occurred, as well as what to look for when using any census index to locate an ancestor.
Cloth, $19.95. Paper, $10.95. 63 pp. .... Vendor G0552

Smith, Leonard H., Jr., comp. **United States Census Key: 1850, 1860, 1870**. 1987.
Paper. $14.95. 193 pp. .... Vendor G0552

Stemmons, Jack. **United States Census Compendium**.
Lists under each state the census records that have been published, as well as any type of document that can be used as a census, such as tax lists, petitions, oaths of allegiance, directories, poll lists, etc.
Paper. $12.50. 143 pp. .... Vendor G0618

Thorndale, William, and William Dollarhide. **Map Guide to the U.S. Federal Censuses, 1790-1920**. (1987) reprint 1997. Illus.
Paper. $39.95. 445 pp. .... Vendor G0010

U.S. Bureau of Census. **Surnames Listed in the 1790 United States Census**.
Paper. $5.95. 44 pp. .... Vendor G0552

U.S. Bureau of Census. **200 Years of U.S. Census Taking; Population and Housing Questions, 1790-1990**.
Paper. $7.95. 91 pp. .... Vendor G0552

United States Bureau of the Census. **Heads of Families at the First Census of the United States Taken in the Year 1790**. 12 vols.
 Each volume is also available separately.
 Connecticut: Cloth, $35.00. Paper, $20.00.
 Maine: Cloth, $31.50. Paper, $16.50.
 Maryland: Cloth, $36.00. Paper, $21.00.
 Massachusetts: Cloth, $50.00. Paper, $35.00.
 New Hampshire: Cloth, $35.00. Paper, $20.00.
 New York: Cloth, $45.00. Paper, $30.00.
 North Carolina: Cloth, $45.00. Paper, $30.00.
 Pennsylvania: Cloth, $56.50. Paper, $41.50.
 Rhode Island: Cloth, $27.50. Paper, $12.50.
 South Carolina: Cloth, $35.00. Paper, $20.00.
 Vermont: Cloth, $27.50. Paper, $12.50.
 Virginia: Cloth, $35.00. Paper, $20.00.
Cloth, $379.50/set. Paper, $199.50. Fiche. $159.00. .... Vendor G0552

United States Bureau of the Census. **Heads of Families at the First Census of the United States Taken in the Year 1790: Connecticut**. (1908) reprint 1992. Indexed. Illus.
Paper. $22.50. 227 pp. .... Vendor G0010

United States Bureau of the Census. **Heads of Families at the First Census of the United States Taken in the Year 1790: Maine**. (1908) reprint 1992. Indexed. Illus.
Paper. $18.50. 105 pp. .... Vendor G0010

United States Bureau of the Census. **Heads of Families at the First Census of the United States Taken in the Year 1790: Maryland**. (1907) reprint 1992. Indexed. Illus.
Contact vendor for information. 189 pp. .... Vendor G0010

United States Bureau of the Census. **Heads of Families at the First Census of the United States Taken in the Year 1790: Massachusetts.** (1908) reprint 1992. Indexed. Illus.
Contact vendor for information. 363 pp. .... Vendor G0010

United States Bureau of the Census. **Heads of Families at the First Census of the United States Taken in the Year 1790: New Hampshire.** (1907) reprint 1992. Indexed. Illus.
Paper. $21.50. 146 pp. .... Vendor G0010

United States Bureau of the Census. **Heads of Families at the First Census of the United States Taken in the Year 1790: New York.** (1908) reprint 1992. Indexed. Illus.
Contact vendor for information. 308 pp. .... Vendor G0010

United States Bureau of the Census. **Heads of Families at the First Census of the United States Taken in the Year 1790: North Carolina.** (1908) reprint 1992. Indexed. Illus.
Contact vendor for information. 292 pp. .... Vendor G0010

United States Bureau of the Census. **Heads of Families at the First Census of the United States Taken in the Year 1790: Pennsylvania.** (1908) reprint 1992. Indexed. Illus.
Contact vendor for information. 426 pp. .... Vendor G0010

United States Bureau of the Census. **Heads of Families at the First Census of the United States Taken in the Year 1790: Rhode Island.** (1908) reprint 1992. Indexed. Illus.
Contact vendor for information. 71 pp. .... Vendor G0010

United States Bureau of the Census. **Heads of Families at the First Census of the United States Taken in the Year 1790: South Carolina.** (1908) reprint 1992. Indexed. Illus.
Contact vendor for information. 150 pp. .... Vendor G0010

United States Bureau of the Census. **Heads of Families at the First Census of the United States Taken in the Year 1790: Vermont.** (1907) reprint 1992. Indexed. Illus.
Contact vendor for information. 95 pp. .... Vendor G0010

United States Bureau of the Census. **Heads of Families at the First Census of the United States Taken in the Year 1790: Virginia.** Records of the State Enumerations: 1782 to 1785. (1907) reprint 1992. Indexed. Illus.
Contact vendor for information. 189 pp. .... Vendor G0010

> ### *Ebenezer Baptist of Ellis County, Texas, 1880–1892*
> *Church Records with Genealogies*
> Publication date: 1990. 338 pages. Indexed. Illus.
> Margaret B. Kinsey
> PO Box 459, Lamesa, TX 79331   (806) 872-3603

Church Records

Heisey, John W. **Church and Tombstone Records**.
Paper. $10.00. 30 pp. .... Vendor G0574

Humling, Virginia, comp. **U.S. Catholic Sources: A Diocesan Research Guide**. 1996.
Paper. $14.95. 112 pp. .... Vendor G0570

Kirkham, E. Kay. **Survey of American Church Records**. Rev. 4th ed.
   Contains religious migrations of some of the major church denominations in the U.S.
Paper. $26.00. 344 pp. .... Vendor G0618

Colonial and Early American

Balderston, Marion. **James Claypoole's Letter Book: London and Philadelphia, 1681-1684**. 1967.
   A fresh, absorbing picture of the early years of the American colony of Pennsylvania seen through the letters of the London Quaker merchant James Claypoole.
Cloth. $12.00. 258 pp. .... Vendor G0611

Bockstruck, Lloyd DeWitt. **Virginia's Colonial Soldiers**. 1990. Indexed.
Cloth. $30.00. 443 pp. .... Vendor G0010

Boorstin. **The Americans: The Colonial Experience**. 1958.
   An excellent account of life in America from the first settlements through the Revolution. A classic in American history. First volume of a trilogy (see listings under "History, Social History, and Folklore" for other volumes).
Paper. $12.00. 434 pp. .... Vendor G0611

Coldham, Peter Wilson. **English Estates of American Colonists**. American Wills and Administrations in the Prerogative Court of Canterbury, 1610-1699. (1980) reprint 1983. Indexed.
Cloth. $7.50. 78 pp. .... Vendor G0011

Coldham, Peter Wilson. **English Estates of American Colonists**. American Wills and Administrations in the Prerogative Court of Canterbury, 1700-1799. (1980) reprint 1991. Indexed.
Paper. $15.00. 151 pp. .... Vendor G0011

Coldham, Peter Wilson. **English Estates of American Settlers**. American Wills and Administrations in the Prerogative Court of Canterbury, 1800-1858. 1981. Indexed. Cloth. $9.50. 103 pp. .... Vendor G0011

Coldham, Peter Wilson. **Lord Mayor's Court of London Depositions Relating to Americans, 1641-1736**. Indexed.
   Abstracts of depositions made before the Lord Mayor's Court of London providing unpublished information regarding American colonials or Englishmen having business interests in America.
Cloth, $12.00. Paper, $10.00. 119 pp. .... Vendor G0627

The Colonial Society of Massachusetts. **Medicine in Colonial Massachusetts, 1620-1820**. 1980.
   A collection of essays covering various aspects of this subject.
Cloth. $23.50. 425 pp. .... Vendor G0611

The Colonial Society of Massachusetts. **Seafaring in Colonial Massachusetts**. 1980. Illus.
   An interesting look at early seafaring with maps and illustrations.
Cloth. $27.50. 240 pp. .... Vendor G0611

Demos. **Entertaining Satan: Witchcraft and the Culture of Early New England**. 1982.
   A fascinating study of witchcraft. Includes 121 pages of extensive footnotes.
Paper. $16.95. 543 pp. .... Vendor G0611

Demos. **A Little Commonwealth: Family Life in Plymouth Colony**. 1970.
   Studies the family during the first two generations of the colony's existence.
Paper. $8.95. 201 pp. .... Vendor G0611

Dobson, David. **Scottish Soldiers in Colonial America, Part 1**.
Contact vendor for information. .... Vendor G0641

Drake, Samuel G. **The Annals of Witchcraft in New England & Elsewhere in the U.S., from Their First Settlement**. (1869) reprint 1994.
Cloth. $35.00. 306 pp. .... Vendor G0259

Feldman, Lawrence H. **Anglo-Americans in Spanish Archives** Lists of Anglo-American Settlers in the Spanish Colonies of America. 1991. Indexed.
Cloth. $22.50. 349 pp. .... Vendor G0011

Gandy, Wallace. **The Association Oath Rolls of the British Plantations [New York, Virginia, Etc.] A.D. 1696**. (1922) reprint 1996. Indexed.
Paper. $10.00. 96 pp. .... Vendor G0011

Greene and Pole, eds. **Colonial British America: Essays in the New History of the Early Modern Era**. Reprint 1991.
   Very interesting scholarly study of colonial British America.
Paper. $16.95. 508 pp. .... Vendor G0611

Hanna, Charles. **The Wilderness Trails**. 2 vols. Reprint 1995. Illus.
   An examination of the influence of both Indian history and colonial trading practices on the developing American colonies. Traces the early development and expansion of the young American colonies westward across the Great Pennsylvania Frontier.
Cloth. $79.95/set. 840 pp. .... Vendor G0554

Hardy, Stella P. **Colonial Families of the Southern States of America**. A History and Genealogy of Colonial Families Who Settled in the Colonies Prior to the Revolution. (1958) reprint 1991. Indexed.
Cloth. $28.00. 643 pp. .... Vendor G0011

Harper. **Guide to the Draper Manuscripts**. 1983. Indexed.
   A vast collection of letters, documents, personal interviews, and clippings containing much genealogical and historical data on frontier America. This guide indexes thousands of early settlers and/or their descendants.
Cloth. $30.00. 464 pp. .... Vendor G0611

Hoffer, Peter Charles. **The Devil's Disciples: Makers of the Salem Witchcraft Trials**. 1996.
   How could a settled community like Salem turn against itself so viciously? The author approaches the subject as a legal and social historian and provides us with a fresh view of one of the most frightening incidents in early American history.
Cloth. $29.95. 279 pp. .... Vendor G0611

Innes, Stephen, ed. **Work and Labor in Early America**. 1988.
   A fascinating collection of essays on various aspects of work in early America.
Paper. $14.95. 297 pp. .... Vendor G0611

Karlsen. **The Devil in the Shape of a Woman: Witchcraft in Colonial New England**. 1987.
   A richly detailed portrait of the women who were persecuted as witches.
Paper. $13.00. 360 pp. .... Vendor G0611

Leach. **Roots of Conflict: British Armed Forces and Colonial Americans, 1677-1763**. 1986.
   Recounts the story of the antagonism between the American colonists and the British armed forces prior to the Revolution. Certain Anglo-American attitudes and stereotypes evolved that became significant in the revolutionary crisis.
Paper. $13.95. 232 pp. .... Vendor G0611

Mackenzie, George Norbury. **Colonial Families of the United States of America**. 7 vols. (1907-1920) reprint 1995. Indexed. Illus.
   Vol. I: 730 pp. $45.00
   Vol. II: 941 pp. $50.00
   Vol. III: 740 pp. $45.00
   Vol. IV: 684 pp. $40.00
   Vol. V: 719 pp. $40.00
   Vol. VI: 600 pp. $40.00
   Vol. VII: 605 pp. $40.00
Cloth. $300.00/set. .... Vendor G0010

Morrison, Patricia J. **Mrs**. **Morrison's A. B. C. Reader**. 1972. Illus.
Paper. $10.00. 32 pp. .... Vendor G0112

Owen, David R., and Michael C. Tolley. **Courts of Admiralty in Colonial America: The Maryland Experience, 1634-1776**. With a Foreword by Frank L. Wiswall, Jr. Indexed.
   An examiniation of the admiralty law system as it was transmitted from England to America.
Cloth. $45.00. 458 pp. .... Vendor G0617

Peirce, Ebenezer Weaver. **Peirce's Colonial Lists**. Civil, Military and Professional Lists of Plymouth and Rhode Island Colonies . . . 1621-1700. (1881) reprint 1995. Indexed.
Paper. $17.00. 156 pp. .... Vendor G0011

Public Record Office. **Records of the American and West Indian Colonies Before 1782**.
Information leaflet. Contact vendor for information. .... Vendor G0558

Purvis, Thomas L. **Revolutionary America, 1763 to 1800**. 1995. Indexed.
   A complete almanac on American life in the Revolutionary period.
Cloth. $75.00. 382 pp. .... Vendor G0611

Rixford, Elizabeth M. Leach. **Three Hundred Colonial Ancestors and War Service—** Their Part in Making American History from 495 to 1934. Bound with Supplement I, Supplement II, and Supplement II, Concluded. (1934, 1938, 1943, 1944) reprint 1991. Indexed. Illus.
Contact vendor for information. 425 pp. in all. .... Vendor G0011

Salmon. **Women and the Law of Property in Early America**. 1986.
   In-depth study of the rights of women in land ownership, dower, inheritance, divorce and separation, and more. The author, an expert in women's history, was not writing for the genealogist, but she has done us a great service in her examination of the legal place of women from 1750 to 1830.
Paper. $14.95. 267 pp. .... Vendor G0611

Shammas, Carole, Marylynn Salmon, and Michel Dahlin. **Inheritance in America: From Colonial Times to the Present**. (1987) reprint 1996.
   Studies all aspects of inheritance in early America. Focuses on the relationship between the inheritance process and changes in capitalism and the structure of the family.
Paper. $19.95. 320 pp. .... Vendor G0611

Stryker-Rodda, Harriet. **Understanding Colonial Handwriting**. (1986) reprint 1996.
Paper. $4.50. 26 pp. .... Vendor G0010

Taylor, John M. **The Witchcraft Delusion: The Story of the Witchcraft Persecutions in Seventeenth-Century New England, Including Original Trial Transcripts**. 1995.
   A study of witchcraft persecution in general and that which occurred in New England in particular.
Cloth. $14.95. 164 pp. .... Vendor G0611

Treese, Lorett. **The Storm Gathering: The Penn Family and the American Revolution**. 1992.
   Recounts the fascinating saga of the Penn family, focusing primarily on Thomas and John Penn, two of the last members of the family to figure significantly in pre-Revolutionary Pennsylvania history.
Contact vendor for information. 245 pp. .... Vendor G0554

Ulrich. **Good Wives: Image and Reality in the Lives of Women in Northern New England, 1650-1750**. 1982.
   Well-researched social history. Lively with scandal and homely detail, this book is history at its best.
Paper. $11.00. 296 pp. .... Vendor G0611

Usner. **Indians, Settlers & Slaves in a Frontier Exchange Economy: The Lower Mississippi Valley before 1783**. 1992.
Economic and cultural interactions between Indians, Europeans, and African slaves of colonial Louisiana. Well documented.
Paper. $13.95. 294 pp. .... Vendor G0611

Waters, Henry F. **Genealogical Gleanings in England**. Abstracts of Wills Relating to Early American Families. 2 vols. (1901) reprint 1997. Indexed. Illus.
Contact vendor for information. 1,779 pp. .... Vendor G0011

Weis, Frederick Lewis. **The Colonial Clergy and the Colonial Churches of New England**. (1936) reprint 1995.
Paper. $24.00. 280 pp. .... Vendor G0011

Weis, Frederick Lewis. **The Colonial Clergy of Maryland, Delaware and Georgia**. (1950) reprint 1991.
Paper. $12.50. 104 pp. .... Vendor G0011

Weis, Frederick Lewis. **The Colonial Clergy of the Middle Colonies,** New York, New Jersey, and Pennsylvania 1628-1776. (1957) reprint 1995.
Paper. $20.00. 184 pp. .... Vendor G0011

Weis, Frederick Lewis. **The Colonial Clergy of Virginia, North Carolina and South Carolina**. (1955) reprint 1996.
Paper. $16.00. 100 pp. .... Vendor G0011

Whittemore, William H. **Genealogical Guide to the First Settlers of America,** with a Brief History of Those of the First Generation. (1898-1906) reprint 1997.
Consists of genealogical notices of 10,000 17th-century settlers.
Paper. $36.50. 442 pp. .... Vendor G0011

Williams. **Riding the Nightmare: Women and Witchcraft from the Old World to Colonial Salem**. 1978.
How myths, folk art, church dogma, and politics linked up during the decline of agrarian society to brew a craze that sent as many as a million people—90 percent of them women—to the gallows.
Paper. $11.00. 228 pp. .... Vendor G0611

✨ Computers ✨

Ames, Stanley R., Ph.D. **How to Write and Publish Your Family History Using WordPerfect. DOS Versions 4.1, 4.2, & 5.0.** 1988.
Using the powerful word processing program, WordPerfect, this book is like a cookbook. Keystroke-by-keystroke instructions are included to help you accomplish each goal in the production of your book.
Paper. $17.95. 160 pp. .... Vendor G0093

Ames, Stanley R., Ph.D. **How to Write and Publish Your Family History Using WordPerfect. DOS Versions 5.1 & 6.0.** 1994.
Paper. $19.95. 160 pp. .... Vendor G0093

Bradley, Alan. **Family History on Your PC:** A Book for Beginners. 1996. Illus.
This is a British book about computers. With a PC and this book, you can trace your family history back to the early 19th century—maybe even earlier.
£11.70 (overseas surface). 224 pp. .... Vendor G0588

Clifford, Karen. **Genealogy and Computers for the Advanced Researcher:** Pulling it All Together. 1995. Indexed. Illus.
Paper. $39.95. 347 pp. .... Vendor G0011

Clifford, Karen. **Genealogy and Computers for the Complete Beginner:** A Step-by-Step Guide to the PAF Computer Program, Automated Data Bases, Family History Centers, and Local Sources. Rev. 2nd ed. 1995. Indexed.
Paper. $32.50. 282 pp. .... Vendor G0011

Clifford, Karen. **Genealogy and Computers for the Determined Researcher**. Revised and expanded edition. 1995. Indexed.
The sequel to *Genealogy and Computers for the Complete Beginner*.
Paper. $39.95 (Includes floppy disk). 355 pp. .... Vendor G0011

Cosgriff, John, and Carolyn Cosgriff. **Turbo Genealogy: An Introduction to Family History Research in the Information Age**. 1997.
Research techniques and information on using computer technology, as well as computer software and hardware pointers.
Paper. $17.95. Approx. 225 pp. .... Vendor G0570

Crowe, Elizabeth Powell. **Genealogy Online: Researching Your Roots**. 1995. Indexed.
An illuminating look at tapping the vast resources of the online community to enhance genealogical research. Countless tips for doing your research faster and cheaper.
Paper. $27.95. 304 pp. .... Vendor G0611

FFHS. **Computer Aided Genealogy**.
A British book published by the Federation of Family History Societies.
£5.85 (overseas surface). .... Vendor G0588

FFHS. **Computers in Family History**. 4th ed.
A British book published by the Federation of Family History Societies.
£4.40 (overseas surface). .... Vendor G0588

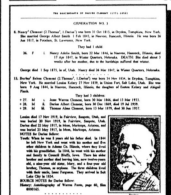
FFHS. **Genealogical Computer Packages**.
A British book published by the Federation of Family History Societies.
£4.00 (overseas surface). .... Vendor G0588

FFHS. **Internet for Genealogy**.
A British book published by the Federation of Family History Societies.
£2.35 (overseas surface). .... Vendor G0588

Hawgood, D. **An Introduction to Using Computers in Genealogy**. 1994.
A British book published by the Federation of Family History Societies.
£3.30 (overseas surface). 51 pp. .... Vendor G0588

Library of Congress. **Internet Resources for the Public**.
Free. Contact vendor for information. 6 pp. .... Vendor G0566

Nichols, Elizabeth L. **Genealogy in the Computer Age: Understanding FamilySearch® (Ancestral File™, International Genealogical Index™, Social Security Death Index)**. Rev. ed. 1994. Illus.
Describes the programs and files published by The Church of Jesus Christ of Latter-day Saints (LDS Church, Mormons, Genealogical Society of Utah)—available in Salt Lake City, Utah, at most of the over 2,000 family history centers (branches of the Mormon Library in Salt Lake City), and at many public and private genealogical societies and libraries. (FamilySearch is not currently available for private purchase.) ALA recommended; book-club featured.
Paper. $11.45. 56 pp. .... Vendor G0203

Nichols, Elizabeth L. **Genealogy in the Computer Age: Understanding FamilySearch®, vol. 2 (Personal Ancestral File® [PAF], Family History Library Catalog™, More Resource Files, and Using Them All in Harmony)**. 1997.

Volume 2 describes additional components of FamilySearch and expands instruction to provide direction on how all FamilySearch programs and files may be used in harmony.

Contact vendor for information. .... Vendor G0203

Nichols, Elizabeth L. **The Genesis of Your Genealogy: Step-by-Step Instruction Books for the Beginner in Family History, 3rd Edition**. 1992. Illus.

Introduces you to family history and genealogy, its sources, resources, forms, terminology, and all the basic how-tos, including computers in finding, organizing, and sharing your information; selected as a required university and community college textbook.

Paper. $10.45. 74 pp. .... Vendor G0203

Przecha, Donna, and Joan Lowrey. **Guide to Genealogy Software**. (1993) reprint 1994.

Contact vendor for information. 206 pp. .... Vendor G0010

Przecha, Donna. **Understanding ROOTS III; More Understanding ROOTS III**. 1990, 1992.

The first book covers how to operate the original program. The second covers the June 1991 update and more information on advanced features such as preparing a family history book (genealogy format report), documentation, splitting and merging, GEDCOM, text files, and install program settings. Sold as a set only.

Paper. $27.00/set. .... Vendor G0575

Taylor, N. C. **Computers in Genealogy Beginners Handbook**. 2nd ed. 1996.

A British book published by the Society of Genealogists.

Paper. £3.70. 76 pp. .... Vendor G0557

Tippey, David. **Genealogy on the MacIntosh**. 1996.

A British book describing methods and genealogy packages useful for recording family history on an Apple Macintosh computer.

£4.20 (overseas surface). 48 pp. .... Vendor G0588

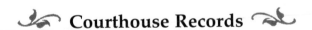

Courthouse Records

Bentley, Elizabeth Petty. **County Courthouse Book. 2nd Edition**. (1995) reprint 1996.

Paper. $34.95. 405 pp. .... Vendor G0010

Franklin, Charles. **Keys to the Courthouse**. 4 vols.
    Volume I: Jurisdictions, 28 pp.
    Volume II: The Records, 40 pp.
    Volume III: Unusual Records, 46 pp.
    Volume IV: Analyzing Records, 73 pp.
Paper. $10.00/Vol. I. $12.00/Vols. II & III. $15.00/Vol. IV. .... Vendor G0574

Meitzler, Leland K., ed. **United States County Courthouse Address Book**. 1988.

Paper. $4.95. 63 pp. .... Vendor G0552

Elizabeth Petty Bentley

COUNTY COURTHOUSE BOOK

2nd edition

First new edition in 5 years!

This is an exhaustive revision of the 1990 classic, featuring updated coverage of 3,125 county jurisdictions and 1,577 New England towns and independent Virginia cities. Also included is detailed coverage of the 18 Vermont probate districts, 9 Massachusetts districts, and 12 Connecticut judicial districts, plus informative state profiles and cross-references to name changes and extinct towns and counties. This new edition of the *County Courthouse Book* is no mere fine-tuning, but is a complete and systematic overhaul of the 1990 edition, and it is up-to-date, comprehensive, and more useful than ever.

Since most genealogical research is organized on county lines, it goes without saying that the researcher needs a reliable guide to American county courthouses, the main repositories of county records. To proceed in his investigations, the researcher needs current addresses and phone numbers, information about the coverage and availability of key courthouse records such as probate, land, naturalization, and vital records, names of courthouse officials, and timely advice on the whole range of services available at the courthouse. He will also need to know whether search services are provided, the fees involved, and whether there are alternative locations for the records, and, if he's a diligent researcher, he'll need to know something about the origins of the county itself—names of parent counties, dates of formation, former names, etc.

Such is the kind of guidebook required, and such a book is Elizabeth P. Bentley's *County Courthouse Book*. Based on her written survey of county courthouses, New England town and probate courts, and Virginia's independent cities, in which she poses a number of questions of vital importance to the genealogist, Mrs. Bentley here presents a systematic digest of the responses to her questionnaire, omitting only certain items of information on those courthouses that failed to respond. Hence we have the names, addresses, phone numbers, and dates of organization of *all* county courthouses, and for those that responded (65 percent), a concise summary of record holdings, personnel, and services.

8½" x 11". 405 pp., paperback. 1995.
Vendor G0010. $34.95

Dictionaries and Glossaries

Black's Law Dictionary With Pronunciations. 6th ed. 1990.
An essential reference work. Certainly every genealogical library should have this reference on the shelf.
Cloth. $37.50. 1,657 pp. .... Vendor G0611

Evans, Barbara J. **A to Zax—A Comprehensive Dictionary for Genealogists & Historians**. 1995.
Paper. $17.95. 300 pp. .... Vendor G0518

FFHS. **Latin Glossary for Family Historians**.
A British book published by the Federation of Family History Societies.
£2.75 (overseas surface). .... Vendor G0588

Harris, Maurine, and Glenn Harris. **Ancestry's Concise Genealogical Dictionary**. 1984.
Paper. $14.95. 259 pp. .... Vendor G0570

Hyamson, Albert M. **A Dictionary of Universal Biography** of All Ages and of All Peoples. (1916) reprint 1995.
Paper. $47.50. 744 pp. .... Vendor G0011

Martin, C. Trice. **The Record Interpreter**. 1993.
Classic reference work giving full Latin/English glossary, dictionaries of alternative and archaic terms and names.
Cloth. £20.00. 512 pp. .... Vendor G0579

Milward, R. **Glossary of Household, Farming & Trade Terms from Probate Inventories**. 3rd ed. 1991.
A British book published by the Federation of Family History Societies.
£4.85 (overseas surface). 62 pp. .... Vendor G0588

Twining, Andrew, and Sandra Twining. **Dictionary of Old Trades and Occupations**. 1995.
Written by an Australian family historian, this book contains a few occupations peculiar to that country. But by and large, this book will be useful to those tracing families in any English-speaking country. A useful reference.
Paper. $13.00. 108 pp. .... Vendor G0611

 # Directories/Catalogues

AGLL. **Where to Write for Vital Records: Births, Deaths, Marriages, and Divorces**.
Pamphlet. $3.50. 20 pp. .... Vendor G0552

Association of Professional Genealogists. **APG Directory of Professional Genealogists**. 1996. Indexed.
Paper. Contact vendor for information. Approx. 150 pp. .... Vendor G0779

Benson, Toni I., comp. **Source Check: A Resource Checklist for United States Genealogical Research**. 1995.
Lists approximately 1,000 sources of family history research common to most areas of the United States.
Paper. $8.50. 29 pp. .... Vendor G0777

Bentley, Elizabeth Petty. **County Courthouse Book. 2nd Edition**. (1995) reprint 1996.
Paper. $34.95. 405 pp. .... Vendor G0010

Bentley, Elizabeth Petty. **Directory of Family Associations**. 3rd ed. 1996.
Paper. $34.95. 355 pp. .... Vendor G0010

Bentley, Elizabeth Petty. **The Genealogist's Address Book, 3rd Edition**. (1995) reprint 1996. Indexed.
Paper. $34.95. 653 pp. .... Vendor G0010

Carson, Dina C. **Directory of Genealogical and Historical Publications in the US and Canada, 1996**. Indexed.
The only source of genealogical and local history research publications you'll need! 6,500 publications listed. Published biennially.
Cloth, $80.00. Paper, $45.00. 500 pp. .... Vendor G0523

Carson, Dina C. **Directory of Genealogical and Historical Societies in the US and Canada, 1996**. Indexed.
An invaluable reference for genealogists who wish to supplement their research or share their findings with other researchers; 13,000 societies listed. Published biennially.
Cloth, $90.00. Paper, $65.00. 750 pp. .... Vendor G0523

Directory of Historical Organizations in the United States and Canada. 1997.
Contact vendor for details. .... Vendor G0457

Heisey, John W. **Works Projects Administration Sources for Genealogists**.
Paper. $12.00. 56 pp. .... Vendor G0574

Jocelyn, Darling & Co. **American Advertising Directory, Manufacturers and Dealers in American Goods for 1831**. (1831) reprint 1977. Indexed.
Cloth, $16.00. Paper, $11.00. 395 pp. .... Vendor G0531

Johnson, Keith A., and Malcolm R. Sainty. **Genealogical Research Directory:** Regional & International, & Guide to Genealogical Societies. Published annually.
Contact vendor for information. .... Vendor G0782

Konrad, J. **Directory of Family "One-Name" Periodicals**.
Paper. $10.00. 65 pp. .... Vendor G0574

Konrad, J. **Family Associations, Societies and Reunions**.
Paper. $10.00. 95 pp. .... Vendor G0574

Konrad, J. **Genealogical & Historical Societies in the U.S.**
Paper. $10.00. 64 pp. .... Vendor G0574

Library of Congress. **Telephone and City Directories in the Library of Congress**. A Finding Guide. By Barbara B. Walsh. 1994.

Elizabeth Petty Bentley

DIRECTORY OF FAMILY ASSOCIATIONS

New 3rd edition!

New features of the 3rd edition—
- Thousands of new and amended listings
- Dates of family reunions
- Frequency and price of family publications

Standard features—
- Addresses
- Phone numbers
- Contact persons
- Publications
- Family associations
- Reunion committees
- One-name societies
- Surname exchanges
- Ancestral name where applicable
- Family newsletters

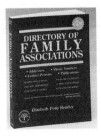

8½" x 11". 355 pp., paperback. 1996.
Vendor G0010.
$34.95

There are many uses for a directory of family associations but undoubtedly the best use for it is for genealogical research—for making contact with family members, sharing information about family history, developing common ground between people of the same surname, arranging reunions, discovering who's out there and where you connect on the family tree, and finding out where you can go with your own research.

And there are a host of other uses—kin searching and heir searching, for example, determining family migration patterns, even marketing your own genealogical research. The possibilities are endless.

Based largely on data received in response to questionnaires sent to family associations, reunion committees, and one-name societies, the 3rd edition of the *Directory of Family Associations* gives you access to a range of possibilities, offering information on approximately 6,500 family associations across the United States. Since by their very nature some of these organizations exist for only a brief period of time or lack the staff to answer queries, Mrs. Bentley has supplemented the available information with details gleaned from notices in the standard family history journals and newsletters.

The result is an immensely useful A–Z directory of family associations giving addresses, phone numbers, contact persons, and publications (if any). So whether you're just starting your genealogical research or already waist deep in your investigations, planning a family reunion or hoping to attend one, or simply curious about your family or your surname, the course you choose from now on will be governed by this indispensable directory.

Genealogical Publishing Co., Inc.

The text of this is available on the Local History and Genealogy Reading Room's home page: http://lcweb.loc.gov/rr/genealogy.
Free. Contact vendor for information. 13 pp. .... Vendor G0566

Meitzler, Leland K., ed. **United States County Courthouse Address Book**. 1988.
Paper. $4.95. 63 pp. .... Vendor G0552

Meyer, Mary Keysor. **Meyer's Directory of Genealogical Societies in the USA and Canada**. 9th ed. 1994.
Paper. $23.00. 123 pp. .... Vendor G0627

Tuttle Antiquarian Books, Inc. **Tuttle's Catalog of Genealogy and Regional Americana #15**. 1996.
A catalogue listing over 7,000 genealogies, town and county histories, and related reference books. All books described are for sale; both new and used material is offered.
Paper. $7.50. 274 pp. .... Vendor G0179

❧ Family History Library ❧ (of The Church of Jesus Christ of Latter-day Saints) Publications (general)

Family History Library. **AIS Census Indexes Resource Guide**.
Free. 4 pp. .... Vendor G0629

Family History Library. **Contributing to Ancestral File**.
Free. 4 pp. .... Vendor G0629

Family History Library. **Correcting Ancestral File**.
Free. 4 pp. .... Vendor G0629

Family History Library. **Discovering Your Family Tree**.
Leaflet. $.40. 20 pp. .... Vendor G0629

Family History Library. **Early Church Information File Guide**.
Free. 4 pp. .... Vendor G0629

Family History Library. **Family History Library Catalog on Compact Disc Guide**.
Free. 4 pp. .... Vendor G0629

Family History Library. **Family History Library on Microfiche Guide**.
Free. 4 pp. .... Vendor G0629

Family History Library. **Family History Publications List**.
Free. 3 pp. .... Vendor G0629

Family History Library. **Finding an International Genealogical Index Source Resource Guide**.
Free. 4 pp. .... Vendor G0629

Elizabeth Petty Bentley

THE GENEALOGIST'S ADDRESS BOOK

New!
3rd edition

The new 3rd edition of the *Genealogist's Address Book* is more accurate, more up-to-date, and more useful than ever—a one-stop resource book needed by everyone engaged in genealogical research, from the beginner to the professional. At least a third larger than the previous edition, it contains thousands of names, addresses, phone numbers, and other information vital to the researcher at each and every turn of the research process. The fast changing world of genealogy demands a book that keeps pace with events, and this new edition of the *Address Book,* reflecting a higher rate of response from organizations that were surveyed, is the only book around that stays abreast of the entire field. The only one!

Featuring hundreds of new entries, with changes to more than 80% of the existing entries, the new 3rd edition of the *Address Book* updates addresses and information, includes hundreds of organizations new to the scene or overlooked in the first edition, contains a Yellow Pages advertising supplement, and has a complete index of genealogical libraries, societies, and institutions, as well as an exhaustive (also unique) index of periodicals and newsletters.

The only nationwide list of genealogical and historical resources, the *Genealogist's Address Book* is the answer to the perennial question, "What's out there in the world of genealogy?" What organizations, institutions, special resources, or publications can help me? Where are they located? Who do I write to or phone? Believe it or not, the solution is simple. By means of a subject-classified and alphabetized list of resources, the *Address Book* puts you in touch with all the key sources of information, providing names, addresses, phone numbers, contact persons, and business hours of government agencies, societies, libraries, archives, professional bodies, periodicals, newspaper columns, publishers, booksellers, services, databases, bulletin boards and much, much more.

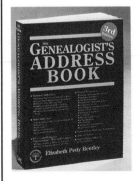

8½" x 11". 653 pp., indexed, paperback. 1995.
Vendor G0010. $34.95

Genealogical Publishing Co., Inc.

Family History Library. **Guide to Research**.
Leaflet. $.40. 24 pp. .... Vendor G0629

Family History Library. **Hiring a Professional Genealogist**.
Free. 4 pp. .... Vendor G0629

Family History Library. **How to Use the Family History Library Catalog**.
Video. $5.00. .... Vendor G0629

Family History Library. **International Genealogical Index (on Compact Disc) Resource Guide**.
Free. 4 pp. .... Vendor G0629

Family History Library. **International Genealogical Index (on Microfiche) Resource Guide**.
Free. 4 pp. .... Vendor G0629

Family History Library. **Introduction to TempleReady Guide**.
Free. 4 pp. .... Vendor G0629

Family History Library. **LDS Records Research Outline**.
Leaflet. $.25. 11 pp. .... Vendor G0629

Family History Library. **Library Services and Resources**.
Free. 4 pp. .... Vendor G0629

Family History Library. **A Member's Guide to Temple and Family History Work**.
Free. 20 pp. .... Vendor G0629

Family History Library. **Members of the Church 1830-1848 Guide**.
Free. 4 pp. .... Vendor G0629

Family History Library. **Military Index Resource Guide**.
Free. 1 p. .... Vendor G0629

Family History Library. **Periodical Source Index (PERSI) Guide**.
Free. 4 pp. .... Vendor G0629

Family History Library. **Personal Ancestral File Brochure**.
Free. 2 pp. .... Vendor G0629

Family History Library. **Research Outline: United States (general)**. All 50 states, & D.C.
Pkg. $10.00. .... Vendor G0629

Family History Library. **Research Outline: United States (general)**.
Leaflet. $.75. 52 pp. .... Vendor G0629

Family History Library. **Research Outline: U.S. Military Records**.
Leaflet. $.50. 39 pp. .... Vendor G0629

Family History Library. **Social Security Death Index Guide**.
Free. 4 pp. .... Vendor G0629

Family History Library. **Using Ancestral FIie Resource Guide**.
Free. 4 pp. .... Vendor G0629

Family History Library. **Using the Family History Library Catalog.**
Leaflet. $.75. 48 pp. .... Vendor G0629

Family History Library. **Why Family History?**
Leaflet. $.25 16 pp. .... Vendor G0629

✒ Genealogy for Children and ✒ Young Adults

Beller, Susan Provost. **Roots for Kids:** A Genealogy Guide for Young People. (1989) reprint 1997. Indexed. Illus.
Paper. $16.95. 128 pp. .... Vendor G0010

Brockman, Terra Castiglia. **A Student's Guide to Italian American Genealogy**. 1996. Indexed. Illus.
Hard-cover. $24.95. 208 pp. .... Vendor G0776

Chorzempa, Rosemary A. **My Family Tree Workbook: Genealogy for Beginners**. Published by Dover Press. 1982.
   A starter book for young genealogists.
Paper. $2.95. 57 pp. .... Vendor G0627

Johnson, Anne E., and Adam Merton Cooper. **A Student's Guide to African American Genealogy**. 1996. Indexed. Illus.
Hard-cover. $24.95. 208 pp. .... Vendor G0776

Johnson, Anne E. **A Student's Guide to British American Genealogy**. 1995. Indexed. Illus.
Hard-cover. $24.95. 208 pp. .... Vendor G0776

Kavasch, E. Barrie. **A Student's Guide to Native American Genealogy**. 1996. Indexed. Illus.
Hard-cover. $24.95. 208 pp. .... Vendor G0776

McKenna, Erin. **A Student's Guide to Irish American Genealogy**. 1996. Indexed. Illus.
Hard-cover. $24.95. 208 pp. .... Vendor G0776

Paddock, Lisa Olson, and Carl Sokolnicki Rollyson. **A Student's Guide to Scandinavian Genealogy**. 1996. Indexed. Illus.
Hard-cover. $24.95. 208 pp. .... Vendor G0776

Robl, Gregory. **A Student's Guide to German American Genealogy**. 1996. Indexed. Illus.
Hard-cover. $24.95. 208 pp. .... Vendor G0776

Rollyson, Carl Sokolnicki, and Lisa Olsen Paddock. **A Student's Guide to Polish American Genealogy**. 1996. Indexed. Illus.
Hard-cover. $24.95. 208 pp. .... Vendor G0776

Ryskamp, George, and Peggy Ryskamp. **A Student's Guide to Mexican American Genealogy**. 1996. Indexed. Illus.
Hard-cover. $24.95. 208 pp. .... Vendor G0776

Schleifer, Jay. **A Student's Guide to Jewish American Genealogy**. 1996. Indexed. Illus.
Hard-cover. $24.95. 208 pp. .... Vendor G0776

She, Colleen. **A Student's Guide to Chinese American Genealogy**. 1996. Indexed. Illus.
Hard-cover. $25.95. 208 pp. .... Vendor G0776

Weitzman. **My Backyard History Book**. 1975.
 History is more than memorizing names of presidents and war dates. This is a collection of history projects intended to bring history alive for children.
Paper. $10.95. 127 pp. .... Vendor G0611

Wolfman, Ira. **Do People Grow on Family Trees?** Genealogy for Kids & Other Beginners. 1991.
 Although this book is very suitable for kids, the adult beginner will find it a very enjoyable introduction to genealogy.
Paper. $9.95. 179 pp. .... Vendor G0611

Yamaguchi, Yoji. **A Student's Guide to Japanese American Genealogy**. 1996. Indexed. Illus.
Hard-cover. $24.95. 208 pp. .... Vendor G0776

⤜ Heraldry ⤛

Bolton, Charles Knowles. **Bolton's American Armory**. (1927) reprint 1989. Indexed. Illus.
Contact vendor for information. 246 pp. .... Vendor G0011

Burke, John. **A Genealogical and Heraldic History of the Commoners of Great Britain and Ireland**. In Four Volumes. Reprinted with the *Index to Pedigrees in Burke's Commoners*, by George Ormerod. (1834-1838, 1907) reprint 1996. Indexed.
 The standard genealogical guide to families in Great Britain and Ireland who enjoyed territorial possession or official rank, but were uninvested with heritable honors.
Paper. $200.00. 3,113 pp. .... Vendor G0011

Burke's Authorised Arms. A Selection of Arms Authorised by the Laws of Heraldry. Illus.
 Pedigrees and arms of over 300 families.
Cloth. £30.00. 244 pp. .... Vendor G0616

Burke's General Armory of England, Scotland, Ireland & Wales.
 The greatest collection of blasons of British arms (about 60,000).
Cloth. £75.00. cxxx + 1,185 pp. .... Vendor G0616

Burke's Prominent Families of the U.S.A.
A "Landed Gentry" of American families; 191 genealogies, illus. of arms.
Cloth. £45.00. 510 pp. .... Vendor G0616

Chesshyre, H., and T. Woodcock, eds. **Dictionary of British Arms. Medieval Ordinary**. Vol. 1. 1992. Indexed.
Both an Ordinary and an Armory with a 132-page Index of Names.
Cloth. £48.00. xvi + 530 pp. .... Vendor G0616

Crozier, William Armstrong. **Crozier's General Armory**. 2nd ed. (1904) reprint 1996.
Contains descriptions of nearly 2,000 coats-of-arms.
Paper. $17.00. 155 pp. .... Vendor G0011

Elvin, C. N. **A Dictionary of Heraldry**. Indexed. Illus.
Cloth. £36.00. 238 pp. .... Vendor G0616

Elvin, Charles Norton. **A Hand-book of Mottoes Borne by the Nobility, Gentry, Cities, Public Companies, Etc.** (1860) reprint 1990. Indexed.
The standard work on heraldic mottoes, those words or sentences associated with coats-of-arms.
Cloth. $25.00. 305 pp. .... Vendor G0011

FFHS. Basic Facts About Heraldry for Family Historians.
A British book published by the Federation of Family History Societies.
£2.00 (overseas surface). .... Vendor G0588

Foster, Joseph. **Some Feudal Coats of Arms from Heraldic Rolls 1298-1418,** Illustrated with 830 Zinco Etchings from Effigies, Brasses and Coats of Arms. (1902) reprint 1994. Illus.
Paper. $26.00. 296 pp. .... Vendor G0011

Friar, Stephen. **Heraldry for the Local Historian and Genealogists**. 1996. Illus.
Paper. $22.95. 288 pp. .... Vendor G0576

Humphery-Smith, C. R. **Anglo-Norman Armory**. 1973. Indexed. Illus.
A collection of essays on medieval heraldry and an edition of the Fitzwilliam roll of arms.
Paper. £16.70. 208 pp. .... Vendor G0562

Humphery-Smith, C. R., Heather E. Peek, Gordon H. Wright, and C. W. Scott-Giles, eds. **Cambridge Armorial**. 1985. Indexed. Illus.
A descriptive history of all the heraldry at the University of Cambridge colleges, the schools, and the city.
Cloth. £18.75. 144 pp. .... Vendor G0562

Innes, Sir Thomas, of Learney. **Scots Heraldry**. A Practical Handbook on the Historical Principles and Modern Application of the Art and Science. 2nd ed., revised and enlarged. (1956) reprint 1994. Indexed. Illus.
Paper. $27.50. 282 pp. plus 46 plates and 106 text figures. .... Vendor G0011

Johnston, G. Harvey. **Scottish Heraldry Made Easy**. 2nd ed. Illus.
Includes lists of crests, mottoes, family histories, glossary, etc.
Cloth. £12.00. xv + 221 pp. .... Vendor G0616

Library of Congress. **Heraldry: A Selected List of References**. Compiled by Paul J. Connor.
   The text of this is available on the Local History and Genealogy Reading Room's home page: http://lcweb.loc.gov/rr/genealogy.
Free. Contact vendor for informaton. 12 pp. .... Vendor G0566

Mandich, D. R., and J. A. Placek. **Russian Heraldry & Nobility**. Ltd. ed. 1992. Indexed. Illus.
Contact vendor for information. iv + 700 pp. .... Vendor G0616

Massicotte, Edouard Z., and Regis Roy. **Armorial Du Canada Francais [Armorial of French-Canada]**. 2 vols. in 1. (1915, 1918) reprint 1994. Indexed. Illus.
   The standard reference for coats-of-arms of officials, civil servants, professional men, and other French Canadians.
Paper. $28.50. 332 pp. in all. .... Vendor G0011

Matthews, John. **Complete American Armoury and Blue Book**. Combining 1903, 1907 and 1911-23 Editions. (1903, 1907, 1923) reprint 1995. Illus.
Paper. $40.00. 544 pp. .... Vendor G0011

Papworth's Ordinary of British Armorials. With a new introduction by J. Brooke-Little.
   Alphabetical dictionary of arms arranged under charges, which enables coats of arms to be identified.
Cloth. £75.00. xxii + 1,125 pp. .... Vendor G0616

Paul, Sir James Balfour. **An Ordinary of Arms**. Contained in the Public Register of All Arms and Bearings in Scotland. 2nd ed. (1903) reprint 1991. Indexed.
Paper. $35.00. 452 pp. .... Vendor G0011

Petchey, W. J. **Armorial Bearings of the Sovereigns of England**. 1977. Illus.
Paper. £2.95. 32 pp. .... Vendor G0579

Pinches, J. H., and R. V. Pinches. **The Royal Heraldry of England**. Illus.
   Arms of all the English royal family lines down to grandchildren of sovereigns. Nine color plates and 258 black-and-white illustrations; 35 pedigrees.
Cloth. £48.00. 352 pp. .... Vendor G0616

Pinches, John H. **European Nobility & Heraldry**. Ltd. ed. 1994. Indexed. Illus.
   A comparative study of the titles of nobility and their heraldic exterior ornaments for each country with historical notes.
Cloth. £48.00. xii + 336 pp. .... Vendor G0616

Pinches, R. V., and A. Wood. **A European Armorial**. Illus.
   An armorial of Knights of the Golden Fleece from a fifteenth-century manuscript. Fine color plates and illustrations.
Cloth. £39.00. 222 pp. .... Vendor G0616

Rietstap's Armorial General. 2 vols.
   Dictionary of arms from all over the world arranged alphabetically under surnames.
Cloth. £150.00. 1,200 + 1,328 pp. .... Vendor G0616

Rolland's Illustrations to Rietstap's Armorial General. 4 vols. in 3.
   Illustrations of approx. 85,000 shields of arms.
Cloth. £320.00. Quarto. .... Vendor G0616

Siddons, Michael Powell. **The Development of Welsh Heraldry**. 1991, 1993.
Contact vendor for information. .... Vendor G0591

Stephenson, Jean. **Heraldry for the American Genealogist**.
Paper. $5.00. 44 pp. .... Vendor G0627

Swinnerton, I. **Heraldry Can Be Fun**. 1988.
£1.75 (overseas surface). 16 pp. .... Vendor G0588

Urquhart, R. M. **Scottish Burgh & County Heraldry**. Illus.
   Blazons and illustrations of all burgh and county arms.
Cloth. £35.00. 296 pp. .... Vendor G0616

Urquhart, R. M. **Scottish Civic Heraldry**. 1979. Illus.
   Regional, islands, and district.
Cloth. £25.00. 112 pp. .... Vendor G0616

Vermont, E. **America Heraldica**. Illus.
   Arms of American families settled before 1800; 400 illustrations.
Cloth. £35.00. 224 pp., quarto. .... Vendor G0616

Wagner, A. R. **Aspilogia I. A Catalogue of English Medieval Rolls of Arms**. Illus.
Cloth. £25.00. .... Vendor G0616

Wagner, A. R. **Aspilogia II. Rolls of Arms of Henry III.** Illus.
Cloth. £15.00 .... Vendor G0616

Wagner, A. R. **Heralds of England**. 1986. Indexed. Illus.
   A history of the Office & College of Arms.
Cloth. £48.00. xxvi + 609 pp., royal quarto. .... Vendor G0616

Whitmore, W. H., ed. **The Heraldic Journal,** Recording the Armorial Bearings and
Genealogies of American Families. 4 vols. in 1. 24 Numbers (all published). (1865-
68) reprint 1996. Indexed. Illus.
Paper. $49.95. 192 pp./vol. .... Vendor G0011

✒ History, Social History, ✒ and Folklore

Boorstin. **The Americans: The Colonial Experience**. 1958.
An excellent account of life in America from the first settlements through the Revolution. A classic in American history. First volume of a trilogy (see below).
Paper. $12.00. 434 pp. .... Vendor G0611

Boorstin. **The Americans: The National Experience**. 1965.
The second volume of Boorstin's classic trilogy covers the period from the Revolution to the Civil War.
Paper. $14.00. 517 pp. .... Vendor G0611

Boorstin. **The Americans: The Democratic Experience**. 1973. ˎ
The final volume of the trilogy covers the century after the Civil War.
Paper. $16.00. 717 pp. .... Vendor G0611

Boydston. **Home & Work: Housework, Wages, and the Ideology of Labor in the Early Republic**. 1990.
This social history of "women's work" yields a fascinating look at women's lives during the period prior to the Civil War.
Paper. $14.95. 222 pp. .... Vendor G0611

Callcott. **Mistress of Riversdale: The Plantation Letters of Rosalie Stier Calvert, 1795-1821**. 1991.
In letters to her European relatives, Calvert provided an uncommonly readable account of America's history and life in early 19th-century Maryland.
Paper. $15.95. 407 pp. .... Vendor G0611

Clinton. **The Plantation Mistress: Woman's World in the Old South**. 1982.
This pioneering study of the much-mythologized Southern belle offers the first serious look at the lives of white women and their harsh and restricted place in the slave society before the Civil War.
Paper. $13.00. 331 pp. .... Vendor G0611

Dayton, Cornelia Hughes. **Women Before the Bar: Gender, Law, & Society in Connecticut: 1639-1789**. 1995.
Explores women's role in the court system in the early 18th century. Includes study of their participation in a range of legal actions such as debt, divorce, illicit sex, rape, and slander.
Paper. $18.95. 382 pp. .... Vendor G0611

Ferrell and Natkiel. **Atlas of American History**. 3rd ed. 1993.
Historical atlases are extremely useful to the genealogist. 8½" x 11".
Paper. $19.95. 192 pp. .... Vendor G0611

FFHS. **Oral History**.
A British book published by the Federation of Family History Societies.
£4.85 (overseas surface). .... Vendor G0588

Friedman. **The Enclosed Garden: Women & Community in the Evangelical South, 1830-1900**. 1985.

How the church and family influenced Southern women's history. Making use of original diaries and letters, this book paints a vivid picture of women's lives during this period.

Paper. $13.95. 180 pp. .... Vendor G0611

Grossberg. **Governing the Hearth: Law and the Family in Nineteenth-Century America**. 1985.

This fascinating study of law and the family will prove useful to genealogical research.

Paper. $19.95. 417 pp. .... Vendor G0611

Hampsten, Elizabeth. **Settlers' Children: Growing up on the Great Plains**. 1991.

An account of the experience of children in the earliest settlements of the American West after the Civil War.

Cloth. $19.95. 252 pp. .... Vendor G0611

Hiner, N. Ray, and Joseph M. Hawes, eds. **Growing Up in America: Children in Historical Perspective**. 1985.

A social history of childhood. Provides illuminating insights on children from infancy to adolescence and from the colonial period to the present.

Paper. $13.95. 310 pp. .... Vendor G0611

Hoffman and Albert. **Women in the Age of the American Revolution**. 1989.

Collection of essays studying the situation of women during this period: inheritance, social history, property rights, white and black women. Extensive footnotes.

Paper. $17.95. 516 pp. .... Vendor G0611

Kolodny. **The Land Before Her: Fantasy and Experience of the American Frontiers, 1630-1860**. 1984.

How did women deal with the tremendous challenge of life in the wilderness, far from the safety of their childhood? Kolodny shows how they constructed their own mythology around their situation to make their home in the wilderness.

Paper. $12.95. 293 pp. .... Vendor G0611

Leavitt. **Brought to Bed: Childbearing in America, 1750-1950**. 1986.

An excellent treatment of this subject, this book goes beyond the childbearing questions to examine women's place in society.

Paper. $11.95. 284 pp. .... Vendor G0611

May. **Great Expectations: Marriage and Divorce in Post-Victorian America**. 1980.

During the late 19th and early 20th centuries, the divorce rate in the U.S. rose a staggering 2,000 percent. May studied over 1,000 divorce cases to determine the reasons.

Paper. $11.95. 200 pp. .... Vendor G0611

Morgan. **Wilderness at Dawn: The Settling of the North American Continent**. 1933.

This easy-to-read, fascinating chronicle of the United States tells the story of the ordinary settlers, women, slaves, and Native Americans who actually shaped the country. Morgan is an engrossing and powerful storyteller who has researched well.

Paper. $15.00. 518 pp. .... Vendor G0611

Namias. **White Captives: Gender and Ethnicity on the American Frontier**. 1993.
Very interesting look at the captivity of white men and women within Indian society.
Paper. $17.95. 378 pp. .... Vendor G0611

Shammas, Carole, Marylynn Salmon, and Michel Dahlin. **Inheritance in America: From Colonial Times to the Present**. (1987) reprint 1996.
Paper. $19.95. 320 pp. .... Vendor G0611

Shryock, Richard Harrison. **Medicine and Society in America: 1660-1860**. 1960.
A history of the medical profession and medicine in America from the 1600s through the 1800s.
Paper. $11.95. 182 pp. .... Vendor G0611

Ulrich. **A Midwife's Tale**. 1990.
Based on Martha Ballard's diary of her midwifery and her life from 1785-1812 in Hallowell, Maine. Many locals are mentioned, but this book is interesting for the portrait of the medical practices, religious squabbles, and sexual mores of the time.
Paper. $13.00. 444 pp. .... Vendor G0611

Humor

Baselt, Fonda D. **The Sunny Side of Genealogy**. 1988.
Paper. $8.95. 102 pp. .... Vendor G0010

Galeener-Moore, Laverne. **Collecting Dead Relatives**. (1987) reprint 1995. Illus.
Paper. $8.95. 155 pp. .... Vendor G0010

Galeener-Moore, Laverne. **Further Undertakings of A Dead Relative Collector**. (1989) reprint 1992.
Paper. $9.95. 167 pp. .... Vendor G0010

Immigration, Emigration, Migration

General References

Anderson, Robert Charles. **The Great Migration Begins: Immigrants to New England 1620-1633**. 3 vols. 1995.
Cloth. $131.00. 717 + 645 + 700 pp. .... Vendor G0406

Bodnar. **The Transplanted: A History of Immigrants in Urban America**. 1985.
Social history of the immigrant experience, 1830-1930.
Paper. $13.95. 294 pp. .... Vendor G0611

IMMIGRANTS TO AMERICA:

❧ From Germany
❧ From France
❧ From Great Britain
❧ From Eastern Europe
Free catalog on request

Westland Publications
POB 117
McNeal, AZ 85617-0117

Colletta, John Phillip. **They Came in Ships: A Guide to Finding Your Immigrant Ancestor's Arrival Record (Revised Edition)**. 1993.
Paper. $9.95. 108 pp. .... Vendor G0570

Daniels. **Coming to America: A History of Immigration and Ethnicity in American Life**. 1990. Illus.
    A comprehensive look at immigration to America, complete with pictures, charts, and maps.
Paper. $16.00. 450 pp. .... Vendor G0611

Filby, William P. **Passenger and Immigration Lists Index**. 3 vols. Published by Gale Research. 1981.
Cloth. $440.00/set. 2,340 pp. .... Vendor G0560

Filby, William P. **Passenger and Immigration Lists Index, 1996 Supplement**. Published by Gale Research.
Cloth. $195.00. 500 pp. .... Vendor G0560

Filby, William P. **Passenger and Immigration Lists Index—Individual Supplements from 1982-1995**. Published by Gale Research.
Cloth. $195.00/supplement. .... Vendor G0560

Filby, William P. **Passenger and Immigration Lists Index—1991-1995 Cumulated Supplements**. Published by Gale Research.
Cloth. $530.00. .... Vendor G0560

Heisey, John W. **American Migration Guide**.
Paper. $10.00. 28 pp. .... Vendor G0574

Higham. **Send These to Me: Immigrants in Urban America**. Rev. ed. 1984.
    Examines overall relations between immigration and other aspects of American history. Interesting ethnic history.
Paper. $14.95. 261 pp. .... Vendor G0611

Jones. **American Immigration**. 2nd ed. 1992.
    Looks at the forces that uprooted emigrants from their roots and their adjustment to American life.
Paper. $18.95. 353 pp. .... Vendor G0611

Library of Congress. **Immigrant Arrivals:** A Guide to Published Sources. Compiled by Virginia Steele Wood.
 The text of this is available on the Local History and Genealogy Reading Room's home page: http://lcweb.loc.gov/rr/genealogy.
Free. Contact vendor for information. 13 pp. .... Vendor G0566

Miller, Olga K. **Migration, Emigration, Immigration**. Vol. 1.
 The book is divided into sections dealing with the colonies, religious and refugee groups, heraldry, states of the United States, and European countries.
Paper. $19.95. 278 pp. .... Vendor G0618

Miller, Olga K. **Migration, Emigration, Immigration**. Vol. 2.
 Vol. 2 of this series contains additional information not found in the first volume concerning migration of gypsies, blacks, Jews, etc. Migration information about several additional foreign countries has also been included.
Paper. $9.25. 148 pp. .... Vendor G0618

National Archives. **Immigrant & Passenger Arrivals**. A Select Catalog of National Archives Microfilm Publications. 1983. 2nd ed. 1991.
Paper. $3.50. 192 pp. .... Vendor G0565

Szucs, Loretto Dennis. **Ellis Island: Gateway to America**. 1986.
 Tells the history of Ellis Island and describes how to trace your family history.
Paper. $2.95. 32 pp. .... Vendor G0570

Yans-McLaughlin. **Immigration Reconsidered: History, Sociology, and Politics**. 1990.
 Offers a scholarly approach to immigration studies.
Paper. $15.95. 342 pp. .... Vendor G0611

British

Public Record Office. **Emigrants: Documents in the Public Record Office**.
Information leaflet. Contact vendor for information. .... Vendor G0558

Public Record Office. **Immigrants: Documents in the PRO**.
Information leaflet. Contact vendor for information. .... Vendor G0558

Public Record Office. **Tracing an Ancestor Who Was an Emigrant**.
Information leaflet. Contact vendor for information. .... Vendor G0558

Public Record Office. **Tracing an Ancestor Who Was an Immigrant**.
Information leaflet. Contact vendor for information. .... Vendor G0558

Smith, Clifford N. **The Immigrant Ancestor: A Survey of Westland Monographs on Emigration from Germany, Great Britain, France, Switzerland, and Eastern Europe**. 1994.
 ISBN 0-915162-71-7.
Paper. $20.00. 28 pp. double-columned. .... Vendor G0491

Smith, Clifford N. **British Deportees to America**. British-American Genealogical Research Series. 8 parts.
Part 1: 1760-1763 (1977; 97 pp.). ISBN 0-915162-25-3.
Part 2: 1764-1765 (1979; 100 pp.). ISBN 0-915162-26-1.
Part 3: 1766-1767 (1981; 73 pp.). ISBN 0-915162-27-X.
Part 4: 1768-1769 (1986; 34 pp. double-columned). ISBN 0-915162-29-6.
Part 5: 1770-1771 (1986; 31 pp. double-columned). ISBN 0-915162-30-X.
Part 6: 1772-1773 (1987; 36 pp. double-columned). ISBN 0-915162-31-8.
Part 7: 1774-1775 (1987; 37 pp. double-columned). ISBN 0-915162-32-6.
Part 8: Cumulative Surname Index, 1760-1775 (1987; 22 pp. double-columned). ISBN 0-915162-33-4.
Paper. $20.00/part. .... Vendor G0491

Smith, Frank. **Immigrants to America Appearing in English Records**.
Contains key information about how to locate former place of residence in the British Isles for immigrant ancestors.
Paper. $11.50. 117 pp. .... Vendor G0618

Canadian

Smith, Leonard H. **Nova Scotia Immigrants to 1867**. 1994.
Cloth. $37.50. 560 pp. .... Vendor G0010

Smith, Leonard H. **Nova Scotia Immigrants to 1867, Volume II**. 1994.
Cloth. $30.00. 304 pp. .... Vendor G0010

Czech

Baca, Leo. **Czech Immigration Passenger Lists, Volume I**. (1983) reprint 1989. Indexed.
Galveston 1848-1861, 1865-1871. New Orleans 1852-1879.
Paper. $17.95. 180 pp. .... Vendor G0481

Baca, Leo. **Czech Immigration Passenger Lists, Volume II**. (1985) reprint 1991. Indexed.
Galveston 1896-1906. New Orleans 1879-1899.
Paper. $17.05. 196 pp. .... Vendor G0481

Baca, Leo. **Czech Immigration Passenger Lists, Volume III**. (1989) reprint 1993. Indexed.
Galveston 1907-1914.
Paper. $17.95. 170 pp. .... Vendor G0481

Baca, Leo. **Czech Immigration Passenger Lists, Volume IV**. (1991) reprint 1994. Indexed.
New York 1847-1869.
Paper. $17.05. 182 pp. .... Vendor G0481

Baca, Leo. **Czech Immigration Passenger Lists, Volume V**. (1993) reprint 1996. Indexed.
New York 1870-1880.
Paper. $19.95. 190 pp. .... Vendor G0481

Baca, Leo. **Czech Immigration Passenger Lists, Volume VI**. 1995. Indexed.
New York 1881-1886. Galveston 1880-1886.
Paper. $19.95. 260 pp. .... Vendor G0481

Danish

Library of Congress. **Danish Immigration to America: An Annotated Bibliography of Resources at the Library of Congress** By Lee Douglas.
The text of this is available on the Local History and Genealogy Reading Room's home page: http://lcweb.loc.gov/rr/genealogy
Free. Contact vendor for information. 8 pp. .... Vendor G0566

Smith, Clifford N. **Emigrants from the Island of Foehr (Formerly Denmark, Now Schleswig-Holstein, Germany) to Australia, Canada, Chile, the United States, and the West Indies**. German-American Genealogical Research Monograph Number 17. 1983.
ISBN 0-915162-19-9.
Paper. $20.00. iii + 33 pp. .... Vendor G0491

Dutch

Brinks, Herbert J. **Dutch American Voices: Letters from the United States, 1850-1930**. 1995.
A fascinating collection of letters from the Dutch Immigrant Letter Collection at Calvin College. Includes an introduction to Dutch immigration history.
Cloth. $35.00. 480 pp. .... Vendor G0611

Swierenga. **The Dutch in America: Immigration, Settlement, and Cultural Change**. 1985.
Well-documented look at Dutch immigration and settlements.
Cloth. $45.00. 303 pp. .... Vendor G0611

Swierenga, Robert P. **Dutch Emigrants to the United States, South Africa, South America, and Southeast Asia, 1835-1880: An Alphabetical Listing by Household Heads and Independent Persons**. 1983. Indexed.
Cloth. $67.50. 346 pp. .... Vendor G0118

Swierenga, Robert P. **Dutch Immigrants in U.S. Ship Passenger Manifests, 1820-1880: An Alphabetical Listing by Household Heads and Independent Persons**. 2 vols. 1983. Indexed.
Cloth. $152.50. .... Vendor G0118

Eastern European

Smith, Clifford N. **The Immigrant Ancestor: A Survey of Westland Monographs on Emigration from Germany, Great Britain, France, Switzerland, and Eastern Europe**. 1994.
    ISBN 0-915162-71-7.
Paper. $20.00. 28 pp. double-columned. .... Vendor G0491

English

Banks, Charles Edward. **The English Ancestry and Homes of the Pilgrim Fathers** Who Came to Plymouth on the Mayflower in 1620, the Fortune in 1621, and the Anne and the Little James in 1623. (1929) reprint 1997. Indexed.
Cloth. $18.50. 187 pp. .... Vendor G0010

Banks, Charles Edward. **Topographical Dictionary of 2885 English Emigrants to New England, 1620-1650**. (1937) reprint 1992. Indexed. Illus.
Cloth. $25.00. 333 pp. .... Vendor G0010

Banks, Charles Edward. **The Winthrop Fleet of 1630**. An Account of the Vessels, the Voyage, the Passengers and Their English Homes, from Original Authorities. (1930) reprint 1994. Indexed. Illus.
Cloth. $15.00. ix + 119 pp. .... Vendor G0010

Brandow, James C. **Omitted Chapters from Hotten's Original Lists of Persons of Quality**. . . And Others Who Went from Great Britain to the American Plantations, 1600-1700. Census Returns, Parish Registers, and Militia Rolls From the Barbados Census of 1679/80. 1983.
Cloth. $20.00. 245 pp. .... Vendor G0010

Coldham, Peter Wilson. **The Bristol Registers of Servants** Sent to Foreign Plantations, 1654-1686. 1988. Indexed.
Cloth. $30.00. 491 pp. .... Vendor G0010

Coldham, Peter Wilson. **Child Apprentices** in America from Christ's Hospital, London, 1617-1778. 1990. Indexed.
Cloth. $21.50. 164 pp. .... Vendor G0010

Coldham, Peter Wilson. **The Complete Book of Emigrants in Bondage, 1614-1775**. 1988.
Cloth. $60.00. 920 pp. .... Vendor G0010

Coldham, Peter Wilson. **Supplement to The Complete Book of Emigrants in Bondage, 1614-1775**. 1992.
Paper. $9.00. 86 pp. .... Vendor G0010

Coldham, Peter Wilson. **The Complete Book of Emigrants, 1607-1660**. (1988) reprint 1992. Indexed.
Contact vendor for information. 600 pp. .... Vendor G0010

Coldham, Peter Wilson. **The Complete Book of Emigrants, 1661-1699**. (1990) reprint 1993. Indexed.
Contact vendor for information. 900 pp. .... Vendor G0010

Coldham, Peter Wilson. **The Complete Book of Emigrants, 1700-1750**. (1992) reprint 1993. Indexed.
Cloth. $44.95. 748 pp. .... Vendor G0010

Coldham, Peter Wilson. **The Complete Book of Emigrants, 1751-1776**. 1993. Indexed.
Cloth. $29.95. 358 pp. .... Vendor G0010

Coldham, Peter Wilson. **Emigrants from England to the American Colonies, 1773-1776**. 1988. Indexed.
Cloth. $22.50. 182 pp. .... Vendor G0010

Coldham, Peter Wilson. **Emigrants in Chains**. A Social History of Forced Emigration to the Americas of Felons, Destitute Children, Political and Religious Non-Conformists, Vagabonds, Beggars and Other Undesirables, 1607-1776. (1992) reprint 1994.
Cloth. $21.95. 196 pp. .... Vendor G0010

Coldham, Peter Wilson. **English Adventurers and Emigrants, 1609-1660** Abstracts of Examinations in the High Court of Admiralty with Reference to Colonial America. (1984) reprint 1991. Indexed.
Cloth. $22.50. 219 pp. .... Vendor G0011

Coldham, Peter Wilson. **English Adventurers and Emigrants, 1661-1733**. 1985. Indexed.
Cloth. $15.00. 238 pp. .... Vendor G0011

Erickson. **Leaving England: Essays on British Emigration in the Nineteenth Century**. 1994.
    A series of essays studies the ship passenger lists of British immigrants and explores the social impact of their arrivals. Also comments on immigrations to Canada and Australia with contrast to America.
Cloth. $39.95. 272 pp. .... Vendor G0611

Erickson, Charlotte. **Invisible Immigrants: The Adaption of English and Scottish Immigrants in 19th-Century America**. (1972) reprint 1990.
    A remarkable collection of letters from people who immigrated to America in the 19th century and who kept in touch with friends and relatives in England and Scotland. Over 200 letters from 25 families are included.
Paper. $18.95. 531 pp. .... Vendor G0611

Fischer. **Albion's Seed: Four British Folkways in America**. 1989.

This is an absolutely fascinating book that should be read and enjoyed by anyone tracing British ancestors who came into America between 1628 and 1775. This is an in-depth look at these immigrants, their customs and their life. Abundant footnotes add to its value as a research tool.

Paper. $24.95. 946 pp. .... Vendor G0611

Fothergill, Gerald. **Emigrants from England 1773-1776**. (1913) reprint 1992. Indexed.

Contact vendor for information. 206 pp. .... Vendor G0011

French, Elizabeth. **List of Emigrants to America from Liverpool, 1697- 1707**. (1913) reprint 1983. Indexed.

Paper. $5.00. 55 pp. .... Vendor G0010

Ghirelli, Michael. **A List of Emigrants from England to America, 1682-1692**. (1968) reprint 1989. Indexed.

Cloth. $11.50. 120 pp. .... Vendor G0011

Hargreaves-Mawdsley, R. **Bristol and America**. A Record of the First Settlers in the Colonies of North America, 1654-1685. (1929, 1931) reprint 1995. Indexed.

Records the name of practically every person who left England for Virginia, Maryland, and the West Indies for the period covered.

Paper. $20.00. 198 pp. .... Vendor G0011

Hotten, John Camden. **The Original Lists of Persons of Quality** Who Went from Great Britain to the American Plantations, 1600-1700. Localities Where They Formerly Lived in the Mother Country, the Names of the Ships in Which They Embarked and Other Interesting Particulars. (1874) reprint 1996. Indexed.
Paper. $45.00. 580 pp. .... Vendor G0011

Jewson, Charles Boardman. **Transcripts of Three Registers of Passengers from Great Yarmouth to Holland and New England, 1637-1639**. (1964) reprint 1990. Indexed.
Cloth. $12.00. 98 pp. .... Vendor G0011

Kaminkow, Marion, and Jack Kaminkow. **A List of Emigrants from England to America, 1718-1759**. (1981) reprint 1989. Indexed.
Cloth. $15.00. 320 pp. .... Vendor G0011

Newsome, A. R., ed. **Records of Emigrants from England and Scotland to North Carolina, 1774-1775**. 4th printing, 1989.
   Contains lists of persons who took passage on ships from Great Britain to North Carolina. The lists include nearly 100 emigrants from England and nearly 500 emigrants, including 100 family groups, from Scotland.
Paper. $3.00. 30 pp. .... Vendor G0586

Nicholson, Gregoe D. P. **Some Early Emigrants to America [and] Early Emigrants to America from Liverpool**. (1965) reprint 1989. Indexed.
Contact vendor for information. 110 pp. .... Vendor G0011

European

Glasgow Family History Society. **European Immigration into Scotland**.
Paper. £4.50. .... Vendor G0555

Record of Indentures [1771-1773] of Individuals Bound Out as Apprentices, Servants, Etc. And of German and Other Redemptioners in the Office of the Mayor of the City of Philadelphia, October 3, 1771, to October 5, 1773. (Excerpted from The Pennsylvania-German Society Proceedings and Addresses, XVI, 1907). (1907, 1973) reprint 1995. Indexed.
   The vast majority of the passengers cited herein sailed from British, Irish, or Dutch ports, though some passengers were of German origin. Information given for each individual includes the port of embarkation, exact date of arrival, name of person to whom apprenticed or indentured, residence here, occupation, term of service, and exact price of apprenticeship or indenture.
Paper. $30.00. 364 pp. .... Vendor G0011

Rupp, Israel Daniel. **A Collection of Upwards of Thirty Thousand Names of German, Swiss, Dutch, French and Other Immigrants in Pennsylvania from 1727 to 1776**. (1876, 1931) reprint 1994. Indexed. Illus.
Cloth. $30.00. 583 pp. .... Vendor G0010

Smith, Clifford N. **Reconstructed Passenger Lists for 1850: Hamburg to Australia, Brazil, Canada, Chile, and the United States**. German and Central European Emigration Monograph Number 1. 4 parts.

Part 1: Passenger Lists 1 Through 25 (1980; 79 pp.).
Part 2: Passenger Lists 26 Through 42 (1980; 86 pp.).
Part 3: Passenger Lists 43 Through 60 (1981; 63 pp.).
Part 4: Supplemental Notes on Emigrants' Places of Origin (1981; 58 pp.).
ISBN 0-915162-50-4 (the set).
Paper. $20.00/part... Vendor G0491

Smith, Clifford N. **Reconstructed Passenger Lists for 1851 via Hamburg: Emigrants from Germany, Austria, Bohemia, Hungary, Poland, Russia, Scandinavia, and Switzerland to Australia, Brazil, Canada, Chile, the United States, and Venezuela**. German and Central European Emigration Monograph Number. 5 parts.
Part 1: Passenger Lists 1 Through 22 (1986; 45 pp. double-columned).
ISBN 0-915162-51-2.
Part 2: Passenger Lists 23 Through 44 (1986; 41 pp. double-columned).
ISBN 0- 915162-52-0.
Part 3: Passenger Lists 45 Through 66 (1986; 53 pp. double-columned).
ISBN 0- 915162-53-9.
Part 4: Passenger Lists 67 Through 85 (1986; 26 pp. double-columned).
ISBN 0- 915162-54-7.
Part 5: Supplemental Notes on Emigrants' Places of Origin: Place Names A Through L (1987; ii + 41 pp. double-columned). ISBN 0-915162-55-5.
Part 5: Supplemental Notes on Emigrants' Places of Origin: Place Names M Through Z (1987; ii + 38 pp. double-columned). ISBN 0-915162-55-5.
Paper. $20.00/part... Vendor G0491

Wyman, Mark. **Round-Trip to America: The Immigrants Return to Europe, 1880-1930**. 1993.
An interesting perspective on the 4 million immigrants who came to America and then returned to their native lands.
Paper. $14.95. 267 pp. .... Vendor G0611

French

Smith, Clifford N. **Emigrants from France (Haut-Rhin Departement) to America** French-American Genealogical Research Monograph Number 2.
Part 1: 1837-1844 (1986; ii + 36 pp. double-columned). ISBN 0-915162-61-X.
Part 2: 1845-1847 (1989; i + 46 pp. double-columned). ISBN 0-915162-62-8.
Part 3: Contact vendor for information.
Paper. $20.00/part... Vendor G0491

Smith, Clifford N. **The Immigrant Ancestor: A Survey of Westland Monographs on Emigration from Germany, Great Britain, France, Switzerland, and Eastern Europe**. 1994.
ISBN 0-915162-71-7.
Paper. $20.00. 28 pp. double-columned. .... Vendor G0491

Smith, Clifford N. **Immigrants to America from France (Haut-Rhin Departement) and Western Switzerland, 1859-1866**. French-American Genealogical Research Monograph Number 1. 1983.
ISBN 0-915162-60-1.
Paper. $20.00. i + 33 pp. double-columned. .... Vendor G0491

Wesner, Doris. **Alsatian Connections, Volume I**. Indexed.
Cloth. $39.95. 474 pp. .... Vendor G0536

German

Burgert, Annette K. **Eighteenth Century Emigrants from Northern Alsace to America**. 1992. Indexed. Illus.
Cloth. $53.50. 714 pp. .... Vendor G0458

Burgert, Annette K. **Eighteenth Century Emigrants from Pfungstadt, Hessen-Darmstadt to Pennsylvania**. 1995. Indexed. Illus.
Paper. $17.00. 50 pp. .... Vendor G0458

Burgert, Annette K. **Eighteenth Century Emigrants, Volume II:** The Western Palatinate. 1985. Indexed. Illus.
Cloth. $43.00. 421 pp. .... Vendor G0458

Master Index to the Emigrants Documented in the Published Works of Annette K. Burgert. 1993.
   Alphabetically arranged.
Paper. $11.50. 70 pp. .... Vendor G0458

Burgert, Annette K., and Henry Z Jones, Jr. **Westerwald to America**. 1989. Indexed. Illus.
   Book # 1132
Cloth. $29.95. 284 pp. .... Vendor G0082

Burgert, Annette K., and Henry Z Jones, Jr. **Westerwald to America:** Some 18th Century Immigrants. 1989. Indexed. Illus.
Cloth. $32.45. 278 pp. .... Vendor G0458

Burgert, Annette K., and Henry Z Jones, Jr. **Westerwald to America:** Some 18th Century German Immigrants. Indexed. Illus.
   Documents the German origins of more than 265 individuals and/or families who immigrated to Pennsylvania, New Jersey, New York, Maryland, and Virginia.
Cloth. $29.95 + $2.50 p&h. 272 pp. .... Vendor G0581

Diffenderffer, Frank R. **The German Immigration into Pennsylvania** through the Port of Philadelphia, from 1700 to 1775, and the Redemptioners. (1900) reprint 1988. Indexed. Illus.
Cloth. $21.50. 328 pp. .... Vendor G0010

Geue, Chester W., and Ethel H. Geue. **A New Land Beckoned**. German Immigration to Texas, 1844-1847. (1972) reprint 11982.
Contact vendor for information. .... Vendor G0011

Geue, Ethel H. **New Homes in a New Land**. German Immigration to Texas, 1847-1861. (1970) reprint 1994. Indexed. Illus.
   Contains information gleaned from the passenger lists of ships that arrived at Galveston between the years 1847 and 1861, with a history of the German immigration to Texas during this formative period.
Paper. $18.50. 175 pp. .... Vendor G0011

Glazier, Ira A., and P. William Filby. **Germans to America: Lists of Passengers Arriving at U.S. Ports, 1850-1893**. Indexed.

Data on German immigrants listed by ship and indexed by surname. Call 800-772-8937 for complete volume breakdown. $77.50 per volume—ongoing publication.

Cloth. $77.50. .... Vendor G0118

Grubb, Farley. **German Immigrant Servant Contracts** Registered at the Port of Philadelphia, 1817-1831. 1994. Indexed.

Cloth. $15.00. 158 pp. .... Vendor G0011

Hacker, Professor Werner. **Eighteenth Century Register of Emigrants from Southwest Germany**.

Contact vendor for information. 516 pp. .... Vendor G0536

Luebke, Frederick C. **Germans in the New World: Essays in the History of Immigration**. 1990.

A history of German immigration to the United States and Brazil.

Cloth. $24.95. 198 pp. .... Vendor G0611

Schenk, Trudy, and Ruth Froelke, comps. **Wuerttemberg Emigration Index (Volumes I, II, III, IV, V, VI)**.

A source of information of individuals who applied to emigrate from Wuerttemberg between 1750 and 1900. Volume I has 240 pages, Volumes II-V have 248 pages, and Volume VI has 496 pages.

Paper. $19.95/Vols. I-V. $29.95/Vol. VI. $89.95/set. .... Vendor G0570

Schrader-Muggenthaler, Cornelia. **The Alsace Emigration Book I**.

Cloth. $24.95. 277 pp. .... Vendor G0536

Schrader-Muggenthaler, Cornelia. **The Alsace Emigration Book II**. Illus.

Cloth. $24.95. 203 pp. .... Vendor G0536

Simmendinger, Ullrich. **True and Authentic Register of Persons . . . Who in The Year 1709 Journeyed . . . from Germany to America**. (1934) reprint 1991.

Paper. $4.00. 20 pp. .... Vendor G0010

Smith, Clifford N. **Eighteenth-Century Emigrants from Kreis Simmern (Hunsrueck), Rheinland-Pfalz, Germany, to Central Europe, Pfalzdorf am Niederrhein, and North America**. German-American Genealogical Research Monograph Number 16. 1982.

ISBN 0-915162-15-6.

Paper. $20.00. iii + 23 pp. .... Vendor G0491

Smith, Clifford N. **Emigrants from Fellbach (Baden-Wuerttemberg, Germany), 1735-1930**. German-American Genealogical Research Monograph Number 14. 1984.

ISBN 0-915162-83-0.

Paper. $20.00. 11 + 48 pp. .... Vendor G0491

Smith, Clifford N. **Emigrants from Saxony (Grandduchy of Sachsen-Weimar-Eisenach) to America, 1854, 1859**. German-American Genealogical Research Monograph Number 4. 1974.

ISBN 0-915162-03-2.

Paper. $20.00. 32 pp. .... Vendor G0491

Smith, Clifford N. **Emigrants from the Former Amt Damme, Oldenburg (Now Niedersachsen), Germany, Mainly to the United States**. German-American Genealogical Research Monograph Number 12. 1981.
   ISBN 0-915162-11-3.
Paper. $20.00. ii + 84 pp. .... Vendor G0491

Smith, Clifford N. **Emigrants from the Island of Foehr (Formerly Denmark, Now Schleswig-Holstein, Germany) to Australia, Canada, Chile, the United States, and the West Indies**. German-American Genealogical Research Monograph Number 17. 1983.
   ISBN 0-915162-19-9.
Paper. $20.00. iii + 33 pp. .... Vendor G0491

Smith, Clifford N. **Emigrants from the Principality of Hessen-Hanau, Germany, 1741-1767**. German-American Genealogical Research Monograph Number 6. 1979.
   ISBN 0-915162-05-9.
Paper. $20.00. 22 pp. .... Vendor G0491

Smith, Clifford N. **Emigrants from the West-German Fuerstenberg Territories (Baden and the Palatinate) to America and Central Europe, 1712, 1737, 1787**. German-American Genealogical Research Monograph Number 9. 1981.
   ISNB 0-915162-08-3.
Paper. $20.00. ii + 46 pp. .... Vendor G0491

Smith, Clifford N. **From Bremen to America in 1850: Fourteen Rare Emigrant Ship Lists**. German-American Genealogical Research Monograph Number 22. 1988.
   ISBN 0-915162-81-4.
Paper. $20.00. iii + 35 pp. double-columned. .... Vendor G0491

Smith, Clifford N. **German Revolutionists of 1848: Among Whom Many Immigrants to America** German-American Genealogical Research Monograph Number 21. 4 parts.
   Part 1: Surnames A Through F (1985; ii + 37 pp. double-columned).
ISBN 0- 915162-77-6.
   Part 2: Surnames G Through K (1985; 38 pp. double-columned).
ISBN 0-915162-78-4.
   Part 3: Surnames L Through R (1985; 33 pp. double-columned).
ISBN 0-915162-79-2.
   Part 4: Surnames S Through Z (1985; 40 pp. double-columned).
ISBN 0-915162-80-6.
Paper. $20.00/part. .... Vendor G0491

Smith, Clifford N. **The Immigrant Ancestor: A Survey of Westland Monographs on Emigration from Germany, Great Britain, France, Switzerland, and Eastern Europe**. 1994.
   ISBN 0-915162-71-7.
Paper. $20.00. 28 pp. double-columned. .... Vendor G0491

Smith, Clifford N. **Immigrants to America (Mainly Wisconsin) from the Former Recklinghausen District (Nordrhein-Westfalen, Germany) Around the Middle of the Nineteenth Century**. German-American Genealogical Research Monograph Number 15. 1983.
   ISBN 0-915162-12-1.
Paper. $20.00. iv + 28 pp. .... Vendor G0491

Smith, Clifford N. **Immigrants to America and Central Europe from Beihingen am Neckar, Baden-Wuerttemberg, Germany**. German-American Genealogical Research Monograph Number 11. 1980.
    ISBN 0-915162-10-5.
Paper. $20.00. 49 pp. .... Vendor G0491

Smith, Clifford N. **Missing Young Men of Wuerttemberg, Germany, 1807: Some Possible Immigrants to America**. German-American Genealogical Research Monograph Number 18. 1983.
    ISBN 0-915162-20-3
Paper. $20.00. vi + 43 pp. double-columned. .... Vendor G0491

Smith, Clifford N. **Nineteenth-Century Emigration from Kreis Simmern (Hunsrueck), Rheinland-Pfalz, Germany, to Brazil, England, Russian Poland, and the United States of America**. German-American Genealogical Research Monograph Number 8. 1980.
    ISBN 0-915162-07-5.
Paper. $20.00. 35 pp. .... Vendor G0491

Smith, Clifford N. **Nineteenth-Century Emigration from the Siegkreis, Nordrhein-Westfalen, Germany, Mainly to the United States**. German-American Genealogical Research Monograph Number 10. 1980.
    ISBN 0-915162-09-1.
Paper. $20.00. 55 pp. .... Vendor G0491

Smith, Clifford N. **Nineteenth-Century Emigration of "Old Lutherans" from Eastern Germany (Mainly Pomerania and Lower Silesia) to Australia, Canada, and the United States**. German-American Genealogical Research Monograph Number 7. 1980.
    ISBN 0-915162-06-7.
Paper. $20.00. 93 pp. double-columned. .... Vendor G0491

Smith, Clifford N. **Passenger Lists (and Fragments Thereof) from Hamburg and Bremen to Australia and the United States, 1846-1849**. German-American Genealogical Research Monograph Number 23. 1988.
    ISBN 0-915162-82-2.
Paper. $20/00. i + 27 pp. double-columned. .... Vendor G0491

Smith, Clifford N. **Political Activists from Hesse, Germany, 1832-1834: Among Whom Many Immigrants to America**. German-American Genealogical Research Monograph Number 29. 1993.
Paper. $20.00. i + 25 pp. double-columned. .... Vendor G0491

Smith, Clifford N. **Reconstructed Passenger Lists for 1850: Hamburg to Australia, Brazil, Canada, Chile, and the United States**. German and Central European Emigration Monograph Number 1. 4 parts.
    Part 1: Passenger Lists 1 Through 25 (1980; 79 pp.).
    Part 2: Passenger Lists 26 Through 42 (1980; 86 pp.).
    Part 3: Passenger Lists 43 Through 60 (1981; 63 pp.).
    Part 4: Supplemental Notes on Emigrants' Places of Origin (1981; 58 pp.).
    ISBN 0-915162-50-4 (the set).
Paper. $20.00/part. .... Vendor G0491

Strassburger, Ralph Beaver, and William John Hinke. **Pennsylvania German Pioneers, 3 Volume Set**. (1937) reprint 1992. Indexed.
Cloth. $175.00. 2,560 pp. .... Vendor G0082

Strassburger, Ralph Beaver. **Pennsylvania German Pioneers: A Publication of the Original Lists of Arrivals in the Port of Philadelphia from 1727 to 1808**. 2 vols. (1934) reprint 1992. Indexed.
Cloth. $75.00. 1,485 pp. total .... Vendor G0010

Strassburger, Ralph Beaver, and William John Hinke. **Pennsylvania German Pioneers: Pennsylvania German Pioneers, 3 Volume Set** A Publication of the Original Lists of Arrivals in the Port of Philadelphia From 1727 to 1808, Signature Volume. (1934) reprint 1992.
    This set, which is commonly known as "Strassburger & Hinke," is the time-honored reference for arrival of German emigrants to America before 1800. It is one of the basic works for genealogical libraries.Volumes 1 and 3 have been reprinted a number of times, but this is the first time this volume (which shows the actual signatures of the emigrants) has been reprinted. This signature volume is important as it may be used to check signatures on wills, deeds, and other documents to ascertain whether they were written by the same man. This volume has been printed the same size and with the same cover as the other currently available volumes so that they will make a matching set. It is being sold separately for purchase by those who already have the other two volumes. It is necessary to have the other volumes in order to use this one as it does not have a separate index. For those who do not have any of this set, all three volumes are available from us as a set for the very special price of $100.00. The other volumes total 1,565 pages. All three are printed on acid-free paper and are Smythe-sewn with cloth bindings.
Cloth. $55.00. 909 pp. .... Vendor G0081

Tribbeko, John, and George Ruperti. **List of Germans from the Palatinate Who Came to England in 1709**. (1909-10) reprint 1996.
Paper. $7.00. 44 pp. .... Vendor G0011

Wesner, Doris. **Alsatian Connections, Volume I**. Indexed.
Cloth. $39.95. 474 pp. .... Vendor G0536

Yoder, Don, ed. **Pennsylvania German Immigrants, 1709-1786** Lists Consolidated from Yearbooks of The Pennsylvania German Folklore Society. (1984) reprint 1989. Indexed. Illus.
Cloth. $25.00. 394 pp. .... Vendor G0010

Zenglein, Dieter, et al. **To the Banks of the Ohio**. Translated from German by Ernest Thode. 1988. Index available. Illus.
    Fascinating German letters; history of migration from Kusel, Palatinate, Germany, to Fearing Twp., Washington County, OH.
Paper. $14.00 postpaid ($14.91 in OH). 64 pp. .... Vendor G0197

Zimmerman, Gary J., and Marion Wolfert. **German Immigrants,** Lists of Passengers Bound from Bremen to New York, 1847-1854, With Places of Origin. (1985) reprint 1993.
Cloth. $22.50. 175 pp. .... Vendor G0010

Zimmerman, Gary J., and Marion Wolfert. **German Immigrants,** Lists of Passengers Bound from Bremen to New York, 1855-1862, With Places of Origin. (1986) reprint 1993.
Cloth. $22.50. xx + 167 pp. .... Vendor G0010

Zimmerman, Gary J., and Marion Wolfert. **German Immigrants,** Lists of Passengers Bound from Bremen to New York, 1863-1867, With Places of Origin. 1988.
Cloth. $21.50. 221 pp. .... Vendor G0010

Zimmerman, Gary J., and Marion Wolfert. **German Immigrants,** Lists of Passengers Bound from Bremen to New York, 1868-1871, With Places of Origin. 1993.
Cloth. $25.00. 218 pp. .... Vendor G0010

German-Russian

Schrader-Muggenthaler, Cornelia. **Baden Emigration Book**.
Cloth. $22.95. 196 pp. .... Vendor G0536

Irish

Adams, Raymond D. **Ulster Emigrants to Philadelphia, 1803-1850**. (1992) reprint 1996.
Paper. $15.00. 102 pp. .... Vendor G0011

Adams, William Forbes. **Ireland and Irish Emigration to the New World** from 1815 to the Famine. (1932) reprint 1993. Indexed.
Paper. $32.50. 444 pp. .... Vendor G0011

Dobson, David. **Irish Emigrants in North America**. In Three Parts. (1994, 1995) reprint 1997.
Contact vendor for information. 54 pp. in all. .... Vendor G0011

Ellis, Eilish. **Emigrants from Ireland, 1847-1852**. State-Aided Emigration Schemes from Crown Estates in Ireland. (1960) reprint 1993.
Paper. $7.50. 68 pp. .... Vendor G0010

Glazier, Ira A., and Michael H. Tepper, eds. **The Famine Immigrants**. Lists of Irish Immigrants Arriving at the Port of New York, 1846-1851. 7 vols. 1983-1986. Indexed.
   Vol. I: January 1846-June 1847. 841 pp. Contact vendor for information.
   Vol. II: July 1847-June 1848. 722 pp. Indexed. 1983.
   Vol. III: July 1848-March 1849. 695 pp. Indexed. 1984.
   Vol. IV: April 1849-September 1849. 814 pp. Indexed. 1984.
   Vol. V: October 1849-May 1850. 638 pp. Indexed. 1985.
   Vol. VI: June 1850-March 1851. 898 pp. Indexed. 1985.
   Vol. VII: April 1851-December 1851. 1,195 pp. Indexed. 1986.
Cloth. $45.00/vol. .... Vendor G0010

Hackett, J. Dominick, and Charles M. Early. **Passenger Lists from Ireland** (Excerpted from Journal of the American Irish Historical Society, Volumes 28 and 29). (1931) reprint 1994.
Paper. $7.50. .... Vendor G0011

Harris, Ruth-Ann, Donald M. Jacobs, and B. Emer O'Keefe. **The Search for Missing Friends: Irish Immigrant Advertisements Placed in the Boston Pilot** (5 vols. to date). 1989-1996.
    Vol. 1: 1831-1850. 684 + lxii pp.
    Vol. 2: 1851-1853. 672 + xx pp.
    Vol. 3: 1854-1856. 672 + xx pp.
    Vol. 4: 1857-1860. 800 pp.
    Vol. 5: 1861-1865. Approx. 800 pp.
Cloth. $48.50/vol. .... Vendor G0406

King, Joseph A. **From Ireland to North America**.
    This book conveys the excitement and the pain of a people forced to risk an uncertain voyage to a hoped-for better life.
Paper. $13.95. .... Vendor G0611

Marshall, William F. **Ulster Sails West**. The Story of the Great Emigration from Ulster to North America in the 18th Century. . . (1950) reprint 1996.
Paper. $7.50. 79 pp. .... Vendor G0010

McDonnell, Frances. **Emigrants from Ireland to America, 1735-1743**. A Transcription of the Report of the Irish House of Commons into Enforced Emigration to America. 1992. Indexed.
Cloth. $18.50. 142 pp. .... Vendor G0010

Miller. **Emigrants & Exiles: Ireland and the Irish Exodus to North America**. 1985.
    In-depth study of Irish emigration to America, 1607-1921. Paints a vivid picture of Ireland and why so many Irish left her. Includes extensive footnotes.
Paper. $18.95. 684 pp. .... Vendor G0611

Miller, Kerby, and Paul Wagner. **Out of Ireland: The Story of Irish Emigration to America**. 1994. Illus.
    This moving portrayal of the history of Irish emigration to the U.S. from the 18th to 20th centuries uses as its primary source the remarkable memoirs and letters by and to Irish immigrants in America. Beautifully illustrated. $8^1/_2$" x 11".
Cloth. $24.95. 132 pp. .... Vendor G0611

Mitchell, Brian. **Irish Emigration Lists, 1833-1839**. Lists of Emigrants Extracted from the Ordnance Survey Memoirs for Counties Londonderry and Antrim. 1989. Indexed.
Cloth. $20.00. 128 pp. .... Vendor G0010

Mitchell, Brian. **Irish Passenger Lists, 1803-1806**. Lists of Passengers Sailing from Ireland to America. 1995. Indexed.
Cloth. $25.00. 154 pp. .... Vendor G0010

Mitchell, Brian. **Irish Passenger Lists, 1847-1871**. (1988) reprint 1992. Indexed.
Cloth. $28.50. 350 pp. .... Vendor G0010

Myers, Albert Cook. **Immigration of the Irish Quakers into Pennsylvania, 1682-1750**. With Their Early History in Ireland. (1902) reprint 1994. Indexed. Illus.
Cloth. $30.00. xxii + 477 pp. .... Vendor G0010

O'Brien, Michael J. **The Irish in America**. Immigration, Land, Probate, Administrations, Birth, Marriage and Burial Records of the Irish in America in and about the Eighteenth Century. (1965) reprint 1996.
Paper. $9.00. 63 pp. .... Vendor G0011

Italian

Glazier, Ira A., and P. William Filby. **Italians to America, 1880-1899: Lists of Passengers Arriving at U.S. Ports**. Indexed.
  Data on Italian immigrants listed by ship and indexed by surname. Call 800-772-8937 for complete volume breakdown. $77.50 per volume—ongoing publication.
Cloth. $77.50. .... Vendor G0118

Rolle. **The Italian Americans: Troubled Roots**. 1984.
  A full-scale "psychohistory of the immigration experience" written by the "dean of Italian immigration historians," this book traces the epic of the Italian Americans.
Paper. $13.95. 222 pp. .... Vendor G0611

Norwegian

Library of Congress. **A Select Bibliography of Works at the Library of Congress on Norwegian-American Immigration and Local History**. Compiled by Lee V. Douglas.
  The text of this is available on the Local History and Genealogy Reading Room's home page: http://lcweb.loc.gov/rr/genealogy.
Free. Contact vendor for information. 8 pp. .... Vendor G0566

Russian

Glazier, Ira A. **Migration from the Russian Empire**. Lists of Passengers Arriving at the Port of New York. Volume 1: January 1875-September 1882. 1995. Indexed.
Cloth. $60.00. 703 pp. .... Vendor G0010

Glazier, Ira A. **Migration from the Russian Empire**. Lists of Passengers Arriving at the Port of New York. Volume 2: October 1882-April 1886. 1995.
Cloth. $60.00. 631 pp. .... Vendor G0010

Glazier, Ira A. **Migration from the Russian Empire**. Lists of Passengers Arriving at the Port of New York. Volume 3: May 1886-December 1887. 1997.
Contact vendor for information. .... Vendor G0010

ROSS RESEARCH

Rt. 1, Box 39
Gladstone, IL 61437
309-924-1879

HENDERSON CO., ILLINOIS RESEARCH FAMILY HISTORY

Glazier, Ira A. **Migration from the Russian Empire**. Lists of Passengers Arriving at the Port of New York. Volume 4: January 1888-June 1889. 1997.
Contact vendor for information. .... Vendor G0010

Scottish

Aberdeen & North East Scotland Family History Society. **Hands Across the Water— Emigration from Northern Scotland to North America**—Proceedings of the 6th Annual Conf. of Scot. Assoc. of FH.
Paper. £2.10. .... Vendor G0555

Anglo Scottish Family History Society. **Dictionary of Scot Emigrants to England Vol. 1**.
Paper. £1.40. .... Vendor G0555

Anglo Scottish Family History Society. **Dictionary of Scot Emigrants to England Vol. 2**.
Paper. £1.40. .... Vendor G0555

Anglo Scottish Family History Society. **Dictionary of Scot Emigrants to England Vol. 3**.
Paper. £1.40. .... Vendor G0555

Anglo Scottish Family History Society. **Dictionary of Scot Emigrants to England Vol. 4**.
Paper. £1.40. .... Vendor G0555

Cameron, Viola R. **Emigrants from Scotland to America, 1774-1775**. (1930) reprint 1990. Indexed.
Cloth. $15.00. 117 pp. .... Vendor G0011

Dobson, David. **Directory of Scots Banished to the American Plantations, 1650-1775**. (1984) reprint 1996.
Paper. 24.00. 239 pp. .... Vendor G0011

Dobson, David. **Directory of Scots in The Carolinas, 1680-1830**. (1986) reprint 1994.
Cloth. $25.00. 322 pp. .... Vendor G0010

Dobson, David. **Directory of Scottish Settlers in North America, 1625-1825. Vol. I**. 1984.
Cloth. $20.00. 267 pp. .... Vendor G0010

Dobson, David. **Directory of Scottish Settlers in North America, 1625-1825. Vol. II**. 1984.
Cloth. $20.00. 216 pp. .... Vendor G0010

Dobson, David. **Directory of Scottish Settlers in North America, 1625-1825. Vol. III**. 1984.
Cloth. $17.50. 194 pp. .... Vendor G0010

Dobson, David. **Directory of Scottish Settlers in North America, 1625-1825. Vol. IV**. 1985.
Cloth. $17.50. 161 pp. .... Vendor G0010

Dobson, David. **Directory of Scottish Settlers in North America, 1625-1825. Vol. V**. 1985.
Cloth. $20.00. 312 pp. .... Vendor G0010

Dobson, David. **Directory of Scottish Settlers in North America, 1625-1825. Vol. VI**. 1986.
Cloth. $15.00. 126 pp. .... Vendor G0010

Dobson, David. **Directory of Scottish Settlers in North America, 1625-1825. Vol. VII**. 1993.
Cloth. $17.50 . 220 pp. .... Vendor G0010

Dobson, David. **Emigrants & Adventurers from Aberdeen & NE, Parts 1 & 2**.
Contact vendor for information. .... Vendor G0641

Dobson, David. **Emigrants & Adventurers from Angus & Perth, Part 1**.
Contact vendor for information. .... Vendor G0641

Dobson, David. **Emigrants & Adventurers from Argyll**.
Contact vendor for information. .... Vendor G0641

Dobson, David. **Emigrants & Adventurers from Moray & Banff, Part 1**.
Contact vendor for information. .... Vendor G0641

Dobson, David. **Emigrants & Adventurers from Orkney & Shetland**.
Contact vendor for information. .... Vendor G0641

Dobson, David. **Emigrants & Adventurers from S. Scotland, Part 1**.
Contact vendor for information. .... Vendor G0641

Dobson, David. **Emigrants & Adventurers from the Lothians, Part 1**.
Contact vendor for information. .... Vendor G0641

Dobson, David. **Scots On the Chesapeake, 1607-1830**. 1992.
Cloth. $20.00. 169 pp. .... Vendor G0010

Erickson, Charlotte. **Invisible Immigrants: The Adaption of English and Scottish Immigrants in 19th-Century America**. (1972) reprint 1990.
    A remarkable collection of letters from people who immigrated to America in the 19th century and who kept in touch with friends and relatives in England and Scotland. Over 200 letters from 25 families are included.
Paper. $18.95. 531 pp. .... Vendor G0611

Fife Family History Society. **Fife Emigrants & Their Ships. Part 1: Aust. & N.Z.**
Paper. £3.00. .... Vendor G0555

Graham, Ian Charles Cargill. **Colonists from Scotland: Emigration to North America, 1707-1783**. (1956) reprint 1996. Indexed.
Paper. $21.50. 223 pp. .... Vendor G0011

Lawson, J. **The Emigrant Scot: Ships' Manifest in Canadian Archives pre-1900**.
Paper. £3.75. .... Vendor G0555

Newsome, A. R., ed. **Records of Emigrants from England and Scotland to North Carolina, 1774-1775**. 4th printing, 1989.

Contains lists of persons who took passage on ships from Great Britain to North Carolina. The lists include nearly 100 emigrants from England and nearly 500 emigrants, including 100 family groups, from Scotland.
Paper. $3.00. 30 pp. .... Vendor G0586

Scottish Genealogy Society. **Scottish Emigration to N. America: Information Leaflet No. 1.**
Paper. £0.10. .... Vendor G0556

Whyte, Donald. **A Dictionary of Scottish Emigrants to Canada Before Confederation.** 2 vols. 1986, 1995.
The two volumes contain information on over 23,000 individuals and their families who emigrated from Scotland to Canada before 1867.
Paper. Each vol. $36.00 (cdn), $37.50 (US). xvi + 441 pp. (Vol. 1); xvi + 433 pp. (Vol. 2) .... Vendor G0568

Whyte, Donald. **A Dictionary of Scottish Emigrants to the U.S.A.** Volume 1. (1972) reprint 1994.
Paper. $37.50. 517 pp. .... Vendor G0011

Swiss

Faust, Albert B., and Gaius M. Brumbaugh. **Lists of Swiss Emigrants in the Eighteenth Century to the American Colonies.** 2 vols. in 1. (1920, 1925, 1972) reprint 1991. Indexed. Illus.
Cloth. $30.00. 122 + 255 pp. .... Vendor G0010

Schrader-Muggenthaler, Cornelia. **Swiss Emigration Book I.**
Cloth. $22.95. 216 pp. .... Vendor G0536

Smith, Clifford N. **The Immigrant Ancestor: A Survey of Westland Monographs on Emigration from Germany, Great Britain, France, Switzerland, and Eastern Europe.** 1994.
ISBN 0-915162-71-7.
Paper. $20.00. 28 pp. double-columned. .... Vendor G0491

Smith, Clifford N. **Immigrants to America from France (Haut-Rhin Departement) and Western Switzerland, 1859-1866** French-American Genealogical Research Monograph Number 1. 1983.
ISBN 0-915162-60-1.
Paper. $20.00. i + 33 pp. double-columned. .... Vendor G0491

U.S.

Elliott, Katherine B. **Emigrations to Other States from Southside Virginia.** 2 vols. (1966) reprint 1983. Indexed.
Paper. $25.00/vol. 138 + 156 pp. .... Vendor G0610

 Indexes

Boyer, Carl, 3rd. **Jacobus' Index to Genealogical Periodicals**. 1995.
Book #1627.
Cloth. $25.00. 373 pp. .... Vendor G0082

Clegg, Michael B., ed. **PERiodical Source Index (PERSI)**. 1986-present (ongoing project).
Indexes articles from the broadest spectrum of English-language and French-Canadian genealogy and local history magazines. Currently over one million citations in 26 volumes. Database searches available. Write for details and price list.
Contact vendor for price. .... Vendor G0485

Family Genealogies in the Carnegie Library. 1993.
An index to a collection of over 2,000 family genealogies accumulated by the Carnegie Library in Oakland, PA, since its founding. Includes family name, author, publication date, and number of pages for most books or records. Listings are national in scope, but primarily cover PA heritage.
Paper. $6.00. 43 pp. .... Vendor G0536

FGS. **Index to NGS and FGS Conferences and Syllabi**.
Paper. $7.00. .... Vendor G0643

Gale Research. **Abridged Biography and Genealogy Master Index**. 3 vols. 1995.
Cloth. $475.00/set. 4,511 pp. .... Vendor G0560

Gale Research. **Biography and Genealogy Master Index, 1991-1995 Cumulation**. 3 vols. 1995.
Cloth. $925.00/set. 4,533 pp. .... Vendor G0560

THE
PERiodical Source Index
1847-1995
over 1,000,000 citations

Are you looking for more source material on your ancestors?

PERSI is the largest index of its kind in the world, indexing articles from the broadest spectrum of English-language and French-Canadian genealogy and local history periodicals. There are thousands upon thousands of articles dealing with cemetery inscriptions, military records, church records, census records and land records, etc. Hundreds of family research articles have also been cited. See our listing under Indexes in this volume or call 219-424-7241 x2227.

Gale Research. **Biography and Genealogy Master Index, 1996**.
Cloth. $315.00. 1,281 pp. .... Vendor G0560

Jacobus, Donald Lines. **Index to Genealogical Periodicals**. 3 vols in 1. (1932, 1948, 1953) reprint 1997.
Contact vendor for information. 365 pp. in all. .... Vendor G0011

Kirkham, E. Kay. **Index to Some of the Bibles and Family Records of the United States**. Vol. 2.
    Index to surnames found in the records of the National Society, DAR. References are from microfilm at the Genealogical Society of Utah.
Paper. $15.50. 300 pp. .... Vendor G0618

McLaughlin, E. **Making the Most of the IGI**.
    A British publication.
Paper. £1.25. .... Vendor G0555

Joel Munsell's Sons. **Index to American Genealogies,** and to Genealogical Material Contained in All Works as Town Histories, County Histories, Local Histories, Historical Society Publications, Biographies, Historical Periodicals, and Kindred Works. 5th ed. With **Supplement, 1900 to 1908**. 2 vols. in 1. (1900, 1908) reprint 1997.
Paper. $36.50. 352 + 107 pp. .... Vendor G0011

Nichols, E. L. **The International Genealogical Index**. 1992 Edition. 1995.
    A British book published by the Society of Genealogists.
Paper. £2.90. 20 pp. .... Vendor G0557

Picton Index. 1995.
    Book #1515.
Windows-based computer program for indexing. $250.00 .... Vendor G0082

Precision Indexing. **The Soundex Reference Guide**. 1990.
    An alphabetical listing of over 125,000 surnames and their corresponding Soundex code. Although a new edition has been issued, this volume is economical for those who do not need foreign names.
Paper. $19.95. 253 pp. .... Vendor G0552

Precision Indexing. **The Soundex Reference Guide**. 2nd ed. 2 vols. 1994.
    A listing of 500,000 surnames, which are coded with both the U.S. and Daitch-Mokotoff Soundex Codes.
Cloth, $129.95. Paper, $99.95. .... Vendor G0552

Reisinger, Joy. **Index to NGS/FGS Conferences and Syllabi, 1978-1992**. 1993. Indexed.
Paper. $6.00. 176 pp. .... Vendor G0627

 Land Records

American State Papers, Public Lands. *The Public Land Records* (9 vols.) and *Grassroots in America* (1 vol. index to the set) by Phillip McMullen (see separate listing below). 1997.
Cloth. $750.00/set. .... Vendor G0610

Barsi. **The Basic Researcher's Guide to Homesteads & Other Federal Land Records**. 1995.
    Explains the process of locating, requesting, and obtaining a copy of the file created for a homestead or other type of federal land claim.
Paper. $12.95. .... Vendor G0611

Carter, Fran. **Searching American Land and Deed Records**. 1993. Illus.
Paper. $7.95. 70 pp. .... Vendor G0552

Hone, E. Wade, with Heritage Consulting and Services. **Land and Property Research in the United States**. 1997.
Cloth. Contact vendor for availability. .... Vendor G0570

Lawson. **Surveying Your Land: A Common-Sense Guide to Surveys, Deeds, and Title Searches**. 1991.
    A surveyor explains surveys, surveyors' terms and calculations, how to research boundaries, and more. Doesn't teach you how to map out land, unfortunately, but useful as general background reading.
Paper. $9.95. 144 pp. .... Vendor G0611

McMullen, Phillip. **Grassroots in America, Index to American State Papers, Land Grants and Claims**. (1972) reprint 1994.
Cloth. $50.00. 490 pp. .... Vendor G0610

McMullen, Phillip. **Grassroots in America: Index to American State Papers, Land Grants and Claims 1789-1837**. (1972) reprint 1991.
Cloth. $52.50. 520 pp. .... Vendor G0064

Public Record Office. **Land Grants in America and American Loyalists' Claims**.
Information leaflet. Contact vendor for information. .... Vendor G0558

Smith, Clifford N., ed. **French and British Land Grants in the Post Vincennes (Indiana) District, 1750-1784**. Selections from The American State Papers. 1996.
    Part 1: ISBN 0-915162-64-4.
    Part 2: ISBN 0-915162-65-2.
    Part 3: ISBN 0-915162-66-0.
    Part 4: ISBN 0-915162-67-9.
Paper. $20.00/part. .... Vendor G0491

Smith, Clifford N. **Spanish and British Land Grants in Mississippi Territory, 1750-1784:** Selections from The American State Papers. 1996.
Part 5: ISBN 0-915162-68-7.
Part 6: ISBN 0-915162-58-X.
Part 7: ISBN 0-915162-59-8.
Additional parts forthcoming.
Paper. $20.00. .... Vendor G0491

Yoshpe, Harry B., and Philip P. Brower. **Preliminary Inventory of the Land Entry Papers of the General Land Office (PI No. 22).** New ed. 1996.
Contact vendor for information. v + 77 pp. .... Vendor G0474

✌ Libraries, Archives, and ✌ Other Institutions

Beers, Henry Putney. **The Confederacy: A Guide to the Archives of the Confederate States of America.** Introduction by Frank C. Burke. (1968) reprint 1986.
A guide to the official archives of the government of the Confederate States of America. The bulk of the book describes materials held by the National Archives, but the book also covers Confederate records maintained at the Library of Congress and at twenty-nine other institutions.
Cloth. $25.00. 536 pp. .... Vendor G0565

Carson, Dina C. **Directory of Genealogical and Historical Society Libraries, Archives and Collections in the US and Canada, 1996.** Indexed.
A welcome resource for genealogists who have exhausted local or state sources; 3,500 collections listed. Published biennially.
Cloth, $80.00. Paper, $45.00. 250 pp. .... Vendor G0523

Filby, P. William. **Directory of American Libraries with Genealogy or Local History Collections.** 1988.
Cloth. $77.50. 330 pp. .... Vendor G0118

Hill, Edward E., comp. **Guide to Records in the National Archives Relating to American Indians.** (1981) reprint 1984. Illus.
Cloth. $25.00. 467 pp. .... Vendor G0565

Library of Congress. **Genealogical Periodicals in the Local History and Genealogy Reading Room:** A Guide for Research. A revision, by Barbara B. Walsh, of a guide prepared in 1983 by Judith P. Reid.
This guide identifies the major genealogical periodicals and indexes that are available in the Library of Congress Local History and Genealogy Reading Room (LH&G).
The text of this is available on the Local History and Genealogy Reading Room's home page: http://lcweb.loc.gov/rr/genealogy.
Free. Contact vendor for information. 12 pp. .... Vendor G0566

Library of Congress. **Genealogical Research at the Library of Congress**.
The text of this is available on the Local History and Genealogy Reading Room's home page: http://lcweb.loc.gov/rr/genealogy.
Free. Contact vendor for information. 11 pp. .... Vendor G0566

Library of Congress. **LH&G News: Recent Acquisitions in the LH&G Reading Room**. Compiled by Judith P. Reid.
Free. Contact vendor for information. Approx. 11 pp. .... Vendor G0566

Library of Congress. **Reference Services and Facilities of the Local History and Genealogy Reading Room**.
The text of this is available on the Local History and Genealogy Reading Room's home page: http://lcweb.loc.gov/rr/genealogy.
Free. Contact vendor for information. 2 pp. .... Vendor G0566

Library of Congress. **A Select Bibliography of Works at the Library of Congress on Norwegian-American Immigration and Local History**. Compiled by Lee V. Douglas.
The text of this is available on the Local History and Genealogy Reading Room's home page: http://lcweb.loc.gov/rr/genealogy.
Free. Contact vendor for information. 8 pp. .... Vendor G0566

Library of Congress. **Telephone and City Directories in the Library of Congress**. A Finding Guide. By Barbara B. Walsh. 1994.
The text of this is available on the Local History and Genealogy Reading Room's home page: http://lcweb.loc.gov/rr/genealogy.
Free. Contact vendor for information. 13 pp. .... Vendor G0566

McPhail, David R. **General Principles of United States Genealogical Research: Using the Family History Library in Salt Lake City**. 1995.
A useful guide to using the Family History Library of Salt Lake City. Geared toward the beginner.
Spiral bound. $13.95. 88 pp. .... Vendor G0611

Munden, Kenneth W., and Henry Putney Beers. **The Union: A Guide to Federal Archives Relating to the Civil War**. (1962) reprint 1986.
G0565
Cloth. $25.00. 721 pp. .... Vendor G0565

National Archives. **The 1790-1890 Federal Population Censuses**. Catalog of National Archives Microfilm. (1979) reprint 1993.
Paper. $3.50. 128 pp. .... Vendor G0565

National Archives. **The 1900 Federal Population Census**. Catalog of National Archives Microfilm. (1978) reprint 1995.
Paper. $3.50. 84 pp. .... Vendor G0565

National Archives. **The 1910 Federal Population Census**. Catalog of National Archives Microfilm. 1982.
Paper. $3.50. 62 pp. .... Vendor G0565

National Archives. **The 1920 Federal Population Census**. Catalog of National Archives Microfilm. 1991.
Paper. $3.50. 96 pp. .... Vendor G0565

National Archives. **American Indians**. A Select Catalog of National Archives Microfilm Publications. 1984. Rev. ed. 1995.
Paper. $3.50. 108 pp. .... Vendor G0565

National Archives. **Black Studies**. A Select Catalog of National Archives Microfilm Publications. 1984.
Paper. $3.50. 112 pp. .... Vendor G0565

National Archives. **Genealogical & Biographical Research**. A Select Catalog of National Archives Microfilm Publications. 1983.
Paper. $3.50. 96 pp. .... Vendor G0565

National Archives. **A Guide to Civil War Maps in the National Archives**. 1964. Rev. ed. 1986. Illus.
Cloth. $30.00. 140 pp. .... Vendor G0565

National Archives. **Guide to Federal Records in the National Archives of the United States**. 3 vols. 1987. Updated 1995. Indexed.
Cloth. $95.00. Approx. 1,500 pp. .... Vendor G0565

National Archives. **Guide to Genealogical Research in the National Archives**. 1982. Rev. ed. 1985. Illus.
Explains what records are preserved in the National Archives and what specific information about individuals is included in each type of record.
Cloth, $35.00. Paper, $25.00. 304 pp. .... Vendor G0565

National Archives. **Immigrant & Passenger Arrivals**. A Select Catalog of National Archives Microfilm Publications. 1983. 2nd ed. 1991.
Paper. $3.50. 192 pp. .... Vendor G0565

National Archives. **Military Service Records**. A Select Catalog of National Archives Microfilm Publications. 1985.
Paper. $3.50. 348 pp. .... Vendor G0565

National Archives. **National Archives Microfilm Resources for Research: A Comprehensive Catalog**. (1986) reprint 1990.
Paper. $5.00. 126 pp. .... Vendor G0565

Neagles, James C. **The Library of Congress: A Guide to Genealogical and Historical Research**. 1990.
Cloth. $39.95. 382 pp. .... Vendor G0570

Newman, Debra L., comp. **Black History: A Guide to the Civilian Records in the National Archives**. 1984. Illus.
Cloth, $25.00. Paper, $15.00. 379 pp. .... Vendor G0565

Walch, Timothy. **Our Family, Our Town**. Essays on Family and Local History Sources in the National Archives. 1987. Illus.
Practical advice and encouragement in the use of federal records in family and local history research. Military pension records, census schedules, ship passenger lists, and court documents are among the materials discussed.
Cloth. $20.00. 223 pp. .... Vendor G0565

✌ Lineage and Hereditary Societies/ ✌ Lineage Records

Colonial Dames of America. **Ancestral Records and Portraits**. 2 vols. (1910) reprint 1997. Indexed. Illus.
   A valuable collection of hundreds of pedigrees and collateral pedigrees of members of Chapter 1 of the Colonial Dames of America.
Paper. $75.00. 835 pp. .... Vendor G0011

Daughters of Founders and Patriots of America, National Society of. **Founders and Patriots of America Index**. (1967) reprint 1993.
Cloth. $22.50. 255 pp. .... Vendor G0010

Daughters of the American Revolution. **Genealogical Guide**. Master Index of Genealogy in the Daughters of the American Revolution Magazine. Volumes 1-84 (1892-1950) Published with Supplement to Genealogical Guide Volumes 85-89 (1950-1955). (1951, 1956) reprint 1994.
Cloth. $20.00. 169 pp. .... Vendor G0010

Daughters of the American Revolution. **Index of the Rolls of Honor (Ancestor's Index) in the Lineage Books of the National Society of the Daughters of the American Revolution**. 4 vols. in 2. (1916-1940) reprint 1988.
Cloth. $75.00. 1,734 pp. total .... Vendor G0010

Davenport, Robert R. **Hereditary Society Blue Book,** 1994 Edition. 1994. Indexed.
Cloth. $38.00. 318 pp. .... Vendor G0010

Finnell, Arthur Louis. **National Society Sons and Daughters of the Pilgrims Lineage Book IV**. 1993.
Cloth. $20.00. 343 pp. .... Vendor G0256

Finnell, Arthur Louis. **National Society Sons and Daughters of the Pilgrims Lineage Book V**. 1995.
Cloth. $20.00. 438 pp. .... Vendor G0256

Hutton, Mary Louise M. **Seventeenth Century Colonial Ancestors** of Members of the National Society Colonial Dames XVII Century, 1915-1975. With Supplement 1 . . . 1975-1979 and Supplement 2 . . . 1979-1988. (1976, 1981, 1988) reprint consolidated edition 1991. Indexed.
Cloth. $30.00. 468 pp. total. .... Vendor G0010

Lineages of Members of the National Society of Sons and Daughters of the Pilgrims. 2 vols. (1929, 1958, 1953) reprint 1988. Indexed.
Cloth. $75.00. 1,004 pp. total. .... Vendor G0010

The Order of the Founders and Patriots of America Register [of] Lineages of Associates, 1896-1993. In Four Volumes. Partially indexed. 1994.
Cloth. $225.00. 3,936 pp. .... Vendor G0011

Rixford, Elizabeth M. Leach. **Three Hundred Colonial Ancestors and War Service**—Their Part in Making American History from 495 to 1934. Bound with Supplement I, Supplement II, and Supplement II, Concluded. (1934, 1938, 1943, 1944) reprint 1991. Indexed. Illus.
Contact vendor for information. 425 pp. .... Vendor G0011

The National Huguenot Society

an organization dedicated to

honoring our Huguenot ancestors

by

perpetuating their memory,

promoting their principles and virtues

and by

commemorating the great events

in their history

For information on
membership requirements, contact

Mr. Arthur Louis Finnell
Executive Director
The National Huguenot Society
9033 Lyndale Avenue South, Suite 108
Bloomington, MN 55420-3535
(612) 885-9776
E-Mail, Compuserve 103336,117

> **Arthur Louis Finnell**
> 9033 Lyndale Ave S. Suite 108
> Bloomington, MN 55420-3535
> **Lineage Society Research**

Sixteen Hundred Lines to Pilgrims of the National Society of the Sons and Daughters of the Pilgrims. (1982) reprint 1996. Indexed.
Cloth. $75.00. 1,048 pp. .... Vendor G0010

Tabb, Jeanne Mitchell Jordan. **Ancestor Lineages of Members Texas Society/National Society Colonial Dames Seventeenth Century**. (1991) reprint 1996. Indexed.
Paper. $40.00. 291 pp. .... Vendor G0011

Thurtle, Robert Glenn, ed. **The General Society of the War of 1812: 1976 Bicentennial Supplement to the 1972 Register**. 1976. Indexed.
Cloth. $20.00. 174 pp. .... Vendor G0011

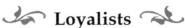 Loyalists

Chadwick, Edward M. **Ontarian Families: Genealogies of United Empire Loyalist & Other Pioneer Families of Upper Canada**. 2 vols. (1895-98) reprint 1990.
    Compiled using a wide variety of sources, this is an invaluable resource for Canadian researchers. The set contains chapters on more than 100 different families with information on over 1,000 surnames.
Paper. $21.50/vol. 203 + 194 pp. .... Vendor G0259

Clark, Murtie J. **Loyalists in the Southern Campaign of the Revolutionary War**. Vol. III, Official Rolls of Loyalists . . . from the Middle Atlantic Colonies . . . 1981. Indexed.
Cloth. $15.00. 494 pp. .... Vendor G0011

Coldham, Peter Wilson. **American Loyalist Claims**. Indexed.
Cloth. $21.50. 615 pp. .... Vendor G0627

Crowder, Norman K. **Early Ontario Settlers:** A Source Book. 1993. Indexed. Illus.
Cloth. $25.00. 259 pp. .... Vendor G0010

DeMond, Robert O. **The Loyalists in North Carolina During the Revolution**. (1940) reprint 1994. Indexed.
Paper. $25.00. 286 pp. .... Vendor G0011

Dwyer, Clifford S. **Index to Series I of American Loyalists Claims**. 1989.
Paper. $14.00. iv + 147 pp. .... Vendor G0632

Fitzgerald, Keith E. **Ontario People: 1796-1803**. 1993. Indexed. Illus.
Contact vendor for information. .... Vendor G0010

Fraser, Alexander. **United Empire Loyalists**. Enquiry into the Losses and Services in Consequence of Their Loyalty. Evidence in Canadian Claims. Second Report of the Bureau of Archives for the Province of Ontario. 2 vols. (1905) reprint 1994. Indexed. Cloth. $87.50. 1,436 pp. total .... Vendor G0010

Gilroy, Marion. **Loyalists and Land Settlement in Nova Scotia**. (1937) reprint 1995. Paper. $16.50. 154 pp. .... Vendor G0011

Holmes, Theodore C. **Loyalists to Canada**. 1993.
 Book #1339
Cloth. $36.50. 346 pp. .... Vendor G0082

Jones, Alfred E. **The Loyalists of Massachusetts,** Their Memorials, Petitions and Claims. (1930) reprint 1995. Indexed. Illus.
Paper. $29.95. 365 pp. .... Vendor G0011

Jones, Caleb, comp. **Orderly Book of the "Maryland Loyalists Regiment," June 18, 1778, to October 12, 1778,** Including General Orders Issued by Sir Henry Clinton, Baron Wilhelm von Kuyphausen, Sir William Erskine, Charles, Lord Cornwallis, General William Tryon and General Oliver De Lancey. Edited by Paul Leicester Ford. (1891) reprint 1996.
Paper. $12.50. 111 pp. .... Vendor G0011

Kelby, William. **Orderly Book of the Three Battalions of Loyalists** Commanded by Brigadier General Oliver De Lancey, 1776-1778. To Which is Appended a List of New York Loyalists in the City of New York During the War of the Revolution. (1917) reprint 1993. Indexed.
Contact vendor for information. 147 pp. .... Vendor G0011

Meyer. **Highland Scots of North Carolina, 1732-1776**.
 Examines the migrations of the Highland Scots into North Carolina during the 18th century, and their tendency to remain Loyalist during the Revolution.
Paper. $12.95. 216 pp. .... Vendor G0611

Ptak, Diane Snyder. **The American Loyalist: Origins and Nominal Lists and Supplement**. 1993.
 An alphabetical listing of all Loyalist biographical and military source materials.
Paper. $16.00. 51 pp. .... Vendor G0663

Public Record Office. **Land Grants in America and American Loyalists' Claims**. Information leaflet. Contact vendor for information. .... Vendor G0558

Reid, William D. **The Loyalists in Ontario**. The Sons and Daughters of the American Loyalists of Upper Canada. (1973) reprint 1994. Indexed.
Cloth. $27.00. 418 pp. .... Vendor G0011

Sabine, Lorenzo. **Biographical Sketches of Loyalists of the American Revolution**. In Two Volumes. (1864) reprint 1994.
Paper. $80.00. 608 + 600 pp. .... Vendor G0011

Smith, Clifford N. **Deserters and Disbanded Soldiers from British, German, and Loyalist Military Units in the South, 1782**. British-American Genealogical Research Monograph Number 10. 1991.
 ISBN 0-915162-36-9.
Paper. $20.00. 26 pp. double-columned. .... Vendor G0491

Stark, J. H. **The Loyalists of Massachusetts,** and the Other Side of the American Revolution. (1910) reprint 1990.
Cloth. $54.00. 509 pp. .... Vendor G0259

United Empire Loyalists Centennial Committee, Toronto. **The Old United Empire Loyalists List.** (1885) reprint 1993.
Cloth. $25.00. 334 pp. .... Vendor G0010

✺ Maps, Atlases, and Gazetteers ✺

All-Name Index to the 1860 Gazetteer of New York State. 1993.
Includes listing of geographic names not in original index. Included with paper version of the 1860 Gazetteer by J. H. French.
Paper. $15.00. 183 pp. .... Vendor G0093

Atlas of the German Empire 1892. Indexed.
This set of maps is an indispensable research tool. 11" x 17".
Paper. $29.95. .... Vendor G0611

Atlas of the World. 4th ed. 1996. Indexed. Illus.
Features fully digitized, computer-generated color maps with international balance and completely up-to-date coverage of the world.
Cloth. $76.00. 400 pp. .... Vendor G0611

Beck, et al. **Historical Atlas of the American West.** 1989.
Fascinating history of the West through maps.
Paper. $21.95. .... Vendor G0611

Blois, John T., and S. L. Hood & Co. **1838 Michigan Gazetteer.** (1838) reprint 1979.
Cloth. $26.00. 424 pp. .... Vendor G0531

Blois, John T. **Gazetteer of the State of Michigan,** in Three Parts. (1840) reprint 1993.
Cloth. $44.00. 418 pp. .... Vendor G0259

Desk Reference Atlas. 1996. Indexed. Illus.
A beautiful, compact atlas with digitized, computer-generated color maps that give remarkable clarity and legibility. This atlas has the latest changes in national boundaries and place names with full-color representations of flags from around the world.
Cloth. $19.00. 208 pp. .... Vendor G0611

Encyclopedic World Atlas, 3rd ed. 1996. Indexed. Illus.
A unique work combining authoritative, full-color maps and informative profiles of every country in the world.
Cloth. $39.95. 272 pp. .... Vendor G0611

Ferrell and Natkiel. **Atlas of American History.** 3rd ed. 1993.
Historical atlases are extremely useful to the genealogist. 8½" x 11".
Paper. $19.95. 192 pp. .... Vendor G0611

French, J. H. **Gazetteer of the State of New York (1860),** Reprinted with an Index of Names Compiled by Frank Place. (1860, 1983) reprint 1995. Indexed. Illus. Cloth. $55.00. 926 pp. .... Vendor G0010

French, J. H. **Gazetteer (1860) of the State of New York.** (1860) reprint 1993. Indexed. Illus.
Long considered a Bible for New York research, which includes almost every place in New York; short histories and facts about events and early settlers; also many statistical tables. Cloth price does not include new, all-name index. Paper price includes new index.
Cloth, $35.00. Paper, $35.00. 784 pp. .... Vendor G0093

Gannett, Henry. **A Gazetteer of Maryland and Delaware** 2 vols. in 1. (1904) reprint 1994.
Paper. $12.50. 99 pp. .... Vendor G0011

Gannett, Henry. **A Gazetteer of Virginia and West Virginia.** 2 vols. in 1. (1904) reprint 1994.
Paper. $26.50. 323 pp. in all. .... Vendor G0011

Gannett, Henry. **A Geographic Dictionary of Massachusetts.** (1894) reprint 1978.
Cloth. $11.50. 126 pp. .... Vendor G0011

Gannett, Henry. **Geographic Dictionary of New Jersey.** (1894) reprint 1993.
Contact vendor for information. 131 pp. .... Vendor G0011

Gardiner. **German Towns in Slovakia and Upper Hungary: A Genealogical Gazetteer.** 1991.
Nearly half of this book is an extremely helpful "how-to" of Czech research, while the second half is the gazetteer that the title promises.
Paper. $17.00. 113 pp. .... Vendor G0611

Gordon, T. F. **Gazetteer of the State of New York,** Comprehending Its Colonial History; General Geography, Geology, Internal Improvements; Its Political State; Minute Description of Its Several Counties, Towns, and Villages; Statistical Tables. (1836) reprint 1990.
Cloth. $79.50. 800 pp. .... Vendor G0259

Gordon, T. F. **A Gazetteer of the State of Pennsylvania.** (1832) reprint 1989.
Cloth. $57.50. 63 + 508 pp. .... Vendor G0259

Gordon, Thomas F. **A Gazetteer of the State of New Jersey.** (1834) reprint 1995. Illus.
Paper. $12.50. 174 pp. .... Vendor G0140

Groome, Francis H., ed. **Ordnance Gazetteer of Scotland:** A Graphic and Accurate Description of Every Place in Scotland. 3 vols. (1902) reprint 1995. Illus.
Alphabetical listing of every city, town, hamlet, village, parish and family seat, with remarkably detailed geographical and social descriptions. Volume III includes an appendix with a brief history and profile of Scotland. Many maps.
    Volume I, A-Foc.
    Volume II, Fod-Moncton.
    Volume III, Monctonhall-end.
Cloth. $55.00/vol., $150.00/set. 1,762 pp. .... Vendor G0259

Harvey. **Maps in Tudor England**. 1993.
This beautiful book traces the cartographic revolution between 1485 and 1603. Those who know England well, or who are tracing families in this time period, will find this collection of maps fascinating. 8½" x 11".
Cloth. $29.95. 120 pp. .... Vendor G0611

Heisey, John W. **Maps, Atlases and Gazetteers**.
Paper. $10.00. 29 pp. .... Vendor G0574

Hough, Franklin B. **Gazetteer of the State of New York,** Embracing a Comprehensive Account of the History & Statistics of the State, with Geological & Topographical Descriptions of Each County, City, Town & Village. (1872) reprint 1993.
Many New York counties were divided several times, and town, township, and village names were often duplicated in every county. This book can help! Very useful for anyone researching New York.
Cloth. $75.00. 745 pp. .... Vendor G0259

Humphery-Smith, Cecil R. **The Phillimore Atlas and Index of Parish Registers**. 1995. Indexed. Illus.
Cloth. £50.00. 320 pp. .... Vendor G0579

Indiana Gazetteer, or Topographical Dictionary of the State of Indiana. 3rd ed. (1850) reprint 1993.
In Indiana today there's one "Madison"; in 1850, there were eleven "Madison Townships"! This book can help you find out which one you're really interested in. Very useful for early state research.
Cloth. $46.00. 440 pp. .... Vendor G0259

Kilbourne, John. **1833 Ohio Gazetteer**. (1833) reprint 1981.
Cloth. $29.00. 494 pp. .... Vendor G0531

Kirkham, E. Kay. **A Genealogical and Historical Atlas of the United States of America**. Illus.
Includes selected maps of 1810, 1823, 1838, 1855, 1866, 1878, 1883, 1909, etc., with an index to maps and historical information.
Paper. $25.00. 328 pp. .... Vendor G0618

Magocsi, Paul Robert. **Historical Atlas of East Central Europe**. 1993. Illus.
For the first time, here is an atlas that covers all of Eastern Central Europe from the early fifth century through 1992. This atlas encompasses the countries of Poland, the Czech Republic, Slovakia, Hungary, Romania, Slovenia, Croatia, Bosnia-Herzegovina, Yugoslavia, Macedonia, Albania, Bulgaria, Greece, and the eastern part of Germany. 9" x 12".
Paper. $39.95. 218 pp. .... Vendor G0611

Monmonier, Mark. **How to Lie with Maps**. 2nd ed. 1996.
This lively, cleverly illustrated essay on the use and abuse of maps teaches us how to evaluate maps critically and promotes a healthy skepticism about these easy-to-manipulate models of reality.
Paper. $14.95. 212 pp. .... Vendor G0611

Morse, Jedidiah. **American Gazetteer**. (1797) reprint 1979.
Cloth. $34.00. 626 pp. .... Vendor G0531

Pease, J., and J. Niles. **Gazetteer of the States of Connecticut & R.I.** Consisting of Two Parts: I, Geogr. & Statistical Desc. of Each State; II, General Geogr. View of Each County, & a Minute & Ample Topographical Desc. of Each Town, Village, Etc. (1819) reprint 1990.
Cloth. $35.00. 339 pp. .... Vendor G0259

Powell. **The North Carolina Gazetteer: A Dictionary of Tar Heel Places.** 1968.
Over 20,000 entries that locate the geographical features of North Carolina.
Paper. $16.95. 561 pp. .... Vendor G0611

Sale and Karn. **American Expansion: A Book of Maps.** 1962.
A fascinating collection of maps showing the rate and direction of expansion across America during the 19th century. Each map is accompanied by descriptive essays.
Paper. $9.95. 28 pp. .... Vendor G0611

Saul, Nigel, ed. **The National Trust Historical Atlas of Britain.** Prehistoric and Medieval. Illus.
Cloth. $53.95. 224 pp. .... Vendor G0576

Smith and Thomsen. **Genealogical Guidebook and Atlas of Denmark.**
Includes terminology, feast days, counties and parishes, maps, and more.
Paper. $17.50. 168 pp. .... Vendor G0611

Smith, Frank. **A Genealogical Gazetteer of England.** An Alphabetical Dictionary of Places, With Their Location, Ecclesiastical Jurisdiction, Population, and the Date of the Earliest Entry in the Registers of Every Ancient Parish in England. (1968) reprint 1995.
Cloth. $35.00. xv + 599 pp. .... Vendor G0010

Smith, Frank. **A Genealogical Gazetteer of Scotland.**
An alphabetical dictionary of places with their locations, population, and date of the earliest entry in the registers of every parish in Scotland.
Paper. $14.00. 140 pp. .... Vendor G0618

Spafford, Horatio Gates. **Gazetteer (1824) of the State of New York.** (1824) reprint 1980.
Cloth. $35.00. 620 pp. .... Vendor G0093

Tanner. **Atlas of Great Lakes Indian History.** 1987.
A beautiful book with exquisite maps and illustrations accompanying a detailed text. 9" x 12".
Paper. $45.00. 224 pp. .... Vendor G0611

Thode, Ernest. **Genealogical Gazetteer of Alsace-Lorraine.**
Paper. $18.00. .... Vendor G0574

Thode, Ernest. **Genealogical Gazetteer of Alsace-Lorraine.** 1986. Illus.
Paper. $17.50 postpaid ($18.64 in OH). 137 pp. .... Vendor G0197

Thrower. **Maps and Civilization: Cartography in Culture and Society.** 1996.
A concise introduction to the history of cartography with rare maps from ancient Egypt to contemporary Western civilization.
Paper. $17.95. 336 pp. .... Vendor G0611

Waldman. **Atlas of the North American Indian**. 1985.
   Over 100 color maps, an informative text and handsome illustrations. Covers the entire history, culture and tribal locations of the Indian peoples of the United States, Canada, and Middle America from pre-historic times to the present day.
Cloth, $35.00. Paper, $18.95. 276 pp. .... Vendor G0611

Wilson, Rev. John. **The Gazetteer of Scotland**. (1882) reprint 1996.
   Facsimile reprint; alphabetic arrangement.
Paper. $32.00. 425 pp. .... Vendor G0669

Marriage Records and Laws (on a nationwide basis)

Bolton, Charles K. **Marriage Records of Marriage Notices, . . . for the Whole U.S.** 1989.
Cloth. $18.00. 139 pp. .... Vendor G0450

Bolton, Charles Knowles. **Marriage Notices, 1785-1794** for the Whole United States from the Massachusetts Centinel and the Columbian Centinel. (1900) reprint 1985.
Cloth. $15.00. 139 pp. .... Vendor G0010

North, S. N. D., and Desmond Walls Allen, ed. **Marriage Laws in the United States, 1887-1906**. 1993.
Paper. $17.95. 91 pp. .... Vendor G0064

Mayflower and Pilgrim

Lineages of Members of the National Society of Sons and Daughters of the Pilgrims. 2 vols. (1929, 1958, 1953) reprint 1988. Indexed.
Cloth. $75.00. 1,004 pp. total. .... Vendor G0010

Banks, Charles Edward. **The English Ancestry and Homes of the Pilgrim Fathers** Who Came to Plymouth on the Mayflower in 1620, the Fortune in 1621, and the Anne and the Little James in 1623. (1929) reprint 1997. Indexed.
   Contains biographical sketches of 112 passengers who sailed on the first four ships to New England.
Cloth. $18.50. 187 pp. .... Vendor G0010

Bowman, George Ernest. **The Mayflower Reader**. A Selection of Articles from *The Mayflower Descendant*. (1899-1905) reprint 1996. Illus.
Paper. $39.95. 537 pp. .... Vendor G0011

Crummer, Larry D. **Crummer Families in the United States and Canada Who Came from Ireland**. 1994. Indexed. Illus.
   Mary Kellogg Crummer line traced to Mayflower and Revolutionary War origin.
Cloth. $58.00. 603 pp. .... Vendor G0192

Davis, W. T. **Genealogical Register of Plymouth Families**. Part II of Ancient Landmarks of Plymouth. (1889) reprint 1994.
Contact vendor for information. 363 pp. .... Vendor G0010

Demos. **A Little Commonwealth: Family Life in Plymouth Colony**. 1970.
Studies the family during the first two generations of the colony's existence.
Paper. $8.95. 201 pp. .... Vendor G0611

General Society of Mayflower Descendants. **Mayflower Families Through Five Generations**.
This series traces descendants of the Pilgrims down through the fifth generation to the birth of the sixth generation children. The volumes are carefully researched and contain the best documented genealogical data that is available.
Volume 1: Francis Eaton, Samuel Fuller, William White, includes addendum & revised index.
Volume 2: James Chilton, Richard More, Thomas Rogers, includes addendum.
Volume 4: Second Edition: Edward Fuller.
Volume 5: Edward Winslow and John Billington.
Volume 6: Stephen Hopkins.
Volume 7: Peter Brown.
Volume 8: Degory Priest.
Cloth. $20.00/Vols. 1, 5, 7 & 8. $25.00/Vols. 2 & 4. $35.00/Vol. 6. . . . Vendor G0620

Harding, Anne Borden, Milton E. Terry, and Alden G. Beaman, eds. **Mayflower Ancestral Index**.
A guide to descendants of *Mayflower* passengers Francis Eaton, Samuel Fuller, William White, James Chilton, Richard More, Thomas Rogers, George Soule, and William Brewster.
Cloth. $15.00. .... Vendor G0620

Hills, Leon Clark. **History and Genealogy of the *Mayflower* Planters** 2 vols. in 1. (1936, 1941) reprint 1996. Indexed.
Paper. $38.50. 461 pp. in all. .... Vendor G0011

Holbrook, Jay Mack. **The Mayflower Descendant 1620-1937**. 1995.
Thirty-four volumes of the quarterly magazine of Pilgrim genealogy and history, with one fiche per volume plus topical index.
Microfiche. $6.00 each or set of 35 fiches for $175.00. .... Vendor G0148

Landis, John T. *Mayflower* **Descendants and Their Marriages for Two Generations After the Landing**. (1922) reprint 1990.
Paper. $5.00. 37 pp. .... Vendor G0011

Mayflower Source Records. Primary Data Concerning Southeastern Massachusetts, Cape Cod, and the Islands of Nantucket and Martha's Vineyard. From The New England Historical and Genealogical Register. Introduction by Gary Boyd Roberts. (1986) reprint 1997. Indexed.
Cloth. $45.00. 832 pp. .... Vendor G0010

Rixford, Elizabeth M. Leach. **Families Directly Descended from All the Royal Families in Europe (495 to 1932) & Mayflower Descendants**. (1932) reprint 1992. Indexed. Illus.
Paper. $28.00. 190 pp. .... Vendor G0011

Roser, Susan E. **Mayflower Births and Deaths**. From the Files of George Ernest Bowman, at the Massachusetts Society of Mayflower Descendants. 2 vols. 1992. Indexed.
Contact vendor for information. 1,075 pp. total. .... Vendor G0010

Roser, Susan E. **Mayflower Deeds & Probates**. From the Files of George Ernest Bowman, at the Massachusetts Society of Mayflower Descendants. 1994. Indexed.
Paper. $44.95. 660 pp. .... Vendor G0010

Roser, Susan E. **Mayflower Increasings**. 2nd ed. (1995) reprint 1996.
Paper. $20.00. 170 pp. .... Vendor G0010

Roser, Susan E. **Mayflower Marriages**. From the Files of George Ernest Bowman, at the Massachusetts Society of Mayflower Descendants. (1990) reprint 1994. Indexed.
Paper. $29.95. 415 pp. .... Vendor G0010

Shaw, H. K., comp. **Families of the Pilgrims**. Compiled for the Massachusetts Society of Mayflower Descendants. (1956) reprint 1994.
Contains biographical sketches and genealogies of several generations of Mayflower descendants, as well as an index to their wills and reference information.
Paper. $19.00. 178 pp. .... Vendor G0259

Simmons, C. H., Jr., scr. **Plymouth Colony Wills and Inventories, Vol. 1, 1633-1669**. 1996. Indexed.
Book #1608.
Cloth. $59.50. 640 pp. .... Vendor G0082

Sixteen Hundred Lines to Pilgrims of the National Society of the Sons and Daughters of the Pilgrims. (1982) reprint 1996. Indexed.
Cloth. $75.00. 1,048 pp. .... Vendor G0010

Stoddard, Francis R. **The Truth About the Pilgrims**. (1952) reprint 1997. Indexed. Illus.
Paper. $22.50. 206 pp. .... Vendor G0011

Stratton, Eugene Aubrey. **Plymouth Colony: Its History and People, 1620-1691**. 1986. Indexed. Illus.
The history and genealogy of Plymouth Colony, with more than 300 biographical sketches of the inhabitants.
Paper. $19.95. 481 pp. .... Vendor G0570

Thacher, James. **History of the Town of Plymouth** from Its Earliest Settlement in 1620 to the Present Time; with a Precise History of the Aborigines of New England & Their Wars with the English. (1835) reprint 1991.
Cloth. $40.00. 401 pp. .... Vendor G0259

Young, Alexander. **Chronicles of the First Planters of the Colony of Massachusetts Bay, from 1623 to 1636**. (1846) reprint 1996. Indexed.
Paper. $45.00. 571 pp. .... Vendor G0011

Young, Alexander. **Chronicles of the Pilgrim Fathers of the Colony of Plymouth from 1602 to 1625**. 2nd ed. (1844) reprint 1995. Indexed. Illus.
Paper. $35.00. 518 pp. .... Vendor G0011

❧ Military ❧

General References

Bond, Col. O. J. **The Story of the Citadel.** (1936) reprint 1989. Indexed.
Cloth. $27.50. 282 pp. .... Vendor G0610

Carter, Fran. **Searching American Military Records.** 1993. Illus.
Paper. $7.95. 62 pp. .... Vendor G0552

Clark, Murtie June. **Colonial Soldiers of the South, 1732-1774.** (1983) reprint 1986.
Indexed.
Contact vendor for information. xxx + 1,245 pp. .... Vendor G0010

Deeter, Judy A. **Veterans Who Applied for Land in Southern California 1851-
1911.** 1993.
Paper. $8.00. 32 pp. .... Vendor G0467

Heisey, John W. **Military Genealogical Sources.**
Paper. $12.00. 44 pp. .... Vendor G0574

Heitman, Francis B. **Historical Register and Dictionary of the United States Army**
from Its Organization, September 29, 1789, to March 2, 1903. 2 vols. (1903) reprint
1994. Indexed.
Cloth. $125.00. 1,069 + 626 pp. .... Vendor G0010

Historical Account of Bouquet's Expedition Against the Indians in 1764. Preface
by Francis Parkman, with a Biographical Sketch of General Bouquet. (1868) reprint
1993.
    This authentic and reliable narrative of one of the earliest British military expedi-
tions into the "Northwest Territory" was originally published in English in 1765 and
in French in 1769.
Cloth, $28.00. Paper, $18.00. xxiii + 162 pp. .... Vendor G0259

Horowitz. **A Bibliography of Military Name Lists from Pre-1675 to 1900: A Guide
to Genealogical Sources.** 1990.
    Extremely useful guide to hundreds of little-known sources. This will expand your
search.
Cloth. $99.50. 1,118 pp. .... Vendor G0611

Johnson. **How to Locate Anyone Who Is or Has Been in the Military.** 6th ed., rev.
1992.
    Covers many of the strategies involved in locating 20th-century persons. Besides
numerous military sources, it includes techniques utilizing driver's licenses and social
security records.
Paper. $19.95. 280 pp. .... Vendor G0611

Knight. **Life and Manners in the Frontier Army.** 1978.
    Highly documented description of the average military post. Very interesting ac-
count.
Paper. $14.95. 280 pp. .... Vendor G0611

National Archives. **Military Service Records**. A Select Catalog of National Archives Microfilm Publications. 1985.
Paper. $3.50. 348 pp. .... Vendor G0565

Neagles, James C. **U.S. Military Records**. 1994.
Cloth. $39.95. 455 pp. .... Vendor G0570

Terry, Rose Caudle. **Military Sources, Queries & Reviews Volume 1**. 1994. Indexed. Illus.
    Queries published free.
Paper. $8.95. 30 pp. .... Vendor G0061

Bacon's Rebellion

Wertenbaker, Thomas J. **Bacon's Rebellion, 1676**. (1957) reprint 1994. Illus.
Paper. $9.50. 60 pp. .... Vendor G0011

Civil War

Angle, Paul M., ed. **Three Years in the Army of the Cumberland**. 1996.
    The diary of Major James Austin Connolly, 123rd Illinois Infantry, constitutes a detailed account of the Civil War in the West.
Paper. $14.95. .... Vendor G0611

Beers, Henry Putney. **The Confederacy: A Guide to the Archives of the Confederate States of America**. Introduction by Frank C. Burke. (1968) reprint 1986.
    A guide to the official archives of the government of the Confederate States of America. The bulk of the book describes materials held by the National Archives, but the book also covers Confederate records maintained at the Library of Congress and at twenty-nine other institutions.
Cloth. $25.00. 536 pp. .... Vendor G0565

Bethel, Elizabeth, comp. **Preliminary Inventory of the War Department Collection of Confederate Records (Record Group 109) in the National Archives**. (1957) reprint 1994. Indexed.
Paper. $28.00. 300 pp. .... Vendor G0632

Boatner. **The Civil War Dictionary**. Rev. ed. 1987.
    More than 4,000 entries.
Paper. $19.00. 974 pp. .... Vendor G0611

Bosse. **Civil War Newspaper Maps: A Historical Atlas**. 1993.
    An important reference for serious students of the Civil War. $8\frac{1}{2}$" x 11".
Cloth. $34.95. 162 pp. .... Vendor G0611

Bracy, Isabel. **157th New York Volunteer (Infantry) Regiment—1862-1865**. 1991. Indexed.
    This is the first published history of the regiment raised in Madison and Cortland counties and fought at Gettysburg.
Paper. $12.00. 128 pp. .... Vendor G0093

Broadfoot Publishing Company. **Confederate Military History**. 19 vols. Indexed. Cloth. $750.00. Contact vendor for pricing options. .... Vendor G0590

Broadfoot Publishing Company. **Confederate Veteran**. 43 vols. 1996. Indexed. Illus.
   A reprint of the complete forty-year run of *Confederate Veteran* magazine, 1893-1932.
Cloth. $1,500.00. Contact vendor for pricing options. .... Vendor G0590

Broadfoot Publishing Company. **Military Order of the Loyal Legion of the United States**. 70 vols.
   First-hand accounts of battles, leaders, and campaigns by men who were active participants in the Civil War.
Cloth. $2,400.00. Contact vendor for pricing options. .... Vendor G0590

Broadfoot Publishing Company. **The Official Records of the Union and Confederate Armies**. 128 vols. Indexed.
Cloth. $2,600.00. Contact vendor for pricing options. .... Vendor G0590

Broadfoot Publishing Company. **The Supplement to the Official Records**. 1996.
   All of the information left out of the original *Official Records*. Being published two volumes per month; final estimated size, 100 volumes.
Cloth. Contact vendor for information. .... Vendor G0590

Broadfoot Publishing Company. **The Official Records of the Union and Confederate Navies**. 31 vols. Indexed.
Cloth. $750.00. Contact vendor for pricing options. .... Vendor G0590

Broadfoot Publishing Company. **Papers of the Military Historical Society of Massachusetts**. 15 vols. Indexed.
Cloth. $500.00. Contact vendor for pricing options. .... Vendor G0590

Broadfoot Publishing Company. **Roster of Confederate Soldiers 1861-1865**. 16 vols. Introduction by Robert K. Krick. 1996.
   The entire Confederate Army in alphabetical order; 1,500,000 names
Cloth. Contact vendor for information. .... Vendor G0590

Broadfoot Publishing Company. **Roster of Union Soldiers 1861-1865**. 33 volumes. 1996. Indexed.
   The entire Union Army in alphabetical order by state; three million names.
Cloth. Contact vendor for information. .... Vendor G0590

Broadfoot Publishing Company. **The Southern Historical Society Papers**. 55 vols. Indexed.
   Includes a history of the Southern Historical Society, biographical sketches of its founders, first-hand battle accounts, diaries, letters, articles, correspondence, and reviews.
Cloth. $1,700.00. Contact vendor for pricing options. .... Vendor G0590

Broadfoot, Tom. **Civil War Books: A Priced Checklist with Advice**. 4th ed. 1996.
   Updated prices and information on over 8,500 titles.
Cloth. $50.00. .... Vendor G0590

Brown, Stuart E., Jr. **The Guns of Harpers Ferry**. (1968) reprint 1996. Indexed. Illus.
Paper. $17.50. 158 pp. .... Vendor G0011

Brumgardt, ed. **Civil War Nurse: The Diary and Letters of Hannah Ropes**. 1993.
Chief nurse of the Union Hospital in Washington, D.C., describes life and stress in the hospital.
Paper. $10.95. 149 pp. .... Vendor G0611

Bumbera, Marlene C. **The Civil War Letters of Cpl. John H. Strathern,** 8th PA Reserve Volunteer Corps. Indexed. Illus.
Paper. $19.95. 146 pp. .... Vendor G0536

Civil War Letter and Diary of Joshua Winters. 1975.
Paper. $10.00. .... Vendor G0660

Clinton and Silber. **Divided Houses: Gender and the Civil War**. 1992.
Interesting study of how the Civil War transformed gender roles. Extensive footnotes.
Paper. $15.95. 418 pp. .... Vendor G0611

Cole. **Civil War Eyewitnesses:** An Annotated Bibliography of Books & Articles, 1955-1986. 1988.
A compilation of nearly 1,400 published diaries, journals, letters, and memoirs written by soldiers, civilians, and foreign travelers. Important sources.
Cloth. $49.95. 351 pp. .... Vendor G0611

Creswell, Stephen, ed. **We Will Know What War Is: The Civil War Diary of Sirene Bunten**. 1993.
The diary begins on the first day of 1863, spans the war years, and ends in the 1870s. In 1901 Sirene Bunten picked up her diary one last time and made a final entry. In her diary we see what war was like for many West Virginians. The diary's postwar entries show the rural life lived by a young West Virginia woman.
Paper. $8.00. .... Vendor G0660

Daniel. **Soldiering in the Army of Tennessee: A Portrait of Life in a Confederate Army**. 1991.
Written from the enlisted man's perspective from journals and letters. Gives a unique glimpse into this experience.
Cloth. $22.50. 231 pp. .... Vendor G0611

Dyer, Frederick H. **A Compendium of the War of the Rebellion**. 2 vols. Indexed.
Cloth. $125.00. 1,796 pp. .... Vendor G0590

Faust, Drew Gilpin. **Mothers of Invention: Women of the Slaveholding South in the American Civil War**. 1996.
A look at the experiences of southern white women in the South during the Civil War and the war's effect on their lives.
Contact vendor for information .... Vendor G0611

Gallagher, Gary, ed. **Campaigns of the Civil War**. 16 vols. 1996. Indexed.
Cloth. $300.00. Contact vendor for pricing options. .... Vendor G0590

Gallagher, Gary, ed. **The Southern Bivouac**. 6 vols. Indexed. Illus.
Sketches of soldiers and articles, stories, and letters related to the southern soldier, the Confederacy, and southern life.
Cloth. $300.00. Contact vendor for pricing options. 3,200+ pp. .... Vendor G0590

Groene, Bertram Hawthorne. **Tracing Your Civil War Ancestor**. (1973) reprint 1995. Indexed. Illus.
A complete guide to tracking down your ancestors' Civil War adventures, North and South.
Paper. $11.95. 119 pp. .... Vendor G0611

Hattaway, Herman, and Archer Jones. **How the North Won: A Military History of the Civil War**. 1996.
This is a superb military history of the Civil War.
Paper. $21.95. 762 pp. .... Vendor G0611

Herrick, Margaret. **A Civil War Soldier's Diary, Peter W. Funk, 150th NY Vol.** 1991. Indexed.
Diary of a foot soldier in the Union Army, 1862-1865; genealogical information and comment by Burton Coon.
Paper. $13.50. 54 pp. .... Vendor G0450

Hughes, Mark. **The Unpublished Roll of Honor**. 1996. Indexed.
Cloth. $35.00. 341 pp. .... Vendor G0010

Inventory of the Louisiana Historical Association Collection on Deposit in the Howard-Tilton Memorial Library, Tulane University.
Detailed guide to the Association's vast Civil War Collection.
Paper. $14.00. 201 pp. .... Vendor G0611

Jones, Virgil Carrington. **The Civil War at Sea**. 3 vols. 1996. Indexed. Illus.
Cloth. $60.00. 506 + 506 + 485 pp. .... Vendor G0590

Jordan, William B., Jr. **Red Diamond Regiment: The 17th Maine Infantry, 1862-1865**. 1995.
This book traces the movements of this regiment, but goes beyond simple military history to show the soldiers' everyday life, their relationships to their home front state, and how their bravery and suffering related to the larger Civil War.
Cloth. $30.00. 438 pp. .... Vendor G0611

Josephy, Alvin M., Jr. **The Civil War in the American West**. 1991.
From Minnesota to Louisiana to Colorado to Texas, the Civil War as fought in the American West is frequently forgotten. Remarkably detailed.
Paper. $15.00. 448 pp. .... Vendor G0611

Joslyn, Mauriel. **The Biographical Roster of the Immortal 600**. 1995.
Includes the histories of individual lives and military service records of the 600 Confederate officers who were imprisoned first in a stockade in Charleston Harbor and then in Fort Pulaski.
Paper. $25.00. 232 pp. .... Vendor G0611

Katcher, Philip. **The Civil War Source Book**. (1992) reprint 1995.
Cloth. $35.00. 318 pp. .... Vendor G0611

Kinney, Shirley Foster, and James P. Kinney, Jr. **Floyd Co. Georgia Confederates —Vol. VIII**. 1992. Indexed.
Cloth. $59.50. 380 pp. .... Vendor G0021

Kraynek, Sharon L. D. **Letters to my Wife . . . A Civil War Diary from the Western Front**. Indexed.

    J. Harvey Greene, a captain in the 8th Wisconsin Infantry, left a wife and daughter behind while he served his duty. The unedited letters of Greene and his wife give one of the most vivid pictures of the thoughts of those who fought and those women who waited throughout the entire war.

Paper. $8.00. 110 pp. .... Vendor G0536

McCammon, Charles S., ed. **Loyal Mountain Troopers: The 2nd & 3rd Volunteer Cavalry (Union) in the Civil War**. 1992. Indexed.

    Memoirs of Cavalry officers written in 1878. Includes complete official roster published 1866.

Cloth. $32.00. .... Vendor G0204

McCawley, Patrick J. **Guide to Civil War Records:** A Guide to the Records in the South Carolina Department of Archives & History. 1994. Indexed. Illus.

Paper. $6.75. 81 pp. .... Vendor G0130

McDonald. **A Woman's Civil War: A Diary with Reminiscences of the War, from March 1862**. 1992.

    The fascinating Civil War diary of Cornelia Peake McDonald, of Winchester, Virginia. A Southern woman's lonely struggle in the midst of chaos.

Paper. $14.95. 303 pp. .... Vendor G0611

McSherry, ed. **Civil War Women: The Civil War Seen Through Women's Eyes in Stories by Louisa May Alcott, Kate Chopin, Eudora Welty, and Other Great Women Writers**. 1988.

    Brings the war to life by way of ten short stories.

Paper. $10.00. 175 pp. .... Vendor G0611

Mills, Gary B. **Southern Loyalists in the Civil War**. A Composite Directory of Case Files Created by the U.S. Commissioner of Claims, 1871-1880, Including Those Appealed to the War Claims Committee of the U.S. House of Representatives and the U.S. Court of Claims. 1994.

Cloth. $45.00. 684 pp. .... Vendor G0010

Mitchell, Reid. **The Vacant Chair: The Northern Soldier Leaves Home**. 1993.

    The author shows that by understanding the links between the homes the troops left behind and the war they had to fight, you can gain critical insight into how they thought, fought, and persevered through four bloody years of combat.

Cloth. $25.00. 201 pp. .... Vendor G0611

Munden, Kenneth W., and Henry Putney Beers. **The Union: A Guide to Federal Archives Relating to the Civil War**. (1962) reprint 1986.

    Studies the vast collection of U.S. government documents in the National Archives that relate to the Civil War.

Cloth. $25.00. 721 pp. .... Vendor G0565

National Archives. **A Guide to Civil War Maps in the National Archives**. (1964. Rev. ed. 1986) reprint 1964. Illus.

Cloth. $30.00. 140 pp. .... Vendor G0565

Neagles, James C. **Confederate Research Sources: A Guide to Archive Collections**. Rev. ed. 1997.
Paper. $15.95. Approx. 286 pp. .... Vendor G0570

Nevins, Allan, James I. Robertson, and Bell I. Wiley. **Civil War Books: A Critical Bibliography**. 2 vols. in 1. Indexed.
Cloth. $75.00. 604 pp. .... Vendor G0590

New York State Archives and Records Administration. **Civil War Records in the New York State Archives**. 1986.
Paper. Free. 5 pp. .... Vendor G0587

Penny, Morris M., and J. Gary Laine. **Law's Alabama Brigade in the War Between the Union and the Confederacy**. 1996.
    The gripping personal stories of the five Alabama regiments known as "Law's Brigade" formed by men from twenty-five of Alabama's sixty-seven counties.
Cloth. $37.50. 480 pp. .... Vendor G0611

Phillips, Marion G., and Valerie Phillips Parsegian. **Richard and Rhoda, Letters from the Civil War**. 1981. Illus.
    Book #1462.
Cloth. $25.00. 128 pp. .... Vendor G0082

Post, Gerald R. **First Guide to Civil War Genealogy and Research**. 2nd ed. 1996. Illus.
Paper. $8.75. 78 pp. .... Vendor G0608

Potter, Johnny L. T. N. **Vidette Cavalry**. Illus.
$12.50 (perfect bound). 42 pp. .... Vendor G0549

Reamy, Martha, and William Reamy. **Index to The Roll of Honor**. With a Place Index to Burial Sites Compiled by Mark Hughes. 1995.
Cloth. $75.00. 1,210 pp. .... Vendor G0010

Roanoke Island Prisoners—Feb. 1862.
    A listing of the prisoners taken at the Battle of Roanoke Island from VA and NC.
Paper. $11.50. .... Vendor G0549

Robertson. **Civil War Virginia: Battleground for a Nation**. 1991.
    A history of Virginia and the Civil War.
Paper. $8.95. 197 pp. .... Vendor G0611

Robertson, James I., Jr., ed. **Medical and Surgical History of the Civil War**. 15 vols. Indexed.
Cloth. $1,400.00. Contact vendor for pricing options. .... Vendor G0590

Robinson. **The Confederate Privateers**. (1928) reprint 1994.
    Recounts the exploits of the Confederacy's privately armed ships and their sea battles with the Union.
Paper. $15.95. 372 pp. .... Vendor G0611

Rouse, Parke Jr. **When the Yankees Came: Civil War and Reconstruction on the Virginia Peninsula**. 1977.
    An inside view to the Civil War and the hard times that followed for the Virginia Peninsula area. Shown through the eyes of George Ben West (1839-1917).
Paper. $15.00. 199 pp. .... Vendor G0611

Schwartz. **A Woman Doctor's Civil War: Esther Hill Hawks' Diary**. 1989.
Paper. $14.95. 289 pp. .... Vendor G0611

Schweitzer, George K. **Civil War Genealogy**. 1996. Illus.
   History of the war, archival records, national publications, state publications, local sources, military unit histories, sites, research techniques.
Paper. $12.00. 76 pp. .... Vendor G0569

Segars, J. H. **In Search of Confederate Ancestors:** The Guide. 1993. Indexed. Illus.
Paper. $12.00. 112 pp. .... Vendor G0011

Sewell. **A House Divided: Sectionalism and Civil War, 1848-1865**. 1988.
   Traces the growth of the bitter sectional discord that led to the Civil War.
Paper. $12.95. 223 pp. .... Vendor G0611

Sibley, F. Ray, Jr. **The Confederate Order of Battle, the Army of Northern Virginia**. 1995.
   A meticulous examination of the organization of the Confederate army during each of its combat operations. 8½" x 11".
Cloth. $80.00. 480 pp. .... Vendor G0611

Martha & INDEX TO THE
William Reamy ROLL OF HONOR

1,210 pp., cloth. 1995.
Vendor G0010. $75.00

   The *Roll of Honor* is the only official memorial to the Union dead ever published. In spite of its omissions and discrepancies, it remains the most comprehensive source of information on Civil War fatalities. Nevertheless, it is not an easy series to work with. Its exhaustive lists of burials in over 300 national cemeteries spread out over 27 volumes has daunted and intimidated generations of researchers, for no index to the work was ever published.
   Until now! In this massive compilation by Martha and William Reamy we at last have a key to the contents of the *Roll of Honor*. The twelve hundred pages of this incredible new index contain the names, in alphabetical order, of the 228,639 Union soldiers listed in the 27 volumes of the *Roll*. Indexed by volume and page number, all names mentioned in this famous series of burial registers are now immediately accessible, and the *Roll of Honor* is at once transformed from an interesting miscellany of fringe history to a reference work of major importance.

G e n e a l o g i c a l   P u b l i s h i n g   C o . ,   I n c .

Sifakis. **Compendium of the Confederate Armies: Alabama**. 1992.
Describes each regiment, the officers, and lists the battles in which they fought.
Cloth. $24.95. 160 pp. .... Vendor G0611

Sifakis. **Compendium of the Confederate Armies: Florida and Arkansas**. 1992.
Describes each regiment, the officers, and lists the battles in which they fought.
Cloth. $24.95. 144 pp. .... Vendor G0611

Sifakis. **Compendium of the Confederate Armies: Kentucky, Maryland, Missouri, the Confederate Units and the Indian Units**. 1995.
Describes the regiments, the officers, and the battles.
Cloth. $27.50. 234 pp. .... Vendor G0611

Sifakis. **Compendium of the Confederate Armies: Louisiana**. 1995.
Describes each regiment, its officers, and its battles.
Cloth. $24.95. 144 pp. .... Vendor G0611

Sifakis. **Compendium of the Confederate Armies: North Carolina**. 1992.
Describes each regiment, the officers, and lists the battles in which they fought.
Cloth. $24.95. 208 pp. .... Vendor G0611

Sifakis. **Compendium of the Confederate Armies: South Carolina and Georgia**. 1995.
Describes each regiment and the officers, and lists the battles in which they fought.
Cloth. $24.95. 311 pp. .... Vendor G0611

Sifakis. **A Compendium of the Confederate Armies: Tennessee**. 1992.
Describes each regiment, the officers, and lists the battles in which they fought.
Cloth. $24.95. 208 pp. .... Vendor G0611

Sifakis. **Compendium of the Confederate Armies: Texas**. 1995.
Describes the regiments, officers, and battles.
Cloth. $24.95. 147 pp. .... Vendor G0611

Sifakis. **Compendium of the Confederate Armies: Virginia**. 1992.
Describes each regiment, the officers, and lists the battles in which they fought.
Cloth. $29.95. 285 pp. .... Vendor G0611

Spratt, Thomas M. **Men in Gray Interments, Volume I**.
A record of Confederate dead buried in Virginia.
Paper. $35.00. ix + 471 pp. .... Vendor G0632

Spratt, Thomas M. **Men in Gray Interments, Volume II**.
Paper. $35.00. iv + 443 pp. .... Vendor G0632

Spratt, Thomas M. **Men in Gray Interments, Volume III**.
Paper. $35.00. iv + 489 pp. .... Vendor G0632

Spratt, Thomas M. **Men in Gray Interments, Volume IV**.
Paper. $35.00. iv + 319 pp. .... Vendor G0632

Spratt, Thomas M. **Men in Gray Interments, Volume V**.
Paper. $35.00. iv + 335 pp. .... Vendor G0632

Steele. **Civil War in the Ozarks**. 1993.
The Ozarks were a volatile and strategically important region during the Civil War.
Paper. $8.95. 136 pp. .... Vendor G0611

Steele, Don. **In A Different Manner**.
An account of the struggle at Gettysburg, written from the southern soldiers point of view. It focuses on Pickett's Division as they attempt to defeat the Union Army on July 3rd, 1863. Contains a listing of the opposing forces of both armies with brigade losses.
Paper. $7.00. 54 pp. .... Vendor G0536

Symonds and Clipson. **A Battlefield Atlas of the Civil War**. 1987. Illus.
Forty-five two-color maps covering the major battles, including a history of each battle.
Cloth. $24.95. 130 pp. .... Vendor G0611

Symonds and Clipson. **Gettysburg: A Battlefield Atlas**. 1992.
Maps showing the deployment of the various companies, and the history of the battles.
Cloth. $24.95. 103 pp. .... Vendor G0611

Turino, Kenneth C., ed. **The Civil War Diary of Lieut. J. E. Hodgkins 1862-1865**. Indexed. Illus.
  Book #1523.
Cloth. $22.50. 224 pp. .... Vendor G0082

U.S. Quartermaster's Dept. **Roll of Honor**. Nos. I-VI. [Together with] Alphabetical Index to Places of Interment of Deceased Union Soldiers in the Various States and Territories as Specified in Rolls of Honor Nos. I-XIII. (1865-66) reprint 1994.
Cloth. $38.50. 615 pp. total. .... Vendor G0010

U.S. Quartermaster's Dept. **Roll of Honor**. Nos. VII-X. (1866) reprint 1994.
Cloth. $42.50. 720 pp. total. .... Vendor G0010

U.S. Quartermaster's Dept. **Roll of Honor**. Nos. XI-XIII. (1866-67) reprint 1994.
Cloth. $44.50. 749 pp. total. .... Vendor G0010

U.S. Quartermaster's Dept. **Roll of Honor**. Nos. XIV-XV. (1868) reprint 1994.
Cloth. $42.50. 720 pp. total. .... Vendor G0010

U.S. Quartermaster's Dept. **Roll of Honor**. Nos. XVI-XVII. (1868) reprint 1994.
Cloth. $52.50. 929 pp. total. .... Vendor G0010

U.S. Quartermaster's Dept. **Roll of Honor**. Nos. XVIII-XIX. (1868-69) reprint 1994.
Cloth. $48.50 . 818 pp. total. .... Vendor G0010

U.S. Quartermaster's Dept. **Roll of Honor**. Nos. XX-XXI. (1869) reprint 1994.
Cloth. $48.50. 808 pp. total. .... Vendor G0010

U.S. Quartermaster's Dept. **Roll of Honor**. Nos. XXII-XXIII. (1869) reprint 1994.
Cloth. $50.00. 847 pp. total. .... Vendor G0010

U.S. Quartermaster's Dept. **Roll of Honor**. Nos. XXIV-XXV. (1869-70) reprint 1994.
Cloth. $35.00. 536 pp. total. .... Vendor G0010

U.S. Quartermaster's Dept. **Roll of Honor**. Nos. XXVI-XXVII and The Final Disposition. (1868, 1871) reprint 1994.
Cloth. $35.00. 536 pp. total. .... Vendor G0010

Van Horne, Thomas. **History of the Army of the Cumberland**. 2 vols. 1996. Indexed. Illus.
The only complete history of the major Union army in the West.
Cloth. $75.00. 1,108 pp. .... Vendor G0590

Ward, Geoffrey. **The Civil War**. 1990.
A text-only edition of the Civil War based on the PBS series.
Paper. $14.00. 348 pp. .... Vendor G0611

Wellikoff, Alan. **Civil War Supply Catalogue: A Comprehensive Source Book of Products From the Civil War Era Available Today**. 1996.
Descriptions rich in Civil War lore, this book is a catalogue to Civil War replicas of such items as uniforms, weapons, foodstuffs, and furnishings. This is a unique source for anyone in search of authentic 19th-century items.
Paper. $23.00. 201 pp. .... Vendor G0611

Wright, John. **Compendium of the Confederacy: An Annotated Bibliography**. 2 vols. Indexed.
Cloth. $150.00. 1,340 pp. .... Vendor G0590

Colonial Wars

Peckham. **The Colonial Wars, 1689-1762**. 1964.
Overview of the various conflicts. Not footnoted, but a good overview. With suggested reading list.
Paper. $13.95. 239 pp. .... Vendor G0611

Forts and Posts

Wright, Mildred S, and William D. Quick. **United States Spanish-American War Fortifications at the Sabine Pass, Texas**. 1982. Indexed. Illus.
Two forts were erected for the protection of the Sabine River. The war ended before they were completed. This book documents their construction, termination, and destruction.
Paper. $15.00. 50 pp. .... Vendor G0145

French and Indian War

Hadden, James. **Washington's and Braddock's Expeditions**. (1910) reprint 1991.
Cloth. $16.00. 139 pp. .... Vendor G0499

Lacock, John Kennedy. **Braddock Road**.
Reprint of scarce booklet originally published about 1908 outlines expeditions of Major-Gen. Edward Braddock and his army. Map of Braddock's Military Road from Cumberland, Maryland to Braddock, Pennsylvania, 1755, denoting encampments.
Paper. $6.00. 38 pp. .... Vendor G0536

Frontier Wars/Indian Wars

Brown, John Henry. **Indian Wars and Pioneers of Texas, 1822-1874**. (1880) reprint 1994. Indexed. Illus.
Cloth. $65.00. 1,152 pp. .... Vendor G0610

Clark, Murtie June. **American Militia in the Frontier Wars, 1790-1796**. 1990. Indexed.
Cloth. Contact vendor for information. 394 pp. .... Vendor G0010

DeHass, Wills. **History of the Early Settlement and Indian Wars of Western Virginia**. (1851) reprint 1989. Illus.
    An early history of what is now West Virginia.
Paper. $14.95. .... Vendor G0660

McWhorter, Lucullus V. **The Border Settlers of Northwestern Virginia, from 1768 to 1795,** Embracing the Life of Jesse Hughes and Other Noted Scouts of the Great Woods of the Trans-Allegheny. (1915) reprint 1996. Illus.
Paper. $37.50. 519 pp. .... Vendor G0011

Murphy, Polly Lewis, comp. **Records of Medical History of Fort Sill, Indian Territory, Feb. 1873-May 1880 and of Fort Sill, OK, 1903-1913**. 1984.
    Includes information on soldiers on sick call and in the hospital and of daily reports of the medical units on the post and on scouting parties. Interesting accounts of military life on the frontier in the late 1880s.
Paper. $15.00. 81 pp. .... Vendor G0661

Volunteer Soldiers in the Cherokee War—1836-1839.
    A listing of over 11,000 volunteers from Tennessee, Georgia, North Carolina, and Alabama who were signed in for the Removal program of the Cherokee Indians to their western homes.
$35.00 (perfect bound). 210 pp. .... Vendor G0549

Whitney, Ellen M. **Black Hawk War 1831-1832, Vols. I-IV**. 1970-78. Indexed.
    Regimental records.
Cloth. $92.00. 1,541 pp. .... Vendor G0501

Withers, Alexander Scott. **Chronicles of Border Warfare,** or A History of the Settlement by the Whites, of Northwestern Virginia, and of the Indian Wars and Massacres in that Section of the State with Reflections, Anecdotes, Etc. Edited and annotated by Reuben Gold Thwaites. (1895) reprint 1994. Indexed.
Paper. $37.50. 467 pp. .... Vendor G0011

Withers, Alexander Scott. **Chronicles of Border Warfare**. Edited and annotated by Reuben Gold Thwaites. (1831) reprint 1989.
    History of the settlement of northern Virginia and of the Indian wars and massacres in that section of the state.
Paper. $14.95. .... Vendor G0660

Wolfe, Barbara. **The Lost Soldiers (1784-1811)**. 4 vols.
    Vol. I Surnames A-E, 90 pp.
    Vol. II Surnames F-L, 82 pp.
    Vol. III Surnames M-R, 74 pp.
    Vol. IV Surnames S-Z, 64 pp.
Paper. $14.00/vol., $48.00/set. .... Vendor G0574

King Philip's War

Bodge, George Madison. **Soldiers in King Philip's War**. Official Lists of the Soldiers of Massachusetts Colony Serving in Philip's War, and Sketches of the Principal Officers, Copies of Ancient Documents and Records Relating to the War. (1906) reprint 1995. Indexed. Illus.
Paper. $35.00. 502 pp. .... Vendor G0011

Drake, Samuel G. **The Old Indian Chronicle**. (1867) reprint 1995.
Cloth. $39.50. 333 pp. .... Vendor G0259

Mexican War

Singletary. **The Mexican War**. 1960.
   A history of the conflict, this book makes good background reading.
Paper. $12.95. 181 pp. .... Vendor G0611

Wolfe, Barbara. **Index to Mexican War Pension Applications**.
Cloth. $49.00. 381 pp. .... Vendor G0574

Navy

Lieutenants in the Navy—1832.
Paper. $5.00. .... Vendor G0549

Pension Records

American Revolutionary War Pensioners—1828.
Paper. $5.00. .... Vendor G0549

Clark, Murtie June. **Index to U.S. Invalid Pension Records, 1801-1815**. 1991. Indexed.
Contact vendor for information. 159 pp. .... Vendor G0010

Clark, Murtie June. **The Pension Lists of 1792-1795**. With Other Revolutionary War Pension Records. (1991) reprint 1996. Indexed.
Cloth. $25.00. 216 pp. .... Vendor G0010

Crowder, Norman K. **British Army Pensioners Abroad, 1772-1899**. 1995. Indexed.
Cloth. $26.50. 351 pp. .... Vendor G0011

Digested Summary and Alphabetical List of Private Claims. 3 vols. (1853) reprint 1970.
Cloth. $150.00. 2,123 pp. .... Vendor G0010

National Genealogical Society. **Index of Revolutionary War Pension Applications**.
   Alphabetically listed Revolutionary War veterans and their widows who applied for pensions and bounty land warrants.
Cloth. $47.50. 658 pp. .... Vendor G0627

Revolutionary War Pensions—1839.
Paper. $8.50. .... Vendor G0549

Scott, Craig R. **The "Lost" Pensions, Settled Accounts of the Act of 6 April 1838.** 1996.
Paper. $32.00. 374 pp. .... Vendor G0669

U.S. Department of State. **A Census of Pensioners** for Revolutionary or Military Services, 1840. [Published with] A General Index to a Census of Pensioners. 2 vols in 1. (1841, 1965) reprint 1996.
Cloth. $35.00. 577 pp. total .... Vendor G0010

U.S. Naval Pensions—1828.
Paper. $5.00. .... Vendor G0549

U.S. Pay Department (War Department). **Pierce's Register**. Register of the Certificates issued by John Pierce, Esquire, Paymaster General and Commissioner of Army Accounts for the United States, to Officers and Soldiers of the Continental Army Under Act of July 4, 1783. (1915) reprint 1987.
Cloth. $25.00. 566 pp. .... Vendor G0010

U.S. War Department. **Pension List of 1820**. Letter from the Secretary of War Transmitting a Report of the Names, Rank and File of Every Person Placed on the Pension List in Pursuance of the Act of the 18th March, 1818, Etc. Washington, 1820. (1820) reprint 1991. Indexed.
Cloth. Contact vendor for information. 672 pp. .... Vendor G0010

U.S. War Department. **The Pension Roll of 1835**. 4 vols. (1835) reprint 1992. Indexed.
Contact vendor for information. 3,183 pp. .... Vendor G0010

U.S. War Department. **Pensioners of the Revolutionary War—Struck Off the Roll**. (1836) reprint 1993.
Contact vendor for information. 103 pp. .... Vendor G0011

U.S. War Department. **Revolutionary Pensioners**. A Transcript of the Pension List of the United States for 1813. (1813) reprint 1997.
Paper. $8.00. 47 pp. .... Vendor G0011

U.S. War Department. **Revolutionary Pensioners of 1818**. (1818) reprint 1996.
Paper. $35.00. 358 pp. .... Vendor G0011

Wolfe, Barbara. **Index to Mexican War Pension Applications.**
Cloth. $49.00. 381 pp. .... Vendor G0574

Revolutionary War

Benson, Adolph B. **Sweden and the American Revolution**. (1926) reprint 1992. Indexed.
Paper. $21.00. 228 pp. .... Vendor G0011

Bockstruck, Lloyd DeWitt. **Revolutionary War Bounty Land Grants** Awarded by State Governments. 1996. Indexed.
Cloth. $45.00. 636 pp. .... Vendor G0010

Bonwick. **The American Revolution**. 1991.
Not a military history, but a social history of the times and conditions that resulted in the American Revolution. Excellent background reading.
Paper. $16.50. 336 pp. .... Vendor G0611

Butterfield, C. W. **Historical Account of the Expedition Against Sandusky** Under Col. William Crawford in 1782, with Biographical Sketches, Personal Reminiscences & Descriptions of Interesting Localities. (1873) reprint 1993.
The Battle of Sandusky and the surrounding events comprised one of the most notable campaigns of the Western Border War of the Revolution. However, little had been written about it when this interesting book, which relied almost exclusively on original sources, was first published.
Cloth. $45.00. 403 pp. .... Vendor G0259

Butterfield, Consul Willshire. **History of the Girtys,** a Concise Acct. of the Girty Bros.—Thomas, Simon, James & George, & Their Half-Brother John Turner—Also of the Part Taken by Them in Lord Dunsmore's War, the Western Border War of the Revolution, and the Indian War, 1790-95. (1905) reprint 1995.
Cloth. $42.50. 425 pp. .... Vendor G0259

Dandridge, Danske. **American Prisoners of the Revolution**. (1911) reprint 1994.
Paper. $36.00. 504 pp. .... Vendor G0011

DeMarce, Virginia Easley. **Mercenary Troops from Anhalt-Zerbst, Germany, Who Served with the British Forces During the American Revolution**. German-American Genealogical Research Monograph Number 19. 1984.
Part 1: Surnames A Through Kr (iv + 54 pp.).
Part 2: Surnames Ku Through Z (50 pp.; appendices).
ISBN 0-915162-21-0 (the set).
Paper. $20.00/part. .... Vendor G0491

Dohla. **A Hessian Diary of the American Revolution**. 1990.
A fascinating look at a Hessian soldier's experience as recorded in his diary.
Paper. $13.95. 276 pp. .... Vendor G0611

Friel, Florence, ed. **The Diary of Job Whitall, Gloucester County, New Jersey 1775-1779**. 1992. Indexed.
Description of everyday life in the midst of opposing armies—"The Battle of Red Bank."
Paper. $16.50. 200 pp. .... Vendor G0069

Godfrey, Carlos E. **The Commander-in-Chief's Guard: Revolutionary War**. (1904) reprint 1995. Illus.
Paper. $28.00. 302 pp. .... Vendor G0011

Hagman, Harlan L. **Nathan Hale and John Andre, Reluctant Heroes of the American Revolution**. 1992. Indexed. Illus.
These two men, soldiers in opposing armies, typify the heroes of many wars where death cuts short the lives of the young and promising.
Cloth. $20.00. 149 pp. .... Vendor G0093

Heitman, Francis B. **Historical Register of Officers of the Continental Army During the War of the Revolution, April 1775 to December 1783**. Revised and enlarged edition. With Addenda by Robert H. Kelby. (1914, 1932) reprint 1997.
Paper. $45.00. 698 pp. .... Vendor G0011

Hilowitz, Harv. **Chronology and Almanac of the Revolutionary War, 1754-1783**. 1995. Illus.
Clear and concise by campaign and date with maps.
Paper. $7.50. 50 pp. .... Vendor G0160

Jones, Mary Helen Eppright, and Lorena Start Jersen, eds. **Steuben: The Baron & The Town**. 1994. Illus.
Biography of Major General Baron Steuben 1730-1794, Drillmaster and Inspector General; stories about the people and history of Steuben, New York, 1786-1994, including Welsh immigration.
Cloth, $27.95. Paper, $17.45. 398 pp. .... Vendor G0070

Kaminkow, Marion, and Jack Kaminkow. **Mariners of the American Revolution**. (1967) reprint 1993.
Cloth. $18.50. 274 pp. .... Vendor G0011

Kelly, Arthur C. M. **Hessian Troops in the American Revolution, Extracts from the Hetrina**. 6 vols. 1991.
Paper. $86.50/set. Volumes also available separately. Contact vendor for price. 534 pp. total. .... Vendor G0450

Leach. **Roots of Conflict: British Armed Forces and Colonial Americans, 1677-1763**. 1986.
Recounts the story of the antagonism between the American colonists and the British armed forces prior to the Revolution. Certain Anglo-American attitudes and stereotypes evolved that became significant in the revolutionary crisis.
Paper. $13.95. 232 pp. .... Vendor G0611

Morrill, Dan L. **Southern Campaigns of the American Revolution**. 1993.
Recounts the story of the "homespun" soldiers of the American Revolution in the South. The determining effects of the war in the South, Dr. Morrill maintains, were not the full-scale engagements "between armies and fleets but engagements between militia, often among neighbors."
Cloth. $29.95. 271 pp. .... Vendor G0611

Muster and Pay Rolls of the War of the Revolution. (1916) reprint 1996. Indexed.
Lists about 8,000 men named in rolls from eleven states, including New York.
Cloth. $45.00. 707 pp. .... Vendor G0010

Neagles, James C., and Lila Lee Neagles. **Locating Your Revolutionary War Ancestor: Guide to Military Records**.
Contains the materials that are available for ancestors who fought in the American Revolution and how to actually find an official record of the military service.
Paper. $14.95. 236 pp. .... Vendor G0618

Neagles, James C. **Summer Soldiers: A Survey and Index of Revolutionary War Courts-Martial**. 1986.
An account orf 3,315 court-martial cases with source documentation from orderly books in the National Archives and the Library of Congress.
Cloth. $19.95. 294 pp. .... Vendor G0570

New York State Archives and Records Administration. **Guide to Records Relating to the Revolutionary War [in the New York State Archives]**. 1994.
Paper. $2.00. 54 pp. .... Vendor G0587

Pancake. **1777: The Year of the Hangman**. 1977.

An account of the Revolution's most crucial year. Burgoyne's Canadian expedition and Howe's Pennsylvania campaign are especially well covered.

Paper. $15.95. 268 pp. .... Vendor G0611

Pancake. **This Destructive War: The British Campaign in the Carolinas, 1780-1782**. 1985.

The story of the guerrilla warfare fought in the Carolinas. Includes numerous references to weaponry, military organization, and the lives of ordinary soldiers in both armies.

Paper. $15.95. 293 pp. .... Vendor G0611

Peterson, Clarence Stewart. **Known Military Dead During the American Revolutionary War, 1775-1783**. (1959) reprint 1997.

Paper. $20.00. 187 pp. .... Vendor G0011

Public Record Office. **The American Revolution: Guides and Lists to Documents in the Public Record Office**.

Information leaflet. Contact vendor for information. .... Vendor G0558

Reid, Arthur. **Reminiscences of the Revolution** or Le Loup's Bloody Trail.

New York's Washington County General Burgoyne's barbarous Indian alliance and the death of Miss McCrea are described in this reprint of the 1859 booklet about the Indian atrocities that rallied the Patriots against the Crown.

Booklet. $6.50 32 pp. .... Vendor G0160

Retzer, Henry J. **German Regiment of Maryland and Pennsylvania**. 1991. Rev. ed. 1996.

Gives information on a little-known unit of Gen. Washington's army.

Paper. $15.00. 183 pp. .... Vendor G0140

Richards, Henry Melchior Muhlenberg. **The Pennsylvania-German in the Revolutionary War, 1775-1783**. (1908) reprint 1991. Indexed. Illus.

Cloth. $27.50. 542 pp. .... Vendor G0011

Royster. **A Revolutionary People at War: The Continental Army and American Character, 1775-1783**. 1979.

Who were these people who fought the War of Independence? Royster examines the relationship of Americans' national character and the military demands of the Revolutionary War to provide a new perspective on the American Revolution and its legacy.

Cloth. $34.95. 452 pp. .... Vendor G0611

Saffell, William T. R. **Records of the Revolutionary War,** Third Edition. [Bound with:] Index to Saffell's List of Virginia Soldiers in the Revolution. (1894, 1913) reprint 1996.

Paper. $45.00. 598 pp. .... Vendor G0011

Schweitzer, George K. **Revolutionary War Genealogy**. 1994. Illus.

History of war, research techniques, archival records, national publications, state publications, local sources, military unit histories, sites.

Paper. $12.00. 110 pp. .... Vendor G0569

Smith, Clifford N. **Annotated Hessian Chaplaincy Record of the American Revo-**

lution, 1776-1784: Christenings, Marriages, Deaths. German-American Genealogical Research Monograph Number 30. 1994.
ISBN 0-915162-72-5.
Paper. $20.00. i + 29 pp. double-columned. .... Vendor G0491

Smith, Clifford N. **British and German Deserters, Dischargees, and Prisoners of War Who May Have Remained in Canada and the United States, 1774-1783.** British-American Genealogical Research Monograph Number 9. 2 parts.
Part 1 (1988; 24 pp. double-columned): ISBN 0-915162-34-2.
Part 2 (1989; 18 pp. double-columned): ISBN 0-915162-35-0.
Paper. $20.00/part. .... Vendor G0491

Smith, Clifford N. **Brunswick Deserter-Immigrants of the American Revolution.** German-American Genealogical Research Monograph Number 1. 1973.
ISBN: 0-915162-00-8.
Paper. $20.00. 54 pp. .... Vendor G0491

Smith, Clifford N. **Mercenaries from Ansbach and Bayreuth, Germany, Who Remained in America After the American Revolution.** German-American Genealogical Research Monograph Number 2. (1974) rev. ed. 1979.
ISBN 0-915162-13-X.
Paper. $20.00. v + 51 pp. .... Vendor G0491

Smith, Clifford N. **Mercenaries from Hessen-Hanau Who Remained in Canada and the United States After the American Revolution.** German-American Genealogical Research Monograph Number 5. 1976.
ISBN 0-915162-04-0.
Paper. $20.00. iv + 105 pp. .... Vendor G0491

Smith, Clifford N. **Muster Rolls and Prisoner-of-War Lists in American Archival Collections Pertaining to the German Mercenary Troops Who Served with the British Forces During the American Revolution.** German-American Genealogical Research Monograph Number 3. 3 parts.
Part 1: Muster Rolls 1-25 (x + 64 pp.).
Part 2: Muster Rolls 26-52 (i + 54 pp.).
Part 3: Muster Rolls 53-72 (i + 57 pp.).
Paper. $20.00/part. .... Vendor G0491

Smith, Clifford N. **Notes on Hessian Soldiers Who Remained in Canada and the United States After the American Revolution.** German-American Genealogical Research Monograph Number 28, Part 4 (in five separately published subparts).
ISBN 0-915162-96-2.
ISBN 0-915162-97-0.
ISBN 0-915162-98-9.
ISBN 0-915162-99-7.
ISBN 0-915162-89-X.
Paper. $20.00/part. .... Vendor G0491

Smith, Clifford N. **Some German-American Participants in the American Revolution: The Rattermann Lists.** German-American Genealogical Research Monograph Number 27. 1990.
ISBN 0-915162-92-X.
Paper. $20.00. ii + 47 pp. double-columned. .... Vendor G0491

Stevens, John Austin. **British Occupation of New York City 1781-1783**. Indexed.
Reprinted from the 1885 Centennial Celebration with a new index and introduction.
Paper. $6.50. 40 pp. .... Vendor G0160

Stewart, Robert Armistead. **The History of Virginia's Navy of the Revolution**. (1934)
reprint 1993. Indexed.
Cloth. $18.50. 279 pp. .... Vendor G0011

Stroh, Oscar H. **The Paxton Rangers**. 1982. Illus.
Cloth, $25.00. Paper, $15.00. 89 pp. .... Vendor G0333

Stroh, Oscar H. **Thompson's Battalion**. (1975) revised 1976. Illus.
The first regiment of the Continental Army.
Cloth, $20.00. Paper, $10.00. 52 pp. .... Vendor G0333

Symonds and Clipson. **A Battlefield Atlas the American Revolution**. 1987.
Forty-one two-color maps covering the major battles, accompanied by a history of
each battle.
Cloth. $24.95. 112 pp. .... Vendor G0611

U.S. War Department. **Pensioners of the Revolutionary War—Struck Off the Roll**.
(1836) reprint 1993.
Contact vendor for information. 103 pp. .... Vendor G0011

U.S. War Department. **Revolutionary Pensioners**. A Transcript of the Pension List of
the United States for 1813. (1813) reprint 1996.
Paper. $7.00. 47 pp. .... Vendor G0011

U.S. War Department. **Revolutionary Pensioners of 1818**. (1818) reprint 1996.
Paper. $35.00. 358 pp. .... Vendor G0011

Waldenmaier, Nellie Protsman. **Some of the Earliest Oaths of Allegiance to the
United States**. (1944) reprint 1995. Indexed.
Paper. $12.00. 99 pp. .... Vendor G0011

Wallace, Lee A., Jr., ed. **The Orderly Book of Captain Benjamin Taliaferro, 2nd
Virginia Detachment, Charleston, South Carolina, 1780**. 1980.
Cloth. $15.00. ix + 185 pp. .... Vendor G0553

White, Katherine Keogh. **The King's Mountain Men**. The Story of the Battle, with
Sketches of the American Soldiers Who Took Part. (1924) reprint 1996. Indexed.
Paper. $25.00. 271 pp. .... Vendor G0011

Spanish-American War

Jones, Janice L. **Diary of Cpl. Davidson—Co. D—Spanish-American War**. 1996.
Paper. $12.50. 6 pp. .... Vendor G0460

War of 1812

Blizzard, Dennis F. **The Roster of The General Society of the War of 1812**. 1989.
Indexed.
Cloth. $15.00. 241 pp. .... Vendor G0011

Fay and Davidson. **Detailed Reports of the War of 1812**. (1815) reprint 1980. Cloth. $28.00. 496 pp. .... Vendor G0531

Hickey. **The War of 1812: A Forgotten Conflict**. 1989.
An in-depth history. Extensive footnotes.
Paper. $14.95. 457 pp. .... Vendor G0611

Peterson, Clarence Stewart. **Known Military Dead During the War of 1812**. (1955) reprint 1997.
Paper. $10.95. 74 pp. .... Vendor G0011

Schweitzer, George K. **War of 1812 Genealogy**. 1995. Illus.
History of war, research techniques, archival sources, national publications, state publications, local sources, military unit histories, sites.
Paper. $12.00. 70 pp. .... Vendor G0569

Scott, Kenneth. **British Aliens in the United States during the War of 1812**. 1979. Indexed.
Cloth. $20.00. 420 pp. .... Vendor G0010

Thurtle, Robert Glenn, ed. **The General Society of the War of 1812: 1976 Bicentennial Supplement to the 1972 Register**. 1976. Indexed.
Cloth. $20.00. 174 pp. .... Vendor G0011

Miscellaneous

California Genealogical Society. **Genealogy Success Stories: Personal Problemsolving Accounts That Encourage, Enlighten and Inspire You**. 1995. Indexed.
Paper. $12.00. 134 pp. .... Vendor G0628

Colorado Genealogical Society, Inc. **CGS Perpetual Calendar**. 1989.
Serves the years 1752-2010, to allow you to check any day-date relationship. Some text material provides background about our present-day Gregorian calendar to assist you in your research.
Cloth. $4.50. .... Vendor G0174

Dixon, Ruth Priest, and Katherine George Eberly. **Index to Seamen's Protection Certificate Applications, Port of Philadelphia, 1796-1823**. 1995.
Paper. $16.50. 152 pp. .... Vendor G0011

Dixon, Ruth Priest. **Index to Seamen's Protection Certificate Applications, Port of Philadelphia, 1824-1861**. (1994) reprint 1997.
Contact vendor for information. 170 pp. .... Vendor G0011

Francis, Elisabeth, and Ethel Moore. **Lost Links**. New Recordings of Old Data from Many States. (1947) reprint 1991. Indexed.
Paper. $39.95. 562 pp. .... Vendor G0011

Heisey, John W. **Genealogy: Helps, Hints, & Hope**. 1995.
A collection of seventy-four articles on a variety of subjects relevant to genealogists today.
Paper. $11.50. 147 pp. .... Vendor G0770

Heiss, Willard. **Working in the Vineyards of Genealogy**. 1993. Indexed. Illus.
Cloth. $27.75. 242 pp. .... Vendor G0109

Medals of John Pinches. Illus.
A catalogue of works struck by the company from 1840 to 1969 by J. H. Pinches. Introduces you to the finest medals in their time; also includes many Wyon medals.
Cloth. £48.00. 288 pp. .... Vendor G0616

Stevenson, Noel C., ed. **The Genealogical Reader**. 1977. Indexed.
A collection of articles by some of America's leading genealogists making for interesting excursions into the byways of genealogy.
Paper. $6.50. 188 pp. .... Vendor G0561

Taylor, Maureen Alice. **Runaways, Deserters, and Notorious Villains**. 1995. Indexed.
   Book #1595.
Cloth. $29.50. 189 pp. .... Vendor G0082

Walch, Timothy. **Our Family, Our Town**. Essays on Family and Local History Sources in the National Archives. 1987. Illus.
Practical advice and encouragement in the use of federal records in family and local history research. Military pension records, census schedules, ship passenger lists, and court documents are among the materials discussed.
Cloth. $10.00. 223 pp. .... Vendor G0565

✌ Names (Given Names, Surnames, ✌ and Nicknames)

Ashley, Leonard R. N. **What's in a Name?** Everything You Wanted to Know. 1989. Rev. ed. 1996.
Paper. $17.95. 265 pp. .... Vendor G0010

Bailey, Rosalie Fellows. **Dutch Systems in Family Naming, New York-New Jersey**.
Paper. $6.50. 21 pp. .... Vendor G0627

Barber, Rev. Henry. **British Family Names—Their Origin and Meaning** . . . (1903) reprint 1990.
Contact vendor for information. 298 pp. .... Vendor G0011

Bardsley, Alan. **First Name Variants**. 1996.
This book lists given names and their variants alphabetically and then groups together those that have a common root. For the genealogist faced with an obscure pet name, it identifies the possible origin and opens up the search for alternatives. The

coverage is primarily for the English-speaking world of the 17th to 19th centuries with the more common Welsh, Irish, and Scottish links.
£6.00 (overseas surface). 108 pp. .... Vendor G0588

Bardsley, Charles W. **Curiosities of Puritan Nomenclature**. (1880) reprint 1996. Indexed.
Paper. $25.00. 264 pp. .... Vendor G0011

Bardsley, Charles Wareing. **A Dictionary of English and Welsh Surnames with Special American Instances**. (Rev. ed., 1901) reprint 1996.
Cloth. $50.00. xvi + 837 pp. .... Vendor G0010

Baring-Gould, Sabine. **Family Names and Their Story**. (1910) reprint 1996. Indexed.
A study of English surnames.
Paper. $32.50. 432 pp. .... Vendor G0011

Beider, Alexander. **Ancient Ashkenazic Surnames: Jewish Surnames from Prague (15th-18th Centuries)**.
Paper. $11.00. 46 pp. .... Vendor G0559

Beider, Alexander. **A Dictionary of Jewish Surnames From the Kingdom of Poland**. 1996.
Cloth. $69.50. 608 pp. .... Vendor G0559

Beider, Alexander. **A Dictionary of Jewish Surnames from the Russian Empire**.
Cloth. $75.00. 784 pp. .... Vendor G0559

Black, G. F. **The Surnames of Scotland**.
£17.99. .... Vendor G0555

Donaldson, G. **Surnames & Ancestry in Scotland**.
Paper. £0.50. .... Vendor G0555

Dorward, D. **Scottish Surnames**.
Paper. £4.99. .... Vendor G0555

Ewen, Cecil Henry L'Estrange. **A History of Surnames of the British Isles**. A Concise Account of Their Origin, Evolution, Etymology, and Legal Status. (1931, 1968) reprint 1995. Indexed.
Paper. $41.50. 539 pp. .... Vendor G0011

FFHS. **Register of One-Name Studies**. 12th ed.
£4.35 (overseas surface). .... Vendor G0588

Fucilla, Joseph G. **Our Italian Surnames**. (1949) reprint 1996. Indexed.
Cloth. $28.50. 299 pp. .... Vendor G0010

General Register Office for Scotland. **Personal Names in Scotland**.
Paper. £2.95 plus shipping. .... Vendor G0589

Gratz, Delbert L. **Was Isch Dini Nahme? What Is Your Name?** Indexed.
   The study of names of Swiss derivation.
Paper. $8.50. 37 pp. .... Vendor G0770

Harrison, Henry. **Surnames of the United Kingdom**. A Concise Etymological Dictionary. 2 vols. in 1. (1912-18) reprint 1996.
Paper. $45.00. 622 pp. .... Vendor G0011

Jones, George F. **German-American Names**. 2nd ed. 1995.
Cloth. $25.00. 320 pp. .... Vendor G0010

Kolatch, Alfred J. **Complete Dictionary of English and Hebrew First Names**. Published by Jonathan David Co.
Cloth. $25.00. 516 pp. .... Vendor G0559

Konrad, J. **Directory of Family "One-Name" Periodicals**.
Paper. $10.00. 65 pp. .... Vendor G0574

Library of Congress. **Surnames:** A Selected List of References about Personal Names. Compiled by Paul J. Connor.
   The text of this is available on the Local History and Genealogy Reading Room's home page: http://lcweb.loc.gov/rr/genealogy.
Free. Contact vendor for information. 15 pp. .... Vendor G0566

Matheson, Sir Robert E. **Special Report On Surnames in Ireland** [together with] Varieties and Synonymes of Surnames and Christian Names in Ireland. (1901, 1909) reprint 1994.
Cloth. $18.50. 78 + 94 pp. .... Vendor G0010

Mitchell, Brian. **The Surnames of Derry.**
Paper. £7.50. .... Vendor G0604

O'Laughlin, M. **The Master Book of Irish Surnames**.
The Master index of 60,000 locations, origins, spellings, and sources for Irish names. The largest collection ever; bonus section includes the surname index to all IGF works and periodicals.
Quality hardbound & gold stamped. $24.00. 320 pp. .... Vendor G0455

Osborne, Joseph F. **Heirlooms of Ireland**. An Easy Reference to Some Irish Surnames and Their Origins. 1995.
Paper. $24.95. 183 pp. .... Vendor G0011

Palgrave, D. A. **Forming a One-Name Group**. 4th ed. 1992.
£2.90 (overseas surface). 16 pp. .... Vendor G0588

Platt, Lyman D. **Hispanic Surnames and Family History**. 1996.
Paper. $19.95. 349 pp. .... Vendor G0010

Precision Indexing. **The Soundex Reference Guide**. 1990.
An alphabetical listing of over 125,000 surnames and their corresponding Soundex code. Although a new edition has been issued, this volume is economical for those who do not need foreign names.
Paper. $19.95. 253 pp. .... Vendor G0552

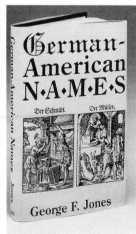

Precision Indexing. **The Soundex Reference Guide**. 2nd ed. 2 vols. 1994.
A listing of 500,000 surnames, which are coded with both the U.S. and Daitch-Mokotoff Soundex Codes.
Cloth, $129.95. Paper, $99.95. .... Vendor G0552

Ptak, Diane Snyder. **Surnames: Their Meaning and Origins**. 1993.
Paper. $14.00. 26 pp. .... Vendor G0663

Rogers, Colin D. **The Surname Detective**. 1996.
This British guide provides the amateur genealogist or family historian with the skills to research the distribution and history of a surname.
£13.00 (overseas surface). 258 pp. .... Vendor G0588

Rose, Christine, CG, CGL, FASG. **Nicknames: Past & Present**. 2nd ed. rev. 1995.
Contact vendor for information. v + 41 pp. .... Vendor G0474

Rowlands, John, and Sheila Rowlands. **The Surnames of Wales** for Family Historians and Others. 1996. Illus.
Paper. $19.95. 229 pp. .... Vendor G0010

Sims, Clifford S. **The Origin and Signification of Scottish Surnames**. (1862) reprint 1995.
Paper. $17.50. 122 pp. .... Vendor G0011

Smith, Clifford N. **Cumulative Surname Index and Soundex to Monographs 1 Through 12 of the German-American Genealogical Research Series**. 1981.
ISBN 0-915162-17-2.
Paper. $20.00. iv + 66 pp. double-columned. .... Vendor G0491

Smith, Clifford N. **Cumulative Surname Soundex to German-American Genealogical Research Monographs 14-19 and 21-25**. German-American Genealogical Research Monograph Number 26. 1990.
ISBN 0-915162-91-1.
Paper. $20.00. i + 41 pp. double-columned. .... Vendor G0491

Smith, Elsdon C. **American Surnames**. (1969) reprint 1995. Indexed.
Paper. $16.95. xx + 370 pp. .... Vendor G0010

Society of Genealogists. **General Register Office One-Name Lists in the Library of the Society of Genealogists**. 1995.
Paper. £1.65. 16 pp. .... Vendor G0557

Society of Genealogists. **Guide to Sources for One-Name Studies in the Society of Genealogists' Library**.
Leaflet. £0.20. .... Vendor G0557

Society of Genealogists. **The Relevance of Surnames**.
A British book published by the Society of Genealogists.
Leaflet. £0.20. .... Vendor G0557

Surnames in the United States Census of 1790. An Analysis of National Origins of the Population . . . (1932) reprint 1995. Indexed.
Lists and classifies thousands of surnames according to the several states in which they were found in 1790, thus enabling researchers to narrow their search to a particular area. English, Scottish, Celitic Irish, Ulster Irish, German, Dutch, French, and Swedish names predominate.
Paper. $28.50. 334 pp. .... Vendor G0011

Swiss Surnames. 3 vols. 1995.
  Book #1630.
Cloth. $149.50. 768 + 704 + 640 pp. .... Vendor G0082

Torrance, D. R. **Scottish Personal Names & Place Names: A Bibliography**.
Paper. £1.75. .... Vendor G0555

Whyte, D. **Scottish Surnames & Families**.
£7.99. .... Vendor G0555

Woulfe, Rev. Patrick. **Irish Names and Surnames**. Sloinnte Gaelheal Is Gall. (1923)
reprint 1993.
Cloth. $40.00. 742 pp. .... Vendor G0010

Woulfe, Rev. Patrick. **Sloinnte Gaedeal is Gall**. Indexed.
"Irish Names and Surnames," the original, classic dictionary of Irish surnames by
the Rev. Patrick Woulfe (1923) with notes on Gaelic origins. All new IGF index.
Includes Irish names for children.
Quality hardbound & gold stamped. $40.00. .... Vendor G0455

Zuercher, Isaac. **Anabaptist-Mennonite Names in Switzerland** Translated by Hannes
Maria Aleman. 1988.
Paper. $9.50. 35 pp. .... Vendor G0150

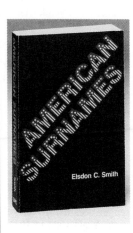

✒ Naturalization ✒

Giuseppi, Montague S. **Naturalizations of Foreign Protestants in the American and West Indian Colonies.** (1921) reprint 1995. Indexed.
Paper. $20.00. 196 pp. .... Vendor G0011

Neagles, James C., and Lila Lee Neagles. **Locating Your Immigrant Ancestor: A Guide to Naturalization Records.**
Paper. $12.95. 153 pp. .... Vendor G0618

Newman, John J. **American Naturalization Processes and Procedures, 1790-1985.** 1985. Illus.
Paper. $8.25. 44 pp. .... Vendor G0109

Schaefer, Christina K. **Guide to Naturalization Records of the United States.** 1997.
Cloth. $25.00. 439 pp. .... Vendor G0010

✒ Newspapers ✒

Albaugh, Gaylord P. **History and Annotated Bibliography of American Religious Periodicals and Newspapers.** 2 vols. 1994.
  Gives locations and/or microform sources for thousands of religious periodicals and newspapers published in America from 1730-1830. Tremendous detailed included. 8½" x 11".
Cloth. $125.00. 1,456 pp. .... Vendor G0611

Henritze, Barbara K. **Bibliographic Checklist of African American Newspapers.** 1995. Indexed.
Cloth. $35.00. 206 pp. .... Vendor G0010

Hosman, Lloyd. **Newspaper Research.**
Paper. $8.00. 26 pp. .... Vendor G0574

Watson, Alan D., comp. & ed. **Index to North Carolina Newspapers, 1784-1789.** 1992.
  Includes an informative introduction, which discusses how newspapers were published in the 18th century.
Paper. $12.00. xxvii + 68 pp. .... Vendor G0586

✒ Passenger Lists, Ships, and ✒ Ship Arrival Records

Allan, Morton. **Morton Allan Directory of European Passenger Steamship Arrivals.** For the Years 1890 to 1930 at the Port of New York, and for the Years 1904 to 1926 at the Ports of New York, Philadelphia, Boston and Baltimore. (1931) reprint 1993.
Cloth. $20.00. 268 pp. .... Vendor G0010

Anuta, Michael J. **Ships of Our Ancestors.** (1983) reprint 1996. Indexed. Illus.
  A compilation of photographs of the steamships that were employed in transporting immigrants to this country.
Paper. $34.95. vii + 380 pp. .... Vendor G0010

Baca, Leo. **Czech Immigration Passenger Lists, Volume I**. (1983) reprint 1989. Indexed.
Galveston 1848-1861, 1865-1871. New Orleans 1852-1879.
Paper. $17.95. 180 pp. .... Vendor G0481

Baca, Leo. **Czech Immigration Passenger Lists, Volume II**. (1985) reprint 1991. Indexed.
Galveston 1896-1906. New Orleans 1879-1899.
Paper. $17.95. 196 pp. .... Vendor G0481

Baca, Leo. **Czech Immigration Passenger Lists, Volume III**. (1989) reprint 1993. Indexed.
Galveston 1907-1914.
Paper. $17.95. 170 pp. .... Vendor G0481

Baca, Leo. **Czech Immigration Passenger Lists, Volume IV**. (1991) reprint 1994. Indexed.
New York 1847-1869.
Paper. $17.95. 182 pp. .... Vendor G0481

Baca, Leo. **Czech Immigration Passenger Lists, Volume V**. (1993) reprint 1996. Indexed.
New York 1870-1880.
Paper. $19.95. 190 pp. .... Vendor G0481

Baca, Leo. **Czech Immigration Passenger Lists, Volume VI**. 1995. Indexed.
New York 1881-1886. Galveston 1880-1886.
Paper. $19.95. 260 pp. .... Vendor G0481

Bangerter, Lawrence. **The Compass**. Vol. 1.
Aid to research of immigrants to America, includes directory of sources: name and

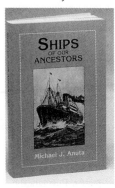

type of ship, ship's ports, registration date of manifest, source from which it was taken. Passenger lists include Port of Baltimore 1820-91, ships coming to North America, Portuguese, LDS Church, Scandinavian and Danish manuscripts.
Paper. $10.95. 184 pp. .... Vendor G0618

Black, John W. **Excursion on the Delaware. A History of Steamboats and Their Men in the Delaware Valley**. 1993. Indexed. Illus.
   A fascinating look at steamships on the Delaware River and the lives they touched.
Paper. $27.50. 280 pp. .... Vendor G0069

Boyer, Carl, 3rd. **Ship Passenger Lists: National and New England, 1600-1825**. (1977) reprint 1992. Indexed.
   Forty-four lists plus Bibliography.
Paper. $27.00. 270 pp. .... Vendor G0198

Boyer, Carl, 3rd. **Ship Passenger Lists: New York and New Jersey, 1600-1825**. (1978) reprint 1992. Indexed.
   Twenty-seven lists plus Bibliography.
Paper. $27.00. 333 pp. .... Vendor G0198

Boyer, Carl, 3rd. **Ship Passenger Lists: Pennsylvania and Delaware, 1641-1825**. (1980) reprint 1992. Indexed.
   Thirty-two lists plus Bibliography.
Paper. $27.00. 289 pp. .... Vendor G0198

Boyer, Carl, 3rd. **Ship Passenger Lists: The South, 1538-1825**. (1979) reprint 1992. Indexed.
   Thirty-four lists plus Bibliography.
Paper. $27.00. 314 pp. .... Vendor G0198

Carr, Peter E. **San Francisco Passenger Departure Lists—Vols. I- IV**. Vol. 1, 1991; Vol. 2, 1992; Vol. 3, 1993. Indexed.
Paper. $15.95/vol. 138 + 160 + 204 pp. .... Vendor G0496

Colletta, John Phillip. **They Came in Ships: A Guide to Finding Your Immigrant Ancestor's Arrival Record (Revised Edition)**. 1993.
Paper. $9.95. 108 pp. .... Vendor G0570

Erickson. **Leaving England: Essays on British Emigration in the Nineteenth Century**. 1994.
   A series of essays studies the ship passenger lists of British immigrants and explores the social impact of their arrivals. Also comments on immigrations to Canada and Australia with contrast to America.
Cloth. $39.95. 272 pp. .... Vendor G0611

Family History Library. **Hamburg Passenger Lists Guide**.
Free. 4 pp. .... Vendor G0629

Filby, William P. **Passenger and Immigration Lists Index**. 3 vols. Published by Gale Research. 1981.
Cloth. $440.00/set. 2,340 pp. .... Vendor G0560

Filby, William P. **Passenger and Immigration Lists Index—Individual Supplements from 1982-1995**. Published by Gale Research.
Cloth. $195.00/supplement. .... Vendor G0560

Filby, William P. **Passenger and Immigration Lists Index, 1996 Supplement**. Published by Gale Research.
Cloth. $195.00. 500 pp. .... Vendor G0560

Filby, William P. **Passenger and Immigration Lists Index—1991-1995 Cumulated Supplements**. Published by Gale Research.
Cloth. $530.00. .... Vendor G0560

Galveston County Genealogical Society. **Port of Galveston, Texas, Ships Passenger List, 1846-1871**. 1984. Indexed.
Cloth. $28.00. 272 pp. .... Vendor G0610

Glazier, Ira A., and Michael H. Tepper, eds. **The Famine Immigrants**. Lists of Irish Immigrants Arriving at the Port of New York, 1846-1851. 7 vols. 1983-1986.
  Vol. I: January 1846-June 1847. 841 pp. Contact vendor for information.
  Vol. II: July 1847-June 1848. 722 pp. Indexed. 1983.
  Vol. III: July 1848-March 1849. 695 pp. Indexed. 1984.
  Vol. IV: April 1849-September 1849. 814 pp. Indexed. 1984.
  Vol. V: October 1849-May 1850. 638 pp. Indexed. 1985.
  Vol. VI: June 1850-March 1851. 898 pp. Indexed. 1985.
  Vol. VII: April 1851-December 1851. 1,195 pp. Indexed. 1986.
Cloth. $45.00/vol. .... Vendor G0010

Glazier, Ira A., and P. William Filby. **Germans to America: Lists of Passengers Arriving at U.S. Ports, 1850-1893**. Indexed.
  Data on German immigrants listed by ship and indexed by surname. Call 800- 772-8937 for complete volume breakdown. $77.50 per volume—ongoing publication.
Cloth. $77.50. .... Vendor G0118

Glazier, Ira A., and P. William Filby. **Italians to America, 1880-1899: Lists of Passengers Arriving at U.S. Ports**. Indexed.
  Data on Italian immigrants listed by ship and indexed by surname. Call 800-772-8937 for complete volume breakdown. $77.50 per volume—ongoing publication.
Cloth. $77.50. .... Vendor G0118

Hackett, J. Dominick, and Charles M. Early. **Passenger Lists from Ireland** (Excerpted from Journal of the American Irish Historical Society, Volumes 28 and 29). (1931) reprint 1994.
Paper. $7.50. 46 pp. .... Vendor G0011

Holcomb, Brent H., comp. **Passenger Arrivals at the Port of Charleston, 1820-1829**. 1994. Indexed.
Cloth. $25.00. 188 pp. .... Vendor G0010

Jewson, Charles Boardman. **Transcripts of Three Registers of Passengers from Great Yarmouth to Holland and New England, 1637-1639**. (1964) reprint 1990. Indexed.
Cloth. $12.00. 98 pp. .... Vendor G0011

Mitchell, Brian. **Irish Emigration Lists, 1833-1839**. Lists of Emigrants Extracted from the Ordnance Survey Memoirs for Counties Londonderry and Antrim. 1989. Indexed.
Cloth. $20.00. 128 pp. .... Vendor G0010

Mitchell, Brian. **Irish Passenger Lists, 1803-1806**. Lists of Passengers Sailing from Ireland to America. 1995. Indexed.
Cloth. $25.00. 154 pp. .... Vendor G0010

Mitchell, Brian. **Irish Passenger Lists, 1847-1871**. (1988) reprint 1992. Indexed.
Cloth. $28.50. 350 pp. .... Vendor G0010

O'Brien, Michael J. **The Irish in America**. Immigration, Land, Probate, Administrations, Birth, Marriage and Burial Records of the Irish in America in and about the Eighteenth Century. (1965) reprint 1996.
Paper. $9.00. 63 pp. .... Vendor G0011

Precision Indexing. **Passenger Ships Arriving in New York Harbor: Vol. 1, 1820-1850**. 1991.
Cloth. $79.95. 352 pp. .... Vendor G0552

Ptak, Diane Snyder. **A Passage in Time: The Ships that Brought Our Ancestors, 1620-1940 and Supplement**. 1992, Supplement 1995.
    Includes a history of immigrant ships from 1700 to 1940, as well as a bibliography of ship-related references.
Paper. $15.00. 26 pp. .... Vendor G0663

Smith, Clifford N. **From Bremen to America in 1850: Fourteen Rare Emigrant Ship Lists**. German-American Genealogical Research Monograph Number 22. 1987.
    ISBN 0-915162-81-4.
Paper. $20.00. iii + 35 pp. double-columned. .... Vendor G0491

Smith, Clifford N. **Passenger Lists (and Fragments Thereof) from Hamburg and Bremen to Australia and the United States, 1846-1849**. German-American Genealogical Research Monograph Number 23. 1988.
    ISBN 0-915162-82-2.
Paper. $20.00. i + 27 pp. double-columned. .... Vendor G0491

Smith, Clifford N. **Reconstructed Passenger Lists for 1850: Hamburg to Australia, Brazil, Canada, Chile, and the United States**. German and Central European Emigration Monograph Number 1. 4 parts.
    Part 1: Passenger Lists 1 Through 25 (1980; 79 pp.).
    Part 2: Passenger Lists 26 Through 42 (1980; 86 pp.).
    Part 3: Passenger Lists 43 Through 60 (1981; 63 pp.).
    Part 4: Supplemental Notes on Emigrants' Places of Origin (1981; 58 pp.). ISBN 0-915162-50-4 (the set).
Paper. $20.00/part. .... Vendor G0491

Smith, Clifford N. **Reconstructed Passenger Lists for 1851 via Hamburg: Emigrants from Germany, Austria, Bohemia, Hungary, Poland, Russia, Scandinavia, and Switzerland to Australia, Brazil, Canada, Chile, the United States, and Venezuela**. German and Central European Emigration Monograph Number 2. 5 parts.
    Part 1: Passenger Lists 1 Through 22 (1986; 45 pp. double-columned).
ISBN 0-915162-51-2.
    Part 2: Passenger Lists 23 Through 44 (1986; 41 pp. double-columned).
ISBN 0- 915162-52-0.
    Part 3: Passenger Lists 45 Through 66 (1986; 53 pp. double-columned).
ISBN 0- 915162-53-9.

Part 4: Passenger Lists 67 Through 85 (1986; 26 pp. double-columned).
ISBN 0- 915162-54-7.
Part 5: Supplemental Notes on Emigrants' Places of Origin: Place Names A Through
L (1987; ii + 41 pp. double-columned). ISBN 0-915162-55-5.
Part 5: Supplemental Notes on Emigrants' Places of Origin: Place Names M Through
Z (1987; ii + 38 pp. double-columned). ISBN 0-915162-55-5.
Paper. $20.00/part. .... Vendor G0491

Strassburger, Ralph Beaver. **Pennsylvania German Pioneers: A Publication of the
Original Lists of Arrivals in the Port of Philadelphia from 1727 to 1808.** 2 vols.
(1934) reprint 1992. Indexed.
Cloth. $75.00. 1,485 pp. total .... Vendor G0010

Strassburger, Ralph Beaver, and William John Hinke. **Pennsylvania German Pioneers: A Publication of the Original Lists of Arrivals in the Port of Philadelphia
from 1727 to 1808, Signature Volume.** (1934) reprint 1992.
This set, which is commonly known as "Strassburger & Hinke," is the time-
honored reference for arrival of German emigrants to America before 1800. It is one
of the basic works for genealogical libraries. Volumes 1 & 3 have been reprinted a
number of times, but this is the first time this volume (which shows the actual signatures of the emigrants) has been reprinted. (See listing on p. 51.)
Cloth. $55.00. 909 pp. .... Vendor G0081

Strassburger, Ralph Beaver, and William John Hinke. **Pennsylvania German Pio-
neers.** 3 vols. (1937) reprint 1992. Indexed.
Book #1345.
Cloth. $175.00. 2,560 pp. .... Vendor G0082

Swierenga, Robert P. **Dutch Immigrants in U.S. Ship Passenger Manifests, 1820-
1880: An Alphabetical Listing by Household Heads and Independent Persons.** 2
vols. 1983. Indexed.
Cloth. $152.50. .... Vendor G0118

Taylor, Maureen A. **Rhode Island Passenger Lists** Port of Providence, 1798-1808,
1820-1872; Ports of Bristol and Warren 1820-1871. 1995.
Cloth. $25.00. 232 pp. .... Vendor G0010

Tepper, Michael. **American Passenger Arrival Records.** A Guide to the Records of
Immigrants Arriving at American Ports by Sail and Steam. Updated and Revised.
(1993) reprint 1996. Illus.
Cloth. $19.95. 144 pp. .... Vendor G0010

Tepper, Michael. **Emigrants to Pennsylvania, 1641-1819.** A Consolidation of Ship
Passenger Lists from the Pennsylvania Magazine of History and Biography. (1877-
1934) reprint 1992. Indexed.
Cloth. $20.00. 302 pp. .... Vendor G0010

Tepper, Michael. **Immigrants to the Middle Colonies.** A Consolidation of Ship Pas-
senger Lists and Associated Data from The New York Genealogical and Biographical
Record. (1879-1970) reprint 1992. Indexed. Illus.
Cloth. $17.50. 191 pp. .... Vendor G0010

Tepper, Michael. **New World Immigrants**. A Consolidation of Ship Passenger Lists and Associated Data from Periodical Literature. 2 vols. 1988. Indexed.
Cloth. $60.00. 568 + 602 pp. .... Vendor G0010

Tepper, Michael H., ed. **Passenger Arrivals at the Port of Baltimore, 1820-1834** from Customs Passenger Lists. Transcribed by Elizabeth P. Bentley. 1982.
Cloth. $38.50. 768 pp. .... Vendor G0010

Tepper, Michael H., ed. **Passenger Arrivals at the Port of Philadelphia, 1800-1819**. Transcribed by Elizabeth P. Bentley. 1986.
Cloth. $45.00. xvii + 913 pp. .... Vendor G0010

Tepper, Michael. **Passengers to America**. A Consolidation of Ship Passenger Lists from The New England Historical and Genealogical Register. (1847-1961) reprint 1988. Indexed.
Cloth. $25.00. 554 pp. .... Vendor G0010

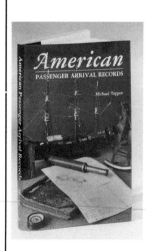

Whitmore, William H. **Port Arrivals and Immigrants to the City of Boston, 1715-1716 and 1762-1769.** (1900) reprint 1996. Indexed.
Paper. $12.50. 111 pp. .... Vendor G0011

Zimmerman, Gary J., and Marion Wolfert. **German Immigrants,** Lists of Passengers Bound from Bremen to New York, 1847-1854, With Places of Origin. (1985) reprint 1993.
Cloth. $22.50. 175 pp. .... Vendor G0010

Zimmerman, Gary J., and Marion Wolfert. **German Immigrants,** Lists of Passengers Bound from Bremen to New York, 1855-1862, With Places of Origin. (1986) reprint 1993.
Cloth. $22.50. xx + 167 pp. .... Vendor G0010

Zimmerman, Gary J., and Marion Wolfert. **German Immigrants,** Lists of Passengers Bound from Bremen to New York, 1863-1867, With Places of Origin. 1988.
Cloth. $21.50. 221 pp. .... Vendor G0010

Zimmerman, Gary J., and Marion Wolfert. **German Immigrants,** Lists of Passengers Bound from Bremen to New York, 1868-1871, With Places of Origin. 1993.
Cloth. $25.00. 218 pp. .... Vendor G0010

Periodicals

Albaugh, Gaylord P. **History and Annotated Bibliography of American Religious Periodicals and Newspapers.** 2 vols. 1994.
Gives locations and/or microform sources for thousands of religious periodicals and newspapers published in America from 1730-1830. Tremendous detail included. 8½" x 11".
Cloth. $125.00. 1,456 pp. .... Vendor G0611

Boyer, Carl, 3rd. **Jacobus' Index to Genealogical Periodicals.** 1995.
Book #1627.
Cloth. $25.00. 373 pp. .... Vendor G0082

Jacobus, Donald Lines. **Index to Genealogical Periodicals.** 3 vols in 1. (1932, 1948, 1953) reprint 1997.
Contact vendor for information. 365 pp. in all. .... Vendor G0011

Konrad, J. **Directory of Family "One-Name" Periodicals.**
Paper. $10.00. 65 pp. .... Vendor G0574

Library of Congress. **Genealogical Periodicals in the Local History and Genealogy Reading Room:** A Guide for Research. A revision, by Barbara B. Walsh, of a guide prepared in 1983 by Judith P. Reid.
The text of this is available on the Local History and Genealogy Reading Room's home page: http://lcweb.loc.gov/rr/genealogy.
Free. Contact vendor for information. 12 pp. .... Vendor G0566

❧ Place Names ❧

Abate, Frank R., ed. **American Places Dictionary:** A Guide to 45,000 Populated Places, Natural Features, and Other Places in the United States. In Four Volumes. Volume 1, Northeast. Volume 2, South. Volume 3, Midwest. Volume 4, West. 1994. Indexed.
Covers states, counties, cities, towns, townships, villages, and boroughs, as well as Indian reservations, military bases, and major geographical features. Entries provide description, precise location, and name origin information; supplemented by maps and indexes.
Hard-cover. Contact vendor for information. .... Vendor G0768

Adams, James N. **Illinois Place Names.** (1969) reprint 1989.
Cloth. $21.50. .... Vendor G0501

All-Name Index to the 1860 Gazetteer of New York State. 1993.
Includes listing of geographic names not in original index. Included with paper version of the 1860 Gazetteer by J. H. French.
Paper. $15.00. 183 pp. .... Vendor G0093

Blois, John T., and S. L. Hood & Co. **1838 Michigan Gazetteer.** (1838) reprint 1979.
Cloth. $26.00. 424 pp. .... Vendor G0531

Blois, John T. **Gazetteer of the State of Michigan,** in Three Parts. (1840) reprint 1993.
Cloth. $44.00. 418 pp. .... Vendor G0259

Espenshade, A. Howry. **Pennsylvania Place Names.** (1925) reprint 1995.
Paper. $32.50. 375 pp. .... Vendor G0011

French, J. H. **Gazetteer of the State of New York (1860),** Reprinted with an Index of Names Compiled by Frank Place. (1860, 1983) reprint 1995. Indexed. Illus.
Cloth. $55.00. 926 pp. .... Vendor G0010

French, J. H. **Gazetteer (1860) of the State of New York**. (1860) reprint 1993. Indexed. Illus.

Long considered a Bible for New York research, which includes almost every place in New York; short histories and facts about events and early settlers; also many statistical tables. Cloth price does not include new, all-name index. Paper price includes new index.

Cloth, $35.00. Paper, $35.00. 784 pp. .... Vendor G0093

Gannett, Henry. **A Gazetteer of Maryland and Delaware**. 2 vols. in 1. (1904) reprint 1994.

Paper. $12.50. 99 pp. .... Vendor G0011

Gannett, Henry. **A Gazetteer of Virginia and West Virginia**. 2 vols. in 1. (1904) reprint 1994.

Paper. $26.50. 323 pp. in all. .... Vendor G0011

Gannett, Henry. **A Geographic Dictionary of Massachusetts**. (1894) reprint 1978.

Cloth. $11.50. 126 pp. .... Vendor G0011

Gannett, Henry. **Geographic Dictionary of New Jersey**. (1894) reprint 1993.

Contact vendor for information. 131 pp. .... Vendor G0011

Gannett, Henry. **The Origin of Certain Place Names in the United States** 2nd ed. (1905) reprint 1996.

Paper. $31.50. 334 pp. .... Vendor G0011

Gardiner. **German Towns in Slovakia and Upper Hungary: A Genealogical Gazetteer**. 1991.

Nearly half of this book is an extremely helpful "how-to" of Czech research, while the second half is the gazetteer that the title promises.

Paper. $17.00. 113 pp. .... Vendor G0611

Gelling, Margaret. **Signposts to the Past**. 1988.

Comprehensive study of British place names.

Cloth. £14.99. 288 pp. .... Vendor G0579

Gordon, T. F. **Gazetteer of the State of New York,** Comprehending Its Colonial History; General Geography, Geology, Internal Improvements; Its Political State; Minute Description of Its Several Counties, Towns, and Villages; Statistical Tables. (1836) reprint 1990.

Cloth. $79.50. 800 pp. .... Vendor G0259

Gordon, T. F. **A Gazetteer of the State of Pennsylvania**. (1832) reprint 1989.

Cloth. $57.50. 63 + 508 pp. .... Vendor G0259

Gordon, Thomas F. **A Gazetteer of the State of New Jersey**. (1834) reprint 1995. Illus.

Paper. $12.50. 174 pp. .... Vendor G0140

Groome, Francis H., ed. **Ordnance Gazetteer of Scotland:** A Graphic and Accurate Description of Every Place in Scotland. 3 vols. (1902) reprint 1995. Illus.

Alphabetical listing of every city, town, hamlet, village, parish and family seat, with

remarkably detailed geographical and social descriptions. Volume III includes an appendix with a brief history and profile of Scotland. Many maps.
Volume I, A-Foc.
Volume II, Fod-Moncton.
Volume III, Monctonhall-end.
Cloth. $55.00/vol., $150.00/set. 1,762 pp. .... Vendor G0259

Hough, Franklin B. **Gazetteer of the State of New York,** Embracing a Comprehensive Account of the History & Statistics of the State, with Geological & Topographical Descriptions of Each County, City, Town & Village. (1872) reprint 1993.
Many New York counties were divided several times, and town, township, and village names were often duplicated in every county. This book can help! Very useful for anyone researching New York.
Cloth. $75.00. 745 pp. .... Vendor G0259

Indiana Gazetteer, or Topographical Dictionary of the State of Indiana. 3rd ed. (1850) reprint 1993.
In Indiana today there's one "Madison"; in 1850, there were eleven "Madison Townships"! This book can help you find out which one you're really interested in. Very useful for early state research.
Cloth. $46.00. 440 pp. .... Vendor G0259

Joyce, P. W. **The Origin and History of Irish Names of Places.** In Three Volumes. (1869-1913) reprint 1995. Indexed.
Paper. $115.00. 1,756 pp. in all. .... Vendor G0011

Kenny, Hamill. **The Placenames of Maryland: Their Origin and Meaning.** Indexed.
An alphabetical listing of the towns and villages, estates and other historic sites, and rivers and streams of Maryland and how they got their names.
Paper. $14.95. 364 pp. .... Vendor G0617

Kilbourne, John. **1833 Ohio Gazetteer.** (1833) reprint 1981.
Cloth. $29.00. 494 pp. .... Vendor G0531

Morse, Jedidiah. **American Gazetteer.** (1797) reprint 1979.
Cloth. $34.00. 626 pp. .... Vendor G0531

Nicolaisen, W. **Scottish Place Names.** The First Cohesive & Systematic Study.
£10.99. .... Vendor G0555

O'Laughlin, M. **The Master Book of Irish Placenames.** Indexed. Illus.
The Master atlas and place-name locator for all of Ireland. Over sixty indexed maps. Seventeenth- and nineteenth-century place-name indexes; spellings; history; appendix; 40,000 listings.
Quality hardbound & gold stamped. $24.00. 250 pp. .... Vendor G0455

Pease, J., and J. Niles. **Gazetteer of the States of Connecticut & R.I.** Consisting of Two Parts: I, Geogr. & Statistical Desc. of Each State; II, General Geogr. View of Each County, & a Minute & Ample Topographical Desc. of Each Town, Village, Etc. (1819) reprint 1990.
Paper. $35.00. 339 pp. .... Vendor G0259

Powell. **The North Carolina Gazetteer: A Dictionary of Tar Heel Places.** 1968.
Over 20,000 entries that locate the geographical features of North Carolina.
Paper. $16.95. 561 pp. .... Vendor G0611

Smith, Frank. **A Genealogical Gazetteer of England**. An Alphabetical Dictionary of Places, With Their Location, Ecclesiastical Jurisdiction, Population, and the Date of the Earliest Entry in the Registers of Every Ancient Parish in England. (1968) reprint 1995.
Cloth. $35.00. xv + 599 pp. .... Vendor G0010

Smith, Frank. **A Genealogical Gazetteer of Scotland**.
An alphabetical dictionary of places with their locations, population, and date of the earliest entry in the registers of every parish in Scotland.
Paper. $14.00. 140 pp. .... Vendor G0618

Spafford, Horatio Gates. **Gazetteer (1824) of the State of New York**. (1824) reprint 1980.
Cloth. $35.00. 620 pp. .... Vendor G0093

T.L.C. Genealogy. **United States Post Offices, 1828-1832**. 1992. Indexed.
A U.S.-wide finding aid for place names.
Paper. $16.00. 224 pp. .... Vendor G0609

Thode, Ernest. **Genealogical Gazetteer of Alsace-Lorraine**.
Paper. $18.00. .... Vendor G0574

Thode, Ernest. **Genealogical Gazetteer of Alsace-Lorraine**. 1986. Illus.
Paper. $17.50 postpaid ($18.64 in OH). 137 pp. .... Vendor G0197

Thode, Ernest. **Interpreting Mispelled Misspelt Misspelled German Place-Names**. 1992.
Paper. $7.50 ($7.99 in OH). .... Vendor G0197

Torrance, D. R. **Scottish Personal Names & Place Names: A Bibliography**.
Paper. £1.75. .... Vendor G0555

Wilson, Rev. John. **The Gazetteer of Scotland**. (1882) reprint 1996.
Facsimile reprint; alphabetic arrangement.
Paper. $32.00. 425 pp. .... Vendor G0669

✑ Probate Records ✑

Carter, Fran. **Searching American Probate Records**. 1993. Illus.
Paper. $7.95. 60 pp. .... Vendor G0552

Coldham, Peter. **American Wills and Administrations** in the Prerogative Court of Canterbury, 1610-1857. 1989. Indexed.
Cloth. $30.00. 416 pp. .... Vendor G0010

Coldham, Peter Wilson. **American Wills Proved in London, 1611-1775**. 1992. Indexed.
Cloth. $30.00. 360 pp. .... Vendor G0010

Dobson, David. **Scottish-American Wills, 1650-1900**. 1991.
Cloth. $20.00. 137 pp. .... Vendor G0010

✿ **Religious and Ethnic Groups** ✿

Acadian/Cajun

Hebert. **Acadian-Cajun Genealogy: Step by Step.** 1993.
An essential guide to this special research. Maps, bibliography.
Paper. $10.00. 146 pp. .... Vendor G0611

African American

Alexander. **Ambiguous Lives: Free Women of Color in Rural Georgia, 1789-1879.**
1991.
Here's an excellent example of the social historian making appropriate use of genealogical methods in her research. The result is a well-written narrative history of a family, which also accomplishes her historical purpose.
Paper. $15.00. 268 pp. .... Vendor G0611

Andrews, William L. **To Tell a Free Story: The First Century of Afro-American Autobiography, 1760-1865.** (1986) reprint 1988.
This is a scholarly look at the history of black America's most innovative literary tradition—the autobiography—from its beginnings to the end of the slavery era. Quite interesting.
Paper. $19.95. 353 pp. .... Vendor G0611

Begley, Paul R., and Steven D. Tuttle. **African American Genealogical Research.**
1991. Illus.
Lists genealogical guidebooks and departmental records available at the South Carolina Department of Archives and History.
Paper. $2.00. 24 pp. .... Vendor G0130

Berlin, Ira, and Ronald Hoffman, eds. **Slavery and Freedom in the Age of the American Revolution.** (1983) reprint 1986.
Examines the war's effect on black lives. An important period in the social history of slavery.
Paper. $12.95. 314 pp. .... Vendor G0611

Blackett, R. J. M. **Beating Against the Barriers: The Lives of Six Nineteenth-Century Afro-Americans.** 1986.
Recounts the lives of six Afro-American abolitionists in the 1800s.
Paper. $17.95. 417 pp. .... Vendor G0611

Blackett, R. J. M. **Building an Antislavery Wall: Black Americans in the Atlantic Abolitionist Movement, 1830-1860.** 1983.
A study of the black Americans who traveled to England in order to win international support for the Atlantic abolitionist movement.
Paper. 15.95. 237pp. .... Vendor G0611

Blockson, Charles L. **Black Genealogy.** Published by Prentice-Hall. (1977) reprint 1991.
Cloth. $14.95. 156 pp. .... Vendor G0627

Chavers-Wright, Madrue. **The Guarantee: P.W. Chavers, Banker, Entrepreneur, Philanthropist in Chicago's Black Belt of the Twenties**. 2nd ed. 1985. Indexed. Illus.

The true story of Chavers adapting to Chicago, a city torn with race riots, after migrating from Columbus, Ohio. His trials in establishing a bank for the community, his crusading legislation to protect bank deposits, and the impact on the family.
Cloth, $29.95. Paper, $18.95. 450 pp. .... Vendor G0006

Crow, Jeffrey J. **The Black Experience in Revolutionary North Carolina**. 4th printing, 1996. Illus.

Includes an appendix of North Carolina blacks who served in the Continental Line or militia.
Paper. $5.00. x + 121 pp. .... Vendor G0586

Crow, Jeffrey J., Paul D. Escott, and Flora J. Hatley. **A History of African Americans in North Carolina**. 2nd printing, 1994. Indexed. Illus.

Includes an appendix that identifies black legislators who served in the North Carolina General Assembly from 1868 through 1900 and a selected list of suggested readings for further study.
Paper. $10.00. xii + 237 pp. .... Vendor G0586

Dickenson, Richard B. **Entitled! Free Papers in Appalachia Concerning Antebellum Freeborn Negroes and Emancipated Blacks of Montgomery County, Virginia**. Edited and indexed by Varney R. Nell.

Freeborn Negroes and emancipated blacks identified from 1830, 1840, 1850, 1860, and 1867 censuses and 1866 Marriage Register of Montgomery County.
Cloth. $18.50. 102 pp. .... Vendor G0627

Duke. **Don't Carry Me Back: Narratives by Former Virginia Slaves**. 1996.

Slave narratives provide first-hand documentary on the slave experience in Virginia.
Paper. $19.95. 264 pp. .... Vendor G0611

Egerton, Douglas R. **Gabriel's Rebellion: The Virginia Slave Conspiracies of 1800-1802**. 1993.

The dramatic story of two related Virginia slave revolts in 1800 and 1802.
Paper. $13.95. 262 pp. .... Vendor G0611

Finley, Randy. **From Slavery to Uncertain Freedom: The Freedmen's Bureau in Arkansas, 1865-1869**. 1996.

A collection of accounts taken from the Freedmen's Bureau in Arkansas, an organization formed after the Civil War to ensure that some measure of freedom was being granted to the new citizens.
Cloth. $28.00. 229 pp. .... Vendor G0611

Forbes, Jack D. **Africans and Native Americans: The Language of Race and the Evolution of Red-Black Peoples**. 1993.

Provides a totally new view of the history of Native American and African American peoples throughout the hemisphere. A very scholarly study, essential to anyone interested in these two ethnic groups.
Paper. $14.95. 344 pp. .... Vendor G0611

Foster, Frances Smith. **Witnessing Slavery: The Development of Ante-Bellum Slave Narratives**. (1979) reprint 1994.

A classic study of the pre-Civil War American slave autobiography. A wonderful book for the students of the American South, slavery, the Civil War, and race issues. Paper. $17.95. 194 pp. .... Vendor G0611

Gale Research. **African American Biography**. 4 vols. 1994.
Profiles 300 notable African Americans from all walks of life.
Cloth. $112.00/set. 812 pp. .... Vendor G0560

Gale Research. **Black Americans Information Directory 1994-95**. 1993. Indexed.
Lists more than 5,200 organizations, agencies, institutions, programs, and publications relating to African American life and culture.
Cloth. $85.00. 556 pp. .... Vendor G0560

Gale Research. **Genealogy Sourcebook Series: African American Genealogical Sourcebook**. 1995.
Cloth. $69.00. 244 pp. .... Vendor G0560

Gale Research. **Historical Statistics of Black America**. 2 vols. 1995. Indexed.
Presents nearly 2,000 tables of statistical information on blacks in North America, from colonial times through 1975.
Cloth. $125.00. 2,244 pp. .... Vendor G0560

Gaspar, David Barry, and Darlene Clark Hine. **More Than Chattel: Black Women and Slavery in the Americas**. 1996.
Slave men's experiences differed from those of slave women, who were exploited both in reproductive as well as productive capacities. Explores slavery and slave society through the lives of black women.
Paper. $18.95. 384 pp. .... Vendor G0611

Gibbs. **Indiana's African American Heritage**. 1993.
A collection of essays from "Black History News & Notes," including extensive footnotes.
Paper. $14.95. 243 pp. .... Vendor G0611

Heinegg, Paul. **Free African Americans of North Carolina and Virginia**. Including the Family Histories of More Than 80% of Those Counted As "All Other Free Persons" in the 1790 and 1800 Census. Expanded 3rd ed. 1997. Indexed.
Contact vendor for information. 831 pp. .... Vendor G0011

Henritze, Barbara K. **Bibliographic Checklist of African American Newspapers**. 1995. Indexed.
Cloth. $35.00. 206 pp. .... Vendor G0010

Holt, Thomas. **Black Over White: Negro Political Leadership in South Carolina During Reconstruction**. (1977) reprint 1979.
Studies not only the identities of the black politicians who gained power in South Carolina during Reconstruction, but also how they functioned within the political system.
Paper. $11.95. 269 pp. .... Vendor G0611

Horton, James Oliver, and Lois E. Horton. **In Hope of Liberty: Culture, Community, and Protest Among Northern Free Blacks, 1700-1860**. 1997.
A seamless narrative that weaves together the stories of courageous men and women

that made up free black society in the North and their struggles for cultural identities and social change.
Cloth. $35.00. 340 pp. .... Vendor G0611

Johnson, Anne E., and Adam Merton Cooper. **A Student's Guide to African American Genealogy**. 1996. Indexed. Illus.
Hard-cover. $24.95. 208 pp. .... Vendor G0776

Joyner. **Down by the Riverside: A South Carolina Slave Community**. 1984.
A fascinating reconstruction of antebellum plantation life in All Saints Parish. Extensive footnotes.
Paper. $11.95. 324 pp. .... Vendor G0611

Krehbiel, Henry Edward. **Afro-American Folksongs**. A Study in Racial and National Music. With a New Introduction by W. K. McNeil. (1914) reprint 1996. Indexed.
Paper. $21.50. 198 pp. .... Vendor G0011

Library of Congress. **Afro-American Genealogical Research:** Published Sources.
The text of this is available on the Local History and Genealogy Reading Room's home page: http://lcweb.loc.gov/rr/genealogy.
Free. Contact vendor for information. 2 pp. .... Vendor G0566

Littlefield, Daniel C. **Rice and Slaves: Ethnicity and the Slave Trade in Colonial South Carolina**. (1981) reprint 1991.
Studies the early slave trade in colonial South Carolina and shows how that led to significant contributions made by African slaves to the development of American institutions. Casts "the enslaved Africans as creative, dynamic forces shaping American culture."—*Georgia Historical Quarterly*
Paper. $15.95. 199 pp. .... Vendor G0611

McBride, David. **The Afro-American in Pennsylvania: A Critical Guide to Sources in the Pennsylvania State Archives**. 1979. Illus.
Paper. $2.95. 36 pp. .... Vendor G0554

Mullin, Michael. **Africa in America: Slave Acculturation and Resistance in the American South and the British Caribbean, 1736-1831**. (1992) reprint 1994.
Extensive archival and anecdotal sources support Mullin's description of slavery as it was practiced in Tidewater Virginia, on the rice coast of the Carolinas, and in Jamaica and Barbados. Through case histories, he offers new and definitive information about how Africans met and often overcame the challenges and deprivations of their new lives through religion, family life, and economic strategies.
Paper. $15.95. 412 pp. .... Vendor G0611

National Archives. **Black Studies**. A Select Catalog of National Archives Microfilm Publications. 1984.
Paper. $3.50. 112 pp. .... Vendor G0565

Newman, Debra L., comp. **Black History: A Guide to the Civilian Records in the National Archives**. 1984. Illus.
Cloth, $25.00. Paper, $15.00. 379 pp. .... Vendor G0565

Pease, Jane H., and William H. Pease. **They Who Would Be Free: Blacks' Search for Freedom, 1830-1861**. (1974) reprint 1990.
An illuminating analysis of the perceptions, attitudes, values, goals, and means of

those Northern blacks who struggled within the abolitionist crusade—and frequently outside it—to achieve meaningful freedom for themselves and their brethren in slavery.
Paper. $14.95. 339 pp. .... Vendor G0611

Peters, Joan W. **Local Sources for African-American Family Historians: Using County Court Records and Census Returns**. 1993. Indexed. Illus.
Local Sources—covers the primary record base, using a local Virginia county as an illustration, found in a judicious use of census returns and court records including the often-overlooked entries found in local County Court Minute Books. The techniques found in this volume can be applied anywhere researchers find county courts. In addition, there are courthouse record forms and pre-1850 federal census forms to help African-American family historians trace their ancestry.
Paper. $24.00. 142 pp. .... Vendor G0074

Plunkett. **Afro-American Sources in Virginia: A Guide to Manuscripts**. 1990.
An extremely valuable collection of sources for African-American research.
Cloth. $35.00. 323 pp. .... Vendor G0611

Schubert, Frank N. **On the Trail of the Buffalo Soldier: Biographies of African-Americans in the U.S. Army, 1866-1917**. 1995. Indexed.
Biographical information (DOB, military service, spouse and children names, prior occupation, etc.) on thousands of black servicemen.
Cloth. $127.50. 520 pp. .... Vendor G0118

Stevenson, Brenda E. **Life in Black and White: Family and Community in the Slave South**. 1996.
This book provides a panoramic portrait of family and community life in and around Loudoun County, Virginia, weaving the fascinating personal stories of planters and slaves, of free blacks and poor to middling whites, into a powerful portrait of southern society from the mid-18th century to the Civil War.
Cloth. 35.00. 457 pp. .... Vendor G0611

Tadman, Michael. **Speculators and Slaves: Masters, Traders, and Slaves in the Old South**. (1989) reprint 1996.
Previously untapped manuscript sources are used in this book to establish that all levels of white society in the antebellum South were deeply involved in a massive interregional trade in slaves. Advances a major thesis of master-slave relationships.
Paper. $17.95. 317 pp. .... Vendor G0611

Underwood, Donald E., and Betty A. Underwood. **Searching for Lost Ancestors: A Guide to Genealogical Research**. 1993. Indexed. Illus.
This compact book covers basic genealogical research techniques as well as more advanced methodology. It also offers special individual chapters on immigrant, black, and Native American research aids and sources.
Paper. $9.00. 191 pp. .... Vendor G0026

Amish

Gingerich, Hugh F., and Rachel W. Kreider. **Amish and Amish-Mennonite Genealogies**. 1986.
Cloth. $75.00. 858 pp. .... Vendor G0150

Hostetler. **Amish Roots: A Treasury of History, Wisdom, and Lore**. 1989.
Using letters, journals, stories, and legends, Hostetler lets the Amish tell their own story. A uniquely authentic view of Amish life from colonial times to the present.
Paper. $16.95. 319 pp. .... Vendor G0611

Hostetler. **Amish Society**. 4th ed. 1993.
A fascinating look at the history and culture of the Amish people.
Paper. $14.95. 435 pp. .... Vendor G0611

Anabaptist

Zuercher, Isaac. **Anabaptist-Mennonite Names in Switzerland**. Translated by Hannes Maria Aleman. 1988.
Paper. $9.50. 35 pp. .... Vendor G0150

Asian American

Gale Research. **Asian American Almanac**. 1996. Indexed. Illus.
Provides information on demography, languages, immigration, important documents, civil rights, education, military, organizations, and much more.
Cloth. $29.00. Approx. 200 pp. .... Vendor G0560

Gale Research. **Asian American Biography**. 2 vols. 1995.
Describes the lives and achievements of 135 notable Asian Americans.
Cloth. $55.00/set. 401 pp. .... Vendor G0560

Gale Research. **Genealogy Sourcebook Series: Asian American Genealogical Sourcebook**. 1995.
Cloth. $69.00. 280 pp. .... Vendor G0560

Baptist

Breed, G. R. **My Ancestors Were Baptists: How Can I Find Out More About Them?** 3rd rev. ed. 1994.
A British book published by the Society of Genealogists.
Paper. £4.99. 104 pp. .... Vendor G0557

Campbell, Jesse H. **Georgia Baptists: Historical and Biographical**. (1847) reprint 1993. Indexed.
Cloth. $33.00. 307 pp. .... Vendor G0610

Hayward, Elizabeth. **American Vital Records from the Baptist Register, 1824-1832 and the New York Baptist Register, 1832-1834**. Indexed.
Abstracts of deaths and marriages from a newspaper published in Utica, NY but area of interest embraces eastern United States. Includes a geographical locator.
Paper. $12.50. 105 pp. .... Vendor G0160

The Historical Records Survey of Virginia/Work Projects Adm. **Guide to the Manuscript Collections of the Virginia Baptist Historical Society, Supplement No. 1:**

Index to Obituary Notices in *The Religious Herald*, **Richmond, Virginia 1828-1938**. (1940) reprint 1996.
Paper. $33.50. 386 pp. .... Vendor G0011

The Historical Records Survey of Virginia/Work Projects Adm. **Guide to the Manuscript Collections of the Virginia Baptist Historical Society, Supplement No. 2: Index to Marriage Notices in** *The Religious Herald*, **Richmond, Virginia 1828-1938**. In Two Volumes. (1941) reprint 1996.
Paper. $56.50. 371 + 316 pp. .... Vendor G0011

Sanford, L. **First Alfred Seventh Day Baptist Church Membership Records, Alfred, NY**. Indexed. Illus.
  From the archives of the Seventh Day Baptist Historical Society. Contains a wealth of biographical material concerning early Rhode Island families and the movement of Seventh Day Baptists as they migrated west.
Paper. $21.00. 107 pp. .... Vendor G0160

Sanford, L. **Membership Records of Seventh Baptists of Central New York State 1797-1940s**. Indexed. Illus.
Paper. $26.00. 127 pp. .... Vendor G0160

Townsend, Leah. **South Carolina Baptists, 1670-1805**. (1935) reprint 1990. Indexed.
Cloth. $23.50. 391 pp. .... Vendor G0011

Belgian

Magee, Joan. **The Belgians in Ontario**. A History. 1987.
Paper. $14.99 (cnd), $13.25 (US). 272 pp. .... Vendor G0640

British

Baxter, Angus. **In Search of Your British & Irish Roots**. 3rd ed. (1994) reprint 1996.
Paper. $16.95. 320 pp. .... Vendor G0010

Johnson, Anne E. **A Student's Guide to British American Genealogy**. 1995. Indexed. Illus.
Hard-cover. $24.95. 208 pp. .... Vendor G0776

Catholic

Doyle, John J. **Genealogical Use of Catholic Records in North America**. (1978) reprint 1992.
Paper. $5.75. 28 pp. .... Vendor G0109

Humling, Virginia, comp. **U.S. Catholic Sources: A Diocesan Research Guide**. 1996.
Paper. $14.95. 112 pp. .... Vendor G0570

Chinese

Low, Jeanie W. Chooey. **China Connection: Finding Ancestral Roots for Chinese in America**. 2nd rev. ed. 1994. Illus.
Emphasis is 1882 to 1960; translate gravestones and dates; "paper names"; and immigration records.
Paper. $13.95. 65 pp. .... Vendor G0502

She, Colleen. **A Student's Guide to Chinese American Genealogy**. 1996. Indexed. Illus.
Hard-cover. $25.95. 208 pp. .... Vendor G0776

Church of the Brethren

Burgert, Annette K. **Brethren from Gimbsheim in the Palatinate to Ephrata and Bermudian in Pennsylvania**. 1994. Indexed. Illus.
Paper. $14.00. 39 pp. .... Vendor G0458

Congregationalist

Clifford, D. J. H. **My Ancestors Were Congregationalists in England and Wales: With a List of Registers**. 1992.
A British book published by the Society of Genealogists.
Paper. £3.90. 94 pp. .... Vendor G0557

Taylor, Richard H. **The Churches of Christ of the Congregational Way in New England**. 1989. Indexed.
Church directory.
Cloth. $33.00. vii +308 pp. .... Vendor G0525

Taylor, Richard H. **The Congregational Churches of the West**. 1992. Indexed.
Church directory.
Cloth. $29.00. viii + 216 pp. .... Vendor G0525

Taylor, Richard H. **Southern Congregational Churches**. 1994. Indexed.
Church directory.
Cloth. $33.00. x + 255 pp. .... Vendor G0525

Czech and Slovak

Bicha. **The Czechs in Oklahoma**. 1980.
A useful booklet.
Paper. $4.95. 81 pp. .... Vendor G0611

Chicago Genealogical Society. **Obituary Dates from the Denni Hlasatel 1891-1899**. 1995.
This and the following two volumes of obituary dates from the Chicago newspaper *Denni Hlasatel* are excellent sources of information for those researching Czech, Moravian, and Slovak ancestors from the Chicago area.
Paper. $3.00. 22 pp. .... Vendor G0742

Chicago Genealogical Society. **Obituary Dates from the Denni Hlasatel 1930-1939**.
1995.
Paper. $8.00. 105 pp. .... Vendor G0742

Chicago Genealogical Society. **Obituary Dates from the Denni Hlasatel 1940-1949**.
1995.
Paper. $9.00. 130 pp. .... Vendor G0742

Dutch

Bailey, Rosalie Fellows. **Dutch Systems in Family Naming, New York-New Jersey**.
Paper. $6.50. 21 pp. .... Vendor G0627

Baughman, J. Ross. **Harvest Time . . . History of the Swiss, German & Dutch Folk
in Early America**. 1994.
Paper. $31.00. 256 pp. .... Vendor G0150

Brinks, Herbert J. **Dutch American Voices: Letters from the United States, 1850-
1930**. 1995.
A fascinating collection of letters from the Dutch Immigrant Letter Collection at
Calvin College. Includes an introduction to Dutch immigration history.
Cloth. $35.00. 480 pp. .... Vendor G0611

Daily, W. N. P. **History of the Montgomery Classis,** to Which Is Added Sketches of
Mohawk Valley Men & Events of Early Days, Etc. (1915?) reprint 1991.
The "classis" is the regional organization of the Dutch Reformed Church. This
history of the Church and the region also contains valuable genealogical & biological
information about early families.
Paper. $24.50. 198 pp. .... Vendor G0259

Elting, Irving. **Dutch Village Communities of the Hudson**.
A reprint of the 1886 study of Dutch influence on the social and political develop-
ment of Hudson River communities. Focuses on New Paltz.
Paper. $8.95. 68 pp. .... Vendor G0160

Epperson, Gwenn F. **New Netherland Roots**. (1994) reprint 1995. Illus.
Cloth. $20.00. 176 pp. .... Vendor G0010

Hall, Rev. Charles. **The Dutch and the Iroquois**. c. 1882.
Outlines the influence the Dutch had and its direct effect on relations with the
Iroquois.
Paper. $8.95. 55 pp. .... Vendor G0160

Hoes, Roswell Randall. **Baptismal and Marriage Registers of the Old Dutch Church
of Kingston, Ulster County, New York, 1660-1809**. (1891) reprint 1997. Indexed.
Cloth. $50.00. 797 pp. .... Vendor G0010

Madden, Joseph P. **Documentary History of Yonkers, New York, Volume Two,
Part Two: The Dutch, the English, and an Incorporated American Village, 1609-
1860**. 1994. Indexed.
Contains detailed historical background from the earliest Dutch and English settle-
ment to the pre-Civil War years.
Paper. $27.50. 286 pp. .... Vendor G0160

O'Callaghan, Edmund B. **The Register of New Netherland, 1626-1674.** (1865) reprint 1996. Indexed.
Paper. $21.50. 198 pp. .... Vendor G0011

Robison, Jeannie F-J., and Henrietta C. Bartlett, eds. **Genealogical Records:** Manuscript Entries of Births, Deaths and Marriages, Taken from Family Bibles, 1581-1917. (1917) reprint 1995. Indexed. Illus.
Contains the genealogical records found in family Bibles of ninety Dutch and English New York families.
Paper. $28.50. 346 pp. .... Vendor G0011

Singleton, Estger. **Dutch New York.** (1909) reprint 1994.
Fascinating social history of early New Amsterdam that is a must-read for anyone of Dutch background.
Cloth. $42.50. 360 pp. .... Vendor G0259

Swierenga. **The Dutch in America: Immigration, Settlement, and Cultural Change.** 1985.
Well-documented look at Dutch immigration and settlements.
Cloth. $45.00. 303 pp. .... Vendor G0611

Swierenga, Robert P. **Dutch Households in U.S. Population Censuses, 1850, 1860, 1870: An Alphabetical Listing by Family Heads.** 1987. Indexed.
Cloth. $182.50. 3 vols. .... Vendor G0118

Van Buren, Augustus H. **A History of Ulster Under the Dutch.**
Paper. $13.95. 146 pp. .... Vendor G0160

Versteeg, Dingman, and Thomas Vermilye, Jr. **Bergen Records: Records of the Reformed Protestant Dutch Church of Bergen in New Jersey, 1666 to 1788.** 3 vols. in 1. (1913-15) reprint 1990. Indexed. Illus.
Includes baptism, marriage, and burial records of the Dutch Church of Bergen. Also included are histories of early New Jersey Dutch families and a history of Bergen.
Cloth. $20.00. 300 pp. in all. .... Vendor G0011

Versteeg, Dingman, trans. **Records of the Reformed Dutch Church of New Paltz, New York,** Containing . . . Registers of Consistories, Members, Marriages, and Baptisms. (1896) reprint 1992. Indexed.
Includes lists of church members and extensive records of marriages and baptisms, with references to several thousand early inhabitants, including those of Huguenot, Dutch, and English origins.
Paper. $22.50. 269 pp. .... Vendor G0011

English

Irvine, Sherry. **Your English Ancestry: A Guide for North Americans.** 1993.
Presents a logical research routine for the family historian based in North America.
Paper. $12.95. 168 pp. .... Vendor G0570

Madden, Joseph P. **Documentary History of Yonkers, New York, Volume Two, Part Two: The Dutch, the English, and an Incorporated American Village, 1609-1860.** 1994. Indexed.

Contains detailed historical background from the earliest Dutch and English settlement to the pre-Civil War years.
Paper. $27.50. 286 pp. .... Vendor G0160

Robison, Jeannie F-J., and Henrietta C. Bartlett, eds. **Genealogical Records:** Manuscript Entries of Births, Deaths and Marriages, Taken from Family Bibles, 1581-1917. (1917) reprint 1995. Indexed. Illus.
Contains the genealogical records found in family Bibles of ninety Dutch and English New York families.
Paper. $28.50. 346 pp. .... Vendor G0011

Episcopal

Axelson, Edith F. **A Guide to Episcopal Church Records in Virginia**. 1988.
A major reference tool for every genealogical researcher who deals with the Church of England in the colonial period and the successor Protestant Episcopal Church.
Paper. 15.95. vi + 136 pp. .... Vendor G0632

Estonian/Latvian

Maldonado, Sigrid Renate. **Estonian Experience and Roots**. Ethnic Estonian Genealogy with Historical Perspective, Social Influences and Possible Family History Resources. 1996. Indexed. Illus.
An aid or guide to those wanting to know some local history and to search for their Estonian (also Latvian) roots, and to professional genealogists.
Cloth. $24.00 + p&h. 128 pp. .... Vendor G0475

French/French Canadian

Conrad. **The Louisiana Purchase Bicentennial Series in Louisiana History, Volume I: The French Experience in Louisiana**. 1995.
History of the French in Louisiana.
Cloth. $40.00. 666 pp. .... Vendor G0611

De Ville, Winston. **Gulf Coast Colonials**. A Compendium of French Families in Early Eighteenth Century Louisiana. Partially indexed. (1968) reprint 1995.
Paper. $8.50. 69 pp. .... Vendor G0011

De Ville, Winston. **The New Orleans French, 1720-1733**. A Collection of Marriage Records Relating to the First Colonists of the Louisiana Province. (1973) reprint 1994. Indexed.
Paper. $13.50. 113 pp. .... Vendor G0011

Konrad, J. **French and French-Canadian Family Research**.
Paper. $10.00. 79 pp. .... Vendor G0574

Potter, Elisha R. **Memoir Concerning the French Settlements and French Settlers in the Colony of Rhode Island**. (1879) reprint 1996. Illus.
Paper. $14.00. 138 pp. .... Vendor G0011

Wittmeyer, Alfred V. **Registers of the Births, Marriages, and Deaths of the "Eglise Francoise a La Nouvelle York" [French Church of New York], from 1688 to 1804.** (1886) reprint 1994. Indexed.
Paper. $25.00. 366 pp. .... Vendor G0011

German

Baughman, J. Ross. **Harvest Time . . . History of the Swiss, German & Dutch Folk in Early America.** 1994.
Paper. $31.00. 256 pp. .... Vendor G0150

Baxter, Angus. **In Search of Your German Roots.** A Complete Guide to Tracing Your Ancestors in the Germanic Areas of Europe. 3rd ed. (1994) reprint 1996.
Paper. $11.95. 122 pp. .... Vendor G0010

Bernheim, Gotthardt D. **History of the German Settlements and of the Lutheran Church in North and South Carolina.** (1872) reprint 1996.
Paper. $40.00. 557 pp. .... Vendor G0011

Brandt, et.al. **Germanic Genealogy:** A Guide to Worldwide Sources and Migration Patterns. 1995.
This remarkable book is jam-packed with essential information. Anyone doing German research should have this book! This replaces the 1991 book called *Research Guide to German-American Genealogy.*
Paper. $24.00. 370 pp. .... Vendor G0611

Brown, John. **Brief Sketch of 1st Settlement of Schoharie.**
A reprint of the 1823 account of the German settlement of Schoharie County.
Stapled booklet. $5.00. 24 pp. .... Vendor G0160

Bucks County, PA Church Records of the 18th Century: Vol. 1, German Church Records. By F. Edward Wright. 1993. Indexed.
Paper. $27.00. 340 pp. .... Vendor G0140

Chambers, T. F. **Early Germans of New Jersey, Their History, Churches, and Genealogy.** (1895) reprint 1991.
Contact vendor for information. 667 pp. .... Vendor G0010

Dearden. **The German Researcher: How to Get the Most out of an L.D.S. Family History Center.** 4th ed. 1990.
Very helpful to those conducting German research in Family History Centers.
Paper. $10.50. 72 pp. .... Vendor G0611

Deiler, J. Hanno. **A History of the German Churches in Louisiana (1823-1893).** Translated and edited by Marie Stella Condon. (1894, 1983) reprint 1995. Indexed.
Paper. $17.50. 155 pp. .... Vendor G0011

Egle, William Henry. **Pennsylvania Genealogies,** Chiefly Scotch-Irish and German. 2nd ed. (1896) reprint 1997. Indexed.
Paper. $49.95. 798 pp. .... Vendor G0011

Eshleman, H. Frank. **Historic Background and Annals of the Swiss and German Pioneer Settlers** of Southeastern Pennsylvania, and of Their Remote Ancestors. (1917) reprint 1991.
Cloth. $25.00. 386 pp. .... Vendor G0010

Faust, Albert Bernhardt. **The German Element in the United States.** With Special Reference to Its Political, Moral, Social, and Educational Influence. In Two Volumes. (1927) reprint 1995. Indexed.
Paper. $85.00. 605 + 730 pp. .... Vendor G0011

Galveston County Genealogical Society. **St. Joseph Catholic Church, Galveston, Texas, Baptismal, Confirmation, Marriage and Death Records 1860-1952.** 1984. Indexed.
    If you have German ancestors who came to Texas, or through Texas to the Midwest, in the mid-1800s, this book is a must. Many Germans came to the Republic of Texas on German land contracts through the port of Galveston and stayed to raise their families. By 1855, Galveston's population was close to one-half German. It was at this time that the Catholic Diocese tried to build a church in Galveston so services could be held in German.
Paper. $27.50. 168 pp. .... Vendor G0610

Glatfelter, Charles H. **Pennsylvania Germans: A Brief Account of Their Influence on Pennsylvania**. 1990.
Covers the entire period of the Germans in Pennsylvania with emphasis on their religion, schooling, and craftsmanship.
Paper. $5.95. 80 pp. .... Vendor G0554

Heavener, Rev. Ulysses S. A. **German New River Settlement: Virginia**. (1929) reprint 1992. Indexed.
Paper. $12.50. 94 pp. .... Vendor G0011

Hocker, Edward W. **Genealogical Data Relating to the German Settlers of Pennsylvania** and Adjacent Territory. From Advertisements in German Newspapers Published in Philadelphia and Germantown, 1743-1800. 1989. Indexed.
Cloth. $17.50. 242 pp. .... Vendor G0010

Jones, George F. **The Germans of Colonial Georgia, 1733-1783**. Rev. ed. 1996. Indexed.
Paper. $17.50. 161 pp. .... Vendor G0011

Kamphoefner, Walter D., Wolfgang Helbich, and Ulrike Sommer, eds. **News from the Land of Freedom: German Immigrants Write Home**. 1991.
A collection of 350 19th-century letters from German immigrants back home to Germany. Captures in their own words the experience of adapting to a profoundly different culture.
Paper. 17.95. 643 pp. .... Vendor G0611

Konrad, J. **German Family Research Made Simple**.
Paper. $12.00. 108 pp. .... Vendor G0574

Levi, Kate, and Albert Faust. **Early German Immigrants in Wisconsin**. (1898, 1909) reprint 1996. Indexed.
Paper. $11.00. 48 pp. .... Vendor G0195

Pennsylvania German Church Records. Births, Baptisms, Marriages, Burials, Etc. from the Pennsylvania German Society Proceedings and Addresses. With an introduction by Don Yoder. 3 vols. 1983. Indexed. Illus.
Cloth. $135.00/set, $45.00/vol. 900 + 700 + 771 pp. .... Vendor G0010

Richards, Henry Melchior Muhlenberg. **The Pennsylvania-German in the Revolutionary War, 1775-1783**. (1908) reprint 1991. Indexed. Illus.
Cloth. $27.50. 542 pp. .... Vendor G0010

Robl, Gregory. **A Student's Guide to German American Genealogy**. 1996. Indexed. Illus.
Hard-cover. $24.95. 208 pp. .... Vendor G0776

Rouse, Parke, Jr. **The Great Wagon Road From Philadelphia to the South: How Scotch-Irish and Germanics Settled the Uplands**. (1973) reprint 1995.
This book is recognized for its insight into the birth of the American South, from the early 1700s until the Civil War. Countless Scotch-Irish, Germanic, and English settlers traveled the road southward from Philadelphia to settle the Appalachian uplands from Pennsylvania to Georgia.
Paper. 1995. 292 pp. .... Vendor G0611

Schuricht, Herrmann. **The German Element in Virginia.** 2 vols. in 1. (1898-1900) reprint 1989. Indexed.
Cloth. $23.95. 433 pp. in all. .... Vendor G0011

Schweitzer, George K. **German Genealogical Research.** 1995. Illus.
German historical background, Germans to America, bridging the Atlantic, types of German records, German record repositories, the German language.
Paper. $21.00. 252 pp. .... Vendor G0569

Smith, Clifford N. **Cumulative Surname Index and Soundex to Monographs 1 Through 12 of the German-American Genealogical Research Series.** 1981.
ISBN 0-915162-17-2.
Paper. $20.00. iv + 66 pp. double-columned. .... Vendor G0491

Smith, Clifford N. **Cumulative Surname Soundex to German-American Genealogical Research Monographs 14-19 and 21-25.** German-American Genealogical Research Monograph Number 26. 1990.
ISBN 0-915162-91-1.
Paper. $20.00. i + 41 pp. double-columned. .... Vendor G0491

Smith, Clifford N. **Early Nineteenth-Century German Settlers in Ohio, Kentucky, and Other States.** German-American Genealogical Research Monograph Number 20. Parts 1-4C.
Part 1 (1984; iv + 36 pp. double-columned). ISBN 0-915162-22-9.
Part 2 (1988; ii + 56 pp. double-columned). ISBN 0-915162-23-7.
Part 3 (1988; ii + 60 pp. double-columned). ISBN 0-915162-25-5.
Part 4A: Surnames A Through J (1991; ii + 34 pp. double-columned).
ISBN 0- 915162-84-9.
Part 4B: Surnames K Through Z (1991; ii + 37 pp. double-columned).
ISBN 0- 915162-85-7.
Part 4C: Appendices (1991; ii + 26 pp. double-columned). ISBN 0-915162-85-7.
Contact vendor for information about additional parts.
Paper. $20.00/part. .... Vendor G0491

Smith, Clifford N. **Some German-American Participants in the American Revolution: The Rattermann Lists.** German-American Genealogical Research Monograph Number 27. 1990.
ISBN 0-915162-92-X.
Paper. $20.00. ii + 47 pp. double-colummned. .... Vendor G0491

Strassburger, Ralph Beaver, and William John Hinke. **Pennsylvania German Pioneers: A Publication of the Original Lists of Arrivals in the Port of Philadelphia from 1727 to 1808, Signature Volume.** (1934) reprint 1992.
This set, which is commonly known as "Strassburger & Hinke," is the time-honored reference for arrival of German emigrants to America before 1800. It is one of the basic works for genealogical libraries. Volumes 1 & 3 have been reprinted a number of times, but this is the first time this volume (which shows the actual signatures of the emigrants) has been reprinted. (See listing on p. 51.)
Cloth. $55.00. 909 pp. .... Vendor G0081

Strassburger, Ralph Beaver, and William John Hinke. **Pennsylvania German Pioneers, 3 Volume Set.** (1937) reprint 1992.
Book #1345.
Cloth. $175.00. 2,560 pp. .... Vendor G0082

Strassburger, Ralph Beaver. **Pennsylvania German Pioneers: A Publication of the Original Lists of Arrivals in the Port of Philadelphia from 1727 to 1808.** 2 vols. (1934) reprint 1992. Indexed.
Cloth. $75.00. 1,485 pp. total .... Vendor G0010

Strobel, P.A. **Salzburgers and Their Descendants, Being the History of a Colony of German, Lutheran, Protestants Who Emigrated to Georgia in 1734.** (1855) reprint 1980. Indexed.
Cloth. $15.00. 320 pp. .... Vendor G0610

Thode, Ernest. **Address Book for Germanic Genealogy.** 6th ed. (1994) reprint 1997. Illus.
Paper. $27.45 postpaid ($29.23 in OH). 196 pp. .... Vendor G0197

Thode, Ernest. **Address Book for Germanic Genealogy.** 6th ed. (1994) reprint 1997.
Paper. $24.95. 195 pp. .... Vendor G0010

Thode, Ernest. **German-English Genealogical Dictionary.** (1992) reprint 1996.
Paper. $29.95. 318 pp. .... Vendor G0010

Thode, Ernest. **German-English Genealogical Dictionary.** 1992. Illus.
Paper. $32.95 ($35.09 in OH). xxxiv + 286 pp. .... Vendor G0197

Von-Maszewski. **Handbook and Registry of German-Texan Heritage**. 1989.
Useful collection of German churches, societies, businesses, more.
Paper. $9.00. 193 pp. .... Vendor G0611

Weiser, Frederick S., translator. **Marriages and Burials from the Frederick, Maryland Evangelical Lutheran Church**. Indexed.
Earliest concentrated settlement of Germans in western Maryland. Burial records often give birthplaces in Europe and birth dates of early settlers.
Cloth. $19.00. 183 pp. .... Vendor G0627

Wust. **The Virginia Germans**. 1969.
A fascinating study of these German immigrants.
Paper. $16.50. 310 pp. .... Vendor G0611

Young, Henry James, trans. **Moravian Families of Graceham, Maryland:** Church Records of Mainly German Families from Pennsylvania & Maryland Who Made Up the Congregation: 1759-1871. 1942. Indexed.
Paper. $11.00. 125 pp. .... Vendor G0140

Hispanic

Carr, Peter E. **Guide to Cuban Genealogical Research**. 1991. Indexed.
The first and only comprehensive book of its kind.
Paper. $19.95. 103 pp. .... Vendor G0496

Gale Research. **Genealogy Sourcebook Series: Hispanic American Genealogical Sourcebook**. 1995.
Cloth. $69.00. 224 pp. .... Vendor G0560

Gale Research. **Hispanic American Almanac**. 1995.
Cloth. $29.00. 213 pp. .... Vendor G0560

Gale Research. **Hispanic American Biography**. 2 vols. 1995.
The lives and times of ninety famous and lesser known Hispanic Americans are profiled, most (but not all) contemporary figures.
Cloth. $55.00/set. 238 pp. .... Vendor G0560

Gale Research. **Hispanic Americans Information Directory 1994-95**. 1994. Indexed.
Offers complete contact information on over 5,000 Hispanic organizations.
Cloth. $85.00. 515 pp. .... Vendor G0560

Konrad, J. **Mexican and Spanish Family Research**.
Paper. $10.00. 70 pp. .... Vendor G0574

Platt, Lyman D. **Hispanic Surnames and Family History**. 1996.
Paper. $19.95. 349 pp. .... Vendor G0010

Ryskamp, George R. **Finding Your Hispanic Roots**. 1997. Indexed. Illus.
Paper. $19.95. 306 pp. .... Vendor G0010

Ryskamp, George, and Peggy Ryskamp. **A Student's Guide to Mexican American Genealogy**. 1996. Indexed. Illus.
Hard-cover. $24.95. 208 pp. .... Vendor G0776

Lyman D. Platt HISPANIC SURNAMES AND FAMILY HISTORY

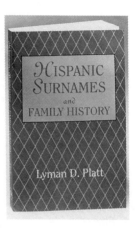

This is a groundbreaking work on Hispanic surnames, the first comprehensive analytical work on Hispanic surnames and the most extensive bibliography of Hispanic family histories ever published. It must be stressed that this is not a study of surnames or family history in Spain; rather, it is an exhaustive review of the development of Spanish surnames in Latin America and the Hispanic United States where there are obvious links between Latin American and Spanish families.

At the very heart of the book is a bibliography of Hispanic family histories in the U.S. and Latin America, certainly the most extensive list of its kind ever compiled. Twenty-five years in preparation, it consists of every Hispanic family history Dr. Platt was able to locate in newspapers, magazines, historical compilations, and monographs. There is nothing like it in existence, and for the genealogist interested in Hispanic ancestry, this is the very first place to begin his research. This section alone is worth the price of the book.

349 pp., paperback. 1996.
Vendor G0010. $19.95

Genealogical Publishing Co., Inc.

Huguenot

Baird, Charles W. **History of the Huguenot Emigration to America**. 2 vols. in 1. (1885) reprint 1991. Indexed. Illus.
Cloth. Contact vendor for information. 354 + 448 pp. .... Vendor G0010

Brock, Robert Alonzo. **Huguenot Emigration to Virginia . . .** With an Appendix of Genealogies Presenting Data of the Fontaine, Maury, Dupuy, Trabue, Marye, Chastain, Cocke, and Other Families. (1886) reprint 1995. Indexed.
Paper. $23.00. 255 pp. .... Vendor G0011

Clute, Robert F. **The Annals and Parish Register of St. Thomas and St. Denis Parish, in South Carolina, from 1680 to 1884**. (1884) reprint 1989.
A collection of parish registers containing "vital records" of the French Huguenot settlement of South Carolina known as the Orange Quarter.
Cloth. $15.00. 111 pp. .... Vendor G0011

Currer-Briggs, Noel, and Royston Gambier. **Huguenot Ancestry**. 1985. Illus.
A British publication.
Cloth. £13.95. 160 pp. .... Vendor G0579

Eakle, Arlene H., Ph.D. **Huguenot Research**. (1993) revised 1996. Illus.
Only book describing *original* sources for Huguenot ancestry; ten maps; settlements, migrations, and locations of churches. Covers nine European countries.
Paper. $19.00. 40 pp. .... Vendor G0504

Finnell, Arthur Louis. **The Huguenot Society of New England 1924-1949 Roster of Members and Ancestors**. 1993. Indexed.
Special Publication No. 1, National Huguenot Society.
Paper. $5.00. 16 pp. .... Vendor G0256

Finnell, Arthur Louis, ed. **National Huguenot Society Bible Records**. Abstracted from the Files of the Society. 1996. Indexed.
Paper. $39.95. 502 pp. .... Vendor G0011

Finnell, Arthur Louis. **1996 Update of Corrections and Additions to the Register of Qualified Huguenot Ancestors of the National Huguenot Society Fourth Edition 1995**. 1996. Indexed.
Paper. $7.00. 37 pp. .... Vendor G0256

Finnell, Arthur Louis. **Register of Qualified Huguenot Ancestors of the National Huguenot Society**. 4th ed. 1995. Indexed. Illus.
Paper. $25.00. 352 pp. .... Vendor G0256

Fontaine, Rev. James. **Memoirs of a Huguenot Family** and Other Family Manuscripts; Comprising an Original Journal of Travels in Virginia, New York, Etc., in 1715 and 1716. Edited by Ann Maury. (1853) reprint 1994. Illus.
Paper. $37.00. 512 pp. .... Vendor G0011

Fosdick, Lucian J. **The French Blood in America**. (1906) reprint 1994. Indexed. Illus.
The purpose of this work is to give a true estimate of the Huguenots as a factor in American life.
Paper. $35.00. 448 pp. .... Vendor G0011

Franklin, Charles M. **Huguenot Genealogical Research**.
Paper. $14.00. 58 pp. .... Vendor G0574

Hirsch, Arthur Henry. **The Huguenots of Colonial South Carolina**. (1928) reprint 1991. Indexed. Illus.
Contact vendor for information. 347 pp. .... Vendor G0011

Jones, William Macfarlane. **The Douglas Register,** Being a Detailed Register of Births, Marriages and Deaths . . . as Kept by the Rev. William Douglas, from 1750 to 1797. [With:] An Index of Goochland Wills and Notes on the French Huguenot Refugees who Lived in Manakin-Town. (1928) reprint 1997.
Paper. $32.50. 408 pp. .... Vendor G0011

Koehler, Albert F. **The Huguenots or Early French in New Jersey**. (1955) reprint 1996. Indexed.
Paper. $9.00. 51 pp. .... Vendor G0011

Lart, Charles Edmund. **Huguenot Pedigrees**. 2 vols. in 1. (1924-28) reprint 1996. Indexed.
Paper. $22.50. 258 pp. in all. .... Vendor G0011

Lawton, Mrs. James M. **Family Names of Huguenot Refugees to America**. (1901) reprint 1991.
Paper. $4.00. 20 pp. .... Vendor G0010

Lee, Grace Lawless. **The Huguenot Settlements in Ireland**. (1936) reprint 1993. Indexed.
Contact vendor for information. 281 pp. .... Vendor G0011

Lee, Hannah F. **The Huguenots in France and America**. 2 vols. in 1. (1843) reprint 1994.
Paper. $45.00. 638 pp. in all. .... Vendor G0011

LeFevre, Ralph. **History of New Paltz, New York, and Its Old Families** (from 1678 to 1820). 2nd ed. (1909) reprint 1996. Indexed. Illus.
    This is the definitive history of New Paltz, one of the oldest Huguenot settlements in America and the cradle of surrounding settlements in Ulster and Orange counties, New York.
Paper. $55.00. 607 pp. .... Vendor G0011

Ravenel, Daniel. **[List of French and Swiss]** . . . **settled in Charleston, on the Santee, and at the Orange Quarter in Carolina** . . . (1888) reprint 1990. Indexed. Illus.
    One of the earliest lists of Huguenot emigrants to South Carolina.
Paper. $8.50. 77 pp. .... Vendor G0011

Reaman, George Elmore. **The Trail of the Huguenots** in Europe, the United States, South Africa and Canada. Addenda and Corrigenda by Milton Rubincam. (1963) reprint 1993. Indexed. Illus.
Cloth. $25.00. 318 pp. .... Vendor G0010

Smiles, Samuel. **The Huguenots:** Their Settlements, Churches, and Industries in England and Ireland. (1868) reprint 1995. Indexed.
Paper. $32.50. 448 pp. .... Vendor G0011

Stapleton, Ammon. **Memorials of Huguenots in America**. With Special Reference to Their Emigration to Pennsylvania. (1901) reprint 1996. Indexed.
Paper. $18.50. 164 pp. .... Vendor G0011

Versteeg, Dingman, trans. **Records of the Reformed Dutch Church of New Paltz, New York,** Containing . . . Registers of Consistories, Members, Marriages, and Baptisms. (1896) reprint 1992. Indexed.
    Includes lists of church members and extensive records of marriages and baptisms, with references to several thousand early inhabitants, including those of Huguenot, Dutch, and English origins.
Paper. $22.50. 269 pp. .... Vendor G0011

Weiss, Professor, et al. **Hope Farm Press Indexes: French Huguenots in America**. (1854) reprint 1994. Indexed.
    Nine indexes, Civil War roster, and French Huguenots' history.
3.5 disk. $11.00. .... Vendor G0160

Allie Pink Genealogical Research, Inc.
Mary Nowell, Researcher
For details send SASE to:
Mary Nowell
P.O. Box 1541
McDonough, GA 30253-4422

Irish

Baxter, Angus. **In Search of Your British & Irish Roots**. 3rd ed. (1994) reprint 1996. Paper. $16.95. 320 pp. .... Vendor G0010

Bayor, Ronald H., and Timothy J. Meagher, eds. **The New York Irish**. 1996.
A sweeping story of the Irish immigrants and the impact of their descendants on the history of New York. The history of the Irish in New York is almost as old as the city itself.
Cloth. $45.00. 743 pp. .... Vendor G0611

Clark, Dennis. **The Irish in Pennsylvania: A People Share a Commonwealth**. 1991. Illus.
A well-written and concise account of the history of the Irish in Pennsylvania and their many contributions to the Commonwealth.
Paper. $4.95. 56 pp. .... Vendor G0554

Collins, E. J. **Irish Family Research Made Simple**.
Paper. $10.00. 76 pp. .... Vendor G0574

Diner. **Erin's Daughters in America: Irish Immigrant Women in the Nineteenth Century**. 1983.
Fascinating look at these immigrant women.
Paper. $14.95. 192 pp. .... Vendor G0611

Elliott, Bruce S., and De Alton Owens. **The McCabe List: Early Irish in the Ottawa Valley**. 1991. Indexed. Illus.
List of early Irish settlers in Ontario.
Paper. $12.00 (cdn), $13.50 (US). 64 pp. .... Vendor G0568

Falley, Margaret D. **Irish and Scotch-Irish Ancestral Research:** A Guide to the Genealogical Records, Methods, and Sources in Ireland. 2 vols. (1962) reprint 1988. Indexed.
Cloth. $60.00. 813 + 354 pp. .... Vendor G0010

Grenham, John. **Tracing Your Irish Ancestors**. (1993) reprint 1996.
Paper. $19.95. 320 pp. .... Vendor G0010

McGee, Thomas D'Arcy. **A History of the Irish Settlers in North America**. (1852) reprint 1989. Indexed.
Cloth. $18.95. 240 pp. .... Vendor G0011

McKenna, Erin. **A Student's Guide to Irish American Genealogy**. 1996. Indexed. Illus.
Hard-cover. $24.95. 208 pp. .... Vendor G0776

Mitchell, Brian. **Pocket Guide to Irish Genealogy**.
Paper. $7.95. 103 pp. .... Vendor G0536

Mitchell, Brian. **Pocket Guide to Irish Genealogy**. (1991) reprint 1996. Illus.
Contact vendor for information. 63 pp. .... Vendor G0011

O'Brien, Michael J. **Irish Settlers in America**. A Consolidation of Articles from The Journal of the American Irish Historical Society. 2 vols. (1979) reprint 1993. Indexed. Illus.
Cloth. $50.00. 644 + 638 pp. .... Vendor G0011

O'Brien, Michael J. **The Irish in America**. Immigration, Land, Probate, Administrations, Birth, Marriage and Burial Records of the Irish in America in and about the Eighteenth Century. (1965) reprint 1996.
Paper. $9.00. 63 pp. .... Vendor G0011

O'Connor, Thomas, Marie E. Daly, and Edward L. Galvin. **Irish in New England.** 1985.
Paper. $4.95. 44 pp. .... Vendor G0406

O'Laughlin, M., and P. Donahue. **Irish Settlers on the American Frontier.** The #1 work on the Irish settling in Missouri westward 1770-1900.
Quality hardbound & gold stamped. $34.00. .... Vendor G0455

Shea, Ann M., and Marion R. Casey. **The Irish Experience in New York City: A Select Bibliography**. 1995.
An extensive research guide to non-archival source material that documents three centuries of the history of the Irish in New York City. Contains over 700 entries, including unpublished materials such as master's theses and doctorate dissertations, as well as published articles, chapters, books, and videos.
Cloth. $29.95. 140 pp. .... Vendor G0611

Italian

Brockman, Terra Castiglia. **A Student's Guide to Italian American Genealogy**. 1996. Indexed. Illus.
Hard-cover. $24.95. 208 pp. .... Vendor G0776

Carmack, Sharon DeBartolo. **Italian-American Family History:** A Guide to Researching and Writing About Your Heritage. 1997.
Paper. $12.95. 139 pp. .... Vendor G0010

Colletta, John Philip. **Finding Italian Roots**. The Complete Guide for Americans. 1993. Rev. ed. 1996. Illus.
Paper. $11.95. 130 pp. .... Vendor G0010

Grifo, Richard D., and Anthony F. Noto. **Italian Presence in Pennsylvania**. 1990.
A stimulating account of the contributions of Italians in Pennsylvania, and their rich heritage in the Commonwealth.
Paper. $4.95. 38 pp. .... Vendor G0554

Kessner. **The Golden Door: Italian and Jewish Immigrant Mobility in New York City, 1880-1915**. 1977.
A fascinating closely documented study tracing these New York City immigrants.
Paper. $14.95. 224 pp. .... Vendor G0611

Rolle. **The Italian Americans: Troubled Roots**. 1984.
A full-scale "psychohistory of the immigration experience" written by the "dean of Italian immigration historians," this book traces the epic of the Italian Americans.
Paper. $13.95. 222 pp. .... Vendor G0611

Japanese

Yamaguchi, Yoji. **A Student's Guide to Japanese American Genealogy.** 1996. Indexed. Illus.
Hard-cover. $24.95. 208 pp. .... Vendor G0776

Jewish

Beider, Alexander. **Ancient Ashkenazic Surnames: Jewish Surnames from Prague (15th-18th Centuries).**
Paper. $11.00. 46 pp. .... Vendor G0559

Beider, Alexander. **A Dictionary of Jewish Surnames from the Kingdom of Poland.** 1996.
Cloth. $69.50. 608 pp. .... Vendor G0559

Beider, Alexander. **A Dictionary of Jewish Surnames from the Russian Empire.**
Cloth. $75.00. 784 pp. .... Vendor G0559

Cohen, Chester G. **Shtetl Finder.**
Lists some 1,200 towns in Central and Eastern Europe identifying famous persons from the town and/or pre-publication subscribers to turn-of-the-century books.
Paper. $25.00. 145 pp. .... Vendor G0559

Edlund, Thomas Kent. **The German Minority Census of 1939: An Introduction and Register.** 1996.
A valuable finding aid for persons who want to use the LDS Family History Library microfilm collection of this important Holocaust-era census.
Paper. $9.50. 64 pp. .... Vendor G0559

Feingold. **The Jewish People in America.** 5 vols. 1992.
A history of the Jewish people in America, 1654 to the present. Extensive footnotes.
Cloth. $145.00/5 vol. boxed set. 1,458 pp. .... Vendor G0611

Greenbaum, Masha. **The Jews of Lithuania: A History of a Remarkable Community 1316-1945.** Published by Gefen Books.
Cloth. $29,95. 416 pp. .... Vendor G0559

Gruber, Ruth Ellen. **Jewish Heritage Travel: A Guide to East-Central Europe.** Published by John Wiley.
Cloth. $16.95. 299 pp. .... Vendor G0559

Gruber, Ruth Ellen. **Upon the Doorposts of Thy House: Jewish Life in East-Central Europe Yesterday and Today.** Published by John Wiley.
Cloth. $24.95. 310 pp. .... Vendor G0559

Guzik, Estelle M. **Genealogical Resources in the New York Metropolitan Area.** Published by Jewish Genealogical Society, Inc.
Definitive resource book for those with ancestors who lived in the New York City area. More than 100 facilities identified. It has one of the most complete annotated lists of yizkor books.
Cloth. $29.95. 404 pp. .... Vendor G0559

Kessner. **The Golden Door: Italian and Jewish Immigrant Mobility in New York City, 1880-1915**. 1977.
A fascinating closely documented study tracing these New York City immigrants.
Paper. $14.95. 224 pp. .... Vendor G0611

Kolatch, Alfred J. **Complete Dictionary of English and Hebrew First Names**. Published by Jonathan David Co.
Cloth. $25.00. 516 pp. .... Vendor G0559

Kurzweil. **From Generation to Generation: How to Trace Your Jewish Genealogy and Family History**.
A completely revised and updated edition of the classic guide to Jewish genealogy. Packed with essential information for a successful search.
Contact vendor for information. .... Vendor G0611

Kurzweil, Arthur, and Miriam Weiner. **Encyclopedia of Jewish Genealogy Volume 1: Sources in the United States and Canada**. Published by Jason Aronson.
Cloth. $40.00. 220 pp. .... Vendor G0559

Levin, Dov, ed. **Pinkas HaKehillot—Lita Encyclopedia of Towns—Lithuania**. Published by Yad Vashem. 1996.
Written in Hebrew.
Cloth. $65.00. 768 pp. .... Vendor G0559

Meshenberg, Michael J. **Documents of Our Ancestors: A Selection of Reproducible Genealogy Forms and Tips for Using Them**. 1996.
Cloth. $19.95. 148 pp. .... Vendor G0559

Mokotoff, Gary. **How to Document Victims and Locate Survivors of the Holocaust**.
Paper. $25.95. 208 pp. .... Vendor G0559

Mokotoff, Gary, and Sallyann Amdur Sack. **Where Once We Walked (WOWW)**. 1991.
Documents more than 21,000 towns in Central and Eastern Europe where Jews lived before the Holocaust. Includes 15,000 alternate names. Gives latitude/longitude, Jewish population before the Holocaust, and cites as many as forty books that reference each town.
Cloth. $69.50. 544 pp. .... Vendor G0559

Mokotoff, Gary. **WOWW Companion: A Guide to the Communities Surrounding Central & Eastern European Towns**.
Lists, in sequence by latitude/longitude, the 21,000 towns identified in *Where Once We Walked*, making it easy to isolate towns that are close to a specific town.
Cloth. $25.95. 208 pp. .... Vendor G0559

Mordy, I. **My Ancestors Were Jewish: How Can I Find Out More About Them?** 1995.
A British book published by the Society of Genealogists.
Paper. £1.80. 30 pp. .... Vendor G0557

Rhode, Harold, and Sallyann Amdur Sack. **Jewish Vital Records, Revision Lists and Other Jewish Holdings in the Lithuanian Archives**. 1996.
Paper. $35.00. .... Vendor G0559

Rosenstein, Neil. **Latter Day Leaders Sages and Scholars**. Published by Computer Center for Jewish Genealogy. 1996.
A bibliographic index of more than 5,500 rabbis from the 18th to early 20th centuries.
Paper. $19.95. 368 pp. .... Vendor G0559

Rosenstein, Neil. **The Unbroken Chain**. 2 vols. 1996.
One of the best-known published Jewish genelogies, it traces the descendants of Rabbi Meir Katzenelnbogen of Padua through sixteen generations to the present.
Cloth. $69.95. 1,344 pp. .... Vendor G0559

Rottenberg, Dan. **Finding Our Fathers**. A Guidebook to Jewish Genealogy. 1977.
Reprinted with a new Preface, 1995.
Paper. $19.95. xxii + 401 pp. .... Vendor G0010

Sack, Sallyann Amdur, and the Israel Genealogical Society. **A Guide to Jewish Genealogical Resources in Israel: Revised Edition**.
Cloth. $35.00. 256 pp. .... Vendor G0559

Schleifer, Jay. **A Student's Guide to Jewish American Genealogy**. 1996. Indexed. Illus.
Hard-cover. $24.95. 208 pp. .... Vendor G0776

Stern, Malcolm H. **Americans of Jewish Descent**.
Paper. $4.50. 11 pp. .... Vendor G0627

Stern, Malcolm H. **First American Jewish Families**. Published by Ottenheimer Publishers Inc.
The definitive work on the Jewish families that arrived during the Colonial/Federal period (1654-1838), tracing many families to the present.
Paper. $75.00. 464 pp. .... Vendor G0559

Tapper, Lawrence F. **A Biographical Dictionary of Canadian Jewry—1909-1914**.
Cloth. $35.00. 256 pp. .... Vendor G0559

Zubatsky, David, and Irwin Berent. **Sourcebook for Jewish Genealogies and Family Histories**. 1996.
Cloth. $69.50. 480 pp. .... Vendor G0559

Lutheran

Bernheim, Gotthardt D. **History of the German Settlements and of the Lutheran Church in North and South Carolina**. (1872) reprint 1996.
Paper. $40.00. 557 pp. .... Vendor G0011

Kleiner, John W., and Helmut T. Lehmann, trans. and eds. **The Correspondence of Henrich Melchior Muhlenberg Vol. 1: 1740-1747**. 1993. Indexed. Illus.
Book #1340.
Cloth. $49.50. 400 pp. .... Vendor G0082

Lehmann, Helmut T. **Missioner Extraordinary**. 1992. Illus.
Paper. $8.50. 25 pp. .... Vendor G0082

Smith, Clifford N. **Nineteenth-Century Emigration of "Old Lutherans" from Eastern Germany (Mainly Pomerania and Lower Silesia) to Australia, Canada, and the United States.** German-American Genealogical Research Monograph Number 7. 1980. ISBN 0-915162-06-7.
Paper. $20.00. 93 pp. double-columned. .... Vendor G0491

Tappert, Theodore G., and John W. Doberstein, trans. **The Journals of Henry Melchior Muhlenberg in 3 Volumes.** (1942) reprint 1993. Indexed. Illus.
Book #1469.
Cloth. $195.00. 2,368 pp. .... Vendor G0082

Melungeon

Bible, Jean P. **Melungeons—Yesterday and Today.**
A full accounting of the lost tribe of Tennessee and North Carolina.
Paper. $12.00. .... Vendor G0549

Kennedy. **The Melungeons: The Resurrection of a Proud People: An Untold Story of Ethnic Cleansing in America.** 1994.
A study of these fascinating people and their origins. Includes genealogical charts of some major families and a list of 260 Melungeon and related families.
Paper. $17.00. 156 pp. .... Vendor G0611

Mennonite

Gingerich, Hugh F., and Rachel W. Kreider. **Amish and Amish-Mennonite Genealogies.** 1986.
Cloth. $75.00. 858 pp. .... Vendor G0150

Zuercher, Isaac. **Anabaptist-Mennonite Names in Switzerland.** Translated by Hannes Maria Aleman. 1988.
Paper. $9.50. 35 pp. .... Vendor G0150

Methodist

Committee on Archives and History. **Guide to Family History Research in the Archival Repositories of the United Church of Canada.** 1996. Indexed.
In a single source, the information to guide researchers through the complete archival network of the United Church of Canada.
Paper. $17.00 (cdn), $18.50 (US). vi + 82 pp. .... Vendor G0568

Fisher, William Scott. **New York City Methodist Marriages 1785-1893.** 2 vols. 1994.
Book #1526.
Cloth. $89.50. 765 + 735 pp. .... Vendor G0082

Hobart, Chauncey. **History of Methodism in Minnesota.** Introduction by Thelma Boeder. (1887) reprint 1992. Indexed. Illus.
Paper. $15.50. 102 pp. .... Vendor G0583

Hope, Louise I. **Index to Niagara Conference Methodist Episcopal Church Baptismal Register, 1849-1886, 2 Parts**. 1994.
Index to an early Methodist Church register which was copied from entries forwarded by the ministers to the Conference.
Paper. $18.00 (cdn), $19.50 (US). 165 pp. .... Vendor G0568

Leary, W. **My Ancestors Were Methodists: How Can I Find Out More About Them?** 2nd ed. (1990) reprint 1993.
A British book published by the Society of Genealogists.
Paper. £3.45. 74 pp. .... Vendor G0557

Peden, Henry C., Jr. **Methodist Records of Baltimore City, Vol. 1: 1799-1829**. 1994. Indexed.
Baltimore (Lovely Lane) was the location of the meeting in 1794 that founded the Methodist Episcopal Church of America. There are few records in the state before 1850 despite the phenomenal growth of Methodist churches in Maryland during this period. From these records the author has abstracted marriages, births, and deaths, as well as information on deaths and removals from the membership and class lists.
Paper. $21.50. 271 pp. .... Vendor G0140

Peden, Henry C., Jr. **Methodist Records of Baltimore City, Vol. 2: 1830-1839**. 1994. Indexed.
Paper. $21.50. 281 pp. .... Vendor G0140

Moravian

Albaugh, Gaylord P. **History and Annotated Bibliography of American Religious Periodicals and Newspapers**. 2 vols. 1994.
Gives locations and/or microform sources for thousands of religious periodicals and newspapers published in America from 1730-1830. Tremendous detail included. 8½" x 11".
Cloth. $125.00. 1,456 pp. .... Vendor G0611

Chicago Genealogical Society. **Obituary Dates from the Denni Hlasatel 1891-1899**. 1995.
This and the following two volumes of obituary dates from the Chicago newspaper *Denni Hlasatel* are excellent sources of information for those researching Czech, Moravian, and Slovak ancestors from the Chicago area.
Paper. $3.00. 22 pp. .... Vendor G0742

Chicago Genealogical Society. **Obituary Dates from the Denni Hlasatel 1930-1939**. 1995.
Paper. $8.00. 105 pp. .... Vendor G0742

Chicago Genealogical Society. **Obituary Dates from the Denni Hlasatel 1940-1949**. 1995.
Paper. $9.00. 130 pp. .... Vendor G0742

Fries, Adelaide L. **The Moravians in Georgia, 1735-1740**. (1905) reprint 1993. Illus.
Contact vendor for information. 252 pp. .... Vendor G0011

Reichel, Rev. Levin T. **The Moravians in North Carolina**. (1857) reprint 1995.
Paper. $20.00. 206 pp. .... Vendor G0011

Young, Henry James, trans. **Moravian Families of Graceham, Maryland:** Church Records of Mainly German Families from Pennsylvania & Maryland Who Made Up the Congregation: 1759-1871. 1942. Indexed.
Paper. $11.00. 125 pp. .... Vendor G0140

Mormon

Bennett. **Mormons at the Missouri, 1846-1852**. 1987.
   This history of the Mormon community at Winter Quarters (Omaha, NE) names many of the members as well.
Cloth. $28.95. 347 pp. .... Vendor G0611

O'Dea. **The Mormons**. 1957.
   A scholarly study of the Mormons and the controversial issues surrounding them.
Paper. $11.00. 289 pp. .... Vendor G0611

Winn. **Exiles in a Land of Liberty: Mormons in America, 1830-1846**. 1989.
   Indispensable reading on early Mormon history.
Paper. $12.95. 284 pp. .... Vendor G0611

Native American/Indian

1832—Country for Indians West of the Mississippi.
Paper. $6.50. 20 pp. .... Vendor G0549

Adams, Richard. **Delaware Indians: A Brief History**. Indexed.
   A turn-of-the-century comprehensive history by a descendant of Chief White Eyes. Includes customs, folklore, religion, and first-person accounts of all their military involvement through the Civil War.
Paper. $8.95. 80 pp. .... Vendor G0160

Anderson, Rufus. **Memoir of Catharine Brown—Cherokee**. Indexed.
$18.50 (perfect bound). .... Vendor G0549

Arellano, Fay Louise Smith, trans. **Delaware Trails: Some Tribal Records, 1842-1907**. 1996.
Cloth. $55.00. 527 pp. .... Vendor G0011

Bowen, Jeff. **Chippewa Indians: Turtle Mountain Reservation Birth and Death Rolls 1924-1935**.
$22.50 (perfect bound). 104 pp. .... Vendor G0549

Bowen, Jeff. **Navajo-Hopi-Pieute: Western Navajo Reservation Birth and Death Rolls 1925-1933**.
$15.00 (perfect bound). 70 pp. .... Vendor G0549

Bowen, Jeff. **Oglala Sioux: Pine Ridge Reservations Births & Deaths, 1924-1935**.
$22.50 (perfect bound). 207 pp. .... Vendor G0549

Brandon. **Indians**. 1961.
An overview of American Indian history.
Paper. $10.95. 419 pp. .... Vendor G0611

Calloway. **New Directions in American Indian History**. 1988.
A collection of essays on various aspects of Native American studies.
Paper. $14.95. 262 pp. .... Vendor G0611

Carpenter, Cecelia Svinth. **How to Research American Indian Blood Lines: A Manual on Indian Genealogical Research**. 1991. Illus.
Paper. $9.00. 108 pp. .... Vendor G0552

Cotterill, R. S. **The Southern Indians: The Story of the Civilized Tribes Before Removal**. 1954. Reprinted.
Centers on the history of the Southern Indians (primarily Cherokees, Choctaws, Creeks, and Chickasaws) in the decades before removal.
Paper. $13.95. 254 pp. .... Vendor G0611

Debo. **A History of the Indians of the United States**. 1970.
An in-depth historical survey of the Indians of the U.S.
Paper. $16.95. 450 pp. .... Vendor G0611

DeWitt. **American Indian Resource Materials in the Western History Collections, University of Oklahoma**. 1990.
Thousands of sources listed.
Cloth. $37.95. 272 pp. .... Vendor G0611

Douthat, James L. **1832 Creek Census**. Indexed.
$22.50 (perfect bound). .... Vendor G0549

Douthat, James L. **Colonel Return Jonathan Meigs—Day Book 2**. Indexed.
Paper. $20.00. .... Vendor G0549

Douthat, James L. **Robert Armstrong; Plat Book of Those Indians Given Reservations After the 1817 Treaty**. Indexed.
Paper. $10.00. .... Vendor G0549

Dowd. **A Spirited Resistance: The North American Indian Struggle for Unity, 1745-1815**. 1992.
Draws on many sources to recapture the beliefs, thoughts, and actions of four principal Indian nations—Delaware, Shawnee, Cherokee, and Creek. Portrays their intertribal campaign to resist the Anglo-American forces, as well as the Native American opposition to the movement for unity.
Paper. $14.95. 261 pp. .... Vendor G0611

Dutton, Bertha P. **American Indians of the Southwest**. (1983) reprint 1994.
This books covers the history and contemporary tribal affairs, arts and crafts, changing lifestyles, and cultural and social characteristics that set apart each Indian group in the Southwest.
Paper. $16.95. 285 pp. .... Vendor G0611

Forbes, Jack D. **Africans and Native Americans: The Language of Race and the Evolution of Red-Black Peoples**. 1993.

Provides a totally new view of the history of Native American and African American peoples throughout the hemisphere. A very scholarly study, essential to anyone interested in these two ethnic groups.
Paper. $14.95. 344 pp. .... Vendor G0611

Foreman. **The Five Civilized Tribes: Cherokee, Chickasaw, Choctaw, Creek and Seminole.** (1934) reprint 1989.
A history of the trek of the five great southeastern Indian tribes from their old homes to the Indian territory west of the Mississippi.
Paper. $15.95. 455 pp. .... Vendor G0611

Gale Research. **Genealogy Sourcebook Series: Native American Genealogical Sourcebook.** 1995.
Cloth. $69.00. 218 pp. .... Vendor G0560

Gale Research. **Native Americans Information Directory.** 1992.
Cloth. $85.00. 371 pp. .... Vendor G0560

Gale Research. **Native North American Almanac.** 2 vols. 1994. Indexed. Illus.
Provides an overview of the culture and civilization of native peoples in the U.S. and Canada, from pre-Columbian times to the present.
Cloth. $55.00/set. 341 pp. .... Vendor G0560

Gale Research. **Native North American Biography.** 2 vols. 1996.
Includes both historical and contemporary figures.
Cloth. $55.00/set. 400 pp. .... Vendor G0560

Gormley, Myra Vanderpool. **Cherokee Connections.** Indexed. Illus.
An introduction to genealogical sources pertaining to the Cherokees, designed for researchers who are trying to prove their heritage for tribal Cherokee ancestry. Also examines some of the myths and folklore surrounding this famous Native American tribe. Includes extensive bibliography.
Paper. $11.95. 64 pp. .... Vendor G0546

Hagerty, Gilbert. **Wampum, War and Trade Goods West of the Hudson.** 1987. Indexed. Illus.
This book uses archaeology to document evidence of the history makers of the Mohawk Valley. A chronicle of Mohawk life during the 17th century. 9 maps, 250 illustrations.
Cloth. $40.00. 312 pp. .... Vendor G0093

Hall, Rev. Charles. **The Dutch and the Iroquois.** c. 1882.
Paper. $8.95. 55 pp. .... Vendor G0160

Hubbard, J. M. **Red Jacket.**
A reprint of the biography of this famous Seneca orator and chief.
Paper. $24.50. 356 pp. .... Vendor G0160

Hubbard, Jeremiah. **Forty Years Among the Indians.** (1913) reprint 1975. Indexed. Illus.
Quaker missionary, Indian territory, mostly Okla., biographies, marriages performed.
Paper. $14.00. 272 pp. .... Vendor G0531

Jacobs. **Dispossessing the American Indian: Indians and Whites on the Colonial Frontier**. 1985. Illus.
A fascinating look at the history of early Indian-white relations. Extensive footnotes, maps, illustrations.
Paper. $14.95. 246 pp. .... Vendor G0611

Kavasch, E. Barrie. **A Student's Guide to Native American Genealogy**. 1996. Indexed. Illus.
Hard-cover. $24.95 208 pp. .... Vendor G0776

Kimm, S. C. **The Iroquois**. A History of the Six Nations. 1900. Reprinted.
Compiles material not generally available to the public about the people of this powerful confederacy who played such an important role in the early history of our colonial life.
Paper. $8.95. 122 pp. .... Vendor G0160

Kirkham, E. Kay. **Our Native Americans: Their Records of Genealogical Value**. Vol. 1.
Includes records from the federal government, Oklahoma Society records, and the Genealogical Society of Utah listings for the American Indian.
Paper. $17.75. 235 pp. .... Vendor G0618

Kirkham, E. Kay. **Our Native Americans: Their Records of Genealogical Value**. Vol. 2.
Records from the federal government, Oklahoma Society, and the Genealogical Society of Utah, along with the 1900 federal census of Native Americans on Indian reservations, religious denominations, and Canadian bands.
Paper. $19.95. 262 pp. .... Vendor G0618

Malone. **The Skulking Way of War: Technology and Tactics Among the New England Indians**. 1991.
Looks at combat in the 17th century and shows how Indians honed their skills, creatively adapting European military technology to fit their own needs.
Paper. $13.95. 172 pp. .... Vendor G0611

McCary, Ben C. **Indians in Seventeenth-Century Virginia**. (1957) reprint 1995. Indexed. Illus.
Paper. $12.00. 102 pp. .... Vendor G0011

Mooney. **Myths and Sacred Formulas of Cherokee**. (1972) reprint 1982.
Cloth, $20.00. Paper, $16.95. 672 pp. .... Vendor G0134

National Archives. **American Indians**. A Select Catalog of National Archives Microfilm Publications. 1984. Rev. ed. 1995.
Paper. $3.50. 108 pp. .... Vendor G0565

New York State Archives and Records Administration. **Guide to Records Relating to Native Americans [in the New York State Archives]**. 1988.
Paper. $2.00. 27 pp. .... Vendor G0587

Newcomb. **The Indians of Texas**. 1990.
An anthropologist's comprehensive survey of the Indians of Texas.
Paper. $12.95. 404 pp. .... Vendor G0611

Oklahoma Genealogical Society. **1880 and 1890 Census, Canadian District, Cherokee Nation, Indian Territory.**
Paper. $8.50. .... Vendor G0729

Oklahoma Genealogical Society. **Records of the Choctaw Nation.**
Choctaw census of 1896; miscellaneous cemetery, church, and marriage records.
16 mm microfilm. $17.00. .... Vendor G0729

Olsen, Monty, comp. **Choctaw Emigration Records 1831-1856, Volume I.** 1990.
Paper. $15.00. 281 pp. .... Vendor G0710

Olsen, Monty, comp. **Choctaw Emigration Records 1831-1856, Volume II.** 1990.
Paper. $15.00. 106 pp. .... Vendor G0710

Reintjes, Afton E. **How to Research "A Little Bit of Indian".** (1989) reprint 1996.
Illus.
Forty maps, Indian genetic markers, index to persons with Indian blood, with documentation, before the Bureau of Indian Affairs.
Paper. $29.50. 109 pp. .... Vendor G0504

Rountree. **The Powhatan Indians of Virginia: Their Traditional Culture.** 1989.
Useful for anyone studying early 17th-century Virginia and the Powhatans.
Paper. $13.95. 221 pp. .... Vendor G0611

Ruttenber, E. **Indian Tribes of Hudson's River Vol. I (to 1700).** Indexed.
The only complete history of all the tribes that were located in, or interacted with, New York State Native Americans.
Paper. $12.05. 208 pp. .... Vendor G0160

Ruttenber, E. **Indian Tribes of Hudson's River Vol. II (1700 to 1850).** Indexed.
Includes 100-page appendix of language and biographical data and complete 2-volume index.
Paper. $12.95. 246 pp. .... Vendor G0160

Strickland. **The Indians in Oklahoma.** 1980. Illus.
An interesting history, with many pictures.
Paper. $11.95. 176 pp. .... Vendor G0611

Tanner. **Atlas of Great Lakes Indian History.** 1987. Illus.
A beautiful book with exquisite maps and illustrations accompanying a detailed text. 9" x 12".
Paper. $45.00. 224 pp. .... Vendor G0611

Underwood, Donald E., and Betty A. Underwood. **Searching for Lost Ancestors: A Guide to Genealogical Research.** 1993. Indexed. Illus.
This compact book covers basic genealogical research techniques as well as more advanced methodology. It also offers special individual chapters on immigrant, black, and Native American research aids and sources.
Paper. $9.00. 191 pp. .... Vendor G0026

Utley, Robert M. **The Indian Frontier of the American West, 1846-1890.** (1984) reprint 1993.
A study of the conflicts between Indians and whites through half a century with

perspectives from both sides. Utley recreates events from the Indian viewpoint while providing an objective appraisal of why the 19th-century white man acted as he did. Paper. $15.95. 325 pp. .... Vendor G0611

Venables. **The Six Nations of New York, Mohawks, Oneidas, Onondagas, Senecas, Tuscaroras: The 1892 United States Extra Census Bulletin.** (1892) reprint 1995.
A collection of census reports, observations, and photographs pertaining to the peoples of the Six Nations of New York.
Paper. $15.95. 89 pp. .... Vendor G0611

Waldman. **Atlas of the North American Indian.** 1985. Illus.
Over 100 color maps, an informative text and handsome illustrations. Covers the entire history, culture, and tribal locations of the Indian peoples of the United States, Canada, and Middle America from prehistoric times to the present day.
Cloth, $35.00. Paper, $18.95. 276 pp. .... Vendor G0611

Weatherford. **Native Roots: How the Indians Enriched America.** 1991.
An interesting look at Native Americans and their essential role in the making of the United States.
Cloth. $21.00. 310 pp. .... Vendor G0611

Williams. **The American Indian in Western Legal Thought: The Discourses of Conquest.** 1990.
Fascinating study of how "civilized" peoples justified their conquest of the American Indian.
Paper. $16.95. 352 pp. .... Vendor G0611

Wright. **A Guide to the Indian Tribes of Oklahoma.** 1986.
Oklahoma is home to sixty-seven Indian tribes, and this guide gives detailed information on the customs, location, and history of each.
Paper. $14.95. 300 pp. .... Vendor G0611

Young, Gloryann Hawkins, comp. **Indian Ancestors? Where to Look.** 1996.
Paper. $15.00. 50 pp. .... Vendor G0671

Palatine

Brink, Benjamin Myer. **Palatines of Olde Ulster.**
A reprint of ten articles from the genealogical and biographical magazine *Olde Ulster* (c. 1905-1914) on this early group of Hudson Valley settlers.
Paper. $9.95. 80 pp. .... Vendor G0160

Dixon, Nancy Wagoner. **Palatine Roots: The 1710 German Settlement in NY as Experienced by Johann Peter Wagner.** 1994. Indexed. Illus.
Book #1521. Tells the story of New York's Palatine settlers by focusing on the experiences of the author's ancestor Johann Peter Wagner and his family.
Cloth. $49.50. 352 pp. .... Vendor G0082

Jones, Henry Z, Jr. **The Palatine Families of Ireland.** Indexed. Illus.
A genealogical study of the German families settled by the British government in Ireland in 1709.
Cloth. $37.50 + $2.50 p&h. 190 pp. .... Vendor G0581

Jones, Henry Z, Jr. **Palatine Families of Ireland**. 1990. Indexed. Illus.
   Book #1109.
   Cloth. $37.50. 192 pp. .... Vendor G0082

Jones, Henry Z, Jr. **The Palatine Families of New York—1710**. 2 vols. Indexed. Illus.
   Winner of the Donald Lines Jacobus Award as Best Genealogical Work of the Year.
   Fully documented study of all 847 Palatine families who arrived in colonial New York
   from Germany in 1710. Includes illustrations, map, name and place index, and
   appendices.
   Cloth. $85.00/set + $4.50 p&h. 1,350 pp. .... Vendor G0581

Jones, Henry Z, Jr. **The Palatine Families of New York**. 2 vols. 1985. Indexed. Illus.
   Book #1113
   Cloth. $85.00. 1,374 pp. .... Vendor G0082

Jones, Henry Z, Jr. **More Palatine Families**. Indexed. Illus.
   A companion volume to *The Palatine Families of New York*. Some immigrants to
   the middle colonies from 1717-1776, and their European origins, plus new discover-
   ies on German families who arrived in colonial New York in 1710. Long buried
   emigration materials found in Germany give ancestral origins of hundreds of New
   York, New Jersey, and Pennsylvania colonists.
   Cloth. $65.00 + $4.50 p&h. 625 pp. .... Vendor G0581

Jones, Henry Z, Jr. **More Palatine Families**. 1991. Indexed. Illus.
   Book #1161.
   Cloth. $65.00. 625 pp. .... Vendor G0082

Knittle, Walter Allen. **Early Eighteenth Century Palatine Emigration**. (1937) reprint 1997. Indexed. Illus.
   Cloth. $25.00. xxi + 320 pp. .... Vendor G0010

MacWethy, Lou D. **The Book of Names** Especially Relating to the Early Palatines
   and the First Settlers in the Mohawk Valley. (1933) reprint 1985. Illus.
   Cloth. $15.00. 209 pp. .... Vendor G0010

Staudt, Ricardo W. **Palatine Church Visitations, 1609 . . . Deanery of Kusel**. (1930)
   reprint 1990. Indexed.
   Contact vendor for information. 147 pp. .... Vendor G0011

Tribbeko, John and George Ruperti. **List of Germans from the Palatinate Who
   Came to England in 1709**. (1965) reprint 1996.
   Paper. $7.00. 44 pp. .... Vendor G0011

Polish

Chorzempa, Rosemary A. **Polish Roots**. (1993, 1994) reprint 1996. Illus.
   Paper. $17.95. 262 pp. .... Vendor G0010

Gnacinski, Jan, and Len Gnacinski. **Polish and Proud**. Rev. ed.
   Paper. $10.00. 103 pp. .... Vendor G0574

Golembiewski, Thomas E. **The Study of Obituaries as a Source for Polish Genealogical Research**. 1984.
Paper. $9.00. 63 pp. .... Vendor G0611

Hoffman, William F. **Polish Surnames: Origins and Meanings**.
Paper. $16.50. 295 pp. .... Vendor G0611

Hollowak, Thomas L, and William F. Hoffman. **Index to the Obituaries and Death
Notices Appearing in the Dziennik Chicagoski 1890-1899**. 1984.
Paper. $11.00. 130 pp. .... Vendor G0611ʹ

Hollowak, Thomas L, and William F. Hoffman. **Index to the Obituaries and Death
Notices Appearing in the Dziennik Chicagoski 1900-1909**. 1987.
Paper. $11.00. 443 pp. .... Vendor G0611

Hollowak, Thomas L, and William F. Hoffman. **Index to the Obituaries and Death
Notices Appearing in the Dziennik Chicagoski 1910-1919**. 1988.
Paper. $11.00. 479 pp. .... Vendor G0611

Hollowak, Thomas L, and William F. Hoffman. **Index to the Obituaries and Death
Notices Appearing in the Dziennik Chicagoski 1920-1929, Part I & II A-Z**. 2 vols.
1991.
Paper. $22.00. 813 pp. .... Vendor G0611

Konrad, J. **Polish Family Research**.
Paper. $10.00. 72 pp. .... Vendor G0574

Rollyson, Carl Sokolnicki, and Lisa Olsen Paddock. **A Student's Guide to Polish
American Genealogy**. 1996. Indexed. Illus.
Hard-cover. $24.95. 208 pp. .... Vendor G0776

Schlyter, Daniel. **Essentials in Polish Genealogical Research**. 1993.
Paper. $3.00. 12 pp. .... Vendor G0611

Presbyterian

Braden, Dorothy B., comp. **Presbyterian Churches in Allegheny County,
Pennsylvania**.
Contains all known Presbyterian churches, past or present.
Paper. $16.00. .... Vendor G0615

Hall. **The Shane Manuscript Collection: A Genealogical Guide to the Kentucky
and Ohio Papers**. 1990.
While many genealogists and historians are familiar with the collection of Rev.
John Dabney Shane's papers in the Draper Manuscripts, it often comes as a surprise
that half of Shane's papers are located at the Presbyterian Historical Association in
Philadelphia, and not in Draper's collection. The collection (36 reels of microfilm)
reflects his interest in the history of the Presbyterian Church in very early KY and
OH, and the migration of congregations into IL, IN, MO.
Paper. $12.00. 133 pp. .... Vendor G0611

Porter, H. Leonard. **Destiny of the Scotch-Irish: A Presbyterian Migrational History.** (1984) reprint 1990. Indexed. Illus.
Paper. $27.95. 120 pp. .... Vendor G0548

Ruston, A. **My Ancestors Were English Presbyterians/Unitarians: How Can I Find Out More About Them?** 1993.
A British book published by the Society of Genealogists.
Paper. £3.00. 64 pp. .... Vendor G0557

Stewart, Reid W. **Scottish Dissenting Presbyterian Churches in Allegheny County, Pennsylvania.** 1994. Indexed. Illus.
Paper. $10.00. 41 pp. .... Vendor G0615

Ware, Lowry. **Associate Reformed Presbyterian Death & Marriage Notices 1843-1863.** 1993. Indexed.
Cloth. $25.00. 209 pp. .... Vendor G0602

Protestant

Revill, Janie. **A Compilation of the Original Lists of Protestant Immigrants to South Carolina, 1763-1773.** (1939) reprint 1996. Indexed.
Paper. $17.50. 163 pp. .... Vendor G0011

Puritan

Hinman, Royal R. **A Catalogue of the Names of the First Puritan Settlers of the Colony of Connecticut;** with the Time of Their Arrival in the Colony and Their Standing in Society . . . (1846) reprint 1996.
Paper. $31.50. 336 pp. .... Vendor G0011

Quaker

Barbour, Hugh, Christopher Densmore, and Elizabeth Moger, eds. **Quaker Crosscurrents: Three Hundred Years of New York Yearly Meetings.** With Nancy Sorel, Alson Van Wagner, and Arthur Worrall. Foreword by Martin Marty. Indexed. Illus.
    The first comprehensive history of the Religious Society of Friends or Quakers of New York, from their earliest appearance in the Dutch colony of New Netherlands in the 1650s to the present.
Paper. $19.95. 500 pp. .... Vendor G0160

Beard, Alice L. **Births, Deaths and Marriages of the Nottingham Quakers, 1680-1889.** 1989. Indexed.
    East and West Nottingham Meetings, Little Britain, Deer Creek, and Eastland Meetings, and the Octorara Meeting, Cecil County, Maryland.
Paper. $24.00. 296 pp. .... Vendor G0140

Berry, Ellen, and David Berry. **Our Quaker Ancestors:** Finding Them in Quaker Records. (1987) reprint 1996.
Cloth. $19.95. 136 pp. .... Vendor G0010

Brown and Stuard. **Witnesses For Change: Quaker Women Over Three Centuries.** 1989.
Very interesting background reading.
Paper. $14.50. 190 pp. .... Vendor G0611

Bucks County, PA Church Records of the 18th Century: Vol. 2, Quaker Records: Falls and Middletown Monthly Meetings. By Anna Miller Watring. 1993. Indexed.
Paper. $32.00. 395 pp. .... Vendor G0140

Bucks County, Pennsylvania Church Records of the 18th Century: Vol. 3, Quaker Records: Wrightstown, Richland, Buckingham, Makefield, and Solebury Monthly Meetings. By Anna Miller Watring. 1994. Indexed.
Paper. $18.00. 233 pp. .... Vendor G0140

Comfort, William Wistar. **The Quakers.** Revised by Edwin B. Bronner. 1986. Illus.
A look at the beginnings of Quakerism in the mid-17th century, followed by details of Quaker life, institutions, and contributions to Pennsylvania history.
Paper. $5.95. 65 pp. .... Vendor G0554

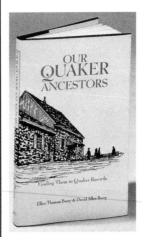

Dorrel, Ruth, and Thomas D. Hamm. **Abstracts of the Records of the Society of Friends in Indiana,** Vol. 1. Rev. ed. 1996. Indexed.
Cloth. $62.75. 318 pp. .... Vendor G0109

Fay, Loren V. **Quaker Census of 1828.** Illus.
Members of the New York Yearly Meeting, The Religious Society of Friends at the time of the Separation.
Cloth. $20.00. 329 pp. .... Vendor G0450

Glenn, Thomas Allen. **Merion in the Welsh Tract.** With Sketches of the Townships of Haverford and Radnor. Historical and Genealogical Collections Concerning the Welsh Barony in the Province of Pennsylvania Settled by the Cymric Quakers in 1682. Partially indexed. (1896) reprint 1994. Illus.
Paper. $32.50. 394 pp. .... Vendor G0011

Haines, G., comp. **Early Quaker Marriages from Various Records in N.J.** (1902) reprint 1987.
Paper. $6.50. 32 pp. .... Vendor G0259

Hamm. **The Transformation of American Quakerism: Orthodox Friends, 1800-1907.** 1988.
Excellent background reading for those with Quaker ancestry. The extensive footnotes and bibliography will prove useful.
Paper. $13.95. 261 pp. .... Vendor G0611

Hazard, Caroline. **The Narragansett Friends' Meeting in the XVIII Century,** with a Chapter on Quaker Beginnings in R. I. (1899) reprint 1992.
Paper. $21.00. 197 pp. .... Vendor G0259

Heiss, Willard, and Thomas D. Hamm. **Quaker Genealogies: A Selected List of Books.** 1985.
Paper. $5.95. 73 pp. .... Vendor G0406

Hinshaw, William Wade. **Encyclopedia of American Quaker Genealogy. Vol. I: (North Carolina Yearly Meeting).** (1936, 1948) reprint 1994. Indexed.
Paper. $75.00 . 1,185 + 12 pp. .... Vendor G0010

Hinshaw, William Wade. **Encyclopedia of American Quaker Genealogy. Vol. II: (New Jersey and Pennsylvania Monthly Meetings).** (1938) reprint 1994. Indexed.
Paper. $75.00. 1,126 pp. .... Vendor G0010

Hinshaw, William Wade. **Encyclopedia of American Quaker Genealogy. Vol. III: (New York Monthly Meetings).** (1940) reprint 1991. Indexed.
Paper. $45.00. 540 pp. .... Vendor G0010

Hinshaw, William Wade. **Encyclopedia of American Quaker Genealogy. Vol. IV: (Ohio Monthly Meetings).** (1946) reprint 1994. Indexed.
Paper. $95.00. 1,424 pp. .... Vendor G0010

Hinshaw, William Wade. **Encyclopedia of American Quaker Genealogy. Vol. V: (Ohio Monthly Meetings).** (1946) reprint 1994. Indexed.
Paper. $75.00. 1,060 pp. .... Vendor G0010

Hinshaw, William Wade. **Encyclopedia of American Quaker Genealogy. Vol. VI: (Virginia).** (1950) reprint 1993. Indexed.
Paper. $75.00. 1,049 pp. .... Vendor G0010

Hoopes, E. Erick, and Christina Hoopes. **A Record of Interments at the Friends Burial Ground, Baltimore, Maryland.** (1995) reprint 1996.
Paper. $10.00. 66 pp. .... Vendor G0011

Hopewell Friends. **Hopewell Friends History, 1734-1934, Frederick County, Virginia.** Records of Hopewell Monthly Meetings and Meetings Reporting to Hopewell. (1936) reprint 1993. Indexed. Illus.
Cloth. $38.50. 671 pp. .... Vendor G0010

Hull, William I. **William Penn and the Dutch Quaker Migration to Pennsylvania.** (1935) reprint 1990. Indexed. Illus.
Cloth. $30.00. 460 pp. .... Vendor G0011

Illiana Genealogical & Historical Society. **Friends of Illiana, 1826.** Indexed.
   Abstracts of Society of Friends meetings.
Spiral binding. $29.50. 391 pp. .... Vendor G0723

Levy. **Quakers and the American Family: British Settlement in the Delaware Valley.** 1988.
   An important social history, this book examines the reasons for the migration of Quaker families from 17th-century England into colonial southeastern Pennsylvania, as well as their life once they arrived there. Many early families mentioned. Extensive footnotes.
Paper. $18.95. 340 pp. .... Vendor G0611

Lucas, S. Emmett, Jr., ed. **Quakers in South Carolina,** Wateree and Bush River, Crane Creek, Piney Grove, and Charleston Meetings. 1892, 1905, 1936. Reprinted in consolidated format 1991. Indexed. Illus.
Paper. $20.00. 150 pp. .... Vendor G0610

Milligan, E. H., and M. J. Thomas. **My Ancestors Were Quakers: How Can I Find Out More About Them?** 1983.
   A British book published by the Society of Genealogists.
Paper. £2.10. 37 pp. .... Vendor G0557

Morris, Jean S. **Pennsylvania Quaker Research: A Bibliography & Guide with Maps.** 1996.
Paper. $13.00. 18 pp. .... Vendor G0521

Myers, Albert Cook. **Immigration of the Irish Quakers into Pennsylvania, 1682-1750.** With Their Early History in Ireland. (1902) reprint 1994. Indexed. Illus.
Cloth. $30.00. xxii + 477 pp. .... Vendor G0010

Myers, Albert Cook. **Quaker Arrivals at Philadelphia 1682-1750.** Being a List of Certificates of Removal Received at Philadelphia Monthly Meeting of Friends. (1902) reprint 1997. Indexed.
Paper. $15.00. 131 pp. .... Vendor G0011

Ohio Historical Society. **Mt. Pleasant & Early Quakers.**
Paper. $4.00. .... Vendor G0619

Peden, Henry C., Jr. **Quaker Records of Southern Maryland, 1658-1800.** 1992. Indexed.
Paper. $10.00. 120 pp. .... Vendor G0140

Pennsylvania Historical Survey. Works Projects Administration. **Inventory of Church Archives Society of Friends in Pennsylvania.** (1941) reprint 1996.
Paper. $35.00. 397 pp. .... Vendor G0011

Putnam, Martha A. **Quaker Records of Southeast Virginia.** 1996. Indexed.
Paper. $6.50. 77 pp. .... Vendor G0140

Reamy, Martha. **Early Church Records of Chester County.** Vol. 1: Quaker Records of Bradford Monthly Meeting. 1995. Indexed.
Paper. $20.00. 260 pp. .... Vendor G0140

Roberts, Clarence V. **Early Friends Families of Upper Bucks** with Some Account of Their Descendants. (1925) reprint 1995. Indexed. Illus.
Paper. $49.95. 680 pp. .... Vendor G0011

Wallace, Paul A. W. **Daniel Boone in Pennsylvania.** Rev. ed. 1987.
Recounts the story of Daniel Boone's early life in Pennsylvania and his later activity in Kentucky, describing his Quaker family and the popular traditions that have survived the years.
Paper. $1.95. 21 pp. .... Vendor G0554

White, Miles, Jr. **Early Quaker Records in Virginia.** (1902, 1903) reprint 1989. Indexed.
Paper. $6.00. 64 pp. .... Vendor G0010

Worrall, Jay, Jr. **The Friendly Virginians.** 1994. Indexed. Illus.
Depicts the rise and progress of Virginia's Quakers since 1655.
Cloth. $29.95. 632 pp. .... Vendor G0632

Wright, F. Edward. **Quaker Records of South River Monthly Meeting, 1756-1800.** 1993.
Paper. $5.00. 74 pp. .... Vendor G0140

Scandinavian

Evjen, John O. **Scandinavian Immigrants in New York, 1630-1674.** (1916) reprint 1996. Illus.
Paper. $36.50. 464 pp. .... Vendor G0011

Magee, Joan. **A Scandinavian Heritage.** 200 Years of Scandinavian Presence in the Windsor—Detroit Border Region. 1985.
Paper. $12.99 (cnd), $11.50 (US). 128 pp. .... Vendor G0640

Paddock, Lisa Olson, and Carl Sokolnicki Rollyson. **A Student's Guide to Scandinavian Genealogy.** 1996. Indexed. Illus.
Hard-cover. $24.95. 208 pp. .... Vendor G0776

Schwenkfelders

Kriebel, Howard W. **The Schwenkfelders in Pennsylvania:** A Historical Sketch. (1904) reprint 1995.
Cloth. $35.00. 246 pp. .... Vendor G0259

Kriebel, Rev. Reuben. **Genealogical Record of the Descendants of the Schwenkfelders** Who Arrived in Pennsylvania in 1733, 1734, 1736, 1737. From the German of the Rev. Balthasar Heebner and from Other Sources. (1879) reprint 1993. Indexed.
Paper. $24.50. 371 pp. .... Vendor G0011

Scots-Irish

Campbell, R. G. **Scotch-Irish Family Research Made Simple.**
Paper. $10.00. 64 pp. .... Vendor G0574

Chalkley, Lyman. **Chronicles of the Scotch-Irish Settlement of Virginia, Extracted from the Original Court Records of Augusta Co., 1745- 1800.** 3 vols. (1912) reprint 1997.
Contact vendor for information. 623 + 652 + 712 pp. .... Vendor G0010

Dobson, David. **Scots-Irish Links, 1575-1725. In Two Parts.** 2 vols. in 1. (1994, 1995) reprint 1997.
Contact vendor for information. 58 pp. .... Vendor G0011

Dunaway, Wayland F. **The Scotch-Irish of Colonial Pennsylvania.** (1944) reprint 1997. Indexed.
Contact vendor for information. 273 pp. .... Vendor G0010

Egle, William Henry. **Pennsylvania Genealogies,** Chiefly Scotch-Irish and German. 2nd ed. (1896) reprint 1997. Indexed.
Paper. $49.95. 798 pp. .... Vendor G0011

Falley, Margaret D. **Irish and Scotch-Irish Ancestral Research:** A Guide to the Genealogical Records, Methods, and Sources in Ireland. 2 vols. (1962) reprint 1988. Indexed.
Cloth. $60.00. 813 + 354 pp. .... Vendor G0010

Ford, Henry Jones. **The Scotch-Irish in America.** (1915) reprint 1995. Indexed.
    This work commences with a discussion of the Scottish migration to Ulster in the 17th century, followed by an examination of the causes of the Scotch-Irish emigration to North America by the end of the century. Ford devotes entire chapters to the Scotch-Irish settlement in New England, New York, the Jerseys, Pennsylvania, and along the colonial frontier, as well as to the history of Scotch-Irish institutions in the U.S.
Paper. $42.50. 607 pp. .... Vendor G0011

Hanna, Charles A. **The Scotch-Irish.** Or the Scot in North Britain, North Ireland and North America. 2 vols. (1902) reprint 1995. Indexed. Illus.
Cloth. $75.00. 623 + 602 pp. .... Vendor G0010

Leyburn. **The Scotch-Irish: A Social History**. (1962) reprint 1991.
These people in Scotland, their removal to Northern Ireland, and their migrations to America. Extensive bibliography.
Paper. $15.95. 377 pp. .... Vendor G0611

Maxwell, Fay. **Franklin County, Ohio Scotch-Irish Nova Scotia Acadians Refugee Tract History**. 1974. Indexed.
ISBN 1-885463-11-1. This is a first. The Scotch-Irish Protestant refugees from General Washington and the Revolutionary War. Coverage includes migratory and military service to the King, their refusal to change Protestant beliefs, and finally settling in the 48½-mile strip called the Refugee Tract in Franklin County, Ohio. Congress waited to eve of War of 1812 before fulfilling land grant promise.
Paper. $35.00. 160 pp. .... Vendor G0135

Porter, H. Leonard. **Destiny of the Scotch-Irish: A Presbyterian Migrational History**. (1984) reprint 1990. Indexed. Illus.
Paper. $27.95. 120 pp. .... Vendor G0548

Reintjes, Afton E. **Scotch-Irish Sources for Research**. (1986) revised 1987. Illus.
Twenty-five maps, immigration to America, migrations patterns in New World, sources for research.
Paper. $20.50. 50 pp. .... Vendor G0504

Rouse, Parke, Jr. **The Great Wagon Road from Philadelphia to the South: How Scotch-Irish and Germanics Settled the Uplands**. (1973) reprint 1995.
This book is recognized for its insight into the birth of the American South, from the early 1700s until the Civil War. Countless Scotch-Irish, Germanic, and English settlers traveled the road southward from Philadelphia to settle the Appalachian uplands from Pennsylvania to Georgia.
Paper. 1995. 292 pp. .... Vendor G0611

Smylie, James H. **Scotch-Irish Presence in Pennsylvania**. 1990.
Focuses on the immigration and life of the Scotch-Irish in Pennsylvania, as well as on their important contributions to Pennsylvania.
Paper. $4.95. 38 pp. .... Vendor G0554

Scottish

Cory, Kathleen. **Tracing Your Scottish Ancestry**. (1990) reprint 1996. Indexed.
Paper. $16.95. 195 pp. .... Vendor G0010

Dobson, David. **Directory of Scots in The Carolinas, 1680-1830**. (1986) reprint 1994.
Cloth. $25.00. 322 pp. .... Vendor G0010

Dobson, David. **Directory of Scottish Settlers in North America, 1625-1825. Vol. I**. (1984) reprint 1988.
Cloth. $20.00. 267 pp. .... Vendor G0010

Dobson, David. **Directory of Scottish Settlers in North America, 1625-1825. Vol. II**. (1984) reprint 1993.
Cloth. $20.00. 216 pp. .... Vendor G0010

Dobson, David. **Directory of Scottish Settlers in North America, 1625-1825.** Vol. **III.** 1984.
Cloth. $17.50. 194 pp. .... Vendor G0010

Dobson, David. **Directory of Scottish Settlers in North America, 1625-1825.** Vol. **IV.** 1985.
Cloth. $17.50. 161 pp. .... Vendor G0010

Dobson, David. **Directory of Scottish Settlers in North America, 1625-1825.** Vol. **V.** 1985.
Cloth. $20.00. 312 pp. .... Vendor G0010

Dobson, David. **Directory of Scottish Settlers in North America, 1625-1825.** Vol. **VI.** 1986.
Cloth. $15.00. 126 pp. .... Vendor G0010

Dobson, David. **Directory of Scottish Settlers in North America, 1625-1825.** Vol. **VII.** 1993.
Cloth. $17.50. 220 pp. .... Vendor G0010

Dobson, David. **The Original Scots Colonists of Early America, 1612- 1783.** (1989) reprint 1995. Indexed.
Cloth. $28.50. 370 pp. .... Vendor G0010

Dobson, David. **Scots On the Chesapeake, 1607-1830.** 1992.
Cloth. $20.00. 169 pp. .... Vendor G0010

Dobson, David. **Scottish-American Court Records, 1733-1783.** 1991. Indexed.
Cloth. $18.00. 105 pp. .... Vendor G0010

Dobson, David. **Scottish-American Heirs, 1683-1883.** (1990) reprint 1992. Indexed.
Cloth. $21.50. 165 pp. .... Vendor G0010

Dobson, David. **Scottish-American Wills, 1650-1900.** 1991.
Cloth. $20.00. 137 pp. .... Vendor G0010

Irvine, Sherry. **Your Scottish Ancestry: A Guide for North Americans.** 1997.
Paper. $17.95. 253 pp. .... Vendor G0570

Konrad, J. **Scottish Family Research.**
Paper. $10.00. 56 pp. .... Vendor G0574

MacDougall, Donald, ed. **Scots and Scots' Descendants in America.** (1917) reprint 1992. Indexed.
Contact vendor for information. 390 pp. .... Vendor G0011

Meyer. **Highland Scots of North Carolina, 1732-1776.**
    Examines the migrations of the Highland Scots into North Carolina during the 18th century, and their tendency to remain Loyalist during the Revolution.
Paper. $12.95. 216 pp. .... Vendor G0611

Patten, Jennie M. **The Argyle Patent** and Accompanying Documents. (1928) reprint 1991.

In 1764, a large number of Scottish Presbyterian colonists succeeded in securing the land grant known as the Argyle Patent, in Washington County, New York, upon which they took up residence. This work comprises a collection of the various documents produced in support of the Argyle claim and features genealogical notices of various Washington County families.
Paper. $9.00. 68 pp. .... Vendor G0011

Stewart, Reid W. **Scottish Dissenting Presbyterian Churches in Allegheny County, Pennsylvania**. 1994. Indexed. Illus.
Paper. $10.00. 41 pp. .... Vendor G0615

Stuart, Margaret. **Scottish Family History:** A Guide to Works of Reference on the History and Genealogy of Scottish Families. (1930) reprint 1994.
Cloth. $25.00. 386 pp. .... Vendor G0010

Spanish

Bolton, Herbert E. **The Spanish Borderlands: A Chronicle of Old Florida and the Southwest**. (1921) reprint 1996.
In narrative prose, Bolton recounts the Spanish exploration and the permanent settlement of Old Florida, New Mexico, Texas, Louisiana, and California.
Paper. $22.50. 320 pp. .... Vendor G0611

Swedish

Johnson, Amandus. **The Swedish Settlements On the Delaware, 1638-1664**. 2 vols. (1911) reprint 1996. Indexed. Illus.
Paper. $80.00. 1,080 pp. in all. .... Vendor G0011

Strand, A. E. **History of the Swedish-Americans of Minnesota**. 3 vols. (1910) reprint 1994.
Cloth. $115.00/set. 1,147 pp. .... Vendor G0259

Swiss

Baughman, J. Ross. **Harvest Time . . . History of the Swiss, German & Dutch Folk in Early America**. 1994.
Paper. $31.00. 256 pp. .... Vendor G0150

Eshleman, H. Frank. **Historic Background and Annals of the Swiss and German Pioneer Settlers** of Southeastern Pennsylvania, and of Their Remote Ancestors. (1917) reprint 1991. Indexed.
Cloth. $25.00. 386 pp. .... Vendor G0010

Steinach, Dr. Adelrich, comp. **Swiss Colonists**. 1995. Indexed.
Book #1607.
Cloth. $49.50. 512 pp. .... Vendor G0082

Welsh

Browning, Charles H. **Welsh Settlement of Pennsylvania**. (1912) reprint 1993. Indexed.
Paper. $42.50. 631 pp. .... Vendor G0011

Glenn, Thomas Allen. **Merion in the Welsh Tract**. With Sketches of the Townships of Haverford and Radnor. Historical and Genealogical Collections Concerning the Welsh Barony in the Province of Pennsylvania Settled by the Cymric Quakers in 1682. Partially indexed. (1896) reprint 1994. Illus.
Paper. $32.50. 394 pp. .... Vendor G0011

Glenn, Thomas Allen. **Welsh Founders of Pennsylvania**. 2 vols. in 1. (1911, 1913) reprint 1991. Indexed. Illus.
Cloth. $31.50. 356 pp. in all. .... Vendor G0011

Rowlands, John, ed. **Welsh Family History**. A Guide to Research. (1993) reprint 1996. Indexed. Illus.
Paper. $19.95. 316 pp. .... Vendor G0010

Royal, Noble, and Notable Descent

Boyer, Carl, 3rd. **Ancestral Lines, 3rd Edition**. 1996. Indexed. Illus.
Includes royal and noble descent of Robert Abell of Leicestershire, England, and Rehoboth, Plymouth Colony, and Welsh royal ancestry of Eleanor (Jones) Evans, wife of Titus Evans of Machynlleth, Wales, and New York City, as well as more than 170 descents from American lines.
Cloth. $73.00. est. 1,000 pp. .... Vendor G0198

Brewer-Ward, Daniel A. **The House of Habsburg: a Genealogy of the Descendants of Empress Maria Theresia**. 1996. Illus.
Paper. $37.50. 466 pp. .... Vendor G0011

Brown, Stuart E., Jr., Lorraine F. Myers, and Eileen M. Chappel. **Pocahontas' Descendants**. A Revision, Enlargement and Extension of the List as Set Out by Wyndham Robertson in His Book Pocahontas and Her Descendants (1887). Combined with two volumes of corrections and additions. (1985, 1992, 1994) reprint 1997. Indexed. Illus.
Cloth. $50.00. 716 pp. .... Vendor G0010

Browning, Charles H. **Americans of Royal Descent**. (1911) reprint 1986. Indexed. Illus.
Cloth. $30.00. 575 pp. total .... Vendor G0010

Browning, Charles H. **The Magna Charta Barons and Their American Descendants [1898]**. Together with the Pedigrees of the Founders of the Order of Runnemede. (1898) reprint 1991. Indexed. Illus.
Cloth. $32.50. 463 pp. .... Vendor G0011

Browning, Charles H. **Magna Charta Barons and Their Descendants [1915]**. (1915) reprint 1991. Indexed. Illus.
Cloth. $31.50. 366 pp. .... Vendor G0011

Buck, J. Orton, Jr., and Timothy F. Beard. **Pedigrees of Some of the Emperor Charlemagne's Descendants**, Volume III. (1978) reprint 1996. Indexed.
Cloth. $30.00. 309 pp. total .... Vendor G0010

Burke, Arthur Meredyth. **The Prominent Families of the United States of America**. (1908) reprint 1991. Indexed.
Cloth. $35.00. 510 pp. .... Vendor G0010

Burke, Ashworth P. **Burke's Family Records**. (1897) reprint 1994. Indexed. Illus.
Traces the descent of some 300 cadet houses of the British nobility from Airey and Groton to Swanzy and Yarker.
Paper. $50.00. 709 pp. .... Vendor G0011

Burke, Sir Bernard. **Burke's American Families with British Ancestry**. (1939) reprint 1996. Illus.
Cloth. $47.50. 494 pp. plus 48 pp. of coats-of-arms. .... Vendor G0010

Burke, Sir Bernard. **A Genealogical History of the Dormant, Abeyant, Forfeited, and Extinct Peerages of the British Empire**. (1883) reprint 1996. Indexed. Illus.
Cloth. $40.00. 642 pp. .... Vendor G0010

Burke, J., and J. B. Burke. **Burke's Extinct & Dormant Baronetcies of England, Ireland & Scotland**. (1841) reprint 1994.
Contact vendor for information. 644 pp. .... Vendor G0010

Burke, J. B., comp. **Roll of Battle Abbey**. (1848) reprint 1989.
A list of several hundred noble companions of William the Conqueror, with biographical and genealogical details.
Contact vendor for information. 127 pp. .... Vendor G0010

Burke, John. **A Genealogical and Heraldic History of the Commoners of Great Britain and Ireland**. In Four Volumes. Reprinted with the *Index to Pedigrees in Burke's Commoners*, by George Ormerod. (1834-1838, 1907) reprint 1996. Indexed. Illus.
The standard genealogical guide to families in Great Britain and Ireland who enjoyed territorial possession or official rank, but were uninvested with heritable honors.
Paper. $200.00. 3,113 pp. .... Vendor G0011

Burke's Prominent Families of the U.S.A.
A "Landed Gentry" of American families; 191 genealogies, illus. of arms.
Cloth. £45.00. 510 pp. .... Vendor G0616

Camp, Anthony J. **My Ancestors Came with the Conqueror,** Those Who Did, and Some of Those Who Probably Did Not. (1988, 1990) reprint 1994.
Paper. $9.50. 89 pp. .... Vendor G0010

Crispin, M. Jackson, and Leonce Macary. **Falaise Roll,** Recording Prominent Companions of William Duke of Normandy at the Conquest of England. (1938) reprint 1994. Indexed. Illus.
Cloth. $30.00. 258 pp. .... Vendor G0010

Crowther, G. Rodney, III. **Surname Index to Sixty-Five Volumes of Colonial and Revolutionary Pedigrees**.
Index and quick search aid to lineages hidden in printed collections of genealogies.
Cloth. $19.00. 143 pp. .... Vendor G0627

Faris, David. **Plantagenet Ancestry of Seventeenth-Century Colonists:** The Descent from the Later Plantagenet Kings of England, Henry III, Edward I, Edward II, and Edward III, of Emigrants from England and Wales to the North American Colonies before 1701. 1996. Indexed.
Cloth. $30.00. 337 pp. .... Vendor G0010

Kent, Dr. Lawrence, ed. **Presidential Families Gazette,** Presidential Families of America.
Concerned with the genealogies and family histories of the Presidents of the U.S.A. Membership is based on consanguinity, direct or collateral, and includes citizens of all nations. The ancestor held in common with a President must have been resident in the area now encompassed by the United States of America. Direct inquiries require a SASE. A roster and a journal are issued.
Life fees are applicable. .... Vendor G0448

Langston, Aileen Lewers, and J. Orton Buck. **Pedigrees of Some of the Emperor Charlemagne's Descendants**. Volume II. With a Foreword by Timothy F. Beard. (1974) reprint 1996. Indexed.
Cloth. $35.00. 516 pp. .... Vendor G0010

Leeson, Francis L. **A Directory of British Peerages**. (1984) reprint 1986.
Paper. $12.50. 174 pp. .... Vendor G0010

The Marquis of Ruvigny and Raineval. **The Blood Royal of Britain**. [Tudor Roll].
Being a Roll of the Living Descendants of Edward IV and Henry VII, Kings of
England, and James III, King of Scotland. (1903) reprint 1994. Indexed. Illus.
Cloth. $45.00. 632 pp. .... Vendor G0010

The Marquis of Ruvigny and Raineval. **The Plantagenet Roll of The Blood Royal**.
The Clarence Volume, Containing the Descendants of George, Duke of Clarence.
(1905) reprint 1994. Indexed. Illus.
Cloth. $50.00. 730 pp. .... Vendor G0010

The Marquis of Ruvigny and Raineval. **The Plantagenet Roll of The Blood Royal**.
The Anne of Exeter Volume, Containing the Descendants of Anne (Plantagenet), Duch-
ess of Exeter. (1907) reprint 1994. Indexed. Illus.
Cloth. $50.00. 842 pp. .... Vendor G0010

David Faris # PLANTAGENET ANCESTRY OF SEVENTEENTH-CENTURY COLONISTS

337 pp., indexed, cloth.
1996. **Vendor G0010.**
$30.00

Since 1950 the standard work linking 17th-cen-
tury colonial immigrants with the kings of England has been *Ancestral Roots of Sixty Colonists*
(seven editions from 1950 to 1992). To give the
work greater definition, however, and to make it
easier to use, it has been decided to replace *Ancestral Roots* and its companion volume, *The Magna
Charta Sureties, 1215*, with a series of volumes presenting the ancestry of 17th-century colonists from
the Plantagenet kings of England, the Magna Charta
Sureties, the feudal English barons, and the Emperor Charlemagne.

The first of this new generation of books is now
available. *Plantagenet Ancestry of Seventeenth-Century
Colonists*, prepared by David Faris, who had assisted with the last two editions of *Ancestral Roots*,
provides the descent from the later Plantagenet
kings of England (Henry III, Edward I, Edward II,
and Edward III) of more than one hundred emigrants from England and Wales to the North American colonies before 1701. Many colonists not included in former editions of *Ancestral Roots* appear
in this book, together with all their lines of descent from the later Plantagenet kings.

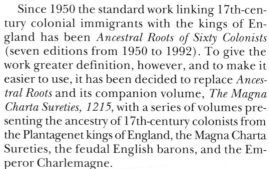

The Marquis of Ruvigny and Raineval. **The Plantagenet Roll of The Blood Royal.** The Isabel of Essex Volume, Containing the Descendants of Isabel (Plantagenet), Countess of Essex and Eu. (1908) reprint 1994. Indexed. Illus.
Cloth. $45.00. 698 pp. .... Vendor G0010

The Marquis of Ruvigny and Raineval. **The Plantagenet Roll of The Blood Royal.** The Mortimer-Percy Volume, Containing the Descendants of Lady Elizabeth Percy, nee Mortimer. (1911) reprint 1994. Indexed. Illus.
Cloth. $45.00 . 650 pp. .... Vendor G0010

The Marquis of Ruvigny and Raineval. **The Blood Royal of Britain [in One Volume] and the Plantagenet Roll of the Blood Royal [in four volumes].** Indexed. Illus.
See above listings.
Cloth. $235.00/set. .... Vendor G0010

Pine, L. G. **New Extinct Peerage.** Illus.
Extinct, dormant, abeyant, and suspended; 1884-1971. Brings Burke's work up-to-date. Arms and pedigrees.
Cloth. £48.00. 368 pp. .... Vendor G0616

Redlich, Marcellus Donald Alexander R. von. **Pedigrees of Some of the Emperor Charlemagne's Descendants,** Volume I. With a Foreword by Prof. Arthur Adams. (1941) reprint 1996. Indexed.
Cloth. $25.00. 320 pp. .... Vendor G0010

Rixford, Elizabeth M. Leach. **Families Directly Descended from All the Royal Families in Europe (495 to 1932) & Mayflower Descendants.** (1932) reprint 1992. Indexed. Illus.
Paper. $28.00. 190 pp. .... Vendor G0011

Roberts, Gary Boyd, and William Addams Reitwiesner. **American Ancestors and Cousins of the Princess of Wales.** 1984. Indexed. Illus.
Cloth. $14.95. 194 pp. .... Vendor G0010

Roberts, Gary Boyd. **Ancestors of American Presidents, First Definitive Edition.** 1995. Indexed. Illus.
Most people with ancestors in America before 1750 are related to one or more presidents, so the extensive ancestor tables, charts, and bibliography will help millions trace their own ancestry.
Cloth. $38.00. xix + 457 pp. .... Vendor G0198

Roberts, Gary Boyd. **Notable Kin.** 1997. Indexed.
Will help millions find their relationships to world leaders, tycoons, movie stars, and rogues.
Contact vendor for information. Approx. 350 pp. .... Vendor G0198

Roberts, Gary Boyd. **The Royal Descents of 500 Immigrants** to the American Colonies or the United States Who Were Themselves Notable or Left Descendants Notable in American History. 1993. Indexed.
Cloth. $45.00. 700 pp. .... Vendor G0010

Robertson, Wyndham, and Robert A. Brock. **Pocahontas, Alias Matoaka,** and Her Descendants Through Her Marriage at Jamestown, Virginia in April, 1614, With John Rolfe, Gentleman. (1887) reprint 1993.
Cloth. $10.00. 84 pp. .... Vendor G0010

Round, J. Horace. **Studies in Peerage and Family History**. (1901) reprint 1996. Indexed.
Paper. $39.95. 496 pp. .... Vendor G0011

Shaw, William A. **The Knights of England**. A Complete Record from the Earliest Time to the Present Day of the Knights of all the Orders of Chivalry in England, Scotland, and Ireland . . . 2 vols. (1906) reprint 1995.
Paper. $95.00. 1,316 pp. in all. .... Vendor G0011

Stuart, Roderick W. **Royalty for Commoners**. The Complete Known Lineage of John of Gaunt, Son of Edward III, King of England, and Queen Philippa. Rev. 2nd ed. 1995. Indexed.
Cloth. $30.00. 277 pp. .... Vendor G0010

Tucker, Leslie R. **Aristocratic and Royal Ancestors**. 1991. Illus.
    All lines traced in Turton and Moriarity. Includes biographical and siblings.
Hard cover. $59.95. 938 pp. .... Vendor G0516

Turton, Lt.-Col. W. H. **The Plantagenet Ancestry,** Being Tables Showing Over 7,000 of the Ancestors of Elizabeth (Daughter of Edward IV and Wife of Henry VII) the Heiress of the Plantagenets. (1928) reprint 1993. Indexed.
Cloth. $50.00. 274 pp. .... Vendor G0010

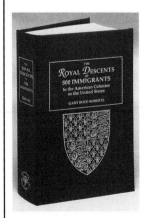

Weis, Frederick Lewis. **Ancestral Roots of Certain American Colonists,** Who Came to America before 1700. The Lineage of Alfred the Great, Charlemagne, Malcomb of Scotland, Robert the Strong, and Some of Their Descendants. With additions and corrections by Walter L. Sheppard, Jr.; assisted by David Faris. 1992. 7th ed. 1995. Indexed.
Cloth. $25.00. 274 pp. .... Vendor G0010

Weis, Frederick Lewis, and Arthur Adams. **The Magna Charta Sureties, 1215**. The Barons Named in the Magna Charta, 1215 and Some of Their Descendants Who Settled in America, 1607-1650. With additions and corrections by Walter L. Sheppard, Jr.; with David Faris. 4th ed. (1991) reprint 1993. Indexed.
Cloth. Contact vendor for information. 196 pp. .... Vendor G0010

ꙮ Textbooks, Guides, and Handbooks ꙮ

Akeret, Robert U. **Family Tales, Family Wisdom**. Published by William Morrow & Co., Inc. 1991.
    Tells how to get parents, grandparents, and other elders to tell the stories of their lives.
Paper. $17.00. 236 pp. .... Vendor G0627

Alessi, Jean, and Jan Miller. **Once Upon a Memory, Your Family Tales and Treasures**. 1987.
    Ideas and techniques to help create an interesting family history; includes tips on everything from interviewing today's senior family members to researching the family tree and writing a family history.
Paper. $7.95. 126 pp. .... Vendor G0611

Allen, Desmond Walls, and Carolyn Earle Billingsley. **Beginner's Guide to Family History Research, Third Edition**. 1997. Indexed. Illus.
Paper. $7.95. 70 pp. .... Vendor G0064

Arnold, Jackie Smith. **Kinship: It's All Relative**. 2nd ed. (1994) reprint 1996.
    The author explains everything there is to know about kinship and all of its complexities.
Paper. $9.95. 120 pp. .... Vendor G0010

Arthur, Stephen, and Julia Arthur. **Your Life and Times**. (1987) reprint 1994.
    With this oral history handbook as a guide, you will be able to record your life experiences on tape.
Paper. $8.95. 50 pp. .... Vendor G0010

Balhuizen, Anne Ross. **Getting Started**. Illus.
Paper. $12.00. 96 pp. + charts. .... Vendor G0574

Balhuizen, Anne Ross. **Searching on Location**. 1992.
    A guide for planning and carrying out a successful research trip.
Paper. $8.95. 112 pp. .... Vendor G0570

Bannister, Shala Mills. **Family Treasures:** Videotaping Your Family History. A Guide for Preserving Your Family's Living History as an Heirloom for Future Generations. 1994. Illus.
Paper. $11.95. 97 pp. .... Vendor G0011

Barnes, Donald R., and Richard S. Lackey. **Write It Right:** A Manual for Writing Family Histories and Genealogies. (1983) reprint 1988. Indexed.
A companion volume to *Cite Your Sources* (see Lackey, Richard S.), providing genealogists with an easily understood guide for writing a family history or genealogical articles or books.
Paper. $7.95 + $1.00 (MD residents must pay sales tax). 124 pp. .... Vendor G0637

Baumann, Roland M., ed. **A Manual of Archival Techniques.** 1982. Illus.
Contains basic and general essays by leading archivists, offering a ground-level approach for those working with smaller collections.
Paper. $5.95. 132 pp. .... Vendor G0554

Baxter, Angus. **Do's and Don'ts for Ancestor-Hunters.** 1988.
Paper. $10.95. 115 pp. .... Vendor G0010

Beach, Mark. **Editing Your Newsletter: How to Produce an Effective Publication Using Traditional Tools and Computers**. 1988.
A guide to managing production of a newsletter from planning through distribution.
Paper. $18.95. 168 pp. .... Vendor G0611

Beach, Mark. **Newsletter Sourcebook**. 1993.
Everything you need to know about producing your own newsletter is here.
Paper. $26.95. 137 pp. .... Vendor G0611

Billingsley, Carolyn Earle, and Desmond Walls Allen. **How to Become a Professional Genealogist**. 1991. Indexed. Illus.
Paper. $5.95. 28 pp. .... Vendor G0064

Boyer, Carl, 3rd. **How to Publish and Market Your Family History**. 4th ed. 1993. Indexed. Illus.
Guaranteed to answer all questions and save much time and money.
Cloth. $20.50. 160 pp. .... Vendor G0198

Brigham, Nancy. **How to Do Leaflets, Newsletters & Newspapers**. 1991.
Includes the latest on desktop publishing, legal rights, computer services, using color, sources for facts and art, and mailing rules and rates.
Paper. $14.95. 176 pp. .... Vendor G0611

Brown, Vandella. **Celebrating the Family: Steps to Planning a Family Reunion**. 1991.
Step-by-step guide to planning a family reunion.
Paper. $9.95. 64 pp. .... Vendor G0570

Buchman, Dian Dincin and Seli Groves. **The Writer's Digest Guide to Manuscript Formats**. 1987.
A complete manual to standard manuscript formats.
Cloth. $18.95. 198 pp. .... Vendor G0611

Bukke, et al. **The Comprehensive Genealogical Feast Day Calendar**. 1983.
A complete guide to feast days.
Spiral bound. $13.95. 119 pp. .... Vendor G0611

Cache Genealogical Library. **Handbook for Genealogical Correspondence**.
An analysis of the problems and procedures involved in genealogical correspondence.
Paper. $20.00. 274 pp. .... Vendor G0618

Camp, A. J. **First Steps in Family History**. 2nd ed. 1996.
A British book published by the Society of Genealogists.
Paper. £1.45. 32 pp. .... Vendor G0557

Carmicheal, David. **Organizing Archival Records: A Practical Method of Arrangement and Description for Small Archives**. 1993. Indexed. Illus.
A clear and concise guide for cataloging and conserving records for small archives and historical societies. Includes step-by-step instructions, as well as illustrations and exercises.
Paper. $9.95. 54 pp. .... Vendor G0554

Carroll, F. Michael. **Portrait of My Family**. n.d.
Cloth. $10.95. Approx. 140 pp. .... Vendor G0010

Carson, Dina C. **Easy and Affordable Video Production for Genealogical and Historical Societies and Their Members: A Step-by-Step Guide to Planning, Equipment Preparation, and Video Production**. 1993. Indexed. Illus.
Cloth, $60.00. Paper, $21.95. 104 pp. .... Vendor G0523

Carson, Dina C. **Easy and Affordable Video Production for Genealogical and Historical Societies and Their Members, Seminar Teaching Guide: Everything You Need to Conduct this Seminar . . . Even if You Have Never Given a Seminar Before**. 1993. Indexed. Illus.
Paper. $69.95. 134 pp. .... Vendor G0523

Carson, Dina C. **The Genealogy and Local History Researcher's Self Publishing Guide—2nd Edition**. 1993. Indexed. Illus.
If compiling and publishing your family history is something you've been wanting to do, and have been putting off, try the approach outlined in this book!
Cloth, $60.00. Paper, $21.95. 204 pp. .... Vendor G0523

Carson, Dina C. **Self-Publishing for Genealogy and Local History Researchers, Seminar Teaching Guide: Everything You Need to Conduct This Seminar . . . Even if You Have Never Given a Seminar Before**. 1992. Indexed. Illus.
Paper. $89.95. 164 pp. .... Vendor G0523

Carter, Fran. **On Teaching Genealogy**. Illus.
Paper. $9.95. .... Vendor G0552

Cerny, Johni, and Arlene Eakle. **Ancestry's Guide to Research: Case Studies in American Genealogy**. 1985.
Step-by-step instruction in genealogical research using the case-study approach.
Paper. $19.95. 364 pp. .... Vendor G0570

Collins, Rae P. **Forward to the Past**. Another Journey in Ancestry. 1995. Indexed. Illus.
A practical guide offering helpful advice to the would-be family researcher. Using her family history as an example, the author describes how a genealogical line can be traced forward.
Paper. $15.95. iv + 156 pp. .... Vendor G0576

Collins, Ron. **A Genealogy Primer and Sources Listing**.
A compilation of public domain articles on how to get started in developing your family history.
Paper. $20.00. 145 pp. .... Vendor G0160

Costello, Margaret F., and Jane Fletcher Fiske. **Guidelines for Genealogical Writing**. 1990.
Paper. $4.00. 24 pp. .... Vendor G0406

Craig, H. **The Family Record: A Unique Way of Recording Your Family Tree**.
Published in Scotland by the Aberdeen & North East Scotland Family History Society.
Paper. £2.40. .... Vendor G0555

Crandall, Ralph J. **Shaking Your Family Tree**. Published by Yankee Publishing. 1986. Indexed. Illus.
A basic guidebook for tracing your family's genealogy.
Paper. $10.95. 256 pp. .... Vendor G0627

Croom, Emily Anne. **The Genealogist's Companion and Sourcebook**. 1994.
Paper. $16.99. 256 pp. .... Vendor G0580

Croom, Emily Anne. **Unpuzzling Your Past: A Basic Guide to Genealogy**. 3rd ed. 1995.
A complete genealogical research guide. Handy forms, sample letters, and a comprehensive resource list.
Paper. $14.99. 176 pp. .... Vendor G0580

Croom, Emily Anne. **The Unpuzzling Your Past Workbook: Essential Forms and Letters for All Genealogists**. 1996.
Includes forty-two genealogical forms designed to make organizing, searching, record-keeping, and presenting information effortless.
Paper. $15.99. 320 pp. .... Vendor G0580

Culligan. **You, Too, Can Find Anybody: A Reference Manual**. 1994.
Written by a private investigator to teach the layman how to locate missing persons through driver's licenses, occupational licenses, nationwide telephone listings, and more.
Paper. $19.95. 368 pp. .... Vendor G0611

Curran, Joan Ferris. **Numbering Your Genealogy: Sound and Simple Systems**. Illus.
Explains the four recommended numbering systems.
Paper. $5.00. 16 pp. .... Vendor G0627

Davis, John. **Not Merely Ancestors**. A Guide for Teaching Genealogy in the Schools. (1993) reprint 1997.
Paper. $12.50. 80 pp. .... Vendor G0011

Doane, Gilbert H., and James B. Bell. **Searching for Your Ancestors: The How and Why of Genealogy**. 6th ed. (1977) reprint 1992. Indexed.
Contact vendor for information. xvii + 334 pp. .... Vendor G0639

Dollarhide, William. **Genealogy Starter Kit**. (1994) reprint 1996.
Paper. $8.95. 32 pp. .... Vendor G0010

Dollarhide, William. **Managing a Genealogical Project**. (1988, rev. 1991) reprint 1996.
Paper. $14.95. 98 pp. .... Vendor G0010

Doyle, John J. **Genealogical Use of Catholic Records in North America**. (1978) reprint 1992.
Paper. $5.75. 28 pp. .... Vendor G0109

Eakle, Arlene H., Ph.D. **American Cities**. 1994. Illus.
Includes all-black towns, Hispanic townsites; 40 maps; Mississippi, Missouri, and Ohio River systems; locations of tobacco inspection warehouses in Virginia.
Paper. $26.50. 53 pp. .... Vendor G0504

Eakle, Arlene H., Ph.D., presenter. **Do Your Family Tree: Instructional Videos**. 2 videos. 1992.

Rated four stars by ABC Video Guide. Programmed learning, from how to fill out a pedigree chart to using occupations to extend your family tree. Part I, 50 minutes; Part II, 75 minutes.

$29.95 each/$53.00/set .... Vendor G0504

Eakle, Arlene H., Ph.D. **8,000 Little-Used Biography and Genealogy Sources**. 1987. Illus.

Guide to key indexes for over 6 million American biographies, chronicles, "mugbooks," unique ancestors; and examples of various formats for biographical data.

Paper. $29.50. 106 pp. .... Vendor G0504

Eakle, Arlene H., Ph.D. **How to Trace Your Pedigree Ladies**. (1988) reprint 1996. Illus.

Eight strategies for tracing women with examples for each strategy. Extensive bibliography of sources. Three search checklists.

Paper. $22.00. 76 pp. .... Vendor G0504

Eakle, Arlene H., Ph.D. **Teacher's Kit: Research Notekeeping and Analysis of Evidence**. (1988) revised 1990. Illus.

William Dollarhide GENEALOGY STARTER KIT

8½" x 11". 32 pp., paperback. 1994.
Vendor G0010. $8.95

This booklet was written as a guide for the raw beginner, although for the more experienced researcher it can be used as a handy guide to essential information sources. It begins with a **How to Start** section in which author William Dollarhide outlines his unique seven-step system for gathering facts essential for any genealogical project: interviewing family members, contacting relatives, writing for death records, following up on death records, census searching, LDS Library searching, and state and county searching. These are the building blocks of genealogical research, the only prerequisites demanded of the researcher. A **Where to Find More** section follows, giving the names and addresses of specific places to obtain more information, including a list of vital records offices for all fifty states, a list of the various branches of the National Archives, and a breakdown, by region, of the major genealogical libraries and societies in the country. Also included are genealogical forms which can be used to keep track of the information gathered.

Genealogical Publishing Co., Inc.

Twelve transparencies, instruction guide, sample case history for student application, coordinated content.
Paper. $56.00. 63 pp. .... Vendor G0504

Eichholz, Alice, ed. **Ancestry's Red Book: American State, County, & Town Sources**. Rev. ed. 1992.
Contains information on the holdings of every county in the United States.
Hard-cover. $49.95. 858 pp. .... Vendor G0570

Eichholz, Alice. **Discovering Your Heritage**. 1987.
An introduction to family history.
Paper. $2.95. 32 pp. .... Vendor G0570

Epperson, Gwenn F. **New Netherland Roots**. (1994) reprint 1995. Illus.
Cloth. $20.00. 176 pp. .... Vendor G0010

Everton Publishers, Inc. **The Handy Book for Genealogists**. 8th ed. Indexed. Illus.
Provides information on how to find information about county and state records. Includes 56 maps. More copies of this research book are in print than any other genealogical publication.
Cloth. $31.95. .... Vendor G0618

FFHS. How to Tackle Your Family History: A Preliminary Guide for the Beginner. Revised and updated. 1992.
A British book published by the Federation of Family History Societies.
£1.55 (overseas surface). 6 pp. .... Vendor G0588

FFHS. Practice Makes Perfect (A Genealogical Workbook). 1993.
A British book published by the Federation of Family History Societies.
£6.50 (overseas surface). 84 pp. .... Vendor G0588

FFHS. Sources for Family History in the Home.
A British book published by the Federation of Family History Societies.
£2.00 (overseas surface). .... Vendor G0588

FGS. Family Associations Organization and Management Handbook.
Paper. $12.95 + $2.00 p&h. .... Vendor G0643

FGS. Guide for the Organization & Management of Genealogical Societies.
Paper. $15.00 + $2.00 p&h. .... Vendor G0643

FGS. Organizing Archival Records.
Paper. $18.00. .... Vendor G0643

FGS. A Primer for Local Historical Societies.
Paper. $16.00 + $2.00 p&h. .... Vendor G0643

Fletcher, William. **Recording Your Family History.** 1986.
Paper. $9.95. 313 pp. .... Vendor G0552

Friedman. **A History of American Law.** 1985.
Excellent background reading.The history of American law from its beginnings in the colonies. Every genealogist will benefit from studying this book.
Paper. $22.00. 781 pp. .... Vendor G0611

Frisch, Karen. **Unlocking the Secrets in Old Photographs.** 1991.
Paper. $14.95. 202 pp. .... Vendor G0570

Gale Research. **Genealogy Sourcebook Series.** 4 vols. Indexed.
Includes *African American Genealogical Sourcebook* (see "Religious and Ethnic Groups—African American"), *Asian American Genealogical Sourcebook* (see "Religious and Ethnic Groups—Asian American"), *Hispanic American Genealogical Sourcebook (see "Religious and Ethnic Groups— Hispanic")*, and *Native American Genealogical Sourcebook* (see "Religious and Ethnic Groups—Native American/ Indian").
Cloth. $239.00/set. Approx. 1,000 pp. .... Vendor G0560

Gandy, M. **Basic Approach to Latin for Family Historians.** 1995.
A British book published by the Federation of Family History Societies.
£2.00 (overseas surface). 16 pp. .... Vendor G0588

Gandy, M. **An Introduction to Planning Research: Short Cuts in Family History.** 1993.
A British book published by the Federation of Family History Societies.
£3.65 (overseas surface). 60 pp. .... Vendor G0588

Ginzburg. **Clues, Myths, and the Historical Method**. 1989.
Explores in a more direct way the questions of historical method and historical knowledge. Push beyond the simple "clues" of historical evidence to tease out the hidden information embedded in them. Ginzberg challenges us to retrieve a cultural and social world that more conventional history does not record.
Paper. $13.95. 231 pp. .... Vendor G0611

Gooldy, Pat. **21 Things I Wish I'd Found**.
Paper. $6.00. 24 pp. .... Vendor G0574

Gooldy, Ray. **Helpful Hints for the Genealogical Librarian**.
Paper. $7.00. 23 pp. .... Vendor G0574

Gouldrup, Lawrence P. **Writing the Family Narrative**. 1987.
A clear and concise explanation of how to write your family history.
Paper. $12.95. 157 pp. .... Vendor G0570

Gouldrup, Lawrence P. **Writing the Family Narrative Workbook**. 1993.
A companion to the above book. Takes you step-by-step through the writing process.
Paper. $16.95. 168 pp. .... Vendor G0570

Greenwood, Val D. **The Researcher's Guide to American Genealogy**. 2nd ed. (1990) reprint 1996. Indexed. Illus.
Cloth. $24.95. 623 pp. .... Vendor G0010

Hackleman, Phyllis A. **Reunion Planner**. (1993) reprint 1995. Indexed. Illus.
Paper. $12.95. 133 pp. .... Vendor G0011

Harper. **Guide to the Draper Manuscripts**. 1983. Indexed.
A vast collection of letters, documents, personal interviews, and clippings containing much genealogical and historical data on frontier descendants.
Cloth. $30.00. 464 pp. .... Vendor G0611

Hatcher, Patricia Law, and John V. Wylie. **Indexing Family Histories**. 1993.
Leads the genealogist step-by-step through the planning and production of a thorough and systematic index that will enhance all types of family histories.
Paper. $5.00. 22 pp. .... Vendor G0627

Hatcher, Patricia Law. **Producing a Quality Family History**. 1996.
Paper. $17.95. 286 pp. .... Vendor G0570

Heisey, John W. **Genealogical Research and Organization**.
Paper. $12.00. 46 pp. .... Vendor G0574

Heisey, John W. **Genealogists' Guide to Washington D.C.**
Paper. $8.00. 24 pp. .... Vendor G0574

Hey. **The Oxford Guide to Family History**. 1993.
An essential guide to family history research. Written by an English family historian, with a decidedly English focus. This beautifully illustrated volume offers authoritative advice on tracing your family and suggests ways of broadening your research to look at the history of their times.
Cloth. $35.00. 246 pp. .... Vendor G0611

Val D. Greenwood

THE RESEARCHER'S GUIDE TO AMERICAN GENEALOGY

2nd edition!

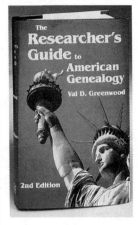

The
**Researcher's
Guide** to
**American
Genealogy**
Val D. Greenwood

2nd Edition

623 pp., illus., indexed, cloth. 1990. **Vendor G0010. $24.95**

In every field of study there is one book that rises above the rest in stature and authority and becomes the standard work in the field. In genealogy that book is Val Greenwood's *Researcher's Guide to American Genealogy.*

This completely revised second edition, updated to include all major developments in the field, is an essential text for the present generation of researchers in American genealogy. While it instructs the researcher in the timeless principles of genealogical research, it also identifies the various classes of records employed in that research, groups them in convenient tables and charts, gives their location, explains their uses, and evaluates each of them in the context of the research process. Designed to answer practically all the researcher's needs, it is both a textbook and an all-purpose reference book. And it is this singular combination that makes *The Researcher's Guide* the book of choice in any genealogical investigation. It is also the reason why if you can afford to buy only one book on American genealogy in a lifetime, this has to be it.

Genealogical Publishing Co., Inc.

Jacobson, Judy. **A Genealogist's Refresher Course**. 2nd ed. 1996.
Paper. $12.00. 96 pp. .... Vendor G0011

Jacobus, Donald Lines, ed. **The American Genealogist 1932-1965, Eleven Volumes**. 1989. Indexed.
Book #1144
Cloth. $825.00. 10,000 pp. .... Vendor G0082

Jacobus, Donald Lines. **Genealogy As Pastime and Profession**. 2nd ed. (1968) reprint 1996.
Paper. $8.95. 120 pp. .... Vendor G0010

Jarausch. **Quantitative Methods for Historians: A Guide to Research, Data, & Statistics**. 1991.
Introduction to quantitative methods specifically for historians.
Paper. $12.95. 246 pp. .... Vendor G0611

Jaussi, Laureen R. **Genealogy Fundamentals**. 1994. Indexed. Illus.
Twelve basic lessons with step-by-step instructions are correlated to each of the thirty-nine chapters. Library reference sections include recommended gazetteers, vital

record repositories, International Genealogical Index batch numbers, card system for note keeping, and sample letters. Emphasizes genealogical research techniques at local repositories and LDS family history centers.
Cloth. $42.95. 405 pp. .... Vendor G0465

Johnson. **How to Locate Anyone Who Is or Has Been in the Military**. 6th ed., rev. 1992.
    Covers many of the strategies involved in locating 20th-century persons. Besides numerous military sources, it includes techniques utilizing driver's licenses and social security records.
Paper. $19.95. 280 pp. .... Vendor G0611

Jones, Henry Z, Jr. **Psychic Roots:** Serendipity and Intuition in Genealogy. (1993) reprint 1996. Indexed.
Paper. $14.95. 236 pp. .... Vendor G0010

Jones, Henry Z, Jr. **More Psychic Roots:** Further Adventures in Serendipity & Intuition in Genealogy. 1997. Indexed.
Paper. $16.95. xiii + 261 pp. .... Vendor G0010

Kammen, Carol. **Plain as Pipestem—Essays about Local History**. 1989.
    Includes nineteen articles originally printed in "New York History" covering a wide range of subjects—designed to give guidance to local and family historians.
Paper. $15.00. 144 pp. .... Vendor G0093

Kanin, Ruth. **Write the Story of Your Life**. (1981) reprint 1997.
Contact vendor for information. 219 pp. .... Vendor G0011

Kemp, Thomas Jay. **International Vital Records Handbook**. 3rd ed. (1994) reprint 1996.
Paper. $29.95. 430 pp. .... Vendor G0010

Kirkham, E. Kay. **The Handwriting of American Records for a Period of 300 Years**.
This is the story behind writing and writing materials—the American alphabet through 300 years including many samples of old handwriting.
Paper. $11.00. 106 pp. .... Vendor G0618

Kirkham, E. Kay. **A Handy Guide to Record Searching in the Larger Cities of the United States**. Indexed. Illus.
Guide to vital records, some maps with street indexes, and other information of genealogical value for some of the larger cities in the U.S.
Paper. $13.00. 133 pp. .... Vendor G0618

Kirkham, E. Kay. **Professional Techniques and Tactics in American Genealogical Research**.
Paper. $9.00. 82 pp. .... Vendor G0618

Kirkpatrick, Kathy. **Basic Genealogy (Including Steps Sometimes Forgotten by the Pros)**. 1995.
A step-by-step guide to researching your family history.
Paper. $15.95. 125 pp. .... Vendor G0769

Kitchel, Dwain L. **Writing and Marketing a Family History in the mid-1990s**. (1990) reprint 1994. Indexed. Illus.
Paper. $9.50. 85 pp. .... Vendor G0183

Lackey, Richard S. **Cite Your Sources:** A Manual for Documenting Family Histories and Genealogical Records. Introduction by Winston DeVille. 1980. Indexed.
Paper. $9.95 + postage. xii + 94 pp. .... Vendor G0638

Latham, William. **How to Find Your Family Roots**. (1994) reprint 1996.
How to trace your family history in an easy and inexpensive manner. Updated in 1996!
Paper. $15.95. 224 pp. .... Vendor G0490

Light. **House Histories: A Guide to Tracing the Genealogy of Your Home**. 1993.
An excellent guide to researching the history of a house.
Paper. $14.95. 300 pp. .... Vendor G0611

Mann. **A Guide to Library Research Methods**. 1986.
Successful research demands a knowledge of techniques, a knowledge of sources, and a great deal of persistence. Problem-solving techniques for the age of the information explosion.
Cloth, $23.00. Paper, $10.95. 199 pp. .... Vendor G0611

Mann. **Library Research Models: A Guide to Classification, Cataloging, and Computers**. 1993.
Most researchers, even with computers, find only a fraction of the sources relevant to their interest. Learn to use the library more effectively.
Cloth, $22.50. Paper, $14.95. 248 pp. .... Vendor G0611

Maxwell, Fay. **Laws and Religions 4713 B.C. to 1948 A.D., First Facts in World Order**. 1968.
ISBN 1-885463-15-4.
Paper. $17.00. 23 pp. .... Vendor G0135

McCusker. **How Much Is That in Real Money?** A Historical Price Index for Use as a Deflator of Money Values in the Economy of the U.S. 1991.
An economic historian, McCusker compiled a complete reference for converting prices from as far back as 1700, even those expressed in colonial currency of pounds, shillings, and pence, to their comparable values in today's dollars. Conversions going back to 1600, England.
Paper. $10.95. 76 pp. .... Vendor G0611

McCusker. **Money & Exchange in Europe and America, 1600-1775: A Handbook**. 1978.
A more far-ranging study of monetary values than the title above, McCusker sets out to examine all of Europe and America during this period. The extensive bibliography and footnotes should prove useful for further study.
Paper. $32.50. 367 pp. .... Vendor G0611

McCutcheon. **The Writer's Guide to Everyday Life in the 1800's**. 1993.
Intended for use by writers of historical fiction, this book will not only help define archaic terms, but also aid in your writing.
Cloth. $18.95. 308 pp. .... Vendor G0611

McDowell, Vera. **When Your Ox Is in the Ditch**. Genealogical How-to Letters. (1995) reprint 1996.
Paper. $19.95. 161 pp. .... Vendor G0010

McGrady, L. J. **How to Publish Your Genealogy**.
Paper. $8.00. 72 pp. .... Vendor G0574

McLaughlin, E. **Interviewing Elderly Relatives**.
A British publication.
Paper. £1.95. .... Vendor G0555

McLaughlin, E. **Laying Out a Pedigree**.
A British publication.
Paper. £1.00. .... Vendor G0555

McLaughlin, E. **No Time for Family History?**
A British publication.
Paper. £1.25. .... Vendor G0555

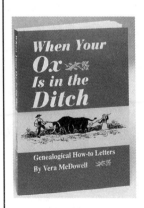

McLaughlin, E. **Reading Old Hand Writing**.
A British publication.
Paper. £1.50. .... Vendor G0555

McLaughlin, E. **Simple Latin for Family Historians**.
A British publication.
Paper. £1.50. .... Vendor G0555

McPhail, David R. **General Principles of United States Genealogical Research:
Using the Family History Library in Salt Lake City**. 1995.
A useful guide to using the Family History Library of Salt Lake City. Geared
toward the beginner.
Spiral bound. $13.95. 88 pp. .... Vendor G0611

Meshenberg, Michael J. **Documents of Our Ancestors: A Selection of Reproducible Genealogy Forms and Tips for Using Them**. 1996.
Paper. $19.95. 148 pp. .... Vendor G0559

Meyerink, Kory L. **Printed Sources: A Guide to Published Genealogical Records**.
1997.
Cloth. $49.95. Contact vendor for availability. .... Vendor G0570

Mokotoff, Gary. **How to Document Victims and Locate Survivors of the
Holocaust**.
Paper. $25.95. 208 pp. .... Vendor G0559

Muran, Lois Kay. **Family Tree Questionnaire**. 1995.
Consists of fill-in-the-blank entries for recording genealogical information on each
member in the family.
Paper. $12.00. 108 pp. .... Vendor G0011

National Archives. **Guide to Federal Records in the National Archives of the United
States**. 3 vols. 1987. Updated 1995. Indexed.
Cloth. $95.00. Approx. 1,500 pp. .... Vendor G0565

National Archives. **Guide to Genealogical Research in the National Archives**. 1982.
Rev. ed. 1985. Illus.
Explains what records are preserved in the National Archives and what specific
information about individuals is included in each type of record.
Cloth, $35.00. Paper, $25.00. 304 pp. .... Vendor G0565

Neagles, James C. **The Library of Congress: A Guide to Genealogical and Historical Research**. 1990.
Cloth. $39.95. 382 pp. .... Vendor G0570

Neubauer, Joan R. **Dear Diary**. 1995.
Tips for writing a creative journal.
Paper. $8.95. 64 pp. .... Vendor G0570

Neubauer, Joan R. **From Memories to Manuscript: The Five-Step Method of Writing Your Life Story**. 1994.
A handbook intended to help you write a quality autobiography.
Paper. $7.95. Also available as a set with Dear Diary (see above listing), $15.50. 40
pp. .... Vendor G0570

Newman, Debra L., comp. **Black History: A Guide to the Civilian Records in the National Archives**. 1984. Illus.
Cloth, $25.00. Paper, $15.00. 379 pp. .... Vendor G0565

Nichols, Elizabeth L. **Genealogy in the Computer Age: Understanding FamilySearch® (Ancestral File™, International Genealogical Index™, Social Security Death Index)**. Rev. ed. 1994. Illus.
Describes the programs and files published by The Church of Jesus Christ of Latter-day Saints (LDS Church, Mormons, Genealogical Society of Utah)—available in Salt Lake City, Utah, at most of the over 2,000 family history centers (branches of the Mormon Library in Salt Lake City), and at many public and private genealogical societies and libraries. (FamilySearch is not currently available for private purchase.) ALA recommended; book-club featured.
Paper. $11.45. 56 pp. .... Vendor G0203

Nichols, Elizabeth L. **Genealogy in the Computer Age: Understanding FamilySearch®, vol. 2 (Personal Ancestral File® [PAF], Family History Library Catalog™, More Resource Files, and Using Them All in Harmony)**. 1997.
Volume 2 describes additional components of FamilySearch and expands instruction to provide direction on how all FamilySearch programs and files may be used in harmony.
Contact vendor for information. .... Vendor G0203

Nichols, Elizabeth L. **The Genesis of Your Genealogy: Step-by-Step Instruction Books for the Beginner in Family History, 3rd Edition**. 1992. Illus.
Introduces you to family history and genealogy, its sources, resources, forms, terminology, and all the basic how-tos, including computers in finding, organizing, and sharing your information; selected as a required university and community college textbook.
Paper. $10.45. 74 pp. .... Vendor G0203

Palgrave-Moore, P. **How to Record Your Family Tree**. 5th ed. 1991.
A British book published by the Federation of Family History Societies.
£2.25 (overseas surface). 32 pp. .... Vendor G0588

Parker, J. Carlyle. **Going to Salt Lake City to Do Family History Research**. 1996. Indexed. Illus.
Third edition, revised and expanded. Also includes the use of Family History Centers, public libraries, and home sources.
Paper. $18.45. 262 pp. .... Vendor G0492

Pehrson, Helga. **Order**.
This is an instruction book that shows you how to record your ancestors and how to number them on pedigree charts.
Paper. $16.00. 190 pp. .... Vendor G0618

Peters, Joan W. **Local Records and Genealogy: A Primer for Family Historians**. (1990) reprint 1992. Illus.
This volume has been called the courthouse researcher's best friend! The use of census returns with the requisite county court records can be of inestimable value to a family historian. This guide helps make these records less intimidating and mysterious to those seeking to compile a history of their family's past.
Paper. $12.95. 71 pp. .... Vendor G0074

Pine, L. G. **Guide to Titles & Forms of Address.**
A useful guide to the puzzling problems of written and spoken address. Origins of various noble and clerical titles are also given.
Paper. £4.50. .... Vendor G0616

Polking, Kirk. **Writing Family Histories and Memoirs.** 1995.
Guides the reader in writing a family history and other areas such as coverage of legal issues, a sample genealogical chart, and a questionnaire to help you get answers from faraway relatives.
Paper. $15.00. 250 pp. .... Vendor G0611

Pols, R. **Dating Old Photographs.** 2nd ed. 1995.
A British book published by the Federation of Family History Societies.
£6.00 (overseas surface). 83 pp. .... Vendor G0588

Pols, R. **Understanding Old Photographs.** 1995.
A British book published by the Federation of Family History Societies.
£6.00 (overseas surface). 86 pp. .... Vendor G0588

Reeder, Josh. **Indexing Genealogy Publications.** 1994. Indexed.
Paper. $13.90 + $2.00 p&h. 48 pp. .... Vendor G0644

Rose, Christine, CG, CGL, FASG. **Family Associations: Organization & Management.** 2nd ed. rev. 1994. Indexed.
Paper. 71 pp. .... Vendor G0474

Rubincam, Milton. **Evidence: An Exemplary Study—A Craig Family Case History.** Indexed.
A study in genealogical evidence. Demonstrates how one goes about assembling data from original sources, evaluating the evidence, arriving at conclusions, and putting the pieces together.
Paper. $6.00. 41 pp. .... Vendor G0627

Rubincam, Milton. **Pitfalls in Genealogical Research.** 1987.
Designed to help the beginning genealogist recognize and avoid the pitfalls and major problems of genealogical research.
Paper. $7.95. 74 pp. .... Vendor G0570

Sagraves, Barbara. **A Preservation Guide: Saving the Past and the Present for the Future.** 1995.
Provides simple instructions for maintaining and storing everything from paper and photographs to motion picture film, sound recording, and textiles.
Paper. $6.95. 48 pp. .... Vendor G0570

Schaefer, Christina K. **The Center:** A Guide to Genealogical Research in the National Capital Area. 1996. Indexed. Illus.
Paper. $19.95. 160 pp. .... Vendor G0010

Schweitzer, George K. **Handbook of Genealogical Sources.** 1994. Illus.
Genealogical sources, what can be obtained from them, where to find them, and how to use them. Descriptions of 132 sources, from adoptions, ads, and archives down through War of 1812, wills, and WPA transcripts.
Paper. $15.00. 217 pp. .... Vendor G0569

*Christina K.
Schaefer*

THE CENTER
A Guide to Genealogical Research in the National Capital Area

From its first appearance in 1965 (as *Lest We Forget*), this popular guidebook has succeeded in leading the researcher through a bewildering maze of agencies, departments, and archives in the Washington, D.C. area, highlighting the unique role the D.C. area plays as a repository of genealogical materials. Completely revised and updated, *The Center* is indispensable in understanding precisely what genealogical resources are available in the nation's capital and where they can be found.

Special attention is given to the most important research facilities in the D.C. area, including the National Archives (both Archives I and Archives II), the Library of Congress, the Bureau of Land Management, the DAR Library, and the National Genealogical Society. Also covered are facilities in the D.C. area for military research, federal government agencies, nearby facilities in Maryland and Virginia, academic institutions with genealogical resources, ethnic and religious research facilities, and societies and professional organizations with genealogical resources.

Under each facility listed there is a survey of key record holdings, with a description of the records, a summary of their contents, an explanation of their organization, and directions for their use. There is also a list of published indexes and finding aids, key addresses for mail requests, publications, phone numbers and hours of business, and **an itemization of those materials available through the Family History Library system**.

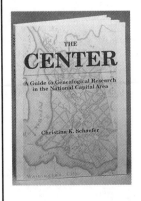

8½" x 11". 160 pp., illus., indexed, paperback. 1996.
Vendor G0010. $19.95

Genealogical Publishing Co., Inc.

Segars, J. H. **In Search of Confederate Ancestors:** The Guide. 1993. Indexed. Illus.
Paper. $12.00. 112 pp. .... Vendor G0011

Segel, Jay D. **Owner Unknown**. Your Guide to Real Estate Treasure Hunting. 1991.
Indexed.
Cloth. $17.95. 129 pp. .... Vendor G0010

Segel, Jay D. **Owner Unknown:** The Workbook. 1992.
Paper. $25.00. 96 pp. .... Vendor G0010

Shea, Jonathan D., and William F. Hoffman. **Following the Paper Trail: A Multilingual Translation Guide.**
Cloth. $29.00. 256 pp. .... Vendor G0559

Shull, Wilma Sadler. **Photographing Your Heritage**. 1988.
    Describes in detail how to use photography in doing genealogical and historical research.
Paper. $10.95. 128 pp. .... Vendor G0570

Smith, Kenneth L. **Estate Inventories: How to Use Them**. 1993.
    This helpful guide provides help in reading and interpreting inventories. Includes sections on handwriting, spelling, foreign words, abbreviations, currencies, wage rates, commodity prices, and a glossary of archaic words.
Paper. $12.50. 100 pp. .... Vendor G0611

Smith, Kenneth L. **Genealogical Dates: A User-friendly Guide**. 1994.
    Book #1396. Comes with computer disk.
Paper. $19.50. 198 pp. .... Vendor G0082

Society of American Archivists. **The WPA Historical Records Survey: A Guide to the Unpublished Inventories, Indexes, and Transcripts**. 1980.
    This guide lists repositories in the United States which hold HRS materials, and summarizes HRS holdings in each state. Detailed lists of counties, municipalities, and denominations that were covered are included on one microfiche.
Paper. $8.50. 42 pp. .... Vendor G0611

Society of Genealogists. **Family Records and Their Layout**. Rev. ed. 1994.
    A British book published by the Society of Genealogists.
Leaflet. £0.20. .... Vendor G0557

Society of Genealogists. **Genealogy as a Career**. Rev. ed. 1994.
    A British book published by the Society of Genealogists.
Leaflet. £0.20. .... Vendor G0557

Society of Genealogists. **Note Taking and Keeping for Genealogists**. Rev. ed. 1994.
    A British book published by the Society of Genealogists.
Leaflet. £0.20. .... Vendor G0557

Society of Genealogists. **Starting Genealogy**. Rev. ed. 1995.
    A British book published by the Society of Genealogists.
Leaflet. £0.20. .... Vendor G0557

Stevenson, Noel C. **Genealogical Evidence: A Guide to the Standard of Proof Relating to Pedigrees, Ancestry, Heirship and Family History**. 1989. Indexed.

Classic study of genealogical evidence written by a lawyer genealogist. Details many tricky genealogical problems. Must reading for all genealogists.
Paper. $18.95. vi + 233 pp. .... Vendor G0611

Stillman, Peter R. **Families Writing**. 1989.
Details why and how to record "the real family treasures."
Paper. $14.95. 189 pp. .... Vendor G0611

Stryker-Rodda, Harriet. **How to Climb Your Family Tree,** Genealogy for Beginners. (1977) reprint 1995.
Paper. $8.95. 144 pp. .... Vendor G0010

Stryker-Rodda, Harriet. **Understanding Colonial Handwriting**. (1986) reprint 1996.
Paper. $4.50. 26 pp. .... Vendor G0010

Stuart, Denis. **Latin for Local and Family Historians**. 1995.
A British publication by Phillimore.
Cloth. £13.95. 144 pp. .... Vendor G0579

Sturm, Duane, and Pat Sturm. **Video Family History**. 1989.
Describes equipment and techniques used in producing a family video.
Paper. $10.95. 123 pp. .... Vendor G0570

Swinnerton, I. **Basic Approach to Keeping Your Family Records**. 1995.
A British book published by the Federation of Family History Societies.
£2.00 (overseas surface). 16 pp. .... Vendor G0588

Szucs, Loretto, and Sandra Luebking. **The Source: A Guidebook of American Genealogy**. 2nd ed. 1997.
Cloth. $49.95. 834 pp. .... Vendor G0570

Terhune, Jim. **Start Your Own Newsletter from Scratch**. 1996. Illus.
Paper. $9.95. 68 pp. .... Vendor G0011

Titford, John. **Writing & Publishing Your Family History**. 1996.
A British book that discusses how to collect your family history material; how to organize and arrange it into book form; how to decide on the size, shape, and number of illustrations; and how to get it published.
£6.00 (overseas surface). 128 pp. .... Vendor G0588

Tuttle, Craig A. **An Ounce of Preservation: A Guide to the Care of Papers and Photographs**. 1995. Indexed.
Guide for recognizing, preventing, and treating damaged papers and photographs.
Paper. $12.95. 111 pp. .... Vendor G0611

Underwood, Donald E., and Betty A. Underwood. **Searching for Lost Ancestors: A Guide to Genealogical Research**. 1993. Indexed. Illus.
This compact book covers basic genealogical research techniques as well as more advanced methodology. It also offers special individual chapters on immigrant, black, and Native American research aids and sources.
Paper. $9.00. 191 pp. .... Vendor G0026

Van Noy, Rosamond. **Your Ancestral Trail—Genealogy for Beginners**. 1995. Illus. with samples of note-keeping forms.
Paper. $10.00. 37 pp. .... Vendor G0245

Walters, Judith Allison. **A Guide to Dating Old Family Photographs**. Indexed. With 145 examples from the 1840s to 1905; descriptions, suggestions. Paper. $14.95. .... Vendor G0726

Warren, Jim, and Paula Warren. **Getting the Most Mileage from Genealogical Research Trips**. 2nd ed. 1993.
Thousands of suggestions that will make your research trip more productive and enjoyable. The authors are professional genealogists who travel extensively. Staplebound. $8.00. 50 pp. .... Vendor G0611

Westin, Jeane Eddy. **Finding Your Roots**. 1977. Reprinted. Indexed. Paper. $5.05 + p&h. Approx. 290 pp. .... Vendor G0772

Where to Write for Birth, Marriage and Death Records. Paper. $3.00. 16 pp. .... Vendor G0574

Whitaker, Beverly DeLong. **Beyond Pedigrees:** Organizing and Enhancing Your Work. 1993. Indexed. Illus.
Provides hundreds of tips for more efficient research and organization. Paper. $12.95. 104 pp. .... Vendor G0570

Whitaker, Beverly DeLong. **Getting Organized**. Paper. $10.00. 72 pp. .... Vendor G0574

Wright, Norman E. **Preserving Your American Heritage: A Guide to Family and Local History**. (1974) reprint 1981. Indexed. Illus.
This book covers the essentials of family history research, invaluable to both beginning and experienced genealogists. Excellent as the text for genealogy classes. Paper. $11.95. viii + 285 pp. .... Vendor G0611

Wright, Norman Edgar. **Adventures in Genealogy:** Case Studies in the Unusual. 1994. Indexed. Illus.
Paper. $24.95. 163 pp. .... Vendor G0011

Wright, Raymond S., III. **The Genealogist's Handbook:** Modern Methods for Researching Family History. 1995. Indexed. Illus.
Cloth. Contact vendor for information. xiv + 190 pp. .... Vendor G0781

Zimmerman, Bill. **How to Tape Instant Oral Biographies**. Published by Gaurineaux Press.
Paper. $8.50. 132 pp. .... Vendor G0559

Vital Records

AGLL. **Where to Write for Vital Records: Births, Deaths, Marriages, and Divorces**.
Pamphlet. $3.50. 20 pp. .... Vendor G0552

Kemp, Thomas Jay. **International Vital Records Handbook**. 3rd ed. (1994) reprint 1996. Paper. $29.95. 430 pp. .... Vendor G0010

Stemmons, Jack, and Diane Stemmons. **Vital Records Compendium.**
This book shows where church, civil, Bible, and other vital records can be found.
Paper. $21.50. 320 pp. .... Vendor G0618

✒ Westward Migration ✒ (Overland Trails)

Butruille, Susan G. **Women's Voices from the Oregon Trail.** 2nd ed.
Part I of this book is a collection of diaries, songs, history, poetry, and recipes creating a masterful narration of women's roles in opening the west. Part II provides a guide to women's history along the trail, showing where to find markers, signposts, landmarks, and historical sites.
Paper. $14.95. 254 pp. .... Vendor G0611

Chamberlain, Welton, ed. **Marching to California on the Emigrant Trail 1852-1853.** From a Journal Kept by Benjamin F. Chamberlain. 1995. Indexed. Illus.
A diary kept by Benjamin F. Chamberlain while traveling the emigrant trail from Dexter, Michigan to California.
Cloth. $14.95. 94 pp. .... Vendor G0735

MacGregor, Greg. **Overland: The California Emigrant Trail of 1841-1870.** 1996.
A fascinating book contrasting memories of the trail between 1841-1870 with black and white present-day photographs of the trail. MacGregor has followed the California-Oregon Trail photographing both the beautiful and the ugly. He provides us with a remarkable glimpse into this portion of our history, and the few traces that remain of it.
Paper. $37.50. 168 pp. .... Vendor G0611

Schlissel, et al. **Far From Home: Families of the Westward Journey.** 1989.
Continuing the approach she began in her previous book, *Women's Diaries of the Westward Journey* (see below), Schlissel and her co-authors use letters and diaries to recreate the lives of three families who ventured west in the mid- to late 19th century. Very interesting reading.
Paper. $14.00. 264 pp. .... Vendor G0611

Schlissel. **Women's Diaries of the Westward Journey.** 1992.
Pioneering was a family matter, and the westering experiences of American women are central to an accurate picture of what life was like on the frontier. Fascinating reading! First-hand accounts.
Paper. $14.00. 278 pp. .... Vendor G0611

Terry, Rose Caudle. **Oregon Trail Sources, Queries & Reviews Volume 1.** 1993. Indexed. Illus.
Paper. $8.95. 37 pp. .... Vendor G0061

Terry, Rose Caudle. **Oregon Trail Sources, Queries & Reviews Volume 2.** 1993. Indexed. Illus.
Paper. $8.95. 43 pp. .... Vendor G0061

Terry, Rose Caudle. **Oregon Trail Sources, Queries & Reviews Volume 3**. 1994. Indexed. Illus.
Paper. $8.95. 48 pp. .... Vendor G0061

Terry, Rose Caudle. **Oregon Trail Sources, Queries & Reviews Volume 4**. 1994. Indexed. Illus.
Queries published free.
Paper. $8.95. .... Vendor G0061

Werner. **Pioneer Children on the Journey West**. 1995.
A remarkable look through the eyes of wagon train children at the treacherous journey to the West. Told through original letters and diaries written by the children.
Cloth. $21.95. 202 pp. .... Vendor G0611

Wexler and Braun. **Atlas of Westward Expansion**. 1994.
Outstanding cartography, informative drawings and photographs, and narrative text. Utilizes historical maps, military maps, cultural maps, and period maps. A solid reference source.
Cloth, $40.00. Paper, $19.95. 288 pp. .... Vendor G0611

SECTION II: WORLD RESOURCES

 Australia

Dobson, David. **Directory of Scots in Australia 1788-1900, Part 1.**
Contact vendor for information. .... Vendor G0641

Garnsey, H., P. McIntyre [?], and A. Phippen. **The Irish Holdings of the Society of Australian Genealogists.** 1996. Indexed.
Paper. $18.50 + postage. 207 pp. .... Vendor G0563

Gray, N. **Compiling Your Family History.** 1996.
Paper. $7.95 plus postage. 80 pp. .... Vendor G0563

Hall, Nick Vine. **Tracing Your Family History in Australia: A Guide to Sources.**
2nd ed. 1994. Indexed.
Hard-cover. Contact vendor for information. 657 pp. .... Vendor G0780

Richards, J., H. Garnsey, and A. Phippen. **Index to the Microform Collection of the SAG [Society of Australian Genealogists].** 1991. Indexed.
Paper. $17.95 + postage. 410 pp. .... Vendor G0563

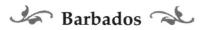 Austria

Thomsen. **Atlas of the Austro-Hungarian Empire, 1892.**
    Useful collection of maps.
Paper. $17.75. .... Vendor G0611

Barbados

Brandow, James C. **Genealogies of Barbados Families,** from *Caribbeana* and *The Journal of the Barbados Museum and Historical Society.* (1983) reprint 1997. Indexed. Illus.
Paper. $49.95. 753 pp. .... Vendor G0011

Brandow, James C. **Omitted Chapters from Hotten's Original Lists of Persons of Quality** . . . And Others Who Went from Great Britain to the American Plantations, 1600-1700. Census Returns, Parish Registers, and Militia Rolls From the Barbados Census of 1679/80. 1983. Indexed.
Cloth. $20.00. 245 pp. .... Vendor G0010

Sanders, Joanne McRee. **Barbados Records: Marriages, 1643-1800**. In Two Volumes. 1982. Indexed.
Many of the early settlers of Barbados eventually moved to the mainland and settled in Virginia, Georgia, the Carolinas, and other colonies.
Cloth. $60.00. 939 pp. .... Vendor G0011

Sanders, Joanne McRee. **Barbados Records: Wills, Vol. II: 1681-1700; Wills, Vol. III: 1701-1725.** 2 vols. 1980-81. Indexed.
Many of the early settlers of Barbados eventually moved to the mainland and settled in Virginia, Georgia, the Carolinas, and other colonies.
Cloth. $30.00/vol. 536 + 526 pp. .... Vendor G0011

✜ Bermuda ✜

Mercer, Julia E. **Bermuda Settlers of the 17th Century**. Genealogical Notes from Bermuda. (1942-1947) reprint 1992. Indexed.
Cloth. $20.00. 276 pp. .... Vendor G0010

✜ Canada ✜

General References

AGLL Canadian Census Listings, 1666-1891.
Arranged according to province, town, and year.
Paper. $15.00. 268 pp. .... Vendor G0552

Baxter, Angus. **In Search of Your Canadian Roots**. 2nd ed. (199) reprint 1995.
Paper. $16.95. 368 pp. .... Vendor G0010

Bousfield, Arthur, and Garry Toffoli. **Canada's Kings & Queens**. 1993.
A genealogical chart presenting Canada's monarchs, their families, interrelationships, and impact on Canada.
Genealogical Chart. $9.99 (cnd), $8.75 (US)....................................... Vendor G0640

Committee on Archives and History. **Guide to Family History Research in the Archival Repositories of the United Church of Canada**. 1996. Illus.
In a single source, the information to guide researchers through the complete archival network of the United Church of Canada.
Paper. $17.00 (cdn), $18.50 (US). vi + 82 pp. .... Vendor G0568

Douglas, Althea, and J. Creighton Douglas. **Canadian Railway Records: A Guide for Genealogists**. 1994.
Tells how to find the companies & archives and what types of records likely to be available.
Paper. $12.50 (cdn), $14.00 (US). 64 pp. .... Vendor G0568

Douglas, Althea. **Here be Dragons! Navigating the Hazards Found in Canadian Family Research: A Guide for Genealogists**. 1996. Illus.
Advises researchers where trouble may lurk as they delve into their Canadian roots.
Paper. $17.00 (cdn), $18.50 (US). vi + 74 pp. .... Vendor G0568

Early Notaries of Canada. With an Introduction by Rene Chartrand. 1977. Indexed.
Names all notaries appointed during the French regime, indicating where their greffes (files) are preserved today. Text in French.
Paper. $8.00. 83 pp. .... Vendor G0561

Eccles, W. J. **The Canadian Frontier, 1534-1760**. 1969. Rev. ed. 1992.
A reliable and authoritative general history of the French era in Canada. Studies the history of New France from the perspective of commerce and society.
Paper. $14.95. 238 pp. .... Vendor G0611

Angus Baxter

New
2nd edition!

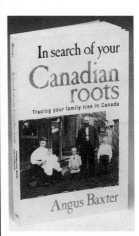

368 pp., paperback. 1994.
Vendor G0010. $16.95

IN SEARCH OF YOUR CANADIAN ROOTS

This is the first book by Angus Baxter to concentrate exclusively on the sources available for research *within* Canada. Handled with the acumen we have come to expect of him, it discusses the great migrations to Canada; describes the National Archives in Ottawa, with its holdings of censuses, parish registers, naturalization records, land and homestead records, military records, and passenger lists; summarizes the holdings of the LDS Church relating to Canada; and explores the vast range of nationwide record sources such as census records and church registers.

But the best is reserved for the province-by-province survey of genealogical sources—a step-by-step guide to the records and record repositories in each of the ten provinces and the Yukon and Northwest territories. This core section gives a detailed breakdown—by province and territory—of vital records, wills, land records, censuses, church records, newspapers, and books, then lists the libraries, societies, and archives and their major holdings and ongoing projects.

Genealogical Publishing Co., Inc.

Family History Library. **Research Outline: Canada**.
Leaflet. $.75. 48 pp. .... Vendor G0629

Holmes, Theodore C. **Loyalists to Canada**. 1993. Indexed. Illus.
Book #1339
Cloth. $36.50. 346 pp. .... Vendor G0082

Konrad, J. **French and French-Canadian Family Research**.
Paper. $10.00. 79 pp. .... Vendor G0574

Martin, Ged, and Jeffrey Simpson. **Canada's Heritage in Scotland**. 1989.
Paper. $14.99 (cnd), $13.25 (US). 245 pp. .... Vendor G0640

National Archives of Canada. **Tracing Your Ancestors in Canada**.
Describes the major genealogical sources available at the National Archives and
makes reference to sources in other Canadian repositories.
Booklet. Free. .... Vendor G0784

The Old Northwest, Pioneer Period, 1815-1840: History of the NW Territory. 2
vols. Reprint 1983.
This two-volume set won the Pulitzer Prize for history in 1950.
Cloth. $41.95. 632 + 686 pp. .... Vendor G0611

Tapper, Lawrence F. **A Biographical Dictionary of Canadian Jewry—1909-1914**.
Cloth. $35.00. 256 pp. .... Vendor G0559

Whyte, Donald. **A Dictionary of Scottish Emigrants to Canada Before Confederation**. 2 vols. 1986, 1995.
The two volumes contain information on over 23,000 individuals and their families
who emigrated from Scotland to Canada before 1867.
Paper. Each vol. $36.00 (cdn), $37.50 (US). xvi + 441 pp. (Vol. 1); xvi + 433 pp.
(Vol. 2). .... Vendor G0568

Alberta

Alberta Genealogical Society. **Alberta Index to Births, Deaths and Marriages, Vol.
1: 1870-1905**. 1995.
Cloth. $55.00. 647 pp. .... Vendor G0614

Alberta Genealogical Society. **Edmonton Resources**. 1991. Updated 1994.
Cloth. $35.00. 330 pp. .... Vendor G0614

Alberta Genealogical Society. **Fiche Index to Alberta Cemetery Records & Other
Sources**.
Over 300,000 names.
Microfiche. $50.00. 24 fiche. .... Vendor G0614

Alberta Genealogical Society. **Tracing Your Ancestors in Alberta**. 1993.
Paper. $20.00. 182 pp. .... Vendor G0614

Nova Scotia

Allison, David. **History of Nova Scotia**. 3 vols. in 2. (1914) reprint 1987. Cloth. $94.00/Vols. I & II. $69.50/Vol. III. 940 + 700 pp. .... Vendor G0259

Brown, George S. **Yarmouth, Nova Scotia, Genealogies.** Transcribed from the Yarmouth Herald. 1993. Indexed. Cloth. $60.00. 956 pp. .... Vendor G0010

Calnek, W. A. **History of the County of Annapolis,** Including Old Port Royal & Acadia, with Genealogical Sketches of Its Early English Settlers & Their Families. Edited by A. W. Savary. (1897) reprint 1988. Cloth. $69.50. 682 pp. .... Vendor G0259

Calnek, W. A. **Supplement to History of the County of Annapolis** (see above listing). Edited by A. W. Savary. (1913) reprint 1988. Cloth. $19.50. May be ordered bound with above book. 142 pp. .... Vendor G0259

Carter, J. Smyth. **Story of Dundas,** Being a History of the Co. of Dundas, 1784 to 1904. With portraits & illustrations. (1905) reprint 1996. Cloth. $49.00. 462 pp. .... Vendor G0259

Crowell, E. **History of Barrington Township & Vicinity, Shelbourne Co., 1604-1870,** with a Biographical & Genealogical Appendix. (1870) reprint 1987. Cloth. $63.00. 610 pp. .... Vendor G0259

Eaton, Arthur W. H. **History of King's Co., Heart of the Acadian Land**. Giving a Sketch of the French & Their Expulsion, & a History of the New England Planters Who Came in Their Stead, with Many Genealogies. (1910) reprint 1992. Cloth. $89.00. 898 pp. .... Vendor G0259

Family History Library. **Research Outline: Nova Scotia**. Leaflet. $.25. 4 pp. .... Vendor G0629

Gilroy, Marion. **Loyalists and Land Settlement in Nova Scotia**. (1937) reprint 1995. Paper. $16.50. 154 pp. .... Vendor G0011

Maxwell, Fay. **Franklin County, Ohio Scotch-Irish Nova Scotia Acadians Refugee Tract History**. 1974. Indexed. ISBN 1-885463-11-1. This is a first. The Scotch-Irish Protestant refugees from General Washington and the Revolutionary War. Coverage includes migratory and military service to the King, their refusal to change Protestant beliefs, and finally settling in the 48½-mile strip called the Refugee Tract in Franklin County, Ohio. Congress waited to eve of War of 1812 before fulfilling land grant promise. Paper. $35.00. 160 pp. .... Vendor G0135

More, James F. **History of Queens County, Nova Scotia**. (1873) reprint 1995. Cloth. $32.00. 255 pp. .... Vendor G0259

Smith, Clifford N. **Whereabouts of Some American Refugees, 1784-1800: The Nova Scotian Land Grants**. British-American Genealogical Research Monograph Number 12.

Part 1: Surnames Aarons-Clapper. ISBN 0-915162-41-5.
Part 2: Surnames Clark-Furnay. ISBN 0-915162-42-3.
Part 3: Surnames Gabriel-Jingo. ISBN 0-915162-43-1.
Part 4: Surnames Johallen-McVie. ISBN 0-915162-44-X.
Part 5: Surnames Mead-Rivers. ISBN 0-915162-45-8.
Part 6: Surnames Roach-Smyth. ISBN 0-915162-46-6.
Part 7: Surnames Snarlock-Way. ISBN 0-915162-69-5.
Part 8: Surnames Wear-Zeneva. ISBN 0-915162-70-9.
Paper. $20.00/part. .... Vendor G0491

Smith, Leonard H. **Nova Scotia Immigrants to 1867**. 1994.
Cloth. $37.50. 560 pp. .... Vendor G0010

Smith, Leonard H. **Nova Scotia Immigrants to 1867, Volume II**. 1994.
Cloth. $30.00. 304 pp. .... Vendor G0010

Ontario

Chadwick, Edward M. **Ontarian Families: Genealogies of United Empire Loyalist & Other Pioneer Families of Upper Canada**. 2 vols. (1895-98) reprint 1990.
    Compiled using a wide variety of sources, this is an invaluable resource for Canadian researchers. The set contains chapters on more than 100 different families with information on over 1,000 surnames.
Paper. $21.50/vol. 203 + 194 pp. .... Vendor G0259

Croupe, Linda, trans. **Lennox and Addington County (Ontario) Marriages 1869 to 1880, Volume 1**. Indexed.
Spiral binding. $45.00. 383 pp. .... Vendor G0771

Crowder, Norman K. **Early Ontario Settlers: A Source Book**. 1993. Indexed. Illus.
Cloth. $25.00. 259 pp. .... Vendor G0010

DesBrisay, Mather Byles. **History of the County of Lunenburg**. 2nd ed. (1895) reprint 1996.
Cloth. $62.00. 586 pp. .... Vendor G0259

Dilts, Bryan Lee (indexed by). **1848 and 1850 Canada West (Ontario) Census Index: An Every-Name Index**. 1984.
Cloth. $39.95. 121 pp. .... Vendor G0552

Elliott, Bruce S., et al. **Index to the 1871 Census of Ontario: Brant**. 1986. Indexed. Illus.
    The 1871 Census was the first census for Ontario (previously Upper Canada and Canada West) after Confederation in 1867.
Paper. $17.00 (cdn), $18.50 (US). 86 pp. .... Vendor G0568

Elliott, Bruce S., et al. **Index to the 1871 Census of Ontario: Bruce**. 1989. Indexed. Illus.
    The 1871 Census was the first census for Ontario (previously Upper Canada and Canada West) after Confederation in 1867.
Paper. $19.50 (cdn), $21.00 (US). 103 pp. .... Vendor G0568

Elliott, Bruce S., et al. **Index to the 1871 Census of Ontario: Durham**. 1991. Indexed. Illus.
The 1871 Census was the first census for Ontario (previously Upper Canada and Canada West) after Confederation in 1867.
Paper. $21.00 (cdn), $22.50 (US). 118 pp. .... Vendor G0568

Elliott, Bruce S., et al. **Index to the 1871 Census of Ontario: Elgin**. 1989. Indexed. Illus.
The 1871 Census was the first census for Ontario (previously Upper Canada and Canada West) after Confederation in 1867.
Paper. $18.00 (cdn), $19.50 (US). 95 pp. .... Vendor G0568

Elliott, Bruce S., et al. **Index to the 1871 Census of Ontario: Essex-Kent**. 1989. Indexed. Illus.
The 1871 Census was the first census for Ontario (previously Upper Canada and Canada West) after Confederation in 1867.
Paper. $27.00 (cdn), $28.50 (US). 193 pp. .... Vendor G0568

Elliott, Bruce S., et al. **Index to the 1871 Census of Ontario: Grey**. 1991. Indexed. Illus.
The 1871 Census was the first census for Ontario (previously Upper Canada and Canada West) after Confederation in 1867.
Paper. $22.50 (cdn), $24.00 (US). 123 pp. .... Vendor G0568

Elliott, Bruce S., et al. **Index to the 1871 Census of Ontario: Haldimand-Norfolk.**
1988. Indexed. Illus.
The 1871 Census was the first census for Ontario (previously Upper Canada and
Canada West) after Confederation in 1867.
Paper. $24.00 (cdn), $25.50 (US). 139 pp. .... Vendor G0568

Elliott, Bruce S., et al. **Index to the 1871 Census of Ontario: Halton-Peel.** 1986.
Indexed. Illus.
The 1871 Census was the first census for Ontario (previously Upper Canada and
Canada West) after Confederation in 1867.
Paper. $22.50 (cdn), $24.00 (US). 129 pp. .... Vendor G0568

Elliott, Bruce S., et al. **Index to the 1871 Census of Ontario: Hamilton-Wentworth.**
1987. Indexed. Illus.
The 1871 Census was the first census for Ontario (previously Upper Canada and
Canada West) after Confederation in 1867.
Paper. $26.00 (cdn), $27.50 (US). 171 pp. .... Vendor G0568

Elliott, Bruce S., et al. **Index to the 1871 Census of Ontario: Hastings-Prince
Edward.** 1991. Indexed. Illus.
The 1871 Census was the first census for Ontario (previously Upper Canada and
Canada West) after Confederation in 1867.
Paper. $30.00 (cdn), $31.50 (US). 217 pp. .... Vendor G0568

Elliott, Bruce S, et al. **Index to the 1871 Census of Ontario: Huron.** 1986. Indexed.
Illus.
The 1871 Census was the first census for Ontario (previously Upper Canada and
Canada West) after Confederation in 1867.
Paper. $25.00 (cdn), $26.50 (US). 155 pp. .... Vendor G0568

Elliott, Bruce S., et al. **Index to the 1871 Census of Ontario: Kingston-Frontenac-
Lennox-Addington.** 1988. Indexed. Illus.
The 1871 Census was the first census for Ontario (previously Upper Canada and
Canada West) after Confederation in 1867.
Paper. $26.00 (cdn), $27.50 (US). 167 pp. .... Vendor G0568

Elliott, Bruce S., et al. **Index to the 1871 Census of Ontario: Lambton.** 1986.
Indexed. Illus.
The 1871 Census was the first census for Ontario (previously Upper Canada and
Canada West) after Confederation in 1867.
Paper. $17.00 (cdn), $18.50 (US). 75 pp. .... Vendor G0568

Elliott, Bruce S., et al. **Index to the 1871 Census of Ontario: Lanark.** 1992. In-
dexed. Illus.
The 1871 Census was the first census for Ontario (previously Upper Canada and
Canada West) after Confederation in 1867.
Paper. $17.00 (cdn), $18.50 (US). 76 pp. .... Vendor G0568

Elliott, Bruce S., et al. **Index to the 1871 Census of Ontario: Leeds-Grenville.**
1990. Indexed. Illus.
The 1871 Census was the first census for Ontario (previously Upper Canada and
Canada West) after Confederation in 1867.
Paper. $24.00 (cdn), $25.50 (US). 144 pp. .... Vendor G0568

Elliott, Bruce S., et al. **Index to the 1871 Census of Ontario: Lincoln-Welland-Niagara**. 1987. Indexed. Illus.
The 1871 Census was the first census for Ontario (previously Upper Canada and Canada West) after Confederation in 1867.
Paper. $25.00 (cdn), $26.50 (US). 155 pp. .... Vendor G0568

Elliott, Bruce S., et al. **Index to the 1871 Census of Ontario: London-Middlesex**. 1990. Indexed. Illus.
The 1871 Census was the first census for Ontario (previously Upper Canada and Canada West) after Confederation in 1867.
Paper. $30.00 (cdn), $31.50 (US). 213 pp. .... Vendor G0568

Elliott, Bruce S., et al. **Index to the 1871 Census of Ontario: Northumberland**. 1990. Indexed. Illus.
The 1871 Census was the first census for Ontario (previously Upper Canada and Canada West) after Confederation in 1867.
Paper. $18.00 (cdn), $19.50 (US). 98 pp. .... Vendor G0568

Elliott, Bruce S., et al. **Index to the 1871 Census of Ontario: Ontario County**. 1991. Indexed. Illus.
The 1871 Census was the first census for Ontario (previously Upper Canada and Canada West) after Confederation in 1867.
Paper. $21.00 (cdn), $22.50 (US). 111 pp. .... Vendor G0568

Elliott, Bruce S., et al. **Index to the 1871 Census of Ontario: Ottawa-Carleton**. 1988. Indexed. Illus.
The 1871 Census was the first census for Ontario (previously Upper Canada and Canada West) after Confederation in 1867.
Paper. $18.00 (cdn), $19.50 (US). 95 pp. .... Vendor G0568

Elliott, Bruce S., et al. **Index to the 1871 Census of Ontario: Oxford**. 1991. Indexed. Illus.
The 1871 Census was the first census for Ontario (previously Upper Canada and Canada West) after Confederation in 1867.
Paper. $25.00 (cdn), $26.50 (US). 150 pp. .... Vendor G0568

Elliott, Bruce S., et al. **Index to the 1871 Census of Ontario: Perth County**. 1991. Indexed. Illus.
The 1871 Census was the first census for Ontario (previously Upper Canada and Canada West) after Confederation in 1867.
Paper. $19.50 (cdn), $21.00 (US). 104 pp. .... Vendor G0568

Elliott, Bruce S., et al. **Index to the 1871 Census of Ontario: Peterborough-Victoria**. 1988. Indexed. Illus.
The 1871 Census was the first census for Ontario (previously Upper Canada and Canada West) after Confederation in 1867.
Paper. $21.00 (cdn), $22.50 (US). 110 pp. .... Vendor G0568

Elliott, Bruce S., et al. **Index to the 1871 Census of Ontario: Renfrew and the North**. 1992. Indexed. Illus.
The 1871 Census was the first census for Ontario (previously Upper Canada and Canada West) after Confederation in 1867.
Paper. $19.50 (cdn), $21.00 (US). 107 pp. .... Vendor G0568

Elliott, Bruce S., et al. **Index to the 1871 Census of Ontario: Simcoe.** 1987. Indexed. Illus.
The 1871 Census was the first census for Ontario (previously Upper Canada and Canada West) after Confederation in 1867.
Paper. $25.00 (cdn), $26.50 (US). 150 pp. .... Vendor G0568

Elliott, Bruce S., et al. **Index to the 1871 Census of Ontario: Stormont-Dundas-Glengarry-Prescott-Russell.** 1987. Indexed. Illus.
The 1871 Census was the first census for Ontario (previously Upper Canada and Canada West) after Confederation in 1867.
Paper. $26.00 (cdn), $27.50 (US). 170 pp. .... Vendor G0568

Elliott, Bruce S., et al. **Index to the 1871 Census of Ontario: Toronto.** 1992. Indexed. Illus.
The 1871 Census was the first census for Ontario (previously Upper Canada and Canada West) after Confederation in 1867.
Paper. $27.00 (cdn), $28.50 (US). 193 pp. .... Vendor G0568

Elliott, Bruce S., et al. **Index to the 1871 Census of Ontario: Waterloo.** 1990. Indexed. Illus.
The 1871 Census was the first census for Ontario (previously Upper Canada and Canada West) after Confederation in 1867.
Paper. $18.00 (cdn), $19.50 (US). 97 pp. .... Vendor G0568

Elliott, Bruce S., et al. **Index to the 1871 Census of Ontario: Wellington.** 1989. Indexed. Illus.
The 1871 Census was the first census for Ontario (previously Upper Canada and Canada West) after Confederation in 1867.
Paper. $25.00 (cdn), 26.50 (US). 152 pp. .... Vendor G0568

Elliott, Bruce S., et al. **Index to the 1871 Census of Ontario: York.** 1992. Indexed. Illus.
The 1871 Census was the first census for Ontario (previously Upper Canada and Canada West) after Confederation in 1867.
Paper. $26.00 (cdn), $27.50 (US). 164 pp. .... Vendor G0568

Elliott, Bruce S., and De Alton Owens. **The McCabe List: Early Irish in the Ottawa Valley.** 1991. Indexed. Illus.
List of early Irish settlers in Ontario.
Paper. $12.00 (cdn), $13.50 (US). 64 pp. .... Vendor G0568

Elliott, Bruce S., Dan Walker, and Fawne Stratford-Devai. **Men of Upper Canada: Militia Nomial Rolls, 1828-1829.** 1995. Illus.
Useful resource for names in a period during which there were no censuses.
Paper. $33.00 (cdn), $34.50 (US). xvii + 356 pp. .... Vendor G0568

Family History Library. **Research Outline: Ontario.**
Leaflet. $.25. 7 pp. .... Vendor G0629

Fitzgerald, Keith E. **Ontario People: 1796-1803.** 1993. Indexed. Illus.
Contact vendor for information. .... Vendor G0010

Graham, Robert J., et al. **Inn-Roads to Ancestry: Pioneer Inns of Ontario. Vol. 1: Head of the Lake & Niagara.** 1996. Indexed. Illus.

A depiction of the inns and innkeepers in one of Ontario's earliest settled regions. Paper. $18.00 (cdn), $19.50 (US). xii + 128 pp. .... Vendor G0568

Herrington, Walter S. **History of the Counties of Lennox & Addington.** (1913) reprint 1993.
Cloth. $45.00. xii + 426 pp. .... Vendor G0259

Higgins, W. H. **Life and Times of Joseph Gould:** Reminiscences of Sixty Years of Active Political and Municipal Life. (1887) reprint 1995.
Along with a biography of the subject, an important early figure in local development, this book contains a history of the township of Uxbridge and surrounding areas.
Cloth. $37.50. 304 pp. .... Vendor G0259

Hope, Louise I. **Index to Niagara Conference Methodist Episcopal Church Baptismal Register, 1849-1886, 2 Parts.** 1994.
Index to an early Methodist Church register which was copied from entries forwarded by the ministers to the Conference.
Paper. $18.00 (cdn), $19.50 (US). 165 pp. .... Vendor G0568

Lancastei, Shirley and David J. Browne. **Strays! An Index to the OGS Strays Project, Volume 1.** 1996. Illus.
The first in a planned series of names of people who "strayed" from Ontario to other parts of the country, including the source of the information.
Paper. $13.00 (cdn), $14.50 (US). viii + 72 pp. .... Vendor G0568

Lauber, Wilfred R. **An Index to the Land Claim Certificates of Upper Canada Militiamen Who Served in the War of 1812-1814.** 1995. Indexed. Illus.
Useful resource for names in a period during which there were no censuses.
Paper. $25.00 (cdn), $26.50 (US). 136 pp. .... Vendor G0568

Leavitt, Thad W. H. **History of Leeds & Grenville, Ontario, from 1749 to 1879,** with Illustrations & Biographical Sketches of Some of Its Prominent Men & Pioneers. (1879) reprint 1996.
Cloth. $32.00. 200 pp. .... Vendor G0259

Magee, Joan. **The Belgians in Ontario.** A History. 1987.
Paper. $14.99 (cnd), $13.25 (US). .... Vendor G0640

Magee, Joan. **A Scandinavian Heritage.** 200 Years of Scandinavian Presence in the Windsor—Detroit Border Region. 1985.
Paper. $12.99 (cnd), $11.50 (US). 128 pp. .... Vendor G0640

McFall, David A., and Jean McFall. **Land Records in Ontario Registry Offices, 3rd Edition.** 1987. Illus.
Handy guide to using Ontario land records.
Paper. $7.00 (cdn), $8.50 (US). 16 pp. .... Vendor G0568

McKenzie, Rev. Donald A. **Death Notices from the Canada Christian Advocate, 1858-1872.** 1992.
Notices from a newspaper published by the Methodist Episcopal Church, primarily relating to Ontario.
Cloth. $27.50. 384 pp. .... Vendor G0561

McKenzie, Rev. Donald A. **Death Notices from the Christian Guardian, 1836-1850**. 1983.
Extracts from a Methodist newspaper of Ontario.
Cloth. $25.00. 375 pp. .... Vendor G0561

McKenzie, Rev. Donald A. **Death Notices from the Christian Guardian, 1851-1860**. 1984.
Cloth. $25.00. 365 pp. .... Vendor G0561

McKenzie, Rev. Donald A. **Obituaries from Ontario's Christian Guardian, 1861-1870**. 1988.
The third volume in the above series.
Cloth. $25.00. 418 pp. .... Vendor G0561

McKenzie, Rev. Donald A. **More Notices from Methodist Newspapers [of Ontario], 1830-1857**. 1986.
Contains death and marriage notices with some births from three papers.
Cloth. $25.00. 432 pp. .... Vendor G0561

McKenzie, Donald A. **Upper Canada Naturalization Records, 1828-1850**. 1991. Indexed.
A resource for tracking early settlers in Ontario before censuses.
Paper. $14.50 (cdn), $16.00 (US). 100 pp. .... Vendor G0568

Merriman, Brenda Dougall. **Genealogy in Ontario: Searching the Records**. 3rd ed. 1996. Indexed. Illus.
The authoritative guide through the genealogical rewards of Ontario, Canada.
Paper. $28.00 (cdn), $29.50 (US). xiv + 278 pp. .... Vendor G0568

Merriman, Brenda Dougall. **Genealogy in Ontario: Searching the Records (3rd Edition)**. 1996.
This is a comprehensive guide to the genealogical resources of this large province. Not only will the book tell you what's available, but will help you access the records from a distance.
Paper. $19.00. 278 pp. .... Vendor G0611

Owen, E. A. **Pioneer Sketches of Long Point Settlement,** or Norfolk's Foundation Builders & Their Family Genealogies. (1898) reprint 1996.
Cloth. $59.50. 578 pp. .... Vendor G0259

Pringle, J. F. **Lunenburgh, or the Old Eastern District,** Its Settlement and Early Progress with Personal Recollections of the Town of Cornwall from 1824. (1890) reprint 1996.
Cloth. $46.00. 423 pp. .... Vendor G0259

Rayburn, Alan. **Lost Names and Places of Eastern Ontario**. 1993. Indexed. Illus.
A help for finding former locations in Eastern Ontario.
Paper. $11.50 (cdn), $13.00 (US). 56 pp. .... Vendor G0568

Reaman, George Elmore. **The Trail of the Black Walnut**. (1957) reprint 1993. Indexed. Illus.
Describes the role of the Pennsylvania Germans in the settlement of Ontario in the

late 18th century and also the role of the French Huguenots and English and Welsh Quakers.
Cloth. $25.00. 288 pp. .... Vendor G0010

Reid, William D. **Death Notices of Ontario [1810-1849]**. (1980) reprint 1997. Indexed.
Contact vendor for information. 417 pp. .... Vendor G0011

Reid, William D. **The Loyalists in Ontario**. The Sons and Daughters of the American Loyalists of Upper Canada. (1973) reprint 1994. Indexed.
Cloth. $27.00. 418 pp. .... Vendor G0010

Reid, William D. **Marriage Notices of Ontario**. 1980. Indexed.
Newspaper notices for 1813-1854, although the majority are after 1830.
Cloth. $25.00. 550 pp. .... Vendor G0561

Reid, William D. **Marriage Notices of Ontario [1813-1854]**. 1980. Indexed.
Cloth. $35.00. 550 pp. .... Vendor G0011

Shepard, Catherine. **Surrogate Court Records at the Archives of Ontario**. 1984. Illus.
A guide to the use of the Surrogate Court Records held by the Archives of Ontario.
Paper. $7.00 (cdn), $8.50 (US). 24 pp. .... Vendor G0568

Taylor, Ryan. **Books You Need to Do Genealogy in Ontario:** An Annotated Bibliography. 1996.
Useful sources and practical advice from one of Ontario's most experienced genealogists make this an essential reference.
Paper. $17.45. 154 pp. .... Vendor G0515

Taylor, Ryan. **Important Genealogical Collections in Ontario Archives and Libraries: A Directory**. 1994.
Identifies which genealogical collections exist and are accessible in Ontario.
Paper. $18.00 (cdn), $19.50 (US). 75 pp. .... Vendor G0568

Wilson, Thomas B., and Emily S. Wilson. **Directory of the Province of Ontario 1857**. 1987.
Lists upwards of 40,000 persons, primarily business and trades men, with place of residence and occupation.
Cloth. $35.00. 712 pp. .... Vendor G0561

Wilson, Thomas B. **Marriage Bonds of Ontario, 1803-1834**. 1985. Indexed.
Gives good coverage to a wide-ranging area of the province, but does not include the Western District (the counties of Essex, Kent, and Lambton).
Cloth. $25.00. 445 pp. .... Vendor G0561

Wilson, Thomas B. **Ontario Marriage Notices [1830-1856]**. (1982) reprint 1997. Indexed.
Contact vendor for information. 435 pp. .... Vendor G0011

Wilson, Thomas B., ed. **The Ontario Register**. 8 vols. 1968-1990.
Devoted solely to the publication of records. Fully indexed.
Contact vendor for contents of the volumes still in print and prices. .. Vendor G0561

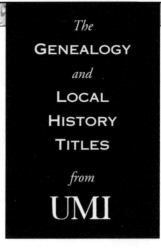

Quebec

Day, Mrs. C. M. **History of the Eastern Townships, Province of Quebec,** Civil & Descriptive, in Three Parts. (1869) reprint 1996.
Cloth. $52.00. 475 pp. .... Vendor G0259

Desaulniers, F. L. **Les Vielles Familles d'Yamachiche.** French language. 2 vols. (1898-99) reprint 1987.
Volume I. Dix Gen.: Les Blois, Lacerte, Lamy, Loranger, Vaillancourt, Gerin-Lajoie, Boucher, Carbonneau, Caron, Comeau.
Volume II. Trois Gen.: Les Desaulniers, Bellemare, Gelinas.
Paper. $25.00/vol. 242 + 303 pp. .... Vendor G0259

Desaulniers, F. L. **Notes Historique sur la Pariosse de St. Guillaume D'Upton.** French language. (1905) reprint 1991.
Paper. $16.00. 143 pp. .... Vendor G0259

Desaulniers, F. L. **Recherches Genealogique sur les Familles Gravel, Cloutiere, Bruneau, et al.** French language. (1902) reprint 1991.
Paper. $21.00. 197 pp. .... Vendor G0259

Family History Library. **Research Outline: Quebec.**
Leaflet. $.25. 6 pp. .... Vendor G0629

Holbrook, Jay Mack. **Ascott, Quebec, Canada 1825 Census.** 1976.
Paper. $2.00. 14 pp. .... Vendor G0148

Holbrook, Jay Mack. **Shipton, Quebec, Canada 1825 Census.** 1976.
Paper. $2.00. 15 pp. .... Vendor G0148

Hubbard, B. F., comp. **Forests & Clearings: History of Stanstead Co., Prov. of Quebec,** with Sketches of More Than Five Hundred Families. Revised & edited by John Lawrence. (1874) reprint 1996.
Cloth. $42.00. 367 pp. .... Vendor G0259

Hubbard, B. F. **The History of Stanstead County, Province of Quebec.** 1874. Reprinted. Indexed.
Stanstead County lies just north of the Vermont border in Quebec. It was first settled in the early 1800s by families from New England, particularly from Vermont and New Hampshire.
Paper. $25.00. 367 pp. .... Vendor G0561

Massicotte, Edouard Z., and Regis Roy. **Armorial Du Canada Francais [Armorial of French-Canada].** 2 vols. in 1. (1915, 1918) reprint 1994.
The standard reference for coats-of-arms of officials, civil servants, professional men, and other French Canadians.
Paper. $28.50. 332 pp. in all. .... Vendor G0011

Thomas, C. **History of the Eastern Townships, Canada.** (1866) reprint 1989. Indexed.
Histories of the townships in Quebec, Canada.
Cloth. $19.95. 387 pp. .... Vendor G0450

White, Jeanne Sauve. **Guide to Quebec Catholic Parishes and Published Parish Marriage Records**. (1993) reprint 1995. Indexed.
Paper. $16.50. 146 pp. .... Vendor G0011

China

Family History Library. **Using the Asian MCC Guide: China**.
Free. 7 pp. .... Vendor G0629

She, Colleen. **A Student's Guide to Chinese American Genealogy**. 1996. Indexed. Illus.
Hard-cover. $25.95. 208 pp. .... Vendor G0776

Cuba

Carr, Peter E. **Censos, Padrones y Matriculas de la Poblacion de Cuba, Siglos 16, 17 y 18**. 1993. Indexed.
Paper. $25.95. 113 pp. .... Vendor G0496

Carr, Peter E. **Guide to Cuban Genealogical Research**. 1991. Indexed.
The first and only comprehensive book of its kind.
Paper. $19.95. 103 pp. .... Vendor G0496

Curaçao

Gehring, Dr. Charles, Translator. **New Netherland Documents: The Curaçao Papers**. 1987. Indexed. Illus.
When Petrus Stuyvesant was transferred from Curaçao to New Amsterdam he brought valuable records concerning the movements of goods to and from the island. These records became a part of the collection of the New York State Library.
Cloth. $50.00. 480 pp. .... Vendor G0093

Czech Republic/Czechoslovakia

Gardiner. **German Towns in Slovakia and Upper Hungary: A Genealogical Gazetteer**. 1991.
Nearly half of this book is an extremely helpful "how-to" of Czech research, while the second half is the gazetteer that the title promises.
Paper. $17.00. 113 pp. .... Vendor G0611

Denmark

Family History Library. **Research Outline: Denmark.**
Leaflet. $.75. 28 pp. .... Vendor G0629

Paddock, Lisa Olson, and Carl Sokolnicki Rollyson. **A Student's Guide to Scandinavian Genealogy.** 1996. Indexed. Illus.
Hard-cover. $24.95. 208 pp. .... Vendor G0776

Renfroe, Vicki. **Finding Your Viking.** 1996. Indexed. Illus.
Source book on researching Danish genealogy.
Paper. $9.95. 20 pp. .... Vendor G0513

Smith and Thomsen. **Genealogical Guidebook and Atlas of Denmark.**
Includes terminology, feast days, counties and parishes, maps, and more.
Paper. $17.50. 168 pp. .... Vendor G0611

Thomsen. **Beginner's Guide to Danish Genealogical Research.**
Useful guide for those just beginning their Danish research.
Paper. $5.25. 24 pp. .... Vendor G0611

Thomsen. **Danish-Norwegian Genealogical Research Sources.**
A guide to sources and how to access from here.
Paper. $9.50. 82 pp. .... Vendor G0611

Thomsen. **Danish-Norwegian Language Guide & Dictionary.**
Useful in understanding the language.
Paper. $10.75. 100 pp. .... Vendor G0611

Thomsen. **Scandinavian Genealogical Research Manual.** 1980.
This volume is a combination of the following books: *Danish/Norwegian Genealogical Research, Danish/Norwegian Language Guide and Dictionary*, and *The Old Handwriting & Names of Denmark and Norway.*
Spiral bound. $19.95. 231 pp. .... Vendor G0611

Eastern Europe

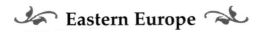

Brandt, Bruce, and Edward Reimer Brandt. **Where to Look for Hard-to-Find German-Speaking Ancestors in Eastern Europe.** Index to 19,720 Surnames in 13 Books, with Historical Background on Each Settlement. 2nd ed. (1993) reprint 1996.
Lists surnames of German-speaking ancestors who emigrated to Russia, Poland, Romania, and elsewhere in Eastern Europe.
Paper. $18.50. 148 pp. .... Vendor G0011

✒ Estonia/Ethnic Estonian ✒

Maldonado, Sigrid Renate. **Estonian Experience and Roots.** Ethnic Estonian Genealogy with Historical Perspective, Social Influences and Possible Family History Resources. 1996. Indexed. Illus.
  An aid or guide to those wanting to know some local history and to search for their Estonian (also Latvian) roots, and to professional genealogists.
Cloth. $24.00 + p&h. 128 pp. .... Vendor G0475

✒ Europe ✒

Baxter, Angus. **In Search of Your European Roots.** 2nd ed. (1994) reprint 1996.
Paper. $16.95. 304 pp. .... Vendor G0010

Eakle, Arlene H., Ph.D. **European Genealogy.** 1996. Illus.
  Boundary changes, handwriting alphabets, new indexes for 51 European countries, 123 maps.
Paper. $28.00. 126 pp. .... Vendor G0504

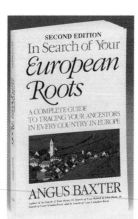

Angus Baxter

**All New
2nd edition!**

304 pp., paperback. 1994.
Vendor G0010. $16.95

IN SEARCH OF YOUR EUROPEAN ROOTS

A Complete Guide to Tracing Your Ancestors in Every Country in Europe

  In Search of Your European Roots is designed to guide the reader through the complexities of genealogical research in Europe, whether the research is conducted in person or by correspondence. It acquaints the researcher with the various types of genealogical records available in each country and explains where they are found and how they are used. With up-to-date information on church, state, and provincial archives (including current addresses), and a discussion of the special characteristics of each area and the ways in which they effect the research process, it opens up a wealth of possibilities for tracing ancestors in Europe.
  This revised edition includes new chapters on Germany and the countries of Eastern Europe.

  "If your ancestors came from Europe, this magnificent guidebook will lead you through the maze of locating records."—**LOS ANGELES TIMES**

Genealogical Publishing Co., Inc.

Magocsi, Paul Robert. **Historical Atlas of East Central Europe**. 1993.
For the first time, here is an atlas that covers all of Eastern Central Europe from the early fifth century through 1992. This atlas encompasses the countries of Poland, the Czech Republic, Slovakia, Hungary, Romania, Slovenia, Croatia, Bosnia-Herzegovina, Yugoslavia, Macedonia, Albania, Bulgaria, Greece, and the eastern part of Germany. 9" x 12".
Paper. $39.95. 218 pp. .... Vendor G0611

Shea, Jonathan D., and William F. Hoffman. **Following the Paper Trail: A Multilingual Translation Guide**.
Cloth. $29.00. 256 pp. .... Vendor G0559

Finland

Paddock, Lisa Olson, and Carl Sokolnicki Rollyson. **A Student's Guide to Scandinavian Genealogy**. 1996. Indexed. Illus.
Hard-cover. $24.95. 208 pp. .... Vendor G0776

Thomsen. **Beginner's Guide to Finnish Genealogical Research**.
Useful guide to beginning your research.
Paper. $5.25. 28 pp. .... Vendor G0611

France

Family History Library. **French Letter-Writing Guide**.
Leaflet. $.25. 8 pp. .... Vendor G0629

Konrad, J. **French and French-Canadian Family Research**.
Paper. $10.00. 79 pp. .... Vendor G0574

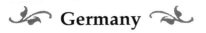

Germany

Atlas of the German Empire 1892. Indexed.
This set of maps is an indispensable research tool. 11" x 17".
Paper. $29.95. .... Vendor G0611

Baxter, Angus. **In Search of Your German Roots**. A Complete Guide to Tracing Your Ancestors in the Germanic Areas of Europe. 3rd ed. (1994) reprint 1996.
Paper. $11.95. 122 pp. .... Vendor G0010

Bentz, Edna M. **Decipher Germanic Records**. 1982.
An extremely useful guide. Has the words and terms you need written out in old German script, then translated to German and English.
Spiral bound. $12.50. 84 pp. .... Vendor G0611

Brandt, et.al. **Germanic Genealogy:** A Guide to Worldwide Sources and Migration Patterns. 1995.
This remarkable book is jam-packed with essential information. Anyone doing German research should have this book! This replaces the 1991 book called *Research Guide to German-American Genealogy*.
Paper. $24.00. 370 pp. .... Vendor G0611

Brandt, Bruce, and Edward Reimer Brandt. **Where to Look for Hard-to-Find German-Speaking Ancestors in Eastern Europe**. Index to 19,720 Surnames in 13 Books, with Historical Background on Each Settlement. 2nd ed. (1993) reprint 1996.
Paper. $18.50. 148 pp. .... Vendor G0011

Burgert, Annette K. **Brethren from Gimbsheim in the Palatinate to Ephrata and Bermudian in Pennsylvania**. 1994. Indexed. Illus.
Paper. $14.00. 39 pp. .... Vendor G0458

Cobb, Sanford H. **Story of the Palatines**. (1897) reprint 1988. Indexed.
Paper. $23.50. 319 pp. .... Vendor G0140

Dearden. **The German Researcher: How to Get the Most out of an L.D.S. Family History Center**. 4th ed. 1990.
Very helpful to those conducting German research in Family History Centers.
Paper. $10.50. 72 pp. .... Vendor G0611

DeMarce, Virginia Easley. **Mercenary Troops from Anhalt-Zerbst, Germany, Who Served with the British Forces During the American Revolution**. German-American Genealogical Research Monograph Number 19. 1984.
Part 1: Surnames A Through Kr (iv + 54 pp.).
Part 2: Surnames Ku Through Z (50 pp.; appendices).
ISBN 0-915162-21-0 (the set).
Paper. $20.00/part. .... Vendor G0491

Deutsche Bundespost. **Das Postleitzahlenbuch**. 1993. Indexed.
Current Zip Code Directory for all of Germany.
Paper. $13.00 postpaid ($13.85 in OH). 990 pp. .... Vendor G0197

Edlund, Thomas Kent. **The German Minority Census of 1939: An Introduction and Register**. 1996.
Paper. $9.50. 64 pp. .... Vendor G0559

The Harrisons from Houston County, Texas, 1835–1993
Publication date: 1994. 297 pages. Indexed. Illus. Cloth. $28.00.
Hilde Shuptrine Farley
10325 Russell Street
Shawnee Mission, KS 66212-1736

Family History Library. **German Letter-Writing Guide.**
Leaflet. $.25. 7 pp. .... Vendor G0629

Family History Library. **Hamburg Passenger Lists Guide.**
Free. 4 pp. .... Vendor G0629

Family History Library. **Research Outline: Germany.**
Leaflet. $.75. 52 pp. .... Vendor G0629

Ferguson, Laraine Kowallis, and Gay P. Kowallis, eds. **German Genealogical Digest, A Quarterly Journal for German Researchers.** 1985-. Indexed.
Histories, sources include Berlin, Pomerania, Palatinate, Hessen, Brandenburg, Schleswig-Holstein, Mecklenburg, Wuerttemberg, Alsace-Lorraine. Send SASE for free 12-year index.
Subscription. $25.00/yr. 140 pp./yr. .... Vendor G0193

German Post Office. **German Zip Code Book and Map.** 1993.
Newly revised and reprinted to reflect the new system of postal codes in the reunified Germany.
Paper. $19.00. .... Vendor G0611

Hall, Charles. **Atlantic Bridge to Germany Vol. 1—Baden-Wuerttemberg.** Illus.
Covers the area of Baden-Wuerttemberg; includes maps.
Paper. $12.50. 166 pp. .... Vendor G0618

Hall, Charles. **Atlantic Bridge to Germany Vol. 2—Hessen, Rheinland-Pfalz.** Illus.
Contains historical orientation, bibliographical orientation, maps, index to communities for Hessen and Rheinland-Pfalz (the Palatinate).
Paper. $11.00. 166 pp. .... Vendor G0618

Hall, Charles. **Atlantic Bridge to Germany Vol. 3—Bavaria.** Illus.
Includes historical and bibliographical data, maps and index to communities, for area of Bavaria, Germany.
Paper. $14.50. 204 pp. .... Vendor G0618

Hall, Charles. **Atlantic Bridge to Germany Vol. 4—Saarland, Alsace-Lorraine and Switzerland.** Illus.
Covers the area of Saarland, Alsace-Lorraine, and Switzerland. Maps are included; historical, bibliographic, and jurisdictional orientation, with an index to the communities.
Paper. $14.50. 169 pp. .... Vendor G0618

Hall, Charles. **Atlantic Bridge to Germany Vol. 5—Bremen, Hamburg, and Schleswig-Holstein.** Illus.
Covers the area of Bremen, Hamburg, and Schleswig-Holstein; includes maps, biographical information, and an index to communities.
Paper. $9.95. 64 pp. .... Vendor G0618

Hall, Charles. **Atlantic Bridge to Germany Vol. 6—Mecklenburg Genealogical Handbook.** Illus.
Covers the area of Mecklenburg; includes maps.
Paper. $8.00. 40 pp. .... Vendor G0618

Hall, Charles. **Atlantic Bridge to Germany Vol. 7—Nordrhein-Westfalen; Northrhine-Westphalia**. Illus.
Includes complete index for about 3,000 repositories of genealogical records; maps.
Paper. $9.95. 64 + xxiv pp. .... Vendor G0618

Hall, Charles M. **Atlantic Bridge to Germany Vol. 8—Prussia** (Brandenburg, East & West Prussia, Pommerania, Posen). Illus.
Includes time line on the history of the former state of Prussia, maps, references to source material, index to Gemeinde, etc.
Paper. $25.00. 245 pp. .... Vendor G0618

Heisey, John W. **German for Genealogy**.
Paper. $10.00. 30 pp. .... Vendor G0574

Konrad, J. **German Family Research Made Simple**.
Paper. $12.00. 108 pp. .... Vendor G0574

Rice, Robert. **German Professions of the Eighteenth and Nineteenth Centuries**.
Paper. $12.00. 103 pp. .... Vendor G0775

Robl, Gregory. **A Student's Guide to German American Genealogy**. 1996. Indexed. Illus.
Hard-cover. $24.95. 208 pp. .... Vendor G0776

Schrader-Muggenthaler, Cornelia. **German Research Aid Audio Cassette Teaching Program**.
Basic German research course. Small booklet includes tips on how to read old script and translation of commonly used German and Latin words in German church books, as well as an archives address list, book list, and form letter.
Booklet/cassette. $7.95 .... Vendor G0536

Schweitzer, George K. **German Genealogical Research**. 1995. Illus.
German historical background, Germans to America, bridging the Atlantic, types of German records, German record repositories, the German language.
Paper. $21.00. 252 pp. .... Vendor G0569

Smelser, Ronald M. **Finding Your German Ancestors**. 1991.
Paper. $2.95. 40 pp. .... Vendor G0570

Smith, Clifford N. **Annotated Hessian Chaplaincy Record of the American Revolution, 1776-1784: Christenings, Marriages, Deaths**. German-American Genealogical Research Monograph Number 30. 1994.
ISBN 0-915162-72-5.
Paper. $20.00. i + 29 pp. double-columned. .... Vendor G0491

Smith, Clifford N. **British and German Deserters, Dischargees, and Prisoners of War Who May Have Remained in Canada and the United States, 1774-1783**. British-American Genealogical Research Monograph Number 9. 2 parts.
Part 1 (1988; 24 pp. double-columned): ISBN 0-915162-34-2.
Part 2 (1989; 18 pp. double-columned): ISBN 0-915162-35-0.
Paper. $20.00/part. .... Vendor G0491

Smith, Clifford N. **Brunswick Deserter-Immigrants of the American Revolution**. German-American Genealogical Research Monograph Number 1. 1973.
ISBN: 0-915162-00-8.
Paper. $20.00. 54 pp. .... Vendor G0491

Smith, Clifford N. **Cumulative Surname Index and Soundex to Monographs 1 Through 12 of the German-American Genealogical Research Series**. 1981.
ISBN 0-915162-17-2.
Paper. $20.00. iv + 66 pp. double-columned. .... Vendor G0491

Smith, Clifford N. **Cumulative Surname Soundex to German-American Genealogical Research Monographs 14-19 and 21-25**. German-American Genealogical Research Monograph Number 26. 1990.
ISBN 0-915162-91-1.
Paper. $20.00. i + 41 pp. double-columned. .... Vendor G0491

Smith, Clifford N. **Deserters and Disbanded Soldiers from British, German, and Loyalist Military Units in the South, 1782**. British-American Genealogical Research Monograph Number 10. 1991.
ISBN 0-915162-36-9.
Paper. $20.00. 26 pp. double-columned. .... Vendor G0491

Smith, Clifford N. **German Revolutionists of 1848: Among Whom Many Immigrants to America**. German-American Genealogical Research Monograph Number 21. 4 parts.
Part 1: Surnames A Through F (1985; ii + 37 pp. double-columned).
ISBN 0- 915162-77-6.
Part 2: Surnames G Through K (1985; 38 pp. double-columned).
ISBN 0-915162-78- 4.
Part 3: Surnames L Through R (1985; 33 pp. double-columned).
ISBN 0-915162-79- 2.
Part 4: Surnames S Through Z (1985; 40 pp. double-columned).
ISBN 0-915162-80- 6.
Paper. $20.00/part. .... Vendor G0491

Smith, Clifford N. **Gold! German Transcontinental Travelers to California, 1849-1851**. German-American Genealogical Research Monograph Number 24. 1988.
ISBN 0-915162-76-8.
Paper. $20.00. iii + 62 pp. .... Vendor G0491

Smith, Clifford N. **Letters Home: Genealogical and Family Historical Data on Nineteenth-Century German Settlers in Australia, Bermuda, Brazil, Canada, and the United States**. Part 1. German-American Genealogical Research Monograph Number 25. 1988.
ISBN 0-915162-90-3.
Paper. $20.00. ii + 36 pp. double-columned. .... Vendor G0491

Smith, Clifford N. **Mercenaries from Ansbach and Bayreuth, Germany, Who Remained in America after the American Revolution**. German-American Genealogical Research Monograph Number 2. (1974) rev. ed. 1979.
ISBN 0-915162-13-X.
Paper. $20.00. v + 51 pp. .... Vendor G0491

Smith, Clifford N. **Mercenaries from Hessen-Hanau Who Remained in Canada and the United States After the American Revolution**. German-American Genealogical Research Monograph Number 5. 1976.
ISBN 0-915162-04-0.
Paper. $20.00. iv + 105 pp. .... Vendor G0491

Smith, Clifford N. **Muster Rolls and Prisoner-of-War Lists in American Archival Collections Pertaining to the German Mercenary Troops Who Served with the British Forces During the American Revolution**. German-American Genealogical Research Monograph Number 3. 3 parts.
Part 1: Muster Rolls 1-25 (x + 64 pp.).
Part 2: Muster Rolls 26-52 (i + 54 pp.).
Part 3: Muster Rolls 53-72 (i + 57 pp.).
ISBN 0-915162-02-4 (the set).
Paper. $20.00/part. .... Vendor G0491

Smith, Clifford N. **Notes on Hessian Soldiers Who Remained in Canada and the United States After the American Revolution**. German-American Genealogical Research Monograph Number 28, Part 4 (in five separately published subparts).
Part 1: ISBN 0-915162-96-2.
Part 2: ISBN 0-915162-97-0.
Part 3: ISBN 0-915162-98-9.
Part 4: ISBN 0-915162-99-7.
Part 5: ISBN 0-915162-89-X.
Paper. $20.00/part. .... Vendor G0491

Smith, Clifford N. **Political Activists from Hesse, Germany, 1832-1834: Among Whom Many Immigrants to America**. German-American Genealogical Research Monograph Number 29. 1993.
ISBN 0-915162-73-3.
Paper. $20.00. i + 25 pp. double-columned. .... Vendor G0491

Smith, Kenneth L. **German Church Books**. 1993. Indexed. Illus.
Book #1150.
Cloth. $29.50. 223 pp. .... Vendor G0082

Staudt, Ricardo W. **Palatine Church Visitations, 1609 . . . Deanery of Kusel**. 1930.
Indexed.
Contact vendor for information. 147 pp. .... Vendor G0011

Thode, Ernest. **Address Book for Germanic Genealogy**. 6th ed. (1994) reprint 1997.
Paper. $24.95. 195 pp. .... Vendor G0010

Thode, Ernest. **Address Book for Germanic Genealogy**. 6th ed. 1997. Illus.
Paper. $27.45 postpaid ($29.23 in OH). 196 pp. .... Vendor G0197

Thode, Ernest. **Genealogical Gazetteer of Alsace-Lorraine**.
Paper. $18.00. .... Vendor G0574

Thode, Ernest. **Genealogical Gazetteer of Alsace-Lorraine**. 1986. Illus.
Paper. $17.50 postpaid ($18.64 in OH). 137 pp. .... Vendor G0197

Thode, Ernest. **German-English Genealogical Dictionary**. (1992) reprint 1996.
Paper. $29.95. 318 pp. .... Vendor G0010

Thode, Ernest. **German-English Genealogical Dictionary**. 1992. Illus.
Paper. $32.95 ($35.09 in OH). xxxiv + 286 pp. .... Vendor G0197

Ernest Thode GERMAN-ENGLISH GENEALOGICAL DICTIONARY

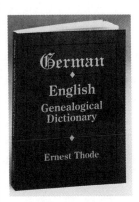

8½" x 11". 318 pp.,
paperback. 1992.
Vendor G0010. $29.95

This book is designed for the family researcher who has little or no knowledge of German but who nevertheless needs to make a translation of German-language documents. With its emphasis on simplicity, the dictionary covers thousands of German terms and defines them in single words or brief phrases. All words, symbols, and abbreviations in the dictionary were chosen on the basis of their association with genealogy, having been noted in church records, civil registration records, family correspondence, genealogical journals, ships' passenger lists, and emigration records. In conjunction with a standard German-English dictionary, the user of this work should be able to make a word-by-word translation of any German document.

Besides the basic word list, the dictionary contains several other features which are tailor-made for the German-American researcher: a map of the German provinces of the 1871–1918 period, samples of German handwriting and Fraktur type, and a guide to genealogical symbols used in Germany.

Genealogical Publishing Co., Inc.

Thode, Ernest. **Interpreting Mispelled Misspelt Misspelled German Place-Names.** 1992.
Paper. $7.50 ($7.99 in OH). .... Vendor G0197

Tribbeko, John, and George Ruperti. **List of Germans from the Palatinate Who Came to England in 1709.** (1965) reprint 1996.
Paper. $7.00. 44 pp. .... Vendor G0011

Uncapher, Wendy, and Linda Herrick. **Brief Look at German/Prussian History.** 1994.
    Timeline, brief history, maps.
Paper. $7.00. 6 pp. .... Vendor G0195

Great Britain

Barber, Rev. Henry. **British Family Names—Their Origin and Meaning . . .** (1903) reprint 1990.
Contact vendor for information. 298 pp. .... Vendor G0011

Baring-Gould, Sabine. **Family Names and Their Story**. (1910) reprint 1996. Indexed.
A study of English surnames.
Paper. $32.50. 432 pp. .... Vendor G0011

Baxter, Angus. **In Search of Your British & Irish Roots**. 3rd ed. (1994) reprint 1996.
Paper. $16.95. 320 pp. .... Vendor G0010

Burke, Ashworth P. **Burke's Family Records**. (1897) reprint 1994. Indexed. Illus.
Traces the descent of some 300 cadet houses of the British nobility from Airey and Groton to Swanzy and Yarker.
Paper. $50.00. 709 pp. .... Vendor G0011

Burke, John. **A Genealogical and Heraldic History of the Commoners of Great Britain and Ireland**. In Four Volumes. Reprinted with the *Index to Pedigrees in Burke's Commoners*, by George Ormerod. (1834-1838, 1907) reprint 1996. Indexed. Illus.
The standard genealogical guide to families in Great Britain and Ireland who enjoyed territorial possession or official rank, but were uninvested with heritable honors.
Paper. $200.00. 3,113 pp. .... Vendor G0011

Chapman, Colin R. **Ecclesiastical Courts, Their Officials and Their Records**. Indexed.
Paper. $12.95. 72 pp. .... Vendor G0552

Chapman, Colin R. **The Growth of British Education and Its Records**. 1991. Illus. Paper. $12.95. 76 pp. .... Vendor G0552

Chapman, Colin R. **Pre-1841 Censuses and Population Listings in the British Isles**. 4th ed. 1996. Indexed. Paper. $15.00. 82 pp. .... Vendor G0010

Chapman, Colin R. **Tracing Your British Ancestors**. 1996. Indexed.
Irish, Scottish, English, and Welsh ancestors, as well as those from the Isle of Man and the Channel Islands, can all be traced using methods described in this book. Paper. $15.00. 108 pp. .... Vendor G0010

Chapman, Colin R. **Weights, Money and Other Measures Used By Our Ancestors**. 1996. Indexed. Paper. $15.00. 92 pp. .... Vendor G0010

Daunton, M. J. **Progress and Poverty: An Economic and Social History of Britain, 1700-1850**. 1995.
British society and the British economy underwent major structural change over the period from 1700 to 1850, as people moved from agriculture and rural life to industry and towns. Combines social, political, and economic history. Paper. $24.00. 620 pp. .... Vendor G0611

Ewen, Cecil Henry L'Estrange. **A History of Surnames of the British Isles**. A Concise Account of Their Origin, Evolution, Etymology, and Legal Status. (1931, 1968) reprint 1995. Indexed. Paper. $41.50. 539 pp. .... Vendor G0011

Fairbairn, James. **Fairbairn's Book of Crests of the Families of Great Britain and Ireland** 2 vols. in 1. (1905) reprint 1993. Illus. Cloth. $60.00. 1,073 pp. .... Vendor G0010

Fischer. **Albion's Seed: Four British Folkways in America**. 1989.
This is an absolutely fascinating book that should be read and enjoyed by anyone tracing British ancestors who came into America between 1628 and 1775. This is an in-depth look at these immigrants, their customs and their life. Abundant footnotes add to its value as a research tool. Paper. $24.95. 946 pp. .... Vendor G0611

Gibson, Jeremy S. W. **Bishops' Transcripts and Marriage Licenses in England, Wales, and Ireland**. 3rd ed. 1992. Paper. $6.00. 40 pp. .... Vendor G0010

Gibson, Jeremy S. W. **Census Returns, 1841-1881 on Microfilm**. 5th ed. 1989. Contact vendor for information. 50 pp. .... Vendor G0010

Gibson, J. S. W., and Colin Rogers. **Electoral Registers Since 1832;** and Burgess Rolls. Second edition. 1990. Paper. $7.50. 60 pp. .... Vendor G0010

Gibson, Jeremy S. W. **The Hearth Tax,** Other Later Stuart Tax Lists, and the Association Oath Rolls. 1990. Paper. $7.50. 60 pp. .... Vendor G0010

Gibson, J. S. W., and Mervyn Medlycott. **Local Census Listings, 1522-1930:** Holdings in the British Isles. 1992.
Paper. $7.50. 60 pp. .... Vendor G0010

Gibson, Jeremy S. W. **Local Newspapers, 1750-1920 in England and Wales, Channel Islands, Isle of Man**. 1989. Illus.
Contact vendor for information. 64 pp. .... Vendor G0010

Gibson, Jeremy S. W. **Marriage, Census and Other Indexes in Great Britain**. 4th ed. 1992.
Paper. $7.50. 60 pp. .... Vendor G0010

Gibson, J. S. W., and Mervyn Medlycott. **Militia Lists and Musters, 1757-1876**. A Directory of Holdings in the British Isles. Second edition. 1990.
Paper. $6.50. 42 pp. .... Vendor G0010

Gibson, J. S. W., and Colin Rogers. **Poll Books c. 1696-1872**. A Directory of Holdings in the British Isles. 2nd ed. 1990.
Paper. $7.50. 60 pp. .... Vendor G0010

Gibson, Jeremy S. W. **Probate Jurisdictions in Great Britain and Ireland**. 3rd ed. (1986) reprint 1989. Illus.
Paper. $7.50. 72 pp. .... Vendor G0010

Gibson, Jeremy S. W. **Quarter Sessions Records in England and Wales**. 3rd ed. 1992.
Paper. $6.50. 47 pp. .... Vendor G0010

Gibson, Jeremy S. W. **Unpublished Personal Name Indexes in Record Offices and Libraries in Great Britain**. 2nd ed. 1989.
Paper. $6.00. 40 pp. .... Vendor G0010

Guppy, Henry Brougham. **Homes of Family Names in Great Britain**. (1890, 1891) reprint 1996. Indexed. Illus.
Paper. $45.00. 667 pp. .... Vendor G0011

Harrison, Henry. **Surnames of the United Kingdom**. A Concise Etymological Dictionary. 2 vols. in 1. (1912-18) reprint 1996.
Paper. $45.00. 622 pp. in all. .... Vendor G0011

Johnson, Anne E. **A Student's Guide to British American Genealogy**. 1995. Indexed. Illus.
Hard-cover. $24.95. 208 pp. .... Vendor G0776

Morgan. **The Oxford History of Britain**. 1988.
    Tells the story of Britain and her peoples over two thousand years. A very useful reference.
Paper. $16.95. 746 pp. .... Vendor G0611

Pelling, George. **Beginning Your Family History in Great Britain**. 4th ed. (1980) reprint 1989. Illus.
Paper. $7.50. 64 pp. .... Vendor G0010

Robbins, Keith. **Nineteenth-Century Britain: Integration and Diversity**. (1988) reprint 1995.

This is a study of how events of the 19th century forged the modern Britain. Paper. $18.95. 205 pp. .... Vendor G0611

Saul, Nigel, ed. **The National Trust Historical Atlas of Britain.** Prehistoric and Medieval. Illus. Cloth. $53.95. 224 pp. .... Vendor G0576

Saul, Pauline, and F.C. Markwell. **The A-Z Guide to Tracing Ancestors in Britain.** 4th ed. 1991. Indexed. Illus. Paper. $17.95. 256 pp. .... Vendor G0010

Society of Genealogists. **Monumental Inscriptions in the Library of the Society of Genealogists.** Part 2 Northern England, Wales, Scotland, Ireland and Overseas. 1987. Paper. £2.40. 46 pp. .... Vendor G0557

Summers, Peter, and John E. Titterton, eds. **Hatchments in Britain, Volume 1: Northamptonshire, Warwickshire, Worcestershire.** 1975. Cloth. £13.95. .... Vendor G0579

Summers, Peter, and John E. Titterton, eds. **Hatchments in Britain, Volume 2: Norfolk and Suffolk.** 1976. Cloth. £13.95. .... Vendor G0579

Summers, Peter, and John E. Titterton, eds. **Hatchments in Britain, Volume 3: Cumbria, Northumberland, Durham, Lancashire, Yorkshire.** 1979. Cloth. £13.95. .... Vendor G0579

Summers, Peter, and John E. Titterton, eds. **Hatchments in Britain, Volume 4: Oxfordshire, Berkshire, Wiltshire, Buckinghamshire, Bedfordshire.** 1982. Cloth. £13.95. .... Vendor G0579

Summers, Peter, and John E. Titterton, eds. **Hatchments in Britain, Volume 5: Kent, Surry, Sussex.** 1985. Cloth. £13.95. .... Vendor G0579

Summers, Peter, and John E. Titterton, eds. **Hatchments in Britain, Volume 6: Essex, Middlesex, Hertfordshire, Cambridgeshire, Hunts.** 1985. Cloth. £13.95. .... Vendor G0579

Summers, Peter, and John E. Tittleton, eds. **Hatchments in Britain, Volume 7: Cornwall, Devon, Dorset, Somerset, Hampshire, Isle of Wight, Gloucestershire.** 1988. Cloth. £13.95. .... Vendor G0579

Summers, Peter, and John E. Titterton, eds. **Hatchments in Britain, Volume 8: Lincolnshire, Nottinghamshire, Cheshire, Staffordshire, Derbyshire, Leicestershire, Rutland.** 1988. Cloth. £13.95. .... Vendor G0579

Summers, Peter, and John E. Titterton, eds. **Hatchments in Britain, Volume 9: Herefordshire, Shropshire, Wales, Scotland, Monmouthshire, Ireland, and Hatchments in Former British Colonies.** 1994. Cloth. £13.95. .... Vendor G0579

Summers, Peter, and John E. Titterton, eds. **Hatchments in Britain, Volume 10: The Development and Use of Hatchments**. 1994.
Cloth. £13.95. .... Vendor G0579

✌ Great Britain—England ✌

General References

Alcock, N. W. **Old Title Deeds: A Guide for Local and Family Historians**. 1994. Illus.
Cloth. £13.95. 112 pp. .... Vendor G0579

Alvey, Norman. **From Chantry to Oxfam: A Short History of Charities and Charity Legislation**. 1995. Illus.
Paper. £6.95. 80 pp. .... Vendor G0579

Atherton, Louise. **"Never Complain, Never Explain"**: Records of the Foreign Office and State Paper Office, 1500-c1960. 1994.
The records of the Foreign Office are vital for research into British foreign relations. It is an indispensable guide for any student of British political history.
£8.95 plus shipping. 189 pp. .... Vendor G0558

Bardsley, Alan. **First Name Variants**. 1996.
This book lists given names and their variants alphabetically and then groups together those that have a common root. For the genealogist faced with an obscure pet name, it identifies the possible origin and opens up the search for alternatives. The coverage is primarily for the English-speaking world of the 17th to 19th centuries with the more common Welsh, Irish, and Scottish links.
£6.00 (overseas surface). 108 pp. .... Vendor G0588

Bardsley, Charles Wareing. **A Dictionary of English and Welsh Surnames with Special American Instances**. (Rev. ed., 1901) reprint 1996.
Cloth. $50.00. xvi + 837 pp. .... Vendor G0010

Beckett, J. V. **Local Taxation**. 1980.
Paper. £2.95. 56 pp. .... Vendor G0579

Bradley, Alan. **Family History on Your PC: A Book for Beginners**. 1996. Illus.
£11.70 (overseas surface). 224 pp. .... Vendor G0588

Breed, G. R. **My Ancestors Were Baptists: How Can I Find Out More About Them?** 3rd rev. ed. 1994.
Paper. £4.99. 104 pp. .... Vendor G0557

The British Public Record Office: History, Description, Record Groups, Finding Aids, and Materials for American History, with Special Reference to Virginia. (1960) reprint 1984.
Paper. $7.95. 178 pp. .... Vendor G0553

Burke, Arthur M. **Key to the Ancient Parish Registers of England and Wales.**
(1908) reprint 1996. Illus.
Paper. $18.00. 163 pp. .... Vendor G0011

Burke, J., and J. B. Burke. **Burke's Extinct & Dormant Baronetcies of England,**
Ireland & Scotland. (1841) reprint 1994.
Contact vendor for information. 644 pp. .... Vendor G0010

Burke, J. B., comp. **Roll of Battle Abbey.** (1848) reprint 1989.
A list of several hundred noble companions of William the Conqueror, with bio-
graphical and genealogical details.
Contact vendor for information. 127 pp. .... Vendor G0010

Cale, Michelle. **An Introduction to Sources for Criminal and Legal History from**
1800. 1996.
An invaluable introduction to modern, post-1800 legal records in the PRO. Covers
both criminal and civil cases.
£12.99 plus shipping. 160 pp. .... Vendor G0558

Camp, A. J. **First Steps in Family History.** 2nd ed. 1996.
Paper. £1.45. 32 pp. .... Vendor G0557

Camp, A. J., comp. **An Index to the Wills Proved in the Prerogative Court of**
Canterbury 1750-1800: Vol. 1 A-Bh. 1976.
Paper. £4.00. 414 pp. .... Vendor G0557

Camp, A. J., comp. **Index to the Wills Proved in the Prerogative Court of Canter-**
bury 1750-1800: Vol. 2 Bi-Ce.
Microfilm. £5.53. 8 fiche. .... Vendor G0557

Camp, A. J., comp. **Index to the Wills Proved in the Prerogative Court of Canter-**
bury 1750-1800: Vol. 3 Ch-G.
Microfilm. £5.11. 7 fiche. .... Vendor G0557

Camp, A. J., comp. **Index to the Wills Proved in the Prerogative Court of Canter-**
bury 1750-1800: Vol. 4 H-M.
Microfilm. £7.15. 7 fiche. .... Vendor G0557

Camp, A. J., comp. **Index to the Wills Proved in the Prerogative Court of Canter-**
bury 1750-1800: Vol. 5 N-Sh. 1991.
Paper. £16.00. 259 pp. .... Vendor G0557

Camp, A. J., comp. **Index to the Wills Proved in the Prerogative Court of Canter-**
bury 1750-1800: Vol. 6 Si-Z. 1992.
Paper. £18.00. 310 pp. .... Vendor G0557

Camp, A. J. **My Ancestors Moved (in England or Wales): How Can I Trace Where**
They Came From? 1994.
Paper. £4.60. 66 pp. .... Vendor G0557

Chapman, C. R. **An Introduction to Using Newspapers and Periodicals.** 1993.
£2.70 (overseas surface). 30 pp. .... Vendor G0588

Clifford, D. J. H. **My Ancestors Were Congregationalists in England and Wales:** With a List of Registers. 1992.
Paper. £3.90. 94 pp. .... Vendor G0557

Coldham, Peter Wilson. **American Wills and Administrations** in the Prerogative Court of Canterbury, 1610-1857. 1989. Indexed.
Cloth. $30.00. 416 pp. .... Vendor G0010

Coldham, Peter Wilson. **American Wills Proved in London, 1611-1775.** 1992.
Cloth. $30.00. 360 pp. .... Vendor G0010

Coldham, Peter Wilson. **English Adventurers and Emigrants, 1661-1733.** 1985. Indexed.
Cloth. $15.00. 238 pp. .... Vendor G0011

Coldham, Peter Wilson. **English Estates of American Colonists.** American Wills and Administrations in the Prerogative Court of Canterbury, 1610-1699. (1980) reprint 1983. Indexed.
Cloth. $7.50. 78 pp. .... Vendor G0011

Coldham, Peter Wilson. **English Estates of American Colonists.** American Wills and Administrations in the Prerogative Court of Canterbury, 1700-1799. (1980) reprint 1991. Indexed.
Paper. $15.00. 151 pp. .... Vendor G0011

Coldham, Peter Wilson. **English Estates of American Settlers.** American Wills and Administrations in the Prerogative Court of Canterbury, 1800-1858. 1981. Indexed.
Cloth. $9.50. 103 pp. .... Vendor G0011

Coldham, Peter Wilson. **Lord Mayor's Court of London Depositions Relating to Americans, 1641-1736.** Indexed.
   Abstracts of depositions made before the Lord Mayor's Court of London providing unpublished information regarding American colonials or Englishmen having business interests in America.
Cloth, $12.00. Paper, $10.00. 119 pp. .... Vendor G0627

Cole, A. **An Introduction to Poor Law Documents Before 1834.** 1993.
£2.70 (overseas surface). 35 pp. .... Vendor G0588

Cornwall, J. **An Introduction to Reading Old Title Deeds.** 1993.
£2.70 (overseas surface). 32 pp. .... Vendor G0588

Craven, Wesley Frank. **The Virginia Company of London, 1606-1624.** (1957) reprint 1995. Illus.
Paper. $10.00. 70 pp. .... Vendor G0011

Culling, J. **An Introduction to Occupations: a Preliminary List.** 1994.
£3.25 (overseas surface). 44 pp. .... Vendor G0588

Currer-Briggs, Noel. **English Adventurers and Virginian Settlers.** 2 vols. 1969.
   Material relating to 17th-century emigrants from East Anglia to Virginia.
Paper. £30.00. .... Vendor G0579

Currer-Briggs, Noel. **The Search for Mr. Thomas Kirbye, Gentleman.** 1986. Illus.

A distinguished professional genealogist reveals his methods in a thirty-year search for an early English settler in the United States.
Cloth. £13.95. 160 pp. .... Vendor G0579

Currie, C. R. J., ed. **English County Histories: A Guide**. A Tribute to C. R. Elrington. Illus.
Cloth. $62.95. 4,496 pp. .... Vendor G0576

des Cognets, Louis, Jr. **English Duplicates of Lost Virginia Records**. (1958) reprint 1990. Indexed.
Cloth. $25.00. 380 pp. .... Vendor G0010

Dunning, Robert. **Local History for Beginners**. 1980. Illus.
Cloth. £7.99. 128 pp. .... Vendor G0579

Dymond, David. **Writing Local History**. 1996.
Paper. £6.95. 112 pp. .... Vendor G0579

Ellis, Mary. **Using Manorial Records**. 1994.
This co-publication with the Royal Commission on Historical Manuscripts explores manorial records held by the PRO as well as the Manorial Documents Register held by the Commission.
£6.95 plus shipping. 109 pp. .... Vendor G0558

Emmison, F. G. **Introduction to Archives**. 1977. Illus.
Paper. £1.50. 52 pp. .... Vendor G0579

Erickson, Charlotte. **Invisible Immigrants: The Adaption of English and Scottish Immigrants in 19th-Century America**. (1972) reprint 1990.
A remarkable collection of letters from people who immigrated to America in the 19th century and who kept in touch with friends and relatives in England and Scotland. Over 200 letters from 25 families are included.
Paper. $18.95. 531 pp. .... Vendor G0611

Evans, Eric J. **Tithes: Maps, Apportionments and the 1836 Act**. 1993. Illus.
Paper. £4.95. 32 pp. .... Vendor G0579

Family History Library. **Research Outline: England**.
Leaflet. $.75. 52 pp. .... Vendor G0629

FFHS. **Army Records for the Family Historian**.
£5.95 (overseas surface). .... Vendor G0588

FFHS. **Basic Sources for Family History**. 3rd ed.
£4.55 (overseas surface). .... Vendor G0588

FFHS. **Book of Trades**. 3 parts.
£3.90 each (overseas surface). .... Vendor G0588

FFHS. **British Genealogical Periodicals**.
£5.55 (overseas surface). .... Vendor G0588

FFHS. **British Genealogical Periodicals: Vol. 2 (Parts 1 & 2) and Vol. 3 (Parts 1 & 2)**.
£5.35 (overseas surface) .... Vendor G0588

FFHS. **British Genealogical Periodicals Vol. 3 Part 2.**
£4.95 (overseas surface). .... Vendor G0588

FFHS. **Computer Aided Genealogy.**
£5.85 (overseas surface). .... Vendor G0588

FFHS. **Computers in Family History.** 4th ed.
£4.40 (overseas surface). .... Vendor G0588

FFHS. **Current Publications by [FFHS] Member Societies.** 8th ed.
£6.00 (overseas surface). .... Vendor G0588

FFHS. **English Genealogy.** 3rd ed.
£5.15 (overseas surface). .... Vendor G0588

FFHS. **Family Historian's Enquire Within.** 5th ed.
£10.80 (overseas surface). .... Vendor G0588

FFHS. **Genealogical Computer Packages.**
£4.00 (overseas surface). .... Vendor G0588

FFHS. **Hatred Pursued Beyond the Grave.**
£11.65 (overseas surface). .... Vendor G0588

FFHS. **How to Tackle Your Family History: A Preliminary Guide for the Beginner.** Revised and updated. 1992.
£1.55 (overseas surface). 6 pp. .... Vendor G0588

FFHS. **Internet for Genealogy.**
£2.35 (overseas surface). .... Vendor G0588

FFHS. **An Introduction to Wills, Probate & Death Duty Records.**
£3.25 (overseas surface). .... Vendor G0588

FFHS. **Latin Glossary for Family Historians.**
£2.75 (overseas surface). .... Vendor G0588

FFHS. **Making Use of the Census.** 2nd ed.
£5.95 .... Vendor G0588

FFHS. **Marriage Laws, Records, Rites, and Customs.**
£6.70 (overseas surface). .... Vendor G0588

FFHS. **Mediaeval Records.**
£5.55 (overseas surface). .... Vendor G0588

FFHS. **Militia Records Since 1757.**
£5.00 (overseas surface). .... Vendor G0588

FFHS. **Monumental Inscriptions.** 4th ed.
£1.80 (overseas surface). .... Vendor G0588

FFHS. **Oral History.**
£4.85 (overseas surface). .... Vendor G0588

FFHS. Records of the RAF.
£4.85 (overseas surface). .... Vendor G0588

FFHS. Register of One-Name Studies. 12th ed.
£4.35 (overseas surface). .... Vendor G0588

FFHS. Sources for Family History in the Home.
£2.00 (overseas surface). .... Vendor G0588

FFHS. Using Marriage Records.
£2.00 (overseas surface).. Vendor G0588

Foot, William. **Maps for Family History.** 1994.
This guide covers the records of the Valuation Office, Tithe and the National Farm Surveys of England and Wales, 1836-1943.
£8.95 plus shipping. 93 pp. .... Vendor G0558

Foster, David. **The Rural Constabulary Act 1839.** 1982.
Paper. £2.95. 56 pp. .... Vendor G0579

Fowler, Simon. **Army Records for Family Historians.** 1992.
A clear and comprehensive guide for people tracing army ancestors. Covers the period from Elizabeth I to the 1960s.
£4.75 plus shipping. 91 pp. .... Vendor G0558

Fowler, Simon, Peter Illiott Roy Nesbit, and Christina Goulter. **RAF Records in the PRO.** 1994.
£8.95 plus shipping. 120 pp. .... Vendor G0558

Fowler, Simon. **Sources for Labour History.** 1995.
This book offers a concise overview to the Labour historian and includes a look at the records of the trade unions, industrial relations and disputes, employment for women, and the political wing of the Labour movement.
£$10.95 plus shipping. 93 pp. .... Vendor G0558

Friar, Stephen. **A Companion to the English Parish Church.** 1996. Illus.
A comprehensive guide to all aspects of the 18,000 English parish churches dating from the post-Roman period to the present day. Subjects include parochial and vestry administration and records, the role of the parish church in the history of a community, hatchments and heraldry, traditions and folklore, and much more.
Cloth. $44.95. 544 pp. .... Vendor G0576

Friar, Stephen. **Heraldry for the Local Historian and Genealogists.** 1996. Illus.
Paper. $22.95. .... Vendor G0576

Gandy, M. **Basic Approach to Latin for Family Historians.** 1995.
£2.00 (overseas surface). 16 pp. .... Vendor G0588

Gandy, M. **An Introduction to Planning Research: Short Cuts in Family History.** 1993.
£3.65 (overseas surface). 60 pp. .... Vendor G0588

Gaskell, S. M. **Building Control.** 1983. Illus.
Paper. £2.95. 76 pp. .... Vendor G0579

Gelling, Margaret. **Signposts to the Past**. 2nd rev. ed. 1988.
Comprehensive study of British place names.
Cloth. £14.99. 288 pp. .... Vendor G0579

Gibbens, L. **An Introduction to Church Registers**. 1994.
£3.25 (overseas surface). 43 pp. .... Vendor G0588

Gibson, J., and C. Rogers. **Coroners' Records in England and Wales**. (1988) reprint
1992.
£2.50 49 pp. .... Vendor G0557

Gibson, J., M. Medlycott, and D. Mills. **Land and Window Tax Assessments**. 1993.
£2.50. 52 pp. .... Vendor G0557

Gibson, J., and H. Creaton. **Lists of Londoners**. 1992. Amended reprint 1993.
£2.50. 39 pp. .... Vendor G0557

Gibson, J., and C. Rogers. **Poor Law Union Records. Part 1: South-east England
and East Anglia**. 1993.
£3.95. 72 pp. .... Vendor G0557

Gibson, J., and C. Rogers. **Poor Law Union Records. Part 2 The Midlands and
Northern England**. 1993.
£3.95. 64 pp. .... Vendor G0557

Gibson, J., and C. Rogers. **Poor Law Union Records. Part 3: South West England,
The Marches & Wales**. 1993.
£3.95. 72 pp. .... Vendor G0557

Gibson, J., and C. Rogers. **Poor Law Union Records. Part 4: Gazetteer of England
and Wales**. 1993.
£3.95. 80 pp. .... Vendor G0557

Gibson, J., and A. Dell. **Protestation Returns 1641-42 and Other Contemporary
Listings**. 1995.
£3.95 84 pp. .... Vendor G0557

Gibson, J., and A. Dell. **Tudor and Stuart Muster Rolls**. 1991.
£2.00. 41 pp. .... Vendor G0557

Gibson, J., and J. Hunter. **Victuallers' Licences: Records for Family and Local
Historians**. 1994.
£2.50. 56 pp. .... Vendor G0557

Gibson, J. S. W., and Pamela Peskett. **Record Offices in England and Wales:** How
to Find Them. 5th ed. 1992. Illus.
Paper. $7.50. 60 pp. .... Vendor G0010

Gillis. **For Better, For Worse: British Marriages, 1600 to the Present**. 1985.
    Social historian Gillis has examined the role marriage and its rituals have played in
the life of the larger community.
Paper. $19.95. 417 pp. .... Vendor G0611

Grace, Frank. **The Late Victorian Town**. 1992. Illus.
Paper. £9.95. 96 pp. .... Vendor G0579

Grannum, Guy. **Tracing Your West Indian Ancestors**. 1995.
This guide brings together for the first time the wide variety of records available for the study of British West Indian ancestry in the PRO in order to develop research into this much neglected field of genealogy.
£8.95 plus shipping. 112 pp. .... Vendor G0558

Gray, Vic, and Bill Liddell. **Running a Local History Fair**. 1989. Illus.
Paper. £2.00. 16 pp. .... Vendor G0579

Hamilton-Edwards, G. **In Search of Ancestry**. 1983.
Cloth. £11.99. 224 pp. .... Vendor G0579

Harvey. **Maps in Tudor England**. 1993.
This beautiful book traces the cartographic revolution between 1485 and 1603. Those who know England well, or who are tracing families in this time period, will find this collection of maps fascinating. 8$^{1}/_{2}$" x 11".
Cloth. $29.95. 120 pp. .... Vendor G0611

Hawgood, D. **An Introduction to Using Computers in Genealogy**. 1994.
£3.30 (overseas surface). 51 pp. .... Vendor G0588

Hawkings, David T. **Criminal Ancestors**. A Guide to Historical Criminal Records in England and Wales. 1996. Illus.
Paper. $23.95. xiv + 448 pp. .... Vendor G0576

Hawkings, David T. **Railway Ancestors**. A Guide to the Staff Records of the Railway Companies of England and Wales 1822-1947. With a Foreword by Lord Teviot. Indexed.
Cloth. $44.95. 384 pp. .... Vendor G0576

Hey, David. **The Oxford Companion to Local and Family History**. 1996.
Over 2,000 entries provide detailed summaries of the latest knowledge in such fields as social, urban, agricultural, legal, family, and ecclesiastical history. Half genealogical encyclopedia, half historical dictionary, this volume is an essential reference for British family history.
Cloth. $45.00. 517 pp. .... Vendor G0611

Hey, David. **The Oxford Guide to Family History**. 1993. Indexed. Illus.
An essential guide to family history research. Written by an English family historian, with a decidedly English focus. This beautifully illustrated volume offers authoritative advice on tracing your family and suggests ways of broadening your research to look at the history of their times.
Cloth. $35.00. 246 pp. .... Vendor G0611

Hoff, Henry B., comp. **English Origins of American Colonists,** from *The New York Genealogical and Biographical Record*. (1903-1916) reprint 1991. Indexed.
Cloth. $28.50. 287 pp. .... Vendor G0010

Holding, N. W. **World War I Army Ancestry**. 2nd ed. 1991.
£4.85. 72 pp. .... Vendor G0588

Holding, N. W. **More Sources of WWI Army Ancestry**. 1991.
£4.85 (overseas surface). 66 pp. .... Vendor G0588

Holdsworth, W. A. **Handy Book of Parish Law.** 1995.
£5.05 (overseas surface). 112 pp. .... Vendor G0588

Hoyle, Richard. **Tudor Taxation Records.** 1994.
This is a guide for academics, and local and family historians, to the nature and use
of Tudor taxation records.
£5.95 plus shipping. 67 pp. .... Vendor G0558

Humphery-Smith, Cecil R. **The Phillimore Atlas and Index of Parish Registers.**
1995. Indexed. Illus.
Cloth. £50.00. 320 pp. .... Vendor G0579

Iredale, David. **Enjoying Archives.** 1985.
Cloth. £12.99. 224 pp. .... Vendor G0579

Irvine, Sherry. **Your English Ancestry: A Guide for North Americans.** 1993.
Presents a logical research routine for the family historian based in North America.
Paper. $12.95. 168 pp. .... Vendor G0570

Kermode and Walker. **Women, Crime and the Courts in Early Modern England.**
1994.
Examines in detail the relationship between the law and women's lives in 17th-
century England.
Paper. $17.95. 216 pp. .... Vendor G0611

Kitching, Christopher. **Archives: The Very Essence of Our Heritage.** 1996. Illus.
Paper. £14.95. 80 pp. .... Vendor G0579

Konrad, J. **English Family Research.**
Paper. $10.00. 65 pp. .... Vendor G0574

Leary, W. **My Ancestors Were Methodists: How Can I Find Out More About
Them?** 2nd ed. (1990) reprint 1993.
Paper. £3.45. 74 pp. .... Vendor G0557

Lewis, Samuel. **A Topographical Dictionary of England.** 4 vols. in 2. (1831) reprint
1996. Illus.
Cloth. $150.00. 2,464 pp. .... Vendor G0010

Library of Congress. **Sources for Research in English Genealogy.** Compiled by
Judith P. Reid.
The text of this is available on the Local History and Genealogy Reading Room's
home page: http://lcweb.loc.gov/rr/genealogy.
Free. Contact vendor for information. 11 pp. .... Vendor G0566

Litton, Pauline. **Using Baptism Records.** 1996.
£2.00 (overseas surface). 16 pp. .... Vendor G0588

Loyd, Lewis C. **The Origins of Some Anglo-Norman Families.** (1951) reprint 1992.
Indexed.
Cloth. $17.50. xvi + 140 pp. .... Vendor G0010

Lumas, Susan. **An Introduction to Census Returns of England & Wales.** 1992.
£1.84 (overseas surface). 21 pp. .... Vendor G0588

Lumas, Susan. **Making Use of the Census**. 2nd ed. 1993.
This book helps the reader understand the complexities and pleasures of census records, which are some of the most used by family historians.
£4.75 plus shipping. 111 pp. .... Vendor G0558

Lynskey, Marie. **Family Trees: A Manual for their Design, Production and Display**. 1996. Illus.
Cloth. £15.95. 112 pp. .... Vendor G0579

Martin, C. Trice. **The Record Interpreter**. 1994.
Classic reference work giving full Latin/English glossary, dictionaries of alternative and archaic terms and names.
Cloth. £20.00. 512 pp. .... Vendor G0579

McLaughlin, E. **Annals of the Poor**.
Paper. £1.00. .... Vendor G0555

McLaughlin, E. **Censuses 1841-91**.
Paper. £1.25. .... Vendor G0555

McLaughlin, E. **Family History from Newspapers**.
Paper. £1.50. .... Vendor G0555

McLaughlin, E. **Illegitimacy**.
Paper. £1.25. .... Vendor G0555

McLaughlin, E. **Interviewing Elderly Relatives**.
Paper. £1.95. .... Vendor G0555

McLaughlin, E. **Laying Out a Pedigree**.
Paper. £1.00. .... Vendor G0555

McLaughlin, E. **Making the Most of the IGI**.
Paper. £1.25. .... Vendor G0555

McLaughlin, E. **No Time for Family History?**
Paper. £1.25. .... Vendor G0555

McLaughlin, E. **Non-conformist Ancestors**.
Paper. £2.00. .... Vendor G0555

McLaughlin, E. **Parish Registers**.
Paper. £1.50. .... Vendor G0555

McLaughlin, E. **Reading Old Hand Writing**.
Paper. £1.50. .... Vendor G0555

McLaughlin, E. **Simple Latin for Family Historians**.
Paper. £1.50. .... Vendor G0555

McLaughlin, E. **Somerset House Wills After 1858**.
Paper. £1.50. .... Vendor G0555

McLaughlin, E. **St. Catherine's House**.
Paper. £1.25. .... Vendor G0555

McLaughlin, E. **Wills Before 1858.**
Paper. £1.25. .... Vendor G0555

Milligan, E. H., and M. J. Thomas. **My Ancestors Were Quakers: How Can I Find Out More About Them?** 1983.
Paper. £2.10. 37 pp. .... Vendor G0557

Milward, R. **Glossary of Household, Farming & Trade Terms from Probate Inventories.** 3rd ed. 1991.
£4.85 (overseas surface). 62 pp. .... Vendor G0588

Mordy, I. **My Ancestors Were Jewish: How Can I Find Out More About Them?** 1995.
Paper. £1.80. 30 pp. .... Vendor G0557

Moulton, Joy Wade. **Genealogical Resources in English Repositories.** 1988 (1992 Supplement). Indexed.
A survey of genealogical sources in 226 key record offices and libraries in England, with special notation of pre-1974 county boundaries, and resources available in repositories worldwide. Winner of the 1993 National Genealogical Society's Book Award for Excellence in Genealogical Sources and Methods. Included with each volume is a Supplement to Genealogical Resources in English Repositories and a 1996 Supplement update. Supplement includes changes in access information, e.g., address, telephone and fax numbers, hours, and also major holdings.
Cloth. $45.00. 648 pp. .... Vendor G0010

Munby, Lionel. **How Much is That Worth?** 1996. Illus.
Paper. £6.95. 48 pp. .... Vendor G0579

Munby, Lionel. **Reading Tudor and Stuart Handwriting.** 1988. Illus.
Paper. £2.00. 16 pp. .... Vendor G0579

Murphy, Michael. **Newspapers and Local History.** 1991. Illus.
Paper. £2.95. 24 pp. .... Vendor G0579

Nichols, E. L. **The International Genealogical Index.** 1992 Edition. 1995.
Paper. £2.90. 20 pp. .... Vendor G0557

Norrington, Valerie. **Recording the Present.** 1988. Illus.
Paper. £2.00. 16 pp. .... Vendor G0579

Palgrave, D. A. **Forming a One-Name Group.** 4th ed. 1992.
£2.90 (overseas surface). 16 pp. .... Vendor G0588

Palgrave-Moore, P. **How to Locate and Use Manorial Records.** 1985.
£2.75 (overseas surface). 25 pp. .... Vendor G0588

Palgrave-Moore, P. **How to Record Your Family Tree.** 5th ed. 1991.
£2.25 (overseas surface). 32 pp. .... Vendor G0588

Palgrave-Moore, P. **Understanding the History & Records of Nonconformity.** 1988.
£2.55 (overseas surface). 32 pp. .... Vendor G0588

Park, P. B. **My Ancestors Were Manorial Tenants: How Can I Find Out More About Them?** 2nd ed. 1994.
Paper. £3.60. 61 pp. .... Vendor G0557

Petchey, W. J. **Armorial Bearings of the Sovereigns of England.** 1977. Illus. Paper. £2.95. 32 pp. .... Vendor G0579

Pols, R. **Dating Old Photographs.** 2nd ed. 1995. £6.00 (overseas surface). 83 pp. .... Vendor G0588

Pols, R. **Understanding Old Photographs.** 1995. £6.00 (overseas surface). 86 pp. .... Vendor G0588

Pratt, David H. **Researching British Probates, 1354-1858: Vol. 1, Northern England, Province of York.** 1992. Indexed. Illus.
  Explains how to search British wills readily available through Family History Library network. "This book should be required reading."—*VA Genealogical Society Newsletter*
Cloth. $77.50. 219 pp. .... Vendor G0118

Preece, Phyllis Pastore, and Floren Stocks Preece. **Handy Guide to English Genealogical Research.**
  Basic instruction on how to begin and continue your genealogical research in England.
Paper. $7.50. 49 pp. .... Vendor G0618

Probert, E. **Company & Business Records for Family Historians.** 1994. £4.85 (overseas surface). 80 pp. .... Vendor G0588

Public Record Office. **Additional Finding Aids: Guides to Places, 1841-1891, and Surname Indexes, 1841-1891.**
Information leaflet. Contact vendor for information. .... Vendor G0558

Public Record Office. **Admiralty Records as Sources for Biography and Genealogy.**
Information leaflet. Contact vendor for information. .... Vendor G0558

Public Record Office. **Air Records as Sources for Biography and Family History.**
Information leaflet. Contact vendor for information. .... Vendor G0558

Public Record Office. **The American Revolution: Guides and Lists to Documents in the Public Record Office.**
Information leaflet. Contact vendor for information. .... Vendor G0558

Public Record Office. **Apprenticeship Records as Sources for Genealogy in the Public Record Office.**
Information leaflet. Contact vendor for information. .... Vendor G0558

Public Record Office. **Army Pension Records.**
Information leaflet. Contact vendor for information. .... Vendor G0558

Public Record Office. **British Army Records as Sources for Biography and Genealogy.**
Information leaflet. Contact vendor for information. .... Vendor G0558

Public Record Office. **Censuses of Population, 1801-1891.**
Information leaflet. Contact vendor for information. .... Vendor G0558

Public Record Office. **Chancery Proceedings (Equity Suits).**
Information leaflet. Contact vendor for information. .... Vendor G0558

Public Record Office. **Customs and Excise Records as Sources for Biography and Family History.**
Information leaflet. Contact vendor for information. .... Vendor G0558

Public Record Office. **The Death Duty Registers.**
Information leaflet. Contact vendor for information. .... Vendor G0558

Public Record Office. **Emigrants: Documents in the Public Record Office.**
Information leaflet. Contact vendor for information. .... Vendor G0558

Public Record Office. **English Local History: A Note for Beginners.**
Information leaflet. Contact vendor for information. .... Vendor G0558

Public Record Office. **Equity Proceedings in the Court of Exchequer.**
Information leaflet. Contact vendor for information. .... Vendor G0558

Public Record Office. **First Visit to the Census Rooms?**
Information leaflet. Contact vendor for information. .... Vendor G0558

Public Record Office. **Genealogy Before the Parish Registers.**
Information leaflet. Contact vendor for information. .... Vendor G0558

Public Record Office. **How to Find a Census Return.**
Information leaflet. Contact vendor for information. .... Vendor G0558

Public Record Office. **Immigrants: Documents in the PRO.**
Information leaflet. Contact vendor for information. .... Vendor G0558

Public Record Office. **The International Genealogical Index (IGI).**
Information leaflet. Contact vendor for information. .... Vendor G0558

Public Record Office. **Land Grants in America and American Loyalists' Claims.**
Information leaflet. Contact vendor for information. .... Vendor G0558

Public Record Office. **Maps and Plans at Chancery Lane.**
Information leaflet. Contact vendor for information. .... Vendor G0558

Public Record Office. **Maps in the Public Record Office.**
Information leaflet. Contact vendor for information. .... Vendor G0558

Public Record Office. **Militia Muster Rolls 1522-1640.**
Information leaflet. Contact vendor for information. .... Vendor G0558

Public Record Office. **Navy, Royal Air Force and Merchant Navy Pension Records.**
Information leaflet. Contact vendor for information. .... Vendor G0558

Public Record Office. **Probate Records: Where to Look for a Will or Grant of Administration.**
Information leaflet. Contact vendor for information. .... Vendor G0558

Public Record Office. **Public Records Outside the Public Record Office.**
Information leaflet. Contact vendor for information. .... Vendor G0558

Public Record Office. **Records of Births, Marriages and Deaths.**
Information leaflet. Contact vendor for information. .... Vendor G0558

Public Record Office. **Records of the American and West Indian Colonies Before 1782.**
Information leaflet. Contact vendor for information. .... Vendor G0558

Public Record Office. **Records of the Registrar General of Shipping and Seamen.**
Information leaflet. Contact vendor for information. .... Vendor G0558

Public Record Office. **Royal Marines Records in the Public Record Office.**
Information leaflet. Contact vendor for information. .... Vendor G0558

Public Record Office. **Tax Records as a Source for Local and Family History, c. 1198 to 1698.**
Information leaflet. Contact vendor for information. .... Vendor G0558

Public Record Office. **Tithe Records in the Public Record Office.**
Information leaflet. Contact vendor for information. .... Vendor G0558

Public Record Office. **Tracing an Ancestor in the Army: Officers.**
Information leaflet. Contact vendor for information. .... Vendor G0558

Public Record Office. **Tracing an Ancestor in the Army: Soldiers.**
Information leaflet. Contact vendor for information. .... Vendor G0558

Public Record Office. **Tracing an Ancestor in the Merchant Navy: Masters and Mates.**
Information leaflet. Contact vendor for information. .... Vendor G0558

Public Record Office. **Tracing an Ancestor in the Merchant Navy: Seamen.**
Information leaflet. Contact vendor for information. .... Vendor G0558

Public Record Office. **Tracing an Ancestor in the Royal Navy: Officers.**
Information leaflet. Contact vendor for information. .... Vendor G0558

Public Record Office. **Tracing an Ancestor in the Royal Navy: Ratings.**
Information leaflet. Contact vendor for information. .... Vendor G0558

Public Record Office. **Tracing an Ancestor Who Was an Emigrant.**
Information leaflet. Contact vendor for information. .... Vendor G0558

Public Record Office. **Tracing an Ancestor Who Was an Immigrant.**
Information leaflet. Contact vendor for information. .... Vendor G0558

Public Record Office. **Using the Rolls Room.**
Information leaflet. Contact vendor for information. .... Vendor G0558

Raymond, S. A. **British Genealogical Periodicals: Miscellaneous Journals, Supplement 1.** 1994.
£8.05 (overseas surface). 80 pp. .... Vendor G0588

Reid, Andy. **The Union Workhouse: A Study Guide for Teachers and Local Historians.** 1994. Illus.
Paper. £10.95. 112 pp. .... Vendor G0579

Reid, Judith Prowse. **Genealogical Research in England's Public Record Office:** A Guide for North Americans. 1996. Indexed. Illus.
Cloth. $22.50. 164 pp. .... Vendor G0010

Richards, T. **Was Your Grandfather a Railwayman?** 3rd ed. 1995.
£6.00 108 pp. .... Vendor G0588

Richardson, John. **The Local Historian's Encyclopedia**. Rev. ed. 1993.
Cloth. £15.95. 264 pp. .... Vendor G0579

Rogers, Colin D. **The Surname Detective**. 1996.
This helpful guide provides the amateur genealogist or family historian with the skills to research the distribution and history of a surname.
£13.00 (overseas surface). 258 pp. .... Vendor G0588

Ruston, A. **My Ancestors Were English Presbyterians/Unitarians: How Can I Find Out More About Them?** 1993.
Paper. £3.00. 64 pp. .... Vendor G0557

Sherwood, George. **American Colonists in English Records**. A Guide to Direct References in Authentic Records, Passenger Lists Not in "Hotten," Etc. 2 vols. in 1. 1932-33. Indexed.
Cloth. $13.50. 216 pp. in all. .... Vendor G0011

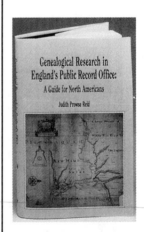

Shorney, David. **Protestant Nonconformity and Roman Catholicism**. 1996.
This guide introduces the reader to the most important records in the development of nonconformity and Catholicism. This includes significant genealogical sources such as the recusant rolls and the non-parochial registers held by the PRO.
£9.99 plus shipping. 136 pp. .... Vendor G0558

Smith, Clifford N. **British and German Deserters, Dischargees, and Prisoners of War Who May Have Remained in Canada and the United States, 1774-1783**.
British-American Genealogical Research Monograph Number 9. 2 parts.
Part 1 (1988; 24 pp. double-columned): ISBN 0-915162-34-2. Part 2 (1989; 18 pp. double-columned): ISBN 0-915162-35-0.
Paper. $20.00/part. .... Vendor G0491

Smith, Clifford N. **British Deportees to America**. British-American Genealogical Research Series. 8 parts.
Part 1: 1760-1763 (1977; 97 pp.). ISBN 0-915162-25-3.
Part 2: 1764-1765 (1979; 100 pp.). ISBN 0-915162-26-1.
Part 3: 1766-1767 (1981; 73 pp.). ISBN 0-915162-27-X.
Part 4: 1768-1769 (1986; 34 pp. double-columned). ISBN 0-915162-29-6.
Part 5: 1770-1771 (1986; 31 pp. double-columned). ISBN 0-915162-30-X.
Part 6: 1772-1773 (1987; 36 pp. double-columned). ISBN 0-915162-31-8.
Part 7: 1774-1775 (1987; 37 pp. double-columned). ISBN 0-915162-32-6.
Part 8: Cumulative Surname Index, 1760-1775 (1987; 22 pp. double-columned).
ISBN 0-915162-33-4.
Paper. $20.00/part. .... Vendor G0491

Smith, Clifford N. **Deserters and Disbanded Soldiers from British, German, and Loyalist Military Units in the South, 1782**. British-American Genealogical Research Monograph Number 10. 1991.
ISBN 0-915162-36-9.
Paper. $20.00. 26 pp. double-columned. .... Vendor G0491

Smith, Frank. **A Genealogical Gazetteer of England**. An Alphabetical Dictionary of Places, With Their Location, Ecclesiastical Jurisdiction, Population, and the Date of the Earliest Entry in the Registers of Every Ancient Parish in England. (1968) reprint 1995.
Cloth. $35.00. xv + 599 pp. .... Vendor G0010

Society of Genealogists. **Army Muster and Description Books**.
Leaflet. £0.20 .... Vendor G0557

Society of Genealogists. **Army Research: Selected Bibliography**. Rev. ed. 1995.
Leaflet. £0.20. .... Vendor G0557

Society of Genealogists. **County Codes**.
Leaflet. £0.20. .... Vendor G0557

Society of Genealogists. **The Data Protection Act and Genealogists**.
Leaflet. £0.20. .... Vendor G0557

Society of Genealogists. **Directories and Poll Books in the Library of the Society of Genealogists**. 6th ed. 1995.
Paper. £7.60. 125 pp. .... Vendor G0557

Society of Genealogists. **Employing a Professional Researcher: A Practical Guide.**
Leaflet. £0.20. .... Vendor G0557

Society of Genealogists. **Essential Addresses.**
Leaflet. £0.20. .... Vendor G0557

Society of Genealogists. **Family Records and Their Layout.** Rev. ed. 1994.
Leaflet. £0.20. .... Vendor G0557

Society of Genealogists. **Genealogy as a Career.** Rev. ed. 1994.
Leaflet. £0.20. .... Vendor G0557

Society of Genealogists. **Genealogy: A Basic Bibliography.** Rev. ed. 1994.
Leaflet. £0.20. .... Vendor G0557

Society of Genealogists. **General Register Office One-Name Lists in the Library of the Society of Genealogists.** 1995.
Paper. £1.65. 16 pp. .... Vendor G0557

Society of Genealogists. **Guide to Sources for One-Name Studies in the Society of Genealogists' Library.**
Leaflet. £0.20. .... Vendor G0557

Society of Genealogists. **Has It Been Done Before?**
Leaflet. £0.20. .... Vendor G0557

Society of Genealogists. **In Search of a Soldier Ancestor.** Rev. ed. 1995.
Leaflet. £0.20. .... Vendor G0557

Society of Genealogists. **Irregular Border Marriages.**
Leaflet. £0.20. .... Vendor G0557

Society of Genealogists. **A List of Parishes in Boyd's Marriage Index.** 6th ed. 1987. Corrected reprint 1994.
Paper. £3.25. 56 pp. .... Vendor G0557

Society of Genealogists. **Marriage Licences: Abstracts and Indexes in the Library of the Society of Genealogists.** 4th ed. 1991.
Paper. £1.80. 26 pp. .... Vendor G0557

Society of Genealogists. **Navy Research: Selected Bibliography.** Rev. ed. 1995.
Leaflet. £0.20. .... Vendor G0557

Society of Genealogists. **Note Taking and Keeping for Genealogists.** Rev. ed. 1994.
Leaflet. £0.20. .... Vendor G0557

Society of Genealogists. **Notes for Americans on Tracing British Ancestry.** Rev. ed. 1995.
Leaflet. £0.20. .... Vendor G0557

Society of Genealogists. **Parish Register Copies in the Library of the Society of Genealogists.** 11th ed. 1995.
Paper. £5.95. 152 pp. .... Vendor G0557

Society of Genealogists. **Protestation Returns of 1641-42.**
Leaflet. £0.20. .... Vendor G0557

Society of Genealogists. **The Relevance of Surnames.**
Leaflet. £0.20. .... Vendor G0557

Society of Genealogists. **The Right to Arms.**
Leaflet. £0.20 .... Vendor G0557

Society of Genealogists. **School, University and College Registers and Histories in the Library of the Society of Genealogists.** 1988.
£1.60 43 pp. .... Vendor G0557

Society of Genealogists. **Society of Genealogists' Bookshop and Order Form.**
Leaflet. Free. .... Vendor G0557

Society of Genealogists. **Society of Genealogists' Floor Guide.**
Leaflet. Free. .... Vendor G0557

Society of Genealogists. **Sources for Anglo-Indian Genealogy in the Library of the Society of Genealogists.** 1990.
Paper. £0.90. 12 pp. .... Vendor G0557

Society of Genealogists. **Starting Genealogy.** Rev. ed. 1995.
Leaflet. £0.20. .... Vendor G0557

Society of Genealogists. **The Trinity House Petitions: A Calendar of the Records of the Corporation of Trinity House, London, in the Library of the Society of Genealogists.** 1987.
Paper. £8.40. 303 pp. .... Vendor G0557

Society of Genealogists. **Using the Library of the Society of Genealogists.** 1996.
Paper. £0.70. 19 pp. .... Vendor G0557

Society of Genealogists. **Vicar-General Marriage Licences Surname Index 1751-1775.** 1996.
Paper. £27.50. 570 pp. .... Vendor G0557

Spring. **Law, Land & Family: Aristocratic Inheritance in England, 1300-1800.** 1993.
    A highly original book on the history of the common law of landholding, especially as it regards female heirs.
Cloth. $29.95. 199 pp. .... Vendor G0611

Stephens, W. B. **Sources for English Local History.** 1994.
Cloth. £16.95. 360 pp. .... Vendor G0579

Stone. **Broken Lives: Separation and Divorce in England, 1660-1857.** 1993.
    Case studies of actual divorces before the enactment of the first Divorce Act of 1857 afford fascinating insights into marital life in early modern England.
Cloth. $35.00. 355 pp. .... Vendor G0611

Stone. **The Family, Sex and Marriage in England, 1500-1800.** 1977.
    An in-depth study of the subject, filled with colorful examples. This abridged edition doesn't contain footnotes, however.
Paper. $16.00. 447 pp. .... Vendor G0611

Storey, R., and L. Madden. **Primary Sources for Victorian Studies**. 1977.
Cloth. £9.95. 88 pp. .... Vendor G0579

Stuart, Denis. **Latin for Local and Family Historians**. 1995.
Cloth. £13.95. 144 pp. .... Vendor G0579

Stuart, Denis. **Manorial Records**. 1992.
Cloth. £12.95. 128 pp. .... Vendor G0579

Swinnerton, I. **Basic Approach to Keeping Your Family Records**. 1995.
£2.00 (overseas surface). 16 pp. .... Vendor G0588

Swinnerton, Col. I. S. **An Introduction to the British Army: Its History, Traditions & Records**. 1996.
£3.25 (overseas surface). 44 pp. .... Vendor G0588

Tarver, Anne. **Church Court Records**. 1994. Illus.
The first practical guide to understanding both Latin and English church court records.
Cloth. £12.95. 160 pp. .... Vendor G0579

Tate, W. E. **The Parish Chest**. 3rd ed. 1983.
Account of the nature and use of parochial archives.
Cloth. £20.00. 400 pp. .... Vendor G0579

Taylor, N. C. **Computers in Genealogy Beginners Handbook**. 2nd ed. 1996.
Paper. £3.70. 76 pp. .... Vendor G0557

Thomas, Garth. **Records of the Militia from 1757**. 1993.
The first guide published specifically relating to the records of Britain's auxiliary forces from the mid-18th century.
£3.95 plus shipping. 59 pp. .... Vendor G0558

Thomas, Garth. **Records of the Royal Marines**. 1994.
Royal Marines have played a distinguished role in British military history. The records featured in this book provide a comprehensive account of their role worldwide.
£8.95 plus shipping. 76 pp. .... Vendor G0558

The Three Charters of the Virginia Company of London. With Seven Related Documents: 1606-1621. With an Introduction by Samuel M. Bemiss. (1957) reprint 1994.
Paper. $15.00. 128 pp. .... Vendor G0011

Tiller, Kate. **English Local History**. An Introduction. Illus.
Paper. $22.95. 256 pp. .... Vendor G0576

Tippey, David. **Genealogy on the Macintosh**. 1996.
A British book describing methods and genealogy packages useful for recording family history on an Apple Macintosh computer.
£4.20 (overseas surface). 48 pp. .... Vendor G0588

Titford, John. **Writing & Publishing Your Family History**. 1996.
A British book that discusses how to collect your family history material; how to

organize and arrange it into book form; how to decide on the size, shape, and number of illustrations; and how to get it published.
£6.00 (overseas surface). 128 pp. .... Vendor G0588

Wagner, Sir Anthony. **English Genealogy**. 1983.
Cloth. £20.00. 496 pp. .... Vendor G0579

Walne, Peter. **English Wills: Probate Records in England and Wales**. (1964) reprint 1981.
Paper. $7.95. 62 pp. .... Vendor G0553

Waters, Henry F. **Genealogical Gleanings in England**. Abstracts of Wills Relating to Early American Families. 2 vols. (1901) reprint 1997. Indexed. Illus.
Contact vendor for information. 1,779 pp. .... Vendor G0011

Watts, C. T., and M. J. Watts. **My Ancestor Was a Merchant Seaman: How Can I Find Out More About Him?** 1991.
Paper. £4.60. 84 pp. .... Vendor G0557

Watts, M. J., and C. T. Watts. **My Ancestor Was in the British Army: How Can I Find Out More About Him?** 1992. Reprint with addenda 1995.
Paper. £5.50. 130 pp. .... Vendor G0557

Webb, C. **Dates and Calendars for the Genealogist**. 1989. Reprint with amendments, 1994.
Paper. £2.70. 34 pp. .... Vendor G0557

Webb, C., comp. **An Index of Wills Proved in the Archdeaconry Court of London 1700-1807**. 1996.
Paper. £8.45. 100 pp. .... Vendor G0557

West, John. **Town Records**. 1983. Illus.
Cloth. £30.00. 384 pp. .... Vendor G0579

West, John. **Village Records**. Rev. ed. 1997. Illus.
Cloth. £30.00. 320 pp. .... Vendor G0579

White, H. L. **Monuments and Their Inscriptions: A Practical Guide**. 1977. 2nd corrected reprint with index, 1987.
Paper. £1.50. 64 pp. .... Vendor G0557

Wilkins, F. **Family History in Scottish Custom Records**.
£10.00. .... Vendor G0555

Willis, Arthur J., and Karin Proudfoot. **Genealogy for Beginners**. 1996. Illus.
Paper. £7.99. 208 pp. .... Vendor G0579

Wiltshire FHS. **The Compleat Parish Officer**. (1734) reprint 1996.
This early 18th-century handbook was published as a guide for parish officers who had to interpret and deal with the complex laws concerning the poor laws and the social problems of this period. This book should prove informative and of the utmost help for family historians endeavoring to discover more about the poor laws, their ancestors who may have been parish officers, and those ancestors who fell foul of the law.
£5.00 (overseas surface). 116 pp. .... Vendor G0588

Withington, Lothrop. **Virginia Gleanings in England**. Abstracts of 17th- and 18th-Century English Wills and Administrations Relating to Virginia and Virginians. 1980. Indexed. Illus.
Cloth. $35.00. 745 pp. .... Vendor G0010

Wood, T. **An Introduction to Civil Registration**. 1994.
£3.30 (overseas surface). 55 pp. .... Vendor G0588

Wood, Tom. **Using Record Offices**. 1996.
£2.00 (overseas surface). 16 pp. .... Vendor G0588

Wrightson. **English Society, 1580-1680**. 1982.
  A fascinating picture of English society and social change, 1580-1680.
Paper. $16.95. 264 pp. .... Vendor G0611

Bedfordshire

Society of Genealogists. **National Index of Parish Registers**. **Vol. 9, Part 1: Bedfordshire, Huntingdonshire**. 1991.
£6.00. 120 pp. .... Vendor G0557

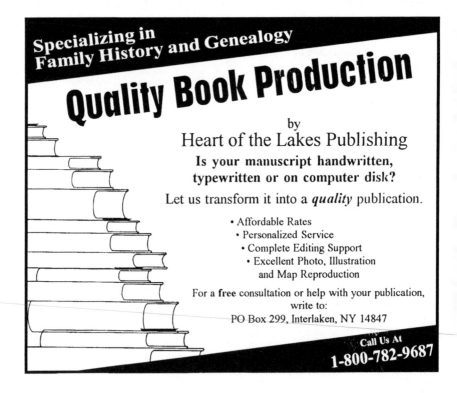

Berkshire

Society of Genealogists. **National Index of Parish Registers. Vol. 8, Part 1: Berkshire**. 1989.
£5.70. 128 pp. .... Vendor G0557

Buckinghamshire

Raymond, S. **A Genealogical Bibliography: Buckinghamshire**. 1993.
£5.85 (overseas surface). 57 pp. .... Vendor G0588

Society of Genealogists. **National Index of Parish Registers. Vol. 9, Part 3: Buckinghamshire**. 1992.
£5.70. 82 pp. .... Vendor G0557

Cambridgeshire

Society of Genealogists. **National Index of Parish Registers. Vol. 7: Cambridgeshire, Norfolk, Suffolk**. 1983.
£9.00. 278 pp. .... Vendor G0557

Cheshire

Raymond, S. **A Genealogical Bibliography: Cheshire Vol. 1,** Cheshire Genealogical Sources. 1995.
£10.55 (overseas surface). 106 pp. .... Vendor G0588

Raymond, S. **A Genealogical Bibliography: Cheshire Vol. 2,** Cheshire Family Histories and Pedigrees. 1995.
£7.75 (overseas surface). 43 pp. .... Vendor G0588

Society of Genealogists. **National Index of Parish Registers. Vol. 10, Part 1: Cheshire**. 1995.
£7.80. 103 pp. .... Vendor G0557

Cornwall

Dudley-Higham, Mary. **The Bellamys and Cornish Cousins of North Cornwall, England**. 1994. Indexed. Illus.
   A case study in Cornish family history research that identifies the Cornish as a distinctively separate people whose unique social history is traced from early times to the 19th century when thousands emigrated to America and other parts of the world. The lifestyle of the Bellamys and their Cornish kin is reconstructed through the analysis of wills, deeds, parish records, land sales, and the common use of the "three-life-lease" system that sustained them for centuries.
Cloth. $40.00 (tax included). 200 pp. .... Vendor G0153

THE BELLAMYS AND CORNISH COUSINS OF NORTH CORNWALL, ENGLAND

The harvesting of thousands of Cornish people who emigrated to America and other parts of the world in the early 19th century. Illustrated church histories, farms, manors, and land ownership maps, all offering insight into the unique and isolated lifestyle of the Cornish. Indexed. $40.00 tax inc.

**Mary Dudley-Higham
GENESIS PUBLICATIONS
5272 Williams Road
Suisun, California 94585**

Raymond, S. **A Genealogical Bibliography: Cornwall.** 2nd ed. 1994.
£9.05 (overseas surface). 84 pp. .... Vendor G0588

Cumberland

Raymond, S. **A Genealogical Bibliography: Cumberland and Westmorland.** 1993.
£5.85 (overseas surface). 68 pp. .... Vendor G0588

Derbyshire

Society of Genealogists. **National Index of Parish Registers. Vol. 6, Part 5: Derbyshire.** 1995.
£8.20 104 pp. .... Vendor G0557

Devon

Raymond, S. **A Genealogical Bibliography: Devon Vol. 1,** Devon Genealogical Sources. 2nd ed. 1994.
£8.80 (overseas surface). 83 pp. .... Vendor G0588

Raymond, S. **A Genealogical Bibliography: Devon Vol. 2,** Devon Family Histories and Pedigrees. 2nd ed. 1994.
£8.40 (overseas surface). 64 pp. .... Vendor G0588

Dorset

Raymond, S. **A Genealogical Bibliography: Dorset.** 1991.
£7.05 (overseas surface). 113 pp. .... Vendor G0588

Essex

Emmison, F. **Essex (England) Wills 1571-1577.** 1986.
Cloth. $21.45. 544 pp. .... Vendor G0406

Emmison, F. G. **Wills of the County of Essex (England), 1558-1565.** Indexed.
Cloth. $35.00. 369 pp. .... Vendor G0627

Society of Genealogists. **National Index of Parish Registers. Vol. 9, Part 4: Essex.** 1993.
£13.50. 264 pp. .... Vendor G0557

Gloucestershire

Raymond, S. **A Genealogical Bibliography: Gloucestershire and Bristol.** 1992.
£7.05 (overseas surface). 88 pp. .... Vendor G0588

Great Yarmouth

Manship, Henry. **History of Great Yarmouth.** Edited by Charles John Palmer. 2 vols. (1856) reprint 1994.
Cloth. $89.95. 435 + 388 pp. .... Vendor G0259

Hampshire

Raymond, S. **A Genealogical Bibliography: Hampshire.** 1995.
£9.45 (overseas surface). 103 pp. .... Vendor G0588

Huntingdonshire

Society of Genealogists. **National Index of Parish Registers. Vol. 9, Part 1: Bedfordshire, Huntingdonshire.** 1991.
£6.00. 120 pp. .... Vendor G0557

Kent

Roberts, Hugh. **Tenterden: The First Thousand Years**. 1995. Indexed. Illus. A history of Tenterden in Kent, England, the home of a number of emigrants to New England in the 17th century. Paper. $30.00 (surface mail delivery). 270 pp. .... Vendor G0731

Lancashire

Gandy, W., ed. **Lancashire Association Oath Rolls 1696**. (1921) reprint 1985. Paper. £3.34. 131 pp. .... Vendor G0557

Raymond, S. **A Genealogical Bibliography: Lancashire Vol. 1**. 1996. Contact vendor for availability. .... Vendor G0588

Raymond, S. **A Genealogical Bibliography: Lancashire Vol. 2**. Registers, Inscriptions, and Wills. 1996. £5.90 (overseas surface). 56 pp. .... Vendor G0588

Raymond, S. **A Genealogical Bibliography: Lancashire Vol. 3**. Lancashire Family Histories and Pedigrees. 1996. £5.85 (overseas surface). 64 pp. .... Vendor G0588

Society of Genealogists. **Sources for Lancashire Genealogy in the Society of Genealogists' Library**. Leaflet. £0.20. .... Vendor G0557

Leicestershire

Society of Genealogists. **National Index of Parish Registers. Vol. 6, Part 3: Leicestershire, Rutland**. 1995. £10.40. 117 pp. .... Vendor G0557

Lincolnshire

Gibbons, A., ed. **Lincoln Marriage Licences**. An Abstract of the Allegation Books Preserved by the Registry of the Bishop of Lincoln, 1598-1628. (1888) reprint 1996. Paper. $19.50. 163 pp. .... Vendor G0259

Raymond, S. **A Genealogical Bibliography: Lincolnshire**. 1995. £8.60 (overseas surface). 108 pp. .... Vendor G0588

Society of Genealogists. **National Index of Parish Registers. Vol. 6, Part 4: Lincolnshire**. 1995. £16.40. 302 pp. .... Vendor G0557

London

Bailey, Paul. **The Oxford Book of London.** 1995.
An anthology of works regarding London, capturing the essence of its allure for visitors and inhabitants from the Middle Ages to the present day.
Cloth. $25.00. 377 pp. .... Vendor G0611

Benton, A. **Irregular Marriage in London Before 1754.** 1993.
Paper. £3.50. 59 pp. .... Vendor G0557

Chester, Col. Joseph Lemuel. **London (England) Marriage Licenses 1521-1869.**
1887. Reprint on microfiche.
Organized alphabetically.
Order no. 197, $46.00. 1,595 pp. .... Vendor G0478

FFHS. **London Poll Book, 1768.**
£15.00 (overseas surface). .... Vendor G0588

Raymond, S. **A Genealogical Bibliography: London/Middlesex.** 1994.
£8.25 (overseas surface). 128 pp. .... Vendor G0588

Raymond, S. **Londoners' Occupations, a Genealogical Guide.** 1994.
£3.85 (surface overseas). 48 pp. .... Vendor G0588

Sharpe, Reginald R., ed. **Calendar of Coroners Rolls of the City of London, A.D. 1300-1378.**
Paper. $29.00. xxvii + 324 pp. .... Vendor G0632

Society of Genealogists. **National Index of Parish Registers. Vol. 9, Part 5: London, Middlesex.** 1995.
£7.80. 90 pp. .... Vendor G0557

Webb, Cliff. **My Ancestors Were Londoners: How Can I Find Out More About Them?** 1996. Illus.
Paper. £3.55. 64 pp. .... Vendor G0557

Middlesex

Raymond, S. **A Genealogical Bibliography: London/Middlesex.** 1994.
£8.25 (overseas surface). 59 pp. .... Vendor G0588

Society of Genealogists. **National Index of Parish Registers. Vol. 9, Part 5: London, Middlesex.** 1995.
£7.80. 90 pp. .... Vendor G0557

Norfolk

FFHS. **Norfolk Poll Book, 1786.** 1996.
£19.20 (overseas surface). .... Vendor G0588

FFHS. **Norfolk Poll Book, 1835.** 1996.
£18.20 (overseas surface). .... Vendor G0588

Raymond, S. **A Genealogical Bibliography: Norfolk.** Rev. ed.
£7.05 (overseas surface). .... Vendor G0588

Raymond, Stuart. **Norfolk Bibliography.** Reprint 1996.
£7.05 (overseas surface). 92 pp. .... Vendor G0588

Society of Genealogists. **National Index of Parish Registers. Vol. 7: Cambridgeshire, Norfolk, Suffolk.** 1983.
£9.00 278 pp. .... Vendor G0557

Northamptonshire

Society of Genealogists. **National Index of Parish Registers. Vol. 9, Part 2: Northamptonshire.** 1991.
£5.00. 86 pp. .... Vendor G0557

Nottinghamshire

Society of Genealogists. **National Index of Parish Registers. Vol. 6, Part 2: Nottinghamshire.** 2nd ed. 1995.
£9.95. 124 pp. .... Vendor G0557

Society of Genealogists. **Sources for Nottinghamshire Genealogy in the Society of Genealogists' Library.**
Leaflet. £0.20. .... Vendor G0557

Oxfordshire

Falkner, J. Meade. **History of Oxfordshire.** (1899) reprint 1993.
Cloth. $39.50. 327 pp. .... Vendor G0259

Raymond, S. **A Genealogical Bibliography: Oxfordshire.** 1993.
£5.85 (overseas surface). 59 pp. .... Vendor G0588

Somerset County

Savage, James. **History of the Hundred of Carhampton, in the County of Somerset.** (1830) reprint 1996.
    History and biography of western Somerset County.
Cloth. $69.00. 662 pp. .... Vendor G0259

Staffordshire

Society of Genealogists. **National Index of Parish Registers. Vol. 6, Part 1: Staffordshire.** 2nd ed. 1992.
£6.30. 100 pp. .... Vendor G0557

Suffolk

Allen, Marion E., and Nesta R. Evans. **Wills from the Archdeaconry of Suffolk, England Volume 1 (1629-1636).** 1986.
Cloth. $28.50. 585 pp. .... Vendor G0406

Allen, Marion E., and Nesta R. Evans. **Wills from the Archdeaconry of Suffolk, England Volume 2 (1637-1640).** 1986.
Cloth. $28.50. 585 pp. .... Vendor G0406

FFHS. **Suffolk Poll Books, 1710.**
£14.30 (overseas surface). .... Vendor G0588

FFHS. **Suffolk Poll Books, 1790.**
£$14.70 (overseas surface). .... Vendor G0588

Society of Genealogists. **National Index of Parish Registers. Vol. 7: Cambridgeshire, Norfolk, Suffolk.** 1983.
£9.00. 278 pp. .... Vendor G0557

Surrey

Society of Genealogists. **National Index of Parish Registers. Vol. 4, Part 1: Surrey.** 1990.
£8.25. 200 pp. .... Vendor G0557

Society of Genealogists. **Sources for Surrey Genealogy in the Society of Genealogists' Library.**
Leaflet. £0.20. .... Vendor G0557

Sussex

Hunnisett, Roy. **Sussex Coroners' Inquests 1558-1603.** 1996.
Written by the foremost authority on the history of the office of coroner, this volume contains the 582 inquests held by Sussex coroners during the reign of Elizabeth, that are known to survive.
£20.00 plus shipping. xivii + 216 pp. .... Vendor G0558

Warwickshire

Alcock, N. W. **People at Home: Living in a Warwickshire Village 1500-1800.**
1993. Illus.
Cloth. £19.95. 256 pp. .... Vendor G0579

Westminster

FFHS. **Westminster Poll Book, 1774.**
£19.65 (overseas surface). .... Vendor G0588

Westmorland

Raymond, S. **A Genealogical Bibliography: Cumberland and Westmorland.** 1993.
£5.85 (overseas surface). 68 pp. .... Vendor G0588

Wiltshire

Raymond, S. **A Genealogical Bibliography: Wiltshire.** 1993.
£7.05 (overseas surface). 82 pp. .... Vendor G0588

Society of Genealogists. **National Index of Parish Registers. Vol. 8, Part 2: Wiltshire.**
1992.
£6.90. 114 pp. .... Vendor G0557

Yorkshire

FFHS. **Yorkshire (West Riding) Poll Book, 1786.**
£23.85 (overseas surface). .... Vendor G0588

Litton, P. M. **Basic Facts About Family History Research in Yorkshire.** 1995.
£2.00 (overseas surface). 16 pp. .... Vendor G0588

৵ Great Britain—Scotland ৵

General References

Aberdeen & North East Scotland Family History Society. **Hands Across the Water—Emigration from Northern Scotland**—Proceedings of the 6th Annual Conf. of Scot. Assoc. of FH.
Paper. £2.10. .... Vendor G0555

Anglo Scottish Family History Society. **Directory of Members' Interests—Anglo Scot FHS.**
Paper. £0.90. .... Vendor G0555

Bigwood, R. **Index to Parishes with Related Sherriff Courts, Commissary Courts & Burgh.**
Paper. £4.00. .... Vendor G0555

Borland, J. **Scottish Family History**. Tracing & Recording Ancestors.
Paper. £3.30. .... Vendor G0555

Burke, J., and J. B. Burke. **Burke's Extinct & Dormant Baronetcies of England, Ireland & Scotland**. (1841) reprint 1994.
Contact vendor for information. 644 pp. .... Vendor G0010

Burness, L. R. **A Scottish Genealogist's Glossary.**
A revised edition is being prepared. Contact vendor for information.
Paper. £1.50. .... Vendor G0555

Carnegie, H. **Harnessing the Wind**. Sea-faring Life in the 19th Century Based on the Logbooks & Letters of Capt. Thomas Mitchel.
Paper. £2.95. .... Vendor G0555

Collins, Ewan. **Beginner's Guide to Scottish Genealogy.**
Paper. £4.50. .... Vendor G0555

Cory, Kathleen B. **Tracing Your Scottish Ancestry**. (1990) reprint 1996. Indexed.
Paper. $16.95. 195 pp. .... Vendor G0010

Cox, M., ed. **Exploring Scottish History**. 1992.
£8.50. 161 pp. .... Vendor G0588

Cross, W. P. **Forgot & Gone: Further Accidents & Disasters in Scotland 1855-99**.
Paper. £2.00. .... Vendor G0555

Cross, W. P. **Hurried into Eternity: Accidents and Disasters in Scotland.**
Paper. £2.95. .... Vendor G0555

Dobson, David. **Directory of Scots in Australia 1788-1900, Part 1.**
Contact vendor for information. .... Vendor G0641

Dobson, David. **Emigrants & Adventurers from S. Scotland, Part 1.**
Contact vendor for information. .... Vendor G0641

Dobson, David. **Jacobites of the '15.**
Paper. £4.50. .... Vendor G0641

Dobson, David. **Scots-Irish Links, 1575-1725. In Two Parts.** 2 vols. in 1. (1994, 1995) reprint 1997.
Contact vendor for information. 58 pp. .... Vendor G0011

Dobson, David. **Scottish Schoolmasters of the 17th Century, Part 1.**
Contact vendor for information. .... Vendor G0641

Dobson, David. **Scottish Seafarers of the 17th Century.**
Contact vendor for information. .... Vendor G0641

Dobson, David. **Scottish Soldiers in Colonial America, Part 1.**
Contact vendor for information. .... Vendor G0641

Dobson, David. **Scottish Whalers Before 1800, Part 1.**
Contact vendor for information. .... Vendor G0641

Donaldson, G. **Dictionary of Scottish History.**
£8.50. .... Vendor G0555

Donaldson, G. **Surnames & Ancestry in Scotland**.
Paper. £0.50. .... Vendor G0555

Dorward, D. **Scottish Surnames**.
Paper. £4.99. .... Vendor G0555

Erickson, Charlotte. **Invisible Immigrants: The Adaption of English and Scottish Immigrants in 19th-Century America**. (1972) reprint 1990.
A remarkable collection of letters from people who immigrated to America in the 19th century and who kept in touch with friends and relatives in England and Scotland. Over 200 letters from 25 families are included.
Paper. $18.95. 531 pp. .... Vendor G0611

Family History Library. **Old Parochial Reg. Index—Scotland Guide**.
Free. 4 pp. .... Vendor G0629

Family History Library. **Scottish Church Records**.
Free. 4 pp. .... Vendor G0629

Ferguson, J. **Directory of Scottish Newspapers**: A Guide to the Whereabouts of Newspapers in Scotland.
£10.00. .... Vendor G0555

Ferguson, J. P. S. **Scottish Family Histories Held in Scottish Libraries**. (1960) reprint 1987.
Cloth. $25.00. 194 pp. .... Vendor G0259

Ford, Henry Jones. **The Scotch-Irish in America**. (1915) reprint 1995. Indexed.
This work commences with a discussion of the Scottish migration to Ulster in the 17th century, followed by an examination of the causes of the Scotch-Irish emigration to North America by the end of the century. Ford devotes entire chapters to the Scotch-Irish settlement in New England, New York, the Jerseys, Pennsylvania, and along the colonial frontier, as well as to the history of Scotch-Irish institutions in the U.S.
Paper. $42.50. 607 pp. .... Vendor G0011

Gandy, M. **Catholic Missions & Registers 1700-1800 in Scotland**.
£6.00. .... Vendor G0555

Genealogical Microform Holdings in Scottish Libraries.
£6.00. .... Vendor G0555

General Register Office for Scotland. **Civil Parish Map Index**. Guide for Researchers: No. 1.
£2.50 plus shipping. .... Vendor G0589

General Register Office for Scotland. **List of Main Records in the Care of the Registrar General**.
Information leaflet. Free. .... Vendor G0589

General Register Office for Scotland. **Personal Names in Scotland**.
Paper. £2.95 plus shipping. .... Vendor G0589

General Register Office for Scotland. **Registration Districts of Scotland from 1855**. Guide for Researchers: No. 2.
£4.50 plus shipping. .... Vendor G0589

Gibbens, L. **Church Registers**.
Paper. £6.00. .... Vendor G0555

Glack, G. F. **The Surnames of Scotland**.
£17.99. .... Vendor G0555

Glasgow Family History Society. **European Immigration into Scotland**.
Paper. £4.50. .... Vendor G0555

Graham, Ian Charles Cargill. **Colonists from Scotland: Emigration to North America, 1707-1783**. (1956) reprint 1996. Indexed.
Paper. $21.50. 223 pp. .... Vendor G0011

Green's Glossary of Scottish Legal Terms.
£11.95. .... Vendor G0555

Groome, Francis H., ed. **Ordnance Gazetteer of Scotland:** A Graphic and Accurate Description of Every Place in Scotland. 3 vols. (1902) reprint 1995. Illus.
Alphabetical listing of every city, town, hamlet, village, parish and family seat, with remarkably detailed geographical and social descriptions. Volume III includes an appendix with a brief history and profile of Scotland. Many maps.
Volume I, A-Foc.
Volume II, Fod-Moncton.
Volume III, Monctonhall-end.
Cloth. $55.00/vol., $150.00/set. 1,762 pp. .... Vendor G0259

Halliday, J. **Scotland: A Concise History**.
Paper. £4.95. .... Vendor G0555

Hamilton-Edwards, G. **In Search of Scottish Ancestry**. 1983.
Cloth. £11.99. 272 pp. .... Vendor G0579

Hanna, Charles A. **The Scotch-Irish**. Or the Scot in North Britain, North Ireland and North America. 2 vols. (1902) reprint 1995. Indexed. Illus.
Cloth. $75.00. 623 + 602 pp. .... Vendor G0010

Innes, Sir Thomas, of Learney. **Scots Heraldry**. A Practical Handbook on the Historical Principles and Modern Application of the Art and Science. 2nd ed., revised and enlarged. (1956) reprint 1994. Indexed.
Paper. $27.50. 282 pp. plus 46 plates and 106 text figures. .... Vendor G0011

Irvine, Sherry. **Your Scottish Ancestry: A Guide for North Americans**. 1997.
Paper. $17.95. 253 pp. .... Vendor G0570

Jacobite Source List—Resources in the SRO.
£6.50. .... Vendor G0555

James, Alwyn. **Scottish Roots: A Step-by-step Guide for Ancestor-hunters**. 1981. Illus.
Describes the wealth of information available on Scottish ancestry, and tells you where it is housed and how to utilize it.
Paper. $13.95. 181 pp. .... Vendor G0611

Johnson, G. **Census Records for Scottish Families**. 2nd ed.
Third edition in preparation.
Paper. £6.00. .... Vendor G0555

The Johnston & Bacon Scottish Clan Histories. Reprint 1993. Illus.
The Clan Cameron, by Charles Ian Fraser (1953).
The Clan Fraser of Lovat, by Charles Ian Fraser, 2nd ed. (1966).
The Clan Gordon, by Jean Dunlop (1955).
The Grahams, by John Stewart (1958).
The Clan Grant, by I.F. Grant (1955).
The Kennedys, by Sir James Fergusson (1958).
The Clan Mackay, by Margaret O. MacDougall (1953).
The Clan Mackenzie, by Jean Dunlop (1953).
The Clan Mackintosh, by Jean Dunlop (1960).
The Clan Maclean, by John Mackechnie (1954).
The Clan MacLeod, by I. F. Grant (1953).
The Clan Morrison, by Alick Morrison (1956).
The Clan Munro, by Charles Ian Fraser (1954).
The Robertsons, by Iain Moncreiffe, 3rd ed. (1979).
The Clan Ross, by Donald Mackinnon (1957).
The Scotts, by Jean Dunlop (1957).
Paper. $8.95/vol. 32 pp./vol. .... Vendor G0011

Kelsall, H. K. **Scottish Lifestyle 300 Years Ago**.
£9.95. .... Vendor G0555

Konrad, J. **Scottish Family Research**.
Paper. $10.00. 56 pp. .... Vendor G0574

Lawson, J. **The Emigrant Scot: Ships' Manifest in Canadian Archives pre 1900**.
Paper. £3.75. .... Vendor G0555

Lewis, Samuel. **A Topographical Dictionary of Scotland**. 2 vols. (1851) reprint 1989.
Cloth. $75.00. 1,233 pp. total. .... Vendor G0010

Leyburn. **The Scotch-Irish: A Social History**. (1962) reprint 1991.
These people in Scotland, their removal to Northern Ireland, and their migrations to America. Extensive bibliography.
Paper. $15.95. 377 pp. .... Vendor G0611

Library of Congress. **Sources for Research in Scottish Genealogy**. Compiled by Judith P. Reid.
The text of this is available on the Local History and Genealogy Reading Room's home page: http://lcweb.loc.gov/rr/genealogy.
Free. Contact vendor for information. 10 pp. .... Vendor G0566

MacLean, John P. **An Historical Account of the Settlements of Scotch Highlanders in America** Prior to the Peace of 1783. (1900) reprint 1996. Illus.
Paper. $35.00. 455 pp. .... Vendor G0011

Martin, Ged, and Jeffrey Simpson. **Canada's Heritage in Scotland**. 1989.
Paper. $14.99 (cnd), $13.25 (US). 245 pp. .... Vendor G0640

McDonnell, Frances. **Jacobites of 1715 and 1745. North East Scotland**. 2 vols. in 1. (1996) reprint 1997.
Contact vendor for information. 96 pp. in all. .... Vendor G0011

McDonnell, Frances. **Scottish Catholic Parents & Their Children 1701-1705**.
Contact vendor for information. .... Vendor G0642

Moody, David. **Scottish Family History**. (1989) reprint 1994. Indexed.
Paper. $18.95. 219 pp. .... Vendor G0010

Moody, David. **Scottish Local History**. (1989) reprint 1994. Indexed.
Paper. $18.95. 178 pp. .... Vendor G0010

Morrison, J. **Scots on the Dijk**. The Scots Church in Rotterdam from Its Beginning in the 17th Century to the Present Day.
Paper. £2.95. .... Vendor G0555

Muster Roll of Prince Charles Edward Stuart's Army 1745-46.
£16.99. .... Vendor G0555

Nicolaisen, W. **Scottish Place Names**. The First Cohesive & Systematic Study.
£10.99. .... Vendor G0555

Paul, Sir James Balfour. **An Ordinary of Arms**. Contained in the Public Register of All Arms and Bearings in Scotland. 2nd ed. (1903) reprint 1991. Indexed.
Paper. $35.00. 452 pp. .... Vendor G0011

Ritchie, G. **Real Price of Fish: Aberdeen Trawler Losees 1887-1961**.
£6.50. .... Vendor G0555

Sail & Steam: Boatbuilders from Portgordon to Cullen.
Paper. £2.50. .... Vendor G0555

Scottish Assoc. of Family History Societies. **Members & Publications 1996 (SAFHS)**.
Paper. £2.75. .... Vendor G0555

Scottish Assoc. of Family History Societies. **Scottish Census Indexes 1841-1871: A Location List**.
Paper. £1.00. .... Vendor G0555

Scottish Genealogy Society. **Beginner's Bibliography: Information Leaflet No. 3**.
Paper. £0.10. .... Vendor G0556

Scottish Genealogy Society. **Burial Grounds in Scotland**.
Paper. £0.80. .... Vendor G0556

Scottish Genealogy Society. **Index to the Scottish Genealogist Vols. 1-28**.
Paper. £2.00. .... Vendor G0556

Scottish Genealogy Society. **Index to the Scottish Genealogist Vols. 29-32**.
Paper. £1.50. .... Vendor G0556

Scottish Genealogy Society. **Index to the Scottish Genealogist Vols. 33-36**.
Paper. £1.50. .... Vendor G0556

Scottish Genealogy Society. **Index to the Scottish Genealogist Vols. 37-40.**
Paper. £1.00. .... Vendor G0556

Scottish Genealogy Society. **Lady Glenorchy's Church Communion Rolls 1785-1835.**
Paper. £5.25. .... Vendor G0556

Scottish Genealogy Society. **Lady Glenorchy's Free Church Baptisms 1845-56.**
Paper. £1.25. .... Vendor G0556

Scottish Genealogy Society. **Starting a Search in New Register House, Edinburgh: Information Leaflet No. 2.**
Paper. £0.10. .... Vendor G0556

Scottish Genealogy Society. **Testaments and Where to Find Them: Information Leaflet No. 4.**
Paper. £0.10. .... Vendor G0556

Scottish Handwriting 1500-1700: A Self-Help Pack.
£7.50. .... Vendor G0555

Short Guide to the Scottish Record Office.
Paper. £1.20. .... Vendor G0555

Sims, Clifford S. **The Origin and Signification of Scottish Surnames.** (1862) reprint 1995.
Paper. $17.50. 122 pp. .... Vendor G0011

Smith, Frank. **A Genealogical Gazetteer of Scotland.**
An alphabetical dictionary of places with their locations, population, and date of the earliest entry in the registers of every parish in Scotland.
Paper. $14.00. 140 pp. .... Vendor G0618

Soutar, D. J. **First Visit to Use the Statutory Records of BMDs New Register House, Edinburgh.**
Paper. £2.00. .... Vendor G0555

Spiers, S. **The Parishes, Registers, and Registrars of Scotland.**
Paper. £3.75. .... Vendor G0555

St. Kilda Heritage.
Paper. £3.00. .... Vendor G0555

Steven, Maisie. **Parish Life in 18th Century Scotland: A Review of the Old Statistical Account.**
£14.95. .... Vendor G0555

Stuart, Margaret. **Scottish Family History:** A Guide to Works of Reference on the History and Genealogy of Scottish Families. (1930) reprint 1994.
Cloth. $25.00. 386 pp. .... Vendor G0010

Taylor, James. **The Great Historic Families of Scotland.** 2nd ed. 2 vols. in 1. (1889) reprint 1995. Indexed.
Cloth. $55.00. 410 + 431 pp. .... Vendor G0010

Torrance, D. R. **Scottish Personal Names & Place Names: A Bibliography**.
Paper. £1.75. .... Vendor G0555

Torrance, D. R. **Scottish Trades and Professions: A Bibliography**.
Paper. £3.75. .... Vendor G0555

Torrance, D. R. **Weights & Measures for the Scottish Family Historian**.
Paper. £3.75. .... Vendor G0555

Tracing Scottish Local History in the SRO.
£7.95. .... Vendor G0555

Tracing Your Scottish Ancestors in the SRO.
£6.95. .... Vendor G0555

Whyte, D. **The Scots Overseas: A Bibliography**.
Paper. £3.00. .... Vendor G0555

Whyte, D. **Scottish Surnames & Families**.
£7.99. .... Vendor G0555

Wilkes, M. **The Scot and His Maps: A Historical Survey from the 16th Century**.
Paper. £4.50. .... Vendor G0555

Willsher, B. **Understanding Scottish Graveyards**.
Paper. £4.99. .... Vendor G0555

Wilson, Rev. John. **The Gazetteer of Scotland**. (1882) reprint 1996.
   Facsimile reprint; alphabetical arrangement.
Paper. $32.00. 425 pp. .... Vendor G0669

Borders Region

Ancestor Hunting in Dumfries Archive Centre.
Paper. £0.60. .... Vendor G0555

Anglo-Scottish Relations & the Borders: B.C.-17th C.
Paper. £1.85. .... Vendor G0555

Borders Family History Society. **Register of Members' Interests, 1995—Borders FHS**.
Paper. £3.00. .... Vendor G0555

Central Region

Central Scotland Family History Society. **Bothkennar & Larbert 1851 Census Indexes**.
Paper. £4.50. .... Vendor G0555

Central Scotland Family History Society. **Dunblane 1851 Census Index**.
Paper. £4.50. .... Vendor G0555

Central Scotland Family History Society. **Stirling Burgess List, Vol. 1 1600-99.** Paper. £3.50. .... Vendor G0555

Central Scotland Family History Society. **Stirling Burgess List, Vol. 2 1700-99.** Paper. £3.50. .... Vendor G0555

Central Scotland Family History Society. **Stirling Burgess List, Vol. 3 1800-1902.** Paper. £3.50. .... Vendor G0555

Dumfries & Galloway Region

Dumfries & Galloway Family History Society. **Applegarth 1851 Census Index.** Paper. £2.00. .... Vendor G0555

Dumfries & Galloway Family History Society. **Balmaclellan 1851 Census Index.** Paper. £2.00. .... Vendor G0555

Dumfries & Galloway Family History Society. **Canonbie 1851 Census Index.** Paper. £4.00. .... Vendor G0555

Dumfries & Galloway Family History Society. **Cummertrees 1851 Census Index.** Paper. £2.00. .... Vendor G0555

Dumfries & Galloway Family History Society. **Durisdeer 1851 Census Index.** Paper. £2.00. .... Vendor G0555

Dumfries & Galloway Family History Society. **Johnstone 1851 Census Index.** Paper. £2.00. .... Vendor G0555

Dumfries & Galloway Family History Society. **Register of Members' Interests— Dumfries & Galloway FHS.** Paper. £3.00. .... Vendor G0555

Dumfries & Galloway Family History Society. **Some Sources for Local & Family Historians, 1851 Census Index and Monumental Inscriptions.** Paper. £3.00. .... Vendor G0555

Johnstone, C. L. **The Historical Families of Dumfriesshire and the Border Wars.** 2nd ed. (1889) reprint 1996. Indexed. Illus. Paper. $22.00. 213 pp. .... Vendor G0011

Fife, Perth, & the Tayside Valley

Campbell, A. J. **Crail Deaths 1794-1854.** 2 vols. Paper. £5.00. .... Vendor G0555

Campbell, S. **Family History Sources in Kirkcaldy Library.** Paper. £5.00. .... Vendor G0555

Dobson, David. **The Burgess Rolls of Fife, 1700-1800, Part 1.** Contact vendor for information. .... Vendor G0641

Dobson, David. **The Burgess Rolls of St. Andrews, 1751-1775.**
Contact vendor for information. .... Vendor G0641

Dobson, David. **Mariners of Angus 1600-1700.**
Contact vendor for information. .... Vendor G0641

Dobson, David. **Mariners of Angus 1700-1800, Part 1.**
Contact vendor for information. .... Vendor G0641

Dobson, David. **Mariners of Angus 1700-1800, Part 2.**
Contact vendor for information. .... Vendor G0641

Dobson, David. **Mariners of Fife 1700-1800.**
Contact vendor for information. .... Vendor G0641

Dobson, David. **Mariners of Kirkcaldy & West Fife 1600-1700.**
Contact vendor for information. .... Vendor G0641

Dobson, David. **Mariners of St. Andrews & East Neuk of Fife 1600-1700.**
Contact vendor for information. .... Vendor G0641

Family History Research: The Ancestor Hunter's ABC in Dunfermline District.
Paper. £1.75. .... Vendor G0555

Fife Family History Society. **Fife Convicts. Transportees 1752-1867.**
Paper. £1.50. .... Vendor G0555

Fife Family History Society. **Fife Emigrants & Their Ships. Part 1: Aust. & N.Z.**
Paper. £3.00. .... Vendor G0555

Fife Family History Society. **Members' Interests Booklet—Fife FHS.**
Paper. £2.75. .... Vendor G0555

Fife Family History Society. **Pedigree Chart Index & Old Parish Registers of Fife & Kinross.**
Paper. £3.00. .... Vendor G0555

Hendry, D. **Cupar Doctors and Their Families.**
Paper. £3.99. .... Vendor G0555

Johnston, M. **With a Name like Lamont.**
Paper. £2.50. .... Vendor G0555

Perth: A Short History.
Paper. £3.50. .... Vendor G0555

Pitmiddle Village and Elcho Nunnery.
Paper. £2.75. .... Vendor G0555

Place Names of Fife and Kinross.
Paper. £3.95. .... Vendor G0555

Smith, A. M. **The Three United Trades of Dundee: Masons, Wrights and Slaters.**
Paper. £3.50. .... Vendor G0555

Tay Valley Family History Society. **Annals of the United Presbyterian Churches in Dundee.**
Paper. £1.50. .... Vendor G0555

Tay Valley Family History Society. **Cases from the Perth Court.**
Paper. £3.20. .... Vendor G0555

Tay Valley Family History Society. **Directory of Members' Interests 1993—Tay Valley FHS.**
Paper. £3.00. .... Vendor G0555

Tay Valley Family History Society. **Maltmen, Customs & Excisemen of Dundee.**
Paper. £2.00. .... Vendor G0555

Tay Valley Family History Society. **North-East Fife Emigrants in Australia.**
Paper. £2.20. .... Vendor G0555

Tay Valley Family History Society. **Source Book 1993: Tay Valley FHS.**
Paper. £3.50. .... Vendor G0555

Tay Valley Family History Society. **Tay Valley People in Australia: 1788-1988.**
Paper. £3.00. .... Vendor G0555

Tay Valley Family History Society. **Tay Valley People in N. America. Vol. 1.**
Paper. £3.00. .... Vendor G0555

Tay Valley Family History Society. **Tay Valley People in N. America. Vol. 2.**
Paper. £3.00. .... Vendor G0555

Tay Valley Family History Society. **Tay Valley People. Vols. 1 & 2.**
Paper. £1.20/vol. .... Vendor G0555

Tay Valley Family History Society. **Tay Valley People. Vol. 3.**
Paper. £1.20. .... Vendor G0555

Tay Valley Family History Society. **Tay Valley People. Vol. 4.**
Paper. £1.20. .... Vendor G0555

Tay Valley Family History Society. **Tay Valley People. Vol. 5.**
Paper. £1.50. .... Vendor G0555

Tay Valley Family History Society. **Tay Valley People. Vol. 6.**
Paper. £2.20. .... Vendor G0555

Tay Valley Family History Society. **Tay Valley People. Vol. 7.**
Paper. £2.00. .... Vendor G0555

Highland Region

Anglo Scottish Family History Society. **Dictionary of Scot Emigrants to England Vol. 5.**
Paper. £5.00. .... Vendor G0555

Highland Family History Society. **Killearnan 1851 Census.**
Paper. £1.20. .... Vendor G0555

Highland Family History Society. **Kiltearn 1851 Census.**
Paper. £1.20. .... Vendor G0555

Highland Family History Society. **Kincardine with Croick 1851 Census.**
Paper. £5.30. .... Vendor G0555

Highland Family History Society. **Knockbain 1851 Census.**
Paper. £2.00. .... Vendor G0555

Highland Family History Society. **Register of Members' Interests 1995—Highland FHS.**
Paper. £2.50. .... Vendor G0555

Highland Family History Society. **Suddie Burial Ground.**
Paper. £1.00. .... Vendor G0555

Highland Family History Society. **Tain-Ross & Cromarty 1851 Census.**
Paper. £1.50. .... Vendor G0555

Highland Family History Society. **Wick 1851 Census.**
Paper. £2.50. .... Vendor G0555

Taylor, J., and L. Taylor. **Highland Rebels.**
Paper. £1.50. .... Vendor G0555

Lothian Region

Dobson, David. **Emigrants & Adventurers from the Lothians, Part 1.**
Contact vendor for information. .... Vendor G0641

Dobson, David. **Mariners of the Lothians 1600-1700, Part 1.**
Contact vendor for information. .... Vendor G0641

Dobson, David. **Mariners of the Lothians 1600-1700, Part 2.**
Contact vendor for information. .... Vendor G0641

Dobson, David. **Mariners of the Lothians 1700-1800, Part 1.**
Contact vendor for information. .... Vendor G0641

Scottish Genealogy Society. **Bathgate Mortality Records 1860-1925.**
£7.00. .... Vendor G0556

Scottish Genealogy Society. **Edinburgh 1851 Census: Canongate.**
£22.00. .... Vendor G0556

Scottish Genealogy Society. **Edinburgh 1851 Census: The Old Town.**
£33.00. .... Vendor G0556

Scottish Genealogy Society. **Edinburgh Police Register 1813-59.**
Paper. £3.00. .... Vendor G0556

Scottish Genealogy Society. **Tron Parish Poll Tax 1694, Edinburgh.**
Paper. £4.50. .... Vendor G0556

Monumental Inscriptions

Aberdeen & North East Scotland Family History Society. **Aberdour Monumental Inscriptions.**
Paper. £1.95. .... Vendor G0555

Aberdeen & North East Scotland Family History Society. **Alford Monumental Inscriptions.**
Paper. £1.95. .... Vendor G0555

Aberdeen & North East Scotland Family History Society. **Alvah Monumental Inscriptions.**
Paper. £1.95. .... Vendor G0555

Aberdeen & North East Scotland Family History Society. **Auchindoir Monumental Inscriptions.**
Paper. £1.95. .... Vendor G0555

Aberdeen & North East Scotland Family History Society. **Belhelvie Monumental Inscriptions.**
Paper. £1.95. .... Vendor G0555

Aberdeen & North East Scotland Family History Society. **Bourtie/Old Meldrum Episcopal Monumental Inscriptions.**
Paper. £1.95. .... Vendor G0555

Aberdeen & North East Scotland Family History Society. **Chapel of Garioch/Logie Durno Monumental Inscriptions.**
Paper. £1.95. .... Vendor G0555

Aberdeen & North East Scotland Family History Society. **Cluny Monumental Inscriptions.**
Paper. £1.95. .... Vendor G0555

Aberdeen & North East Scotland Family History Society. **Crimond/Rattray Monumental Inscriptions.**
Paper. £1.95. .... Vendor G0555

Aberdeen & North East Scotland Family History Society. **Culsalmond Monumental Inscriptions.**
Paper. £1.95. .... Vendor G0555

Aberdeen & North East Scotland Family History Society. **Daviot Monumental Inscriptions.** 1996.
Paper. £1.95. .... Vendor G0555

Aberdeen & North East Scotland Family History Society. **Drumblade Monumental Inscriptions.**
Paper. £1.95. .... Vendor G0555

Aberdeen & North East Scotland Family History Society. **Dunnottar Monumental Inscriptions.**
Paper. £1.95. .... Vendor G0555

Aberdeen & North East Scotland Family History Society. **Durris Monumental Inscriptions.**
Paper. £1.95. .... Vendor G0555

Aberdeen & North East Scotland Family History Society. **Dyce Monumental Inscriptions.**
Paper. £1.95. .... Vendor G0555

Aberdeen & North East Scotland Family History Society. **Echt Monumental Inscriptions.**
Paper. £1.95. .... Vendor G0555

Aberdeen & North East Scotland Family History Society. **Fetterangus Monumental Inscriptions.**
Paper. £1.95. .... Vendor G0555

Aberdeen & North East Scotland Family History Society. **Forglen Monumental Inscriptions.**
Paper. £1.95. .... Vendor G0555

Aberdeen & North East Scotland Family History Society. **Fyvie Monumental Inscriptions.**
Paper. £1.95. .... Vendor G0555

Aberdeen & North East Scotland Family History Society. **Glenbervie Monumental Inscriptions.** 1996.
Paper. £1.95. .... Vendor G0555

Aberdeen & North East Scotland Family History Society. **Hatton of Fintray Monumental Inscriptions.**
Paper. £1.95. .... Vendor G0555

Aberdeen & North East Scotland Family History Society. **Inverkeithny Monumental Inscriptions.**
Paper. £1.95. .... Vendor G0555

Aberdeen & North East Scotland Family History Society. **John Knox (Aberdeen) Monumental Inscriptions.**
Paper. £1.95. .... Vendor G0555

Aberdeen & North East Scotland Family History Society. **Keithhall & Kinkell Monumental Inscriptions.**
Paper. £1.95. .... Vendor G0555

Aberdeen & North East Scotland Family History Society. **Kincardine O'Neil Monumental Inscriptions.**
Paper. £1.95. .... Vendor G0555

Aberdeen & North East Scotland Family History Society. **King Edward Monumental Inscriptions.**
Paper. £1.95. .... Vendor G0555

Aberdeen & North East Scotland Family History Society. **Leslie Monumental Inscriptions.**
Paper. £1.95. .... Vendor G0555

Aberdeen & North East Scotland Family History Society. **Lonmay Monumental Inscriptions.**
Paper. £1.95. .... Vendor G0555

Aberdeen & North East Scotland Family History Society. **Marnoch Monumental Inscriptions.**
Paper. £1.95. .... Vendor G0555

Aberdeen & North East Scotland Family History Society. **Millbrex & Woodhead of Fyvie Monumental Inscriptions.**
Paper. £1.95. .... Vendor G0555

Aberdeen & North East Scotland Family History Society. **Monymusk Monumental Inscriptions.**
Paper. £1.95. .... Vendor G0555

Aberdeen & North East Scotland Family History Society. **Newhills Monumental Inscriptions.**
Paper. £1.95. .... Vendor G0555

Aberdeen & North East Scotland Family History Society. **Oldmeldrum Monumental Inscriptions.**
Paper. £1.95. .... Vendor G0555

Aberdeen & North East Scotland Family History Society. **Peathill Monumental Inscriptions.**
Paper. £1.95. .... Vendor G0555

Aberdeen & North East Scotland Family History Society. **Peterculter Monumental Inscriptions.**
Paper. £1.95. .... Vendor G0555

Aberdeen & North East Scotland Family History Society. **Rathen Monumental Inscriptions.**
Paper. £1.95. .... Vendor G0555

Aberdeen & North East Scotland Family History Society. **Rhynie Monumental Inscriptions.**
Paper. £1.95. .... Vendor G0555

Aberdeen & North East Scotland Family History Society. **St. Clements (Aberdeen) Monumental Inscriptions.**
Paper. £1.95. .... Vendor G0555

Aberdeen & North East Scotland Family History Society. **Strachan Monumental Inscriptions.**
Paper. £1.95. .... Vendor G0555

Aberdeen & North East Scotland Family History Society. **Tough Monumental Inscriptions.**
Paper. £1.95. .... Vendor G0555

Aberdeen & North East Scotland Family History Society. **Tyrie Monumental Inscriptions.**
Paper. £1.95. .... Vendor G0555

Aberdeen & North East Scotland Family History Society. **Udny Monumental Inscriptions**. 1996.
Paper. £1.95. .... Vendor G0555

Borders Family History Society. **[Berwickshire] Fogo Monumental Inscriptions**.
Paper. £5.00. .... Vendor G0555

Borders Family History Society. **[Berwickshire] Mertoun Monumental Inscriptions**.
Paper. £5.00. .... Vendor G0555

Borders Family History Society. **[Berwickshire] Polwarth Monumental Inscriptions**.
Paper. £5.00. .... Vendor G0555

Borders Family History Society. **[Roxburghshire] Crayling and Nisbet Monumental Inscriptions**.
Paper. £5.00. .... Vendor G0555

Borders Family History Society. **[Roxburghshire] Eckford Monumental Inscriptions**.
Paper. £4.50. .... Vendor G0555

Borders Family History Society. **[Roxburghshire] Edgerston Monumental Inscriptions**.
Paper. £5.00. .... Vendor G0555

Borders Family History Society. **[Roxburghshire] Ednam Monumental Inscriptions**.
Paper. £4.50. .... Vendor G0555

Borders Family History Society. **[Roxburghshire] Hounam & Linton Monumental Inscriptions**.
Paper. £4.50. .... Vendor G0555

Borders Family History Society. **[Roxburghshire] Kelso Monumental Inscriptions**.
Paper. £7.00. .... Vendor G0555

Borders Family History Society. **[Roxburghshire] Makerstoun Monumental Inscriptions**.
Paper. £5.00. .... Vendor G0555

Borders Family History Society. **[Roxburghshire] Maxton Monumental Inscriptions**.
Paper. £5.00. .... Vendor G0555

Borders Family History Society. **[Roxburghshire] Morebattle Monumental Inscriptions**.
Paper. £4.50. .... Vendor G0555

Borders Family History Society. **[Roxburghshire] Oxnam Monumental Inscriptions**.
Paper. £5.00. .... Vendor G0555

Borders Family History Society. **[Roxburghshire] Roxburgh Monumental Inscriptions.**
Paper. £5.00. .... Vendor G0555

Borders Family History Society. **[Roxburghshire] Smailholm Monumental Inscriptions.**
Paper. £5.00. .... Vendor G0555

Borders Family History Society. **[Roxburghshire] Sprouston & Lempitlaw Monumental Inscriptions.**
Paper. £4.50. .... Vendor G0555

Borders Family History Society. **[Roxburghshire] Stichill & Hume Monumental Inscriptions.**
Paper. £5.00. .... Vendor G0555

Borders Family History Society. **[Roxburghshire] Yetholm Monumental Inscriptions.**
Paper. £4.50. .... Vendor G0555

Caputh, Perthshire Monumental Inscriptions.
Paper. £3.50. .... Vendor G0555

Cramond, Edinburgh Monumental Inscriptions.
Paper. £3.50. .... Vendor G0555

Crosbie Kirkyard, Ayr, Monumental Inscriptions.
Paper. £1.50. .... Vendor G0555

Dumfries & Galloway Family History Society. **Portpatrick Old Kirkyard Monumental Inscriptions.**
Paper. £3.75. .... Vendor G0555

Dunkeld Cathedral Monumental Inscriptions.
Paper. £2.50. .... Vendor G0555

Highland Family History Society. **Avoch Monumental Inscriptions.**
Paper. £2.50. .... Vendor G0555

Highland Family History Society. **Fortrose Abbey Monumental Inscriptions.**
Paper. £2.00. .... Vendor G0555

Highland Family History Society. **Geddes Monumental Inscriptions, Nairn.**
Paper. £1.20. .... Vendor G0555

Highland Family History Society. **Killearnan Monumental Inscriptions.**
Paper. £2.00. .... Vendor G0555

Highland Family History Society. **Kilmuir Monumental Inscriptions.**
Paper. £1.85. .... Vendor G0555

Highland Family History Society. **St. Clement's, Dingwall Monumental Inscriptions.**
Paper. £4.00. .... Vendor G0555

Lagganallachie Kirkyard Monumental Inscriptions.
Paper. £2.00. .... Vendor G0555

Little Dunkeld Monumental Inscriptions.
Paper. £4.50. .... Vendor G0555

Scottish Genealogy Society. **[Monumental Inscriptions] Angus—Vol. 2: Seacoast.**
£6.00. .... Vendor G0556

Scottish Genealogy Society. **[Monumental Inscriptions] Angus—Vol. 3: Environs of Dundee.**
Paper. £3.50. .... Vendor G0556

Scottish Genealogy Society. **Angus—Vol. 4: Dundee & Broughty Ferry.**
Paper. £4.00. .... Vendor G0556

Scottish Genealogy Society. **Bute Monumental Inscriptions.**
£5.00. .... Vendor G0556

Scottish Genealogy Society. **Caithness Monumental Inscriptions Vol. 1.**
£6.10. .... Vendor G0556

Scottish Genealogy Society. **Caithness Monumental Inscriptions Vol. 2.**
£6.10. .... Vendor G0556

Scottish Genealogy Society. **Caithness Monumental Inscriptions Vol. 3.**
£6.10. .... Vendor G0556

Scottish Genealogy Society. **Caithness Monumental Inscriptions Vol. 4.**
£6.10. .... Vendor G0556

Scottish Genealogy Society. **Carrick Monumental Inscriptions.**
£8.50. .... Vendor G0556

Scottish Genealogy Society. **Dean Cemetery Edinburgh Monumental Inscriptions.**
£6.75. .... Vendor G0556

Scottish Genealogy Society. **Duddington Monumental Inscriptions & Poll Tax 1694-99.**
Paper. £1.75. .... Vendor G0556

Scottish Genealogy Society. **Dunfermline Abbey Monumental Inscriptions.**
Paper. £3.00. .... Vendor G0556

Scottish Genealogy Society. **Eileen Munde Monumental Inscriptions: Argyll.**
Paper. £1.00. .... Vendor G0556

Scottish Genealogy Society. **Inverness-shire (West) Monumental Inscriptions.**
£6.00. .... Vendor G0556

Scottish Genealogy Society. **Kilmarnock & Louden Monumental Inscriptions.**
£7.75. .... Vendor G0556

Scottish Genealogy Society. **Kincardine & the Mearns Monumental Inscriptions.**
£12.00. .... Vendor G0556

Scottish Genealogy Society. **Kinlochlaigh & Keil in Appin Monumental Inscriptions**.
Paper. £1.00. .... Vendor G0556

Scottish Genealogy Society. **Lochaber & Skye Monumental Inscriptions**.
£5.00. .... Vendor G0556

Scottish Genealogy Society. **Peebleshire Monumental Inscriptions**.
£6.00. .... Vendor G0556

Scottish Genealogy Society. **Renfrewshire Monumental Inscriptions Vol. 1**.
£8.00. .... Vendor G0556

Scottish Genealogy Society. **Renfrewshire Monumental Inscriptions Vol. 2**.
£8.00. .... Vendor G0556

Scottish Genealogy Society. **Speyside Monumental Inscriptions**.
£6.50. .... Vendor G0556

Scottish Genealogy Society. **Stewartry of Kirkcudbright Monumental Inscriptions Vol. 1**.
£5.00. .... Vendor G0556

Scottish Genealogy Society. **Stewartry of Kirkcudbright Monumental Inscriptions Vol. 2**.
Paper. £4.00. .... Vendor G0556

Scottish Genealogy Society. **Stewartry of Kirkcudbright Monumental Inscriptions Vol. 3**.
£6.00. .... Vendor G0556

Scottish Genealogy Society. **Stewartry of Kirkcudbright Monumental Inscriptions Vol. 4**.
£6.00. .... Vendor G0556

Scottish Genealogy Society. **Stewartry of Kirkcudbright Monumental Inscriptions Vol. 5**.
£8.00. .... Vendor G0556

Scottish Genealogy Society. **Stewartry of Kirkcudbright Monumental Inscriptions Vol. 6**.
Paper. £3.00. .... Vendor G0556

Scottish Genealogy Society. **Sutherland Monumental Inscriptions**.
£11.50. .... Vendor G0556

Scottish Genealogy Society. **Upper Deeside Monumental Inscriptions**.
£5.00. .... Vendor G0556

Scottish Genealogy Society. **Upper Donside Monumental Inscriptions**.
Paper. £4.50. .... Vendor G0556

Scottish Genealogy Society. **Wester Ross Monumental Inscriptions**.
Paper. £2.50. .... Vendor G0556

St. Mary's Episcopal Church Birnam, Dunkeld Monumental Inscriptions.
Paper. £2.50. .... Vendor G0555

Tay Valley Family History Society. **Inchture Monumental Inscriptions.**
Paper. £2.50. .... Vendor G0555

Tay Valley Family History Society. **Longforgan Monumental Inscriptions.**
Paper. £2.50. .... Vendor G0555

Troon Family History Society. **Coylton Monumental Inscriptions.**
Paper. £1.80. .... Vendor G0555

Troon Family History Society. **Craigie Monumental Inscriptions.**
Paper. £1.80. .... Vendor G0555

Troon Family History Society. **Dundonald Monumental Inscriptions.**
Paper. £1.80. .... Vendor G0555

Troon Family History Society. **Kyle Graveyards (6) Monumental Inscriptions—
Barnwell, Culzean, Fairfield, Newton-on-Ayr, Coodham, St. Margaret's RC.**
Paper. £1.80. .... Vendor G0555

Troon Family History Society. **Monkton Churchyard Monumental Inscriptions.**
Paper. £1.80. .... Vendor G0555

Troon Family History Society. **Old Alloway Kirk Monumental Inscriptions.**
Paper. £1.80. .... Vendor G0555

Troon Family History Society. **St. Nicholas, Prestwick Monumental Inscriptions.**
Paper. £1.80. .... Vendor G0555

Troon Family History Society. **St. Quivox Monumental Inscriptions.**
Paper. £1.80. .... Vendor G0555

Troon Family History Society. **Symington Monumental Inscriptions.**
Paper. £1.80. .... Vendor G0555

Northeast Scotland

Aberdeen & North East Scotland Family History Society. **[Aberdeenshire Poll Book]
Aberdeen & Freedom Lands Poll Book 1696.**
Paper. £1.95. .... Vendor G0555

Aberdeen & North East Scotland Family History Society. **[Aberdeenshire Poll Book]
Aberdour & Tyrie Poll Book 1696.**
Paper. £1.95. .... Vendor G0555

Aberdeen & North East Scotland Family History Society. **[Aberdeenshire Poll Book]
Auchredie (New Deer) Poll Book.**
Paper. £1.95. .... Vendor G0555

Aberdeen & North East Scotland Family History Society. **[Aberdeenshire Poll Book]
Drumoak Poll Book 1696.**
Paper. £1.95. .... Vendor G0555

Aberdeen & North East Scotland Family History Society. **[Aberdeenshire Poll Book]**
Fraserburgh & New Pitsligo Poll Book 1696.
Paper. £1.95. .... Vendor G0555

Aberdeen & North East Scotland Family History Society. **[Aberdeenshire Poll Book]**
Lonmay & Crimond Poll Book 1696.
Paper. £1.95. .... Vendor G0555

Aberdeen & North East Scotland Family History Society. **[Aberdeenshire Poll Book]**
Old Deer & Longside Poll Book 1696.
Paper. £1.95. .... Vendor G0555

Aberdeen & North East Scotland Family History Society. **[Aberdeenshire Poll Book]**
Peterhead Poll Book 1696.
Paper. £1.95. .... Vendor G0555

Aberdeen & North East Scotland Family History Society. **[Aberdeenshire Poll Book]**
Rathen & Strichen Poll Book 1696.
Paper. £1.95. .... Vendor G0555

Aberdeen & North East Scotland Family History Society. **[Aberdeenshire Poll Book]**
Strathbogie Poll Book 1696 Vol. 1: Dumbennan, Gartly, Rhynie, Essie.
Paper. £1.95. .... Vendor G0555

Aberdeen & North East Scotland Family History Society. **[Aberdeenshire Poll Book]**
Strathbogie Poll Book 1696 Vol. 2: Glass, Kinnoir, Ruthven/Botarie.
Paper. £1.95. .... Vendor G0555

Aberdeen & North East Scotland Family History Society. **[Census] Craig Near**
Montrose 1788, with Description of 1791.
Paper. £1.95. .... Vendor G0555

Aberdeen & North East Scotland Family History Society. **[Census] Peterhead Parish 1801.**
Paper. £3.60. .... Vendor G0555

Aberdeen & North East Scotland Family History Society. **Index to Names in**
Banffshire 1851 Census Vol. 1: Marnoch, Forglen, Inverkeithny and Rothiemay.
Paper. £5.00. .... Vendor G0555

Aberdeen & North East Scotland Family History Society. **Index to Names in**
Banffshire 1851 Census Vol. 2: Gamrie and Alvah.
Paper. £5.00. .... Vendor G0555

Aberdeen & North East Scotland Family History Society. **Index to Names in**
Banffshire 1851 Census Vol. 3: Banff (Town & County), Boyndie, Ordiquhill.
Paper. £5.00. .... Vendor G0555

Aberdeen & North East Scotland Family History Society. **Index to Names In**
Banffshire 1851 Census Vol. 4: Fordyce, Cullen and Deskford. 1996.
Paper. £5.00. .... Vendor G0555

Aberdeen FHS. **Directory of Members' Interests 1987.**
Paper. £0.50. .... Vendor G0555

Adams, D. G. **Bothy Nichts & Days.**
£7.50. .... Vendor G0555

Adams, N. **Hangman's Brae: Crime and Punishment in Aberdeen.**
£7.95. .... Vendor G0555

Aitken, W. **Leaves of a Tree.**
Paper. £1.95. .... Vendor G0555

Alexander, William. **Rural Life in Victorian Aberdeenshire.**
£6.95. .... Vendor G0555

Auld Ellon with 1916 Plan of Ellon.
Paper. £2.50. .... Vendor G0555

Baxter, R. **Free St. Clements Aberdeen 1843-59.**
Paper. £1.95. .... Vendor G0555

Baxter, R. **St. Clements Parish Vol. 1.**
Paper. £1.95. .... Vendor G0555

Beverly, W., and S. Beverly. **30 Years at Portlethen: Day Book 1840-1869 of the Rev. William Low.**
Paper. £4.50. .... Vendor G0555

Bing, C. **The Lairds of Arbuthnott.**
£6.99. .... Vendor G0555

The Broch As It Was: Fraserburgh of Old.
Paper. £3.95. .... Vendor G0555

Buchan, David. **St. Combs, My Buchan.**
£7.50. .... Vendor G0555

Buckie in Old Picture Postcards.
£9.95. .... Vendor G0555

Buckie Past and Present.
Paper. £2.25. .... Vendor G0555

Cameron, D. K. **Cornkister Days.**
£12.95. .... Vendor G0555

Campbell, D., and F. Watson. **The Hospitals of Peterhead & District.**
Paper. £1.50. .... Vendor G0555

The Christian Watt Papers: The Fascinating Account of a Broadsea Fisherwoman in the 19th Century.
£9.95. .... Vendor G0555

Churches of Moray.
Paper. £2.00. .... Vendor G0555

Clark, A. **Reminiscences of a Police Officer in the Granite City.**
Paper. £4.00. .... Vendor G0555

Clemo, M. **Historic Insch.**
Paper. £3.00. .... Vendor G0555

Dalgarno, J. **From Brig'o Balgownie to the Bullers o'Buchan—A Travel Guide from the 1890s.**
£5.95. .... Vendor G0555

Diack, Lesley. **North-East Roots: A Guide to Sources.** 3rd rev. ed.
Repositories and sources as of March 1996.
Paper. £1.95. .... Vendor G0555

The Diary of a Canny Man, 1818-28: Adam Mackie of Fyvie.
£6.95. .... Vendor G0555

Dobson, David. **Emigrants & Adventurers from Aberdeen & NE, Part 1.**
Contact vendor for information. .... Vendor G0641

Dobson, David. **Emigrants & Adventurers from Aberdeen & NE, Part 2.**
Contact vendor for information. .... Vendor G0641

Dobson, David. **Emigrants & Adventurers from Moray & Banff, Part 1.**
Contact vendor for information. .... Vendor G0641

Dobson, David. **Mariners of Aberdeen & N. Scotland 1600-1700.**
Contact vendor for information. .... Vendor G0641

Dobson, David. **Mariners of Aberdeen & N. Scotland 1700-1800, Part 1.**
Contact vendor for information. .... Vendor G0641

Dobson, David. **Whalers of Dundee, 1750-1850.**
Contact vendor for information. .... Vendor G0641

Donnelly, T. **The Aberdeen Granite Industry.**
£9.50. .... Vendor G0555

Downie, D., D. Morrison, and A. Muirhead. **Tales o' the Maisters: A History of Kemnay School.**
£9.90. .... Vendor G0555

Duncan, M. **Kemnay Parish Church 1994.**
Paper. £2.25. .... Vendor G0555

Fenton, A. **The Turra Coo:** The Complete Tale of This Famous "Riot" in Turriff in 1913.
Paper. £4.99. .... Vendor G0555

Fenton, A. **Wirds an' Wark 'e Seasons Roon: Everyday Life on an Aberdeenshire Farm.**
Paper. £4.95. .... Vendor G0555

Ferguson. **Shipwrecks of N.E. Scotland 1440-1990.**
£6.95. .... Vendor G0555

Ferguson, K. **Black Kalendar of Aberdeen: 1746-1878.**
Victims and perpetrators of crime.
Paper. £1.95. .... Vendor G0555

Fermfolk & Fisherfolk. **Rural Life in North of Scotland in 18th & 19th Century.**
£6.99. .... Vendor G0555

Findlay, D. **Banffshire Churches.**
Paper. £3.00. .... Vendor G0555

Fraser, G. M. **Aberdeen Street Names.**
£9.95. .... Vendor G0555

From Aberdeen to Ottawa in 1845: The Diary of Alexander Muir.
£5.95. .... Vendor G0555

Haddow, A. H. **The History of Methlick Church.**
£5.00. .... Vendor G0555

Henderson, I. **Discovering Angus and the Mearns.**
£7.50. .... Vendor G0555

Henderson, M. **Harvest: 150 Years of Bucksburn Church (formerly Newhills Free Church).**
Paper. £3.00. .... Vendor G0555

Highways and Byways Around Stonehaven.
£7.95. .... Vendor G0555

Hustwick, Ian. **Moray Firth Ships and Trade.**
£12.95. .... Vendor G0555

Jack, R. **Maud: A Glimpse Into the Past.**
Paper. £2.50. .... Vendor G0555

Jack, R. **New Pitsligo: A Glimpse into the Past.**
Paper. £3.00. .... Vendor G0555

Jackson, R. **The Joint Station 1867-1992.**
Paper. £2.50. .... Vendor G0555

Jamieson. **Education in Fraserburgh.**
Paper. £3.95. .... Vendor G0555

Keith, A. **A Thousand Years of Aberdeen.**
£13.99. .... Vendor G0555

Keith Past and Present.
Paper. £2.25. .... Vendor G0555

Laich O'Moray Past and Present.
Paper. £2.00. .... Vendor G0555

Land of Lonach: History of the Forbes and the Strathdon Area.
£7.50. .... Vendor G0555

Leith, R. **Membership Roll Frederick Street Congregational Chapel Aberdeen 1807-1859.**
Paper. £1.95. .... Vendor G0555

Lunan's Diary (Blairdaff 1729-69, Luthermuir 1770-1817).
Paper. £4.25. .... Vendor G0555

Macdonald, W. **Boats & Boatbuilders Around Fraserburgh.**
£8.95. .... Vendor G0555

Macduff and Its Harbour 1783-1983.
Paper. £1.50. .... Vendor G0555

Marshall, Christian Watt. **A Stranger on the Bars.**
£5.99. .... Vendor G0555

McDonnell, Frances. **Alumni & Graduates in Arts of the Aberdeen Colleges 1840-49.**
Contact vendor for information. .... Vendor G0642

McDonnell, Frances. **Alumni & Graduates in Arts of the Aberdeen Colleges 1850-60.**
Contact vendor for information. .... Vendor G0642

McDonnell, Frances. **Birth Briefs of Aberdeen 1637-1705.**
Contact vendor for information. .... Vendor G0642

McDonnell, Frances. **Burgess Roll of Elgin.**
Contact vendor for information. .... Vendor G0642

McDonnell, Frances. **Burgesses of Banff 1549-1892.**
Contact vendor for information. .... Vendor G0642

McDonnell, Frances. **Register of Merchants & Trade Burgesses of Aberdeen 1600-20.**
Contact vendor for information. .... Vendor G0642

McDonnell, Frances. **Register of Merchants & Trade Burgesses of Aberdeen 1621-39.**
Contact vendor for information. .... Vendor G0642

McDonnell, Frances. **Register of Merchants & Trade Burgesses of Aberdeen 1640-59.**
Contact vendor for information. .... Vendor G0642

McDonnell, Frances. **Register of Merchants & Trade Burgesses of Aberdeen 1660-79.**
Contact vendor for information. .... Vendor G0642

McDonnell, Frances. **Register of Merchants & Trade Burgesses of Aberdeen 1680-1700.**
Contact vendor for information. .... Vendor G0642

McDonnell, Frances. **Register of Merchants & Trade Burgesses of Old Aberdeen 1605-1725.**
Contact vendor for information. .... Vendor G0642

McDonnell, Frances. **Register of Merchants & Trade Burgesses of Old Aberdeen 1726-1885.**
Contact vendor for information. .... Vendor G0642

McDonnell, Frances. **Roll of Apprentices Burgh of Aberdeen 1622-99.**
Contact vendor for information. .... Vendor G0642

McDonnell, Frances. **Roll of Apprentices Burgh of Aberdeen 1700-50.**
Contact vendor for information. .... Vendor G0642

McDonnell, Frances. **Roll of Apprentices Burgh of Aberdeen 1751-96.**
Contact vendor for information. .... Vendor G0642

McGregor, R. **Gregor Willox, Warlock of Kirkmichael 1705?-1833.**
Paper. £5.00. .... Vendor G0555

Meldrum, Ed. **Aberdeen of Old.**
£7.80. .... Vendor G0555

Morayshire Described: A Reprint of the 1868 Edition.
£8.50. .... Vendor G0555

Morgan, Diane. **Footdee.**
£10.95. .... Vendor G0555

Murray, J. **Schooling in the Cove: A History of Schools in This Small Kincardine Fishing Village.**
Paper. £1.00. .... Vendor G0555

Needham-Hurst, K. **Aspects of Alford.**
Paper. £4.50. .... Vendor G0555

Peterhead and the Edinburgh Merchant Co. 1728-1987.
Paper. £3.00. .... Vendor G0555

A Pictorial History of the Garioch.
Paper. £3.00. .... Vendor G0555

Rathen West Church: A History.
Paper. £2.50. .... Vendor G0555

Salter, M. **The Castles of Grampian & Angus.**
£9.00. .... Vendor G0555

Scotland's North Sea Gateway: Aberdeen Harbour 1136-1986.
£7.90. .... Vendor G0555

Seton, Mike. **Distilleries of Moray.**
Paper. £0.99. .... Vendor G0555

Shepherd, I. **Gordon: An Illustrated Architectural Guide.**
£8.99. .... Vendor G0555

Simpson, E. **Discovering Banff, Moray & Nairn.**
£7.95. .... Vendor G0555

Smith, J. **Old Aberdeen: Bishops, Burghers & Buildings.**
£6.99. .... Vendor G0555

Smith, R. **Discovering Aberdeenshire.**
£8.95. .... Vendor G0555

Smith, R. **One Foot in the Sea:** A Journey Along the Coastal Trail from Montrose to the Moray Firth.
£8.50. .... Vendor G0555

Smith, S., and M. Wilson. **Aberdeen Royal Infirmary Deaths Recorded Vol. 1: 1743-1822.**
Paper. £3.90. .... Vendor G0555

Speyside Past and Present.
Paper. £2.25. .... Vendor G0555

St. Ninian's Church, Turriff, 1795-1995.
Paper. £3.00. .... Vendor G0555

Stevenson, D. **From Lairds to Loons: Country and Burgh Life in Aberdeen 1600-1800.**
Paper. £4.99. .... Vendor G0555

Stewart, D. **Lossie War Memorial 1939-45.**
£5.00. .... Vendor G0555

Stonehaven of Old, Vol. 2.
Paper. £3.00. .... Vendor G0555

Survey of the Province of Moray: A Reprint of the 1793 Edition.
£9.50. .... Vendor G0555

Sutherland, G. **Whaling Years: Peterhead 1788-1893.**
£6.95 .... Vendor G0555

Tak Tent O'Lear: History of Dunnottar School.
Paper. £2.80. .... Vendor G0555

Taylor, J. **Fraserburgh Means Fish.**
Paper. £3.50. .... Vendor G0555

Taylor, J., and L. Taylor. **North East Neuk.**
Paper. £4.50. .... Vendor G0555

Taylor, J. **Photographic Memories of the N.E. Coast.**
£5.95. .... Vendor G0555

Thomson, F. **Discovering Speyside.**
£7.50. .... Vendor G0555

Three Score Years and Ten 1913-83. Bert Murray's Memories of Aberdeen.
Paper. £4.00. .... Vendor G0555

Toulmin, D. **The Tillycorthie Story:** An Account of James Duncan Who Made a Vast Fortune in Bolivia.
Paper. £4.50. .... Vendor G0555

Walkin' the Mat: Old Photos of the City [Aberdeen].
£12.00. .... Vendor G0555

Walks About Buchan.
Paper. £2.00. .... Vendor G0555

Wallace, M., N. Wallace, and D. Merson. **Grange Kirk Session Records 1694-1702.**
Paper. £4.50. .... Vendor G0555

Watson, F. **In Sickness and in Health.**
Paper. £1.95. .... Vendor G0555

Watt, A. **A Goodly Heritage: Famous People of Stonehaven & District.**
£6.95. .... Vendor G0555

Waulken, G. **About Banchory.**
Paper. £2.50. .... Vendor G0555

Where and What is Kildrummy?
£6.00. .... Vendor G0555

Whyte, D. **Walter MacFarlane, Clan Chief and Antiquary.**
Paper. £1.95. .... Vendor G0555

Youngblood, M. **Bourtie Kirk 800 Years.**
Paper. £4.50. .... Vendor G0555

Orkney & Shetland

Beattie, A. **Shetland Pre-1855 Parish Sources.**
Paper. £3.50. .... Vendor G0555

Dobson, David. **Emigrants & Adventurers from Orkney & Shetland.**
Contact vendor for information. .... Vendor G0641

Evie & Rendall, Orkney 1851 Census.
Microfiche (2). £3.00. .... Vendor G0555

Firth & Stenness, Orkney 1851 Census.
Microfiche (2). £3.00. .... Vendor G0555

Hoy & Graemsay, Orkney 1851 Census.
Microfiche (1). £3.00. .... Vendor G0555

Orphir, Orkney 1821 Census.
Microfiche (1). £3.00. .... Vendor G0555

Orphir, Orkney 1851 Census.
Microfiche (2). £3.00. .... Vendor G0555

S. Ronaldsay & Burray, Orkney 1851 Census.
Microfiche (3). £3.00. .... Vendor G0555

Strommess, Orkney 1821 Census.
Microfiche (1). £3.00. .... Vendor G0555

Strommess, Orkney 1851 Census.
Microfiche (3). £3.00. .... Vendor G0555

Walls & Flotta, Orkney 1851 Census.
Microfiche (2). £3.00. .... Vendor G0555

Strathclyde Region

Aitken, W. **Leaves of a Tree, Vol. 2.**
Paper. £3.30. .... Vendor G0555

Dobson, David. **Emigrants & Adventurers from Argyll.**
Contact vendor for information. .... Vendor G0641

Dobson, David. **Mariners of the Clyde & W. Scotland 1600-1700.**
Contact vendor for information. .... Vendor G0641

Dobson, David. **Mariners of the Clyde & W. Scotland 1700-1800, Part 1.**
Contact vendor for information. .... Vendor G0641

Glasgow Family History Society. **Burial Grounds—Glasgow.**
Paper. £1.20. .... Vendor G0555

Glasgow Family History Society. **Strathclyde Sources.** 2nd ed.
Paper. £3.50. .... Vendor G0555

McDonnell, Frances. **Burgh of Paisley Poll Tax Roll 1695, Part 1.**
Contact vendor for information. .... Vendor G0642

McDonnell, Frances. **Burgh of Paisley Poll Tax Roll 1695, Part 2.**
Contact vendor for information. .... Vendor G0642

Sources for Family History in Ayrshire.
Paper. £2.50. .... Vendor G0555

Troon Family History Society. **Directory of Members' Interests 1995—Troon FHS.**
Paper. £1.50. .... Vendor G0555

Troon Family History Society. **Dundonald Burial Register.**
Paper. £1.80. .... Vendor G0555

Troon Family History Society. **Newton Green Burial Ground.**
Paper. £2.10. .... Vendor G0555

Troon Family History Society. **Sources for Family History in Ayrshire.**
Paper. £2.50. .... Vendor G0555

West of Scotland Census Returns and OPRs.
Paper. £1.50. .... Vendor G0555

✨ Great Britain—Wales ✨

Bardsley, Charles Wareing. **A Dictionary of English and Welsh Surnames with Special American Instances.** (Rev. ed., 1901) reprint 1996.
Cloth. $50.00. xvi + 837 pp. .... Vendor G0010

Burke, Arthur M. **Key to the Ancient Parish Registers of England and Wales.** (1908) reprint 1996. Illus.
Paper. $18.00. 163 pp. .... Vendor G0011

Camp, A. J. **My Ancestors Moved (in England or Wales): How Can I Trace Where They Came From?** 1994.
Paper. £4.60. 66 pp. .... Vendor G0557

Family History Library. **Research Outline: Wales.**
Leaflet. $.75. 36 pp. .... Vendor G0629

FFHS. **The Family Historian's Guide to Wales.** 1996.
£6.50 (overseas surface). Approx. 100 pp. .... Vendor G0588

Foot, William. **Maps for Family History.** 1994.
    This guide covers the records of the Valuation Office, Tithe and the National Farm Surveys of England and Wales, 1836-1943.
Paper. £8.95. 93 pp. .... Vendor G0558

Gibson, J., and C. Rogers. **Coroners' Records in England and Wales.** (1988) reprint 1992.
£2.50 49 pp. .... Vendor G0557

Gibson, J., and C. Rogers. **Poor Law Union Records. Part 3: South West England, The Marches & Wales.** 1993.
£3.95. 72 pp. .... Vendor G0557

Gibson, J., and C. Rogers. **Poor Law Union Records (in England and Wales). Part 4: Gazetteer of England and Wales.** 1993.
£3.95 80 pp. .... Vendor G0557

Gibson, J. S. W., and Pamela Peskett. **Record Offices in England and Wales:** How to Find Them. 5th ed. 1992. Illus.
Paper. $7.50. 60 pp. .... Vendor G0010

Hawkings, David T. **Criminal Ancestors.** A Guide to Historical Criminal Records in England and Wales. (1992) reprint 1996. Indexed. Illus.
Paper. $23.95. xiv + 448 pp. .... Vendor G0576

Hawkings, David T. **Railway Ancestors.** A Guide to the Staff Records of the Railway Companies of England and Wales 1822-1947. With a Foreword by Lord Teviot. Indexed.
Cloth. $44.95. 384 pp. .... Vendor G0576

Library of Congress. **Sources for Research in Welsh Genealogy.** Compiled by Judith P. Reid.

The text of this is available on the Local History and Genealogy Reading Room's home page: http://lcweb.loc.gov/rr/genealogy.
Free. Contact vendor for information. 9 pp. .... Vendor G0566

Lumas, Susan. **An Introduction to Census Returns of England & Wales**. 1992.
£1.84 (overseas surface). 21 pp. .... Vendor G0588

Roberts, T. R. **A Short Biographical Dictionary of Welshmen Who Have Obtained Distinction from the Earliest Times to the Present**. (1908) reprint 1995. Illus.
Paper. $45.00. 613 pp. .... Vendor G0011

Rowlands, John, and Sheila Rowlands. **The Surnames of Wales** for Family Historians and Others. 1996. Illus.
Paper. $19.95. 229 pp. .... Vendor G0010

Rowlands, John, ed. **Welsh Family History**. A Guide to Research. (1993) reprint 1996. Indexed. Illus.
Paper. $19.95. 316 pp. .... Vendor G0010

Siddons, Michael Powell. **The Development of Welsh Heraldry**. 3 vols. 1991, 1993. Illus.
Contact vendor for information. .... Vendor G0591

John & Sheila Rowlands # THE SURNAMES OF WALES
For Family Historians and Others

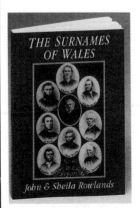

It has been estimated that by mid-nineteenth century, fully 90 percent of the Welsh population shared fewer than 100 surnames, while the 10 most common surnames were shared by roughly half the population. Any attempt to distinguish the individual from the mass would thus be a daunting task, and the prospect of a successful genealogical search would appear to be very slim indeed.

In reality, however, this is more misconception than fact, for as the authors demonstrate in this new study, a good understanding of the historical development of surnames in Wales, together with a knowledge of the relative incidence of individual names in different parts of the country, can often lead to a successful search. It is the purpose of their book, therefore, to provide the reader with a detailed insight into the origins and occurrence of common Welsh surnames, together with some consideration of those surnames which are associated with particular locales, thus helping to suggest a likely place of origin within Wales.

229 pp., illus., paperback.
1996. **Vendor G0010.**
$19.95

Walne, Peter. **English Wills: Probate Records in England and Wales.** (1964) reprint 1981.
Paper. $7.95. 62 pp. .... Vendor G0553

Williams, C. J., and J. Watts-Williams, comps. **Cofrestri Plwyf Cymru—Parish Registers of Wales.** 1986. Indexed. Illus.
Cloth. Contact vendor for information. xxx + 217 pp. .... Vendor G0591

✌ Greece ✌

Mattheou, Antonia S. **Tracing Your Greek Ancestry—Reference to Cyprus.** 1992. Indexed. Illus.
Paper. $12.00. 54 pp. .... Vendor G0473

> ***Tracing Your Greek Ancestry - Reference To Cyprus***
> A guide devoted entirely to step by step research in Greek genealogy in USA and Greece.
> It includes sources and services available in both countries, and other useful information.
> ($12.00 per copy, shipping & handling included)
> Send checks and inquiries: Antonia S. Mattheou. 75-21 177 Street, Flushing, NY 11366.

✌ Hungary ✌

Brandt, Edward Reimer. **Contents and Addresses of Hungarian Archives.** With Supplementary Information for Research on German-Speaking Ancestors from Hungary. 2nd ed. 1993.
Cloth. $15.00. 88 pp. .... Vendor G0011

✌ Ireland ✌

General References

Adams, William Forbes. **Ireland and Irish Emigration to the New World** from 1815 to the Famine. (1932) reprint 1993. Indexed.
Paper. $32.50. 444 pp. .... Vendor G0011

The Ancestor Trail in Ireland.
Paper. £2.35. .... Vendor G0555

Baxter, Angus. **In Search of Your British & Irish Roots**. 3rd ed. (1994) reprint 1996. Paper. $16.95. 320 pp. .... Vendor G0010

Bolton, Charles Knowles. **Scotch Irish Pioneers in Ulster and America**. 1910. Reprint. Indexed. Illus.
Covers the conditions in Ulster that prompted the immigration of the Scotch-Irish to the New World about 1718, and their various settlements.
Paper. $26.50. 398 pp. .... Vendor G0140

Burke, J., and J. B. Burke. **Burke's Extinct & Dormant Baronetcies of England, Ireland & Scotland**. (1841) reprint 1994.
Contact vendor for information. 644 pp. .... Vendor G0010

Burke, John. **A Genealogical and Heraldic History of the Commoners of Great Britain and Ireland**. In Four Volumes. Reprinted with the *Index to Pedigrees in Burke's Commoners*, by George Ormerod. (1834-1838, 1907) reprint 1996. Indexed. Illus.
The standard genealogical guide to families in Great Britain and Ireland who enjoyed territorial possession or official rank, but were uninvested with heritable honors.
Paper. $200.00. 3,113 pp. .... Vendor G0011

Campbell, R. G. **Scotch-Irish Family Research Made Simple**.
64 pp. .... Vendor G0574

Chapman, Colin. **Tracing Your British Ancestors**. 1996. Indexed.
Irish, Scottish, English, and Welsh ancestors, as well as those from the Isle of Man and the Channel Islands, can all be traced using methods described in this book.
Paper. $15.00. 108 pp. .... Vendor G0010

Clare, Rev. Wallace. **A Guide to Copies & Abstracts of Irish Wills**. (1930) reprint 1989.
Contact vendor for information. 111 pp. .... Vendor G0011

Collins, E. J. **Irish Family Research Made Simple**.
Paper. $10.00. 76 pp. .... Vendor G0574

D'Alton. **King James Irish Army List 1689**. (1855) reprint 1996.
Cloth. $95.00 .... Vendor G0259

Davis, B. **An Introduction to Irish Research**. 2nd ed. 1994.
£5.55 (overseas surface). 100 pp. .... Vendor G0588

Diner. **Erin's Daughters in America: Irish Immigrant Women in the Nineteenth Century**. 1983.
Paper. $14.95. 192 pp. .... Vendor G0611

Dobson, David. **Scots-Irish Links, 1575-1725. In Two Parts**. 2 vols. in 1. (1994, 1995) reprint 1997.
Contact vendor for information. 58 pp. .... Vendor G0011

Eustace, P. Beryl, ed. **Registry of Deeds, Dublin Abstract of Wills,** Volume I, 1708-1745; Volume II, 1746-1785. (1956, 1954) reprint 1996. Indexed.
Paper. $65.00. 430 + 453 pp. .... Vendor G0011

Ewen, Cecil Henry L'Estrange. **A History of Surnames of the British Isles**. A Concise Account of Their Origin, Evolution, Etymology, and Legal Status. (1931, 1968) reprint 1995. Indexed.
Paper. $41.50. 539 pp. .... Vendor G0011

Fairbairn, James. **Fairbairn's Book of Crests of the Families of Great Britain and Ireland** 2 vols. in 1. (1905) reprint 1993.
Cloth. $60.00. 1,073 pp. .... Vendor G0010

Falley, Margaret D. **Irish and Scotch-Irish Ancestral Research:** A Guide to the Genealogical Records, Methods, and Sources in Ireland. 2 vols. (1962) reprint 1988. Indexed.
Cloth. $60.00. 813 + 354 pp. .... Vendor G0010

Family History Library. **Ireland Householders Index Guide**.
Free. 4 pp. .... Vendor G0629

Family History Library. **Research Outline: Ireland**.
Leaflet. $.75. 48 pp. .... Vendor G0629

Farrar, Henry. **Irish Marriages** Being an Index to the Marriages in Walker's Hibernian Magazine, 1771-1812. With an Appendix from the Notes of Sir Arthur Vicars . . . 2 vols. in 1. (1897) reprint 1996.
Paper. $37.50. 532 pp. .... Vendor G0011

FFHS. **Ancestor Trail in Ireland**.
£3.10 (overseas surface). .... Vendor G0588

FFHS. **Clans and Families of Ireland**. Illus.
Cloth. £17.85 (overseas surface). .... Vendor G0588

FFHS. **Tracing Your Irish Ancestry**.
£13.10 (overseas surface). .... Vendor G0588

Ford, Henry Jones. **The Scotch-Irish in America**. (1915) reprint 1995. Indexed.
Paper. $42.50. 607 pp. .... Vendor G0011

Foster, ed. **The Oxford History of Ireland**. 1989.
    An account of over 2,000 years of Irish history, from pre-Christian times to the present-day. Includes a chronology of Irish history, bibliography, and maps. Useful reference.
Paper. $14.95. 346 pp. .... Vendor G0611

Foster, ed. **The Oxford Illustrated History of Ireland**. 1989.
    The text is as in *The Oxford History of Ireland* (see above listing), but contains hundreds of beautiful photographs, drawings, and maps to illustrate.
Paper. $22.50. 382 pp. .... Vendor G0611

Garnsey, H., P. McIntyre(?), and A. Phippen. **The Irish Holdings of the Society of Australian Genealogists**. 1996. Indexed.
Paper. $18.50+ postage. 207 pp. .... Vendor G0563

General Alphabetical Index to the Townlands and Towns, Parishes and Baronies of Ireland, Based on the Census of Ireland for the Year 1851. (1861) reprint 1992.
Contact vendor for information. 968 pp. .... Vendor G0010

General Register Office, Dublin. **Registering the People—150 Years of Civil Registration**. 1995. Illus.
Establishment and history of civil registration in Ireland.
£1(Irl) plus postage. 24 pp. .... Vendor G0584

Gibson, Jeremy S. W. **Bishops' Transcripts and Marriage Licenses in England, Wales, and Ireland**. 3rd ed. 1992.
Paper. $6.00. 40 pp. .... Vendor G0010

Gibson, Jeremy S. W. **Probate Jurisdictions in Great Britain and Ireland**. 3rd ed. (1986) reprint 1989.
Paper. $7.50. 72 pp. .... Vendor G0010

Grehan, Ida. **Irish Family Histories**. 1993.
All the known spellings for each major Irish surname are presented followed by geographical distribution and information on emigration to America and elsewhere. 8½" x 11".
Paper. $16.95. 400 pp. .... Vendor G0611

Grenham, John. **Tracing Your Irish Ancestors**. (1993) reprint 1996.
Paper. $19.95. 320 pp. .... Vendor G0010

Hanna, Charles A. **The Scotch-Irish**. Or the Scot in North Britain, North Ireland and North America. 2 vols. (1902) reprint 1995. Indexed. Illus.
Cloth. $75.00. 623 + 602 pp. .... Vendor G0010

Harrison, Henry. **Surnames of the United Kingdom**. A Concise Etymological Dictionary. 2 vols. in 1. (1912-18) reprint 1996.
Paper. $45.00. 622 pp. .... Vendor G0011

Index to the Act or Grant Books, and to the Original Wills, of the Diocese of Dublin [c. 1638] to the Year 1800. From the Appendix to the Twnety-sixth Report of the Deputy Keeper of the Public Records and Keeper of the State Papers in Ireland. (1895) reprint 1997.
Records of the Diocese of Dublin, an ancient jurisdiction which today encompasses all of the city of Dublin and County Dublin, as well as parts of Counties Carlow, Kildare, Leix, Wexford, and Wicklow.
Paper. $65.00. 1,097 pp. .... Vendor G0011

Jones, Henry Z, Jr. **Palatine Families of Ireland**. 1990. Indexed. Illus.
Book #1109.
Cloth. $37.50. 192 pp. .... Vendor G0082

Jones, Henry Z, Jr. **Palatine Families of Ireland**. Indexed. Illus.
A genealogical study of the German families settled by the British government in Ireland in 1709.
Cloth. $37.50 + $2.50 p&h. 190 pp. .... Vendor G0581

Joyce, P. W. **The Origin and History of Irish Names of Places**. In Three Volumes. (1869-1913) reprint 1995. Indexed.
Paper. $115.00. 1,756 pp. in all. .... Vendor G0011

Keating, Geoffrey. **Keatings History of Ireland**. Complete 3 vol. set. Translated by O'Mahoney. Indexed.
New index with genealogies. Nowhere else in print. Priceless footnotes and folk history.
Quality hardbound & gold stamped. $125.00. .... Vendor G0455

King, Joseph A. **From Ireland to North America**.
This book conveys the excitement and the pain of a people forced to risk an uncertain voyage to a hoped-for better life.
Paper. $13.95. .... Vendor G0611

Lewis, Samuel. **A Topographical Dictionary of Ireland**. 2 vols. (1837) reprint 1995.
Cloth. $85.00. 1,480 pp. total. .... Vendor G0010

Leyburn. **The Scotch-Irish: A Social History**. (1962) reprint 1991.
These people in Scotland, their removal to Northern Ireland, and their migrations to America. Extensive bibliography.
Paper. $15.95. 377 pp. .... Vendor G0611

Library of Congress. **Sources for Research in Irish Genealogy**. Compiled by Judith P. Reid.
The text of this is available on the Local History and Genealogy Reading Room's home page: http://lcweb.loc.gov/rr/genealogy.
Free: Contact vendor for information. 19 pp. .... Vendor G0566

McGee, Thomas D'Arcy. **A History of the Irish Settlers in North America**. (1852) reprint 1989. Indexed.
Cloth. $18.95. 240 pp. .... Vendor G0011

McKenna, Erin. **A Student's Guide to Irish American Genealogy.** 1996. Indexed. Illus.
Hard-cover. $24.95. 208 pp. .... Vendor G0776

Miller. **Emigrants & Exiles: Ireland and the Irish Exodus to North America.** 1985.
In-depth study of Irish emigration to America, 1607-1921. Paints a vivid picture of Ireland and why so many Irish left her. Includes extensive footnotes.
Paper. $18.95. 684 pp. .... Vendor G0611

Miller, Kerby, and Paul Wagner. **Out of Ireland: The Story of Irish Emigration to America.** 1994.
This moving portayal of the history of Irish emigration to the U.S. from the 18th to 20th centuries uses as its primary source the remarkable memoirs and letters by and to Irish immigrants in America. Beautifully illustrated. 8½" x 11".
Cloth. $24.95. 132 pp. .... Vendor G0611

Mitchell, Brian. **Family History Pack—How to Trace Your Irish Ancestors.**
Paper. £3.00. .... Vendor G0604

Mitchell, Brian. **A Guide to Irish Churches and Graveyards.** (1990) reprint 1995.
Cloth. $30.00. 253 pp. .... Vendor G0010

Mitchell, Brian. **A Guide to Irish Parish Records.** (1988) reprint 1995.
Cloth. $25.00. 151 pp., quarto .... Vendor G0010

Mitchell, Brian. **A New Genealogical Atlas of Ireland.** (1986) reprint 1996. Illus.
Paper. $18.95. 123 pp. .... Vendor G0010

Mitchell, Brian. **Parish Maps (Depicting All Townlands in the Four Ulster Counties of Armagh, Donegal, Londonderry and Tyrone).**
Paper. $29.95. 288 pp. .... Vendor G0536

Mitchell, Brian S. **Pocket Guide to Irish Genealogy.**
Paper. $7.95. 103 pp. .... Vendor G0536

Mitchell, Brian. **Pocket Guide to Irish Genealogy.** (1991) reprint 1996. Illus.
Contact vendor for information. 63 pp. .... Vendor G0011

Mitchell, Brian. **Tracing Your Irish Ancestors.**
Paper. £3.00. .... Vendor G0604

Musgrave, Sir Richard. **Memoirs of the Different Rebellions in Ireland . . .** (1802) reprint 1995. Indexed. Illus.
Vivid eyewitness accounts of the 1798 Rebellion with new index of 10,600 references to people and places involved.
Cloth. $54.20. xxv + 982 pp. .... Vendor G0515

O'Laughlin, M., ed. **The Book of Irish Families Great & Small.**
Includes coats of arms; native & settler families found nowhere else. Families from all of Ireland; 1,800 families. Our bestselling Irish family history book; 10,000 Irish family names with history and location, sources.
Quality hardbound & gold stamped. $28.00. 320 pp. .... Vendor G0455

O'Laughlin, M. **The Beginners Guide to Irish Family Research**. Illus.
The common sense guide for the beginner.
Paper. $12.00. .... Vendor G0455

O'Laughlin, M. **Complete Book for Tracing Your Irish Ancestors**. 7th printing.
Illus.
All the steps needed for finding your ancestors.
Quality hardbound & gold stamped. $26.00. 300+ pp. .... Vendor G0455

O'Laughlin, M. **The Irish Book of Arms**.
The largest illustrated collection of Irish arms. Specific families. Complete archival
collection; over 1,000 arms, b&w.
Quality hardbound & gold stamped. $30.00. .... Vendor G0455

O'Laughlin, M. **The Master Book of Irish Placenames**.
The Master atlas and place-name locator for all of Ireland. Over sixty indexed
maps. Seventeenth- and nineteenth-century place-name indexes; spellings; history;
appendix; 40,000 listings.
Quality hardbound & gold stamped. $24.00. 250 pp. .... Vendor G0455

O'Laughlin, M. **The Master Book of Irish Surnames**.
The Master index of 60,000 locations, origins, spellings, and sources for Irish names.

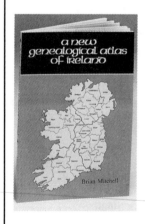

The largest collection ever; bonus section includes the surname index to all IGF works and periodicals.
Quality hardbound & gold stamped. $24.00. 320 pp. .... Vendor G0455

O'Neill, Robert K. **Guide to Libraries and Archives of N. Ireland**. 1996.
Paper. £8.00 + £1.00 surface mail. 160 pp. .... Vendor G0564

Ortelius, A. **Ortelius Map of Ireland**.
  Originally published 1572 A.D., showing location of Irish families and chieftains.
Quality hardbound & gold stamped. $20.00. .... Vendor G0455

Osborne, Joseph F. **Heirlooms of Ireland**. An Easy Reference to Some Irish Surnames and Their Origins. 1995.
Paper. $24.95. 183 pp. .... Vendor G0011

Phillimore, William P. W., and Gertrude Thrift, eds. **Indexes to Irish Wills**. 5 vols. in 1. (1909-20) reprint 1997. Illus.
Cloth. $50.00. 827 pp. .... Vendor G0010

Public Record Office of N. Ireland. **An Irish Genealogical Source & Guide to Church Records**. 1996.
Paper. UK£20.00 + £3.70 surface mail. .... Vendor G0564

Radford, Dwight A., and Kyle J. Betit. **Ireland: A Genealogical Guide for North Americans**. 1994.
  Discusses each of the major record types and their uses, and indicates how the records can be obtained both in Ireland and in North America.
Paper. $14.95. .... Vendor G0611

Return of Owners of Land in Ireland, 1876. (1876) reprint 1996.
Contact vendor for information. 325 pp. .... Vendor G0010

Ryan, James G., ed. **Irish Church Records:** Their History, Availability & Use in Family and Local History Research. Indexed. Illus.
  Includes the following sections: Records of the Church of Ireland, Presbyterian Church Records, Methodist Records in Ireland, Huguenot Church Registers, Irish Quaker Records, Catholic Church Records, Irish Jewish Records, and Irish Baptist Church Records.
Cloth. IR£24.00. 207 pp. .... Vendor G0619

Ryan, James G. **Irish Records: Sources for Family and Local History**. Rev. ed. 1997.
Cloth. $49.95. Contact vendor for availability. 612 pp. .... Vendor G0570

Schlegel, Donald M. **Irish Genealogical Abstracts** from the *Londonderry Journal*, 1772-1784. 1990. Indexed.
Cloth. $21.00. 189 pp. .... Vendor G0011

Society of Genealogists. **Monumental Inscriptions in the Library of the Society of Genealogists**. Part 2 Northern England, Wales, Scotland, Ireland and Overseas. 1987.
Paper. £2.40. 46 pp. .... Vendor G0557

Ulster Historical Foundation. **Directory of Irish Family History Research**. Published annually.
Paper. UK£6.95 + £1.00 surface mail. Approx. 100 pp. .... Vendor G0564

Ulster Historical Foundation. **Familia: Ulster Genealogical Review.** Published annually.
Paper. UK£5.95 + £1.00 surface mail. Approx. 100 pp. .... Vendor G0564

Vicars, Sir Arthur. **Index to the Prerogative Wills of Ireland 1536-1810.** (1897)
reprint 1997.
Cloth. $35.00. 512 pp. .... Vendor G0010

Woulfe, Rev. Patrick. **Irish Names and Surnames.** Sloinnte Gaelheal Is Gall. (1923)
reprint 1993.
Cloth. $40.00. 742 pp. .... Vendor G0010

Woulfe, Rev. Patrick. **Sloinnte Gaedeal is Gall.**
"Irish Names and Surnames," the original, classic dictionary of Irish surnames by
the Rev. Patrick Woulfe (1923) with notes on Gaelic origins. All new IGF index.
Includes Irish names for children.
Quality hardbound & gold stamped. $40.00. .... Vendor G0455

Clare

O'Laughlin, M. **The Families of Co. Clare.** Illus.
Over 1,000 families.
Quality hardbound & gold stamped. $32.00. .... Vendor G0455

White, P. **History of Clare & the Dalcassian Clans of Tipperary, Limerick &
Galway,** with an Ancient & a Modern Map. (1893) reprint 1992.
Contains not only a history of the County of Clare that will be of interest to anyone
with ancestral ties to Clare but also a chapter on Clare in the 1890s, and a map and
appendix that will help the genealogist researching the county.
Cloth. $43.00. 398 pp. .... Vendor G0259

Cork

Masterson, Josephine. **County Cork, Ireland, a Collection of 1851 Census Records.**
(1994) reprint 1996. Indexed.
Paper. $17.50. 117 pp. .... Vendor G0011

Donegal

Duffy, Godfrey F. **A Guide to Tracing Your Donegal Ancestors.** 1996. Indexed.
Illus.
Paper. $18.50. 96 pp. .... Vendor G0619

Dublin

Ryan, James G. **A Guide to Tracing Your Dublin Ancestors.** Indexed. Illus.
Paper. IR£5.95/US$14.20 incl. airmail shipping. 96 pp. .... Vendor G0619

Galway

O'Donovan, John. **Tribes & Customs of Hy Many.**
Quality hardbound & gold stamped. $104.00. .... Vendor G0455

Kerry

O'Connor, Michael H. **A Guide to Tracing Your Kerry Ancestors.** Indexed. Illus.
Paper. IR£6.50/US$15.00 incl. airmail shipping. 96 pp. .... Vendor G0619

O'Laughlin, M. **The Families of Co. Kerry.** Illus.
Quality hardbound & gold stamped. $32.00. 272 pp. .... Vendor G0455

Londonderry

Mitchell, Brian. **County Londonderry—Sources for Family History.**
Paper. £3.00. .... Vendor G0604

Mitchell, Brian. **The Making of Derry—An Economic History.**
Paper. £7.50. .... Vendor G0604

Mitchell, Brian. **The Surnames of Derry.**
Paper. £7.50. .... Vendor G0604

Longford

Leahy, David. **County Longford & Its People: Index to the 1901 Census.** Indexed.
Illus.
Paper. IR£18.50/US$35.00 incl. airmail shipping. 214 pp. .... Vendor G0619

Mayo

O'Donovan, John. **Tribes-Customs of Hy Fiachrach.**
Quality hardbound & gold stamped. $129.00. .... Vendor G0455

Monumental Inscriptions

Co Down Monumental Inscriptions Vol. 19, Lower Iveagh.
£7.50. .... Vendor G0555

Heart of Down Monumental Inscriptions.
£7.50. .... Vendor G0555

Munster

MacCarthy. **Historical Essays on The Kingdom of Munster**.
Quality hardbound & gold stamped. $30.00. 315 pp. .... Vendor G0455

Roscommon

O'Donovan, John. **Tribes & Customs of Hy Many**.
Quality hardbound & gold stamped. $104.00. .... Vendor G0455

Sligo

O'Donovan, John. **Tribes-Customs of Hy Fiachrach**.
Quality hardbound & gold stamped. $129.00. .... Vendor G0455

⚜ Israel ⚜

Sack, Sallyann Amdur, and the Israel Genealogical Society. **A Guide to Jewish Genealogical Resources in Israel: Revised Edition**.
Cloth. $35.00. 256 pp. .... Vendor G0559

⚜ Italy ⚜

Brockman, Terra Castiglia. **A Student's Guide to Italian American Genealogy**. 1996. Indexed. Illus.
Hard-cover. $24.95. 208 pp. .... Vendor G0776

Carmack, Sharon DeBartolo. **Italian-American Family History:** A Guide to Researching and Writing About Your Heritage. 1997.
Paper. $12.95. 139 pp. .... Vendor G0010

Cole, Trafford. **Italian Genealogical Records: How to Use Italian Civil, Ecclesiastical, and Other Records in Family History Research**. 1995.
Hard-cover. $34.95. 265 pp. .... Vendor G0570

Colletta, John Philip. **Finding Italian Roots**. The Complete Guide for Americans. 1993. Rev. ed. 1996. Illus.
Paper. $11.95. 130 pp. .... Vendor G0010

Fucilla, Joseph G. **Our Italian Surnames**. (1949) reprint 1996. Indexed.
Cloth. $28.50. 299 pp. .... Vendor G0010

Pastore, Phyllis, and Floren S. Preece. **Handy Guide to Italian Genealogical Research**.
Paper. $7.00. 30 pp. .... Vendor G0618

John Philip Colletta **FINDING ITALIAN ROOTS**
The Complete Guide for Americans

130 pp., maps, illus.,
paperback. (1993),
corrected edition 1996.
Vendor G0010. $11.95

    In ever increasing numbers, Americans of Italian descent are becoming interested in tracing their families back to the Old Country and visiting their ancestral villages; but few people know where to begin or how to obtain information from Italy. This guide explains it all! It describes the resources available here in the United States for climbing your family tree back to your immigrant ancestor, then shows how you can tap into the wealth of information available in the town halls, archives, churches, and libraries of Italy.
    Whether you choose to conduct your family research by travelling to Italy or by writing to town archives and other repositories of family information, this is the *complete* guide for you.
    Major changes in this edition concern the new civil record repositories and a map of contemporary Italy. Other changes involve the usual updates and corrections expected in a work of this nature.

Genealogical Publishing Co., Inc.

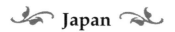 Japan

Family History Library. **Using the Asian MCC Guide: Japan**.
Free. 4 pp. .... Vendor G0629

Yamaguchi, Yoji. **A Student's Guide to Japanese American Genealogy**. 1996. Indexed. Illus.
Hard-cover. $24.95. 208 pp. .... Vendor G0776

 Korea

Family History Library. **Using the Asian MCC Guide: Korea**.
Free. 4 pp. .... Vendor G0629

🌿 Latin America 🌿

Family History Library. **Research Outline: Latin America**.
Leaflet. $.75. 34 pp. .... Vendor G0629

🌿 Lithuania 🌿

Greenbaum, Masha. **The Jews of Lithuania: A History of a Remarkable Community 1316-1945**. Published by Gefen Books. 1996.
Cloth. $29.95. 416 pp. .... Vendor G0559

Levin, Dov, ed. **Pinkas HaKehillot—Lita Encyclopedia of Towns—Lithuania**. 1996.
   Written in Hebrew.
Cloth. $65.00. 768 pp. .... Vendor G0559

Rhode, Harold, and Sallyann Amdur Sack. **Jewish Vital Records, Revision Lists and Other Jewish Holdings in the Lithuanian Archives**. 1996.
Paper. $35.00. .... Vendor G0559

🌿 Mexico 🌿

Konrad, J. **Mexican and Spanish Family Research**.
Paper. $10.00. 70 pp. .... Vendor G0574

Ryskamp, George, and Peggy Ryskamp. **A Student's Guide to Mexican American Genealogy**. 1996. Indexed. Illus.
Hard-cover. $24.95. 208 pp. .... Vendor G0776

Texas State Archives. **Nacagdoches Archives**.
   Selected records of Spanish and Mexican colonial government in East Texas.
Microfilm (35 mm). $17.50/roll. 27 rolls. .... Vendor G0601

Williams, Villamae. **Stephen F. Austin's Register of Families**. (1984) reprint 1996. Indexed.

The Templins of Ohio
Publication date: 1995. Indexed. Illus.
Ronald R. Templin
2256 River Oak Lane SE
Fort Myers, FL 33905   (813) 694-8347

In 1811 Mexico declared its independence from Spain and established itself as a republic. The new government made contracts with Empresarios (contractors) to bring specific numbers of families into the State of Coahuila and Texas. Stephen Austin was the first and most successful of the Empresarios, and he began granting land to settlers in 1824. These records provide information on about 3,000 Anglo-American settlers of Mexican Texas.
Cloth. $20.00. 198 pp. .... Vendor G0011

✄ The Netherlands ✄

Franklin, Charles M. **Dutch Genealogical Research**. Rev. ed.
Paper. $15.00. 128 pp. .... Vendor G0574

Morrison, J. **Scots on the Dijk**. The Scots Church in Rotterdam from Its Beginning in the 17th Century to the Present Day.
Paper. £2.95. .... Vendor G0555

✄ New Zealand ✄

Society of Genealogists. **Genealogical Research in New Zealand**.
Leaflet. £0.20. .... Vendor G0557

✄ Norway ✄

Family History Library. **Research Outline: Norway**.
Leaflet. $.75. 24 pp. .... Vendor G0629

Paddock, Lisa Olson, and Carl Sokolnicki Rollyson. **A Student's Guide to Scandinavian Genealogy**. 1996. Indexed. Illus.
Hard-cover. $24.95. 208 pp. .... Vendor G0776

Thomsen. **Beginner's Guide to Norwegian Genealogical Research**.
Useful to those just beginning their Norwegian research.
Paper. $5.25. 25 pp. .... Vendor G0611

Thomsen. **Danish-Norwegian Genealogical Research Sources**.
Paper. $9.50. 82 pp. .... Vendor G0611

Thomsen. **Danish-Norwegian Language Guide & Dictionary**.
Useful in understanding the language.
Paper. $10.75. 100 pp. .... Vendor G0611

Thomsen. **Genealogical Maps and Guide to the Norwegian Parish Registers.**
An essential book to have on your shelf if you have Norwegian ancestry.
Paper. $9.25. 64 pp. .... Vendor G0611

Thomsen. **Scandinavian Genealogical Research Manual.** 1980.
This volume is a combination of the following books: *Danish/Norwegian Genea-*
logical Research, Danish/Norwegian Language Guide and Dictionary, and *The Old*
Handwriting & Names of Denmark and Norway.
Spiral bound. $19.95. 231 pp. .... Vendor G0611

ᔭᑉ Philippines ᕞᒥ

Family History Library. **Research Outline: Philippines.**
Leaflet. $.75. 24 pp. .... Vendor G0629

ᔭᑉ Poland ᕞᒥ

Beider, Alexander. **A Dictionary of Jewish Surnames from the Kingdom of Po-**
land. 1996.
Cloth. $69.50. 608 pp. .... Vendor G0559

Chorzempa, Rosemary A. **Polish Roots.** (1993, 1994) reprint 1996. Illus.
Paper. $17.95. 262 pp. .... Vendor G0010

Gnacinski, Jan, and Len Gnacinski. **Polish and Proud.** Rev. ed.
Paper. $10.00. 103 pp. .... Vendor G0574

Golembiewski, Thomas E. **The Study of Obituaries as a Source for Polish Genea-**
logical Research. 1984.
Paper. $9.00. 63 pp. .... Vendor G0611

Hoffman, William F. **Polish Surnames: Origins and Meanings.**
Paper. $16.50. 295 pp. .... Vendor G0611

Hollowak, Thomas L., and William F. Hoffman. **Index to the Obituaries and Death**
Notices Appearing in the Dziennik Chicagoski 1890-1899. 1984.
Paper. $11.00. 130 pp. .... Vendor G0611

Hollowak, Thomas L., and William F. Hoffman. **Index to the Obituaries and Death**
Notices Appearing in the Dziennik Chicagoski 1900-1909. 1987.
Paper. $11.00. 443 pp. .... Vendor G0611

Hollowak, Thomas L., and William F. Hoffman. **Index to the Obituaries and Death**
Notices Appearing in the Dziennik Chicagoski 1910-1919. 1988.
Paper. $11.00. 479 pp. .... Vendor G0611

Hollowak, Thomas L., and William F. Hoffman. **Index to the Obituaries and Death Notices Appearing in the Dziennik Chicagoski 1920-1929, Part I & II A-Z.** 2 vols. 1991.
Paper. $22.00. 813 pp. .... Vendor G0611

Konrad, J. **Polish Family Research.**
Paper. $10.00. 72 pp. .... Vendor G0574

Mullerowa, Lidia. **Roman Catholic Parishes in the People's Republic in 1984.** 1995.
Paper. $20.00. 157 pp. .... Vendor G0611

Oshrin, Joyce Schneider. **Koden: A Shtetl No More.**
A Yiskor (Memorial) book about the town of Koden, Lublin, in Poland.
Microfiche. $10.00. 3 fiche. .... Vendor G0732

Rosemary A. Chorzempa

POLISH ROOTS
Korzenie Polskie

262 pp., illus., maps, paperback. 1993.
Vendor G0010. $17.95

The primary focus of this book is on research in Poland, and here the aim is to show the reader what records are available, where they can be found, how to obtain them, and how to make the best use of them. Mrs. Chorzempa first provides an informative essay on Polish history and society, then very carefully describes the ethnic groups and religions of Poland, the country's unique geography and ethnic spread, its political divisions, place names, and topographical features. The bulk of the book, however, shows the reader how to find and use church and civil records; how and where to locate research services, libraries, and archives; how to make sense of Polish names and the naming practices of the major ethnic groups; and how, ultimately, to deal with the Polish language. And in this regard it covers not only Polish—its vocabulary, grammar, and pronunciation—but also German, Russian, Latin, even Ukrainian. Again with the researcher in mind, translations of numbers, dates, and terms and phrases found in vital records figure prominently, and to clinch it there is a letter-writing guide, a transliteration of queries and requests to be sent to Polish churches, civil records offices, and institutions for purposes of obtaining assistance.

G e n e a l o g i c a l   P u b l i s h i n g   C o . ,   I n c .

Peckwas, Edward A. **A Historical Bibliography of Polish Towns, Villages, and Regions (except Warsaw and Krakow)**. 1990.
  Also includes form letters in English and Polish for requesting searches.
  Paper. $10.00. 104 pp. .... Vendor G0611

Rollyson, Carl Sokolnicki, and Lisa Olsen Paddock. **A Student's Guide to Polish American Genealogy**. 1996. Indexed. Illus.
  Hard-cover. $24.95. 208 pp. .... Vendor G0776

Schlyter, Daniel. **Essentials in Polish Genealogical Research**. 1993.
  Paper. $3.00. 12 pp. .... Vendor G0611

✦ Russia ✦

Anuta, Michael J. **East Prussians from Russia,** Bound With Supplement to East Prussians from Russia. (1979) reprint 1994. Indexed. Illus.
  Paper. $26.00. 295 pp. in all. .... Vendor G0011

Beider, Alexander. **A Dictionary of Jewish Surnames from the Russian Empire**.
  Cloth. $75.00. 784 pp. .... Vendor G0559

✦ Spain ✦

Konrad, J. **Mexican and Spanish Family Research**.
  Paper. $10.00. 70 pp. .... Vendor G0574

Texas State Archives. **Nacagdoches Archives**.
  Selected records of Spanish and Mexican colonial government in East Texas.
  Microfilm (35 mm). $17.50/roll. 27 rolls. .... Vendor G0601

✦ Sweden ✦

Benson, Adolph B. **Sweden and the American Revolution**. (1926) reprint 1992. Indexed.
  Paper. $21.00. 228 pp. .... Vendor G0011

Family History Library. **Research Outline: Sweden**.
  Leaflet. $.75. 23 pp. .... Vendor G0629

Paddock, Lisa Olson, and Carl Sokolnicki Rollyson. **A Student's Guide to Scandinavian Genealogy**. 1996. Indexed. Illus.
  Hard-cover. $24.95. 208 pp. .... Vendor G0776

Thomsen. **Beginner's Guide to Swedish Genealogical Research.**
Useful guide for those just starting in Sweden.
Spiral bound. $5.25. 23 pp. .... Vendor G0611

Thomsen. **Genealogical Guidebook & Atlas of Sweden.**
Essential reference for Swedish research.
Paper. $13.95. 115 pp. .... Vendor G0611

✺ Switzerland ✺

Gratz, Delbert L. **Was Isch Dini Nahme? What Is Your Name?** Indexed.
The study of names of Swiss derivation.
Paper. $8.50. 37 pp. .... Vendor G0770

Schelbert, Leo, ed. **America Experienced:** Eighteenth and Nineteenth Century Accounts of Swiss Immigrants to the United States. Translated by Hedwig Rappolt.
1996. Indexed. Illus.
Book #1530.
Cloth. $35.00. 448 pp. .... Vendor G0082

Steinach, Dr. Adelrich, comp. **Swiss Colonists.** 1995. Indexed.
Book #1607.
Cloth. $49.50. 512 pp. .... Vendor G0082

Swiss Surnames. 3 vols. 1995.
Book #1630.
Cloth. $149.50. 768 + 704 + 640 pp. .... Vendor G0082

VonMoos, Mario. **Bibliography of Swiss Genealogies.** 1993. Indexed.
Book #1490.
Cloth. $59.50. 848 pp. .... Vendor G0082

Zuercher, Isaac. **Anabaptist-Mennonite Names in Switzerland.** Translated by Hannes Maria Aleman. 1988.
Paper. $9.50. 35 pp. .... Vendor G0150

✺ West Indies ✺

Carr, Peter E., ed. **Caribbean Historical & Genealogical Journal.** Indexed.
Published quarterly.
$24.00/yr. U.S.; $30.00/yr. outside U.S. Approx. 42 pp. .... Vendor G0496

Grannum, Guy. **Tracing Your West Indian Ancestors.** 1995.
This guide brings together for the first time the wide variety of records available for

the study of British West Indian ancestry in the PRO in order to devleop research into this much neglected field of genealogy.
Paper. £8.95. 112 pp. .... Vendor G0558

Oliver, Vere Langford. **More Monumental Inscriptions: Tombstones of the British West Indies**. (1927) reprint 1989. Indexed. Illus.
Paper. $24.00. viii + 267 pp. .... Vendor G0632

Public Record Office. **Records of the American and West Indian Colonies Before 1782**.
Information leaflet. Contact vendor for information. .... Vendor G0558

Author Index

Abate, Frank R., 110
Aberdeen & North East
Scotland Family History
Society, 55, 247, 259,
260, 261, 262, 266, 267
Aberdeen FHS, 267
Adams, Arthur, 164
Adams, D. G., 268
Adams, James N., 110
Adams, N., 268
Adams, Raymond D., 52
Adams, Richard, 141
Adams, William Forbes,
52, 278
AGLL, 23, 184
Aitken, W., 268, 275
Akeret, Robert U., 164
Albaugh, Gaylord P., 2,
102, 109, 140
Albert, _____, 36
Alberta Genealogical Society, 192
Alcock, N. W., 218, 246
Alessi, Jean, 164
Alexander, _____, 114
Alexander, Susan R., 5
Alexander, William, 268
Allan, Morton, 102
Allen, Desmond Walls,
72, 164, 166
Allen, Marion E., 245
Allison, David, 193
Alvey, Norman, 218
Ames, Stanley R., 19
Anderson, Robert
Charles, 37
Anderson, Rufus, 141
Andrews, William L., 114
Angle, Paul M., 77
Anglo Scottish Family
History Society, 55,
247, 257
Anuta, Michael J., 102,
294

Arellano, Fay Louise
Smith, 141
Arnold, Jackie Smith,
164
Arthur, Julia, 164
Arthur, Stephen, 164
Ashley, Leonard R. N.,
96
Association of Professional Genealogists, 23
Atherton, Louise, 218
Axelson, Edith F., 124

Baca, Leo, 40, 41, 103
Bailey, Paul, 243
Bailey, Rosalie Fellows,
96, 122
Baird, Charles W., 131
Bakeless, _____, 5
Baker, Ruthe, 5
Balderston, Marion, 14
Balhuizen, Anne Ross,
164
Bangerter, Lawrence, 103
Banks, Charles Edward,
42, 72
Bannister, Shala Mills,
165
Barber, Rev. Henry, 96,
213
Barbour, Hugh, 149
Bardsley, Alan, 96, 218
Bardsley, Charles
Wareing, 97, 218, 276
Baring-Gould, Sabine,
97, 214
Barnes, Donald R., 165
Barsi, _____, 60
Bartlett, Henrietta C.,
123, 124
Baselt, Fonda D., 37
Baughman, J. Ross, 122,
125, 157
Baumann, Roland M.,
165

Baxter, Angus, 120, 125,
134, 165, 190, 206,
207, 214, 279
Baxter, R., 268
Bayor, Ronald H., 134
Beach, Mark, 166
Beaman, Alden G., 74
Beard, Alice L., 149
Beard, Timothy F., 159
Beattie, A., 274
Beck, _____, 68
Beckett, J. V., 218
Beers, Henry Putney, 61,
62, 77, 81
Begley, Paul R., 114
Beider, Alexander, 97,
98, 136, 292, 294
Bell, James B., 168
Beller, Susan Provost, 29
Bennett, _____, 141
Benson, Adolph B., 89,
294
Benson, Toni I., 24
Bentley, Elizabeth Petty,
21, 24
Benton, A., 243
Bentz, Edna M., 208
Berent, Irwin, 138
Berlin, Ira, 114
Bernheim, Gotthardt D.,
125, 138
Berry, David, 150
Berry, Ellen, 150
Bethel, Elizabeth, 77
Betit, Kyle J., 285
Beverly, S., 268
Beverly, W., 268
Bible, Jean P., 139
Bicha, _____, 121
Bigwood, R., 247
Billingsley, Carolyn
Earle, 164, 166
Bing, C., 268
Black, G. F., 98

298

Author Index

Title Index

Famine Immigrants, The, 52, 105
Far From Home: Families of the West-
ward Journey, 186
Fermfolk & Fisherfolk. Rural Life in
North of Scotland in 18th & 19th
Century, 270
Fetterangus Monumental Inscriptions, 260
Fiche Index to Alberta Cemetery
Records & Other Sources, 192
Fife Convicts. Transportees 1752-1867,
256
Fife Emigrants & Their Ships. Part 1:
Aust. & N.Z, 56, 256
Finding an International Genealogical
Index Source Resource Guide, 26
Finding Italian Roots, 135, 288
Finding Our Fathers, 138
Finding Your German Ancestors, 210
Finding Your Hispanic Roots, 130
Finding Your Roots, 184
Finding Your Viking, 205
First Alfred Seventh Day Baptist
Church Membership Records, Alfred,
NY, 120
First American Jewish Families, 138
First Guide to Civil War Genealogy and
Research, 82
First Name Variants, 96, 218
First Steps in Family History, 166, 219
First Visit to the Census Rooms?, 230
First Visit to Use the Statutory Records
of BMDs New Register House,
Edinburgh, 253
Firth & Stenness, Orkney 1851 Census,
274
Five Civilized Tribes, The: Cherokee,
Chickasaw, Choctaw, Creek and
Seminole, 143
Floyd Co. Georgia Confederates—Vol.
VIII, 80
Following the Paper Trail: A Multilin-
gual Translation Guide, 182, 207
Footdee, 272
For Better, For Worse: British Mar-
riages, 1600 to the Present, 224
Forests & Clearings: History of
Stanstead Co., Prov. of Quebec, 203
Forglen Monumental Inscriptions, 260
Forgot & Gone: Further Accidents &
Disasters in Scotland 1855-99, 247
Forming a One-Name Group, 99, 228
Fortrose Abbey Monumental Inscrip-
tions, 263

Forty Years Among the Indians, 143
Forward to the Past, 167
Founders and Patriots of America Index,
64
Franklin County, Ohio Scotch-Irish
Nova Scotia Acadians Refugee Tract
History, 155, 193
Fraserburgh Means Fish, 273
Free African Americans of North Caro-
lina and Virginia, 116
Free St. Clements Aberdeen 1843-59, 268
French and British Land Grants in the
Post Vincennes (Indiana) District,
1750-1784, 60
French and French-Canadian Family
Research, 124, 192, 207
French Blood in America, The, 132
French Letter-Writing Guide, 207
Friendly Virginians, The, 153
Friends of Illiana, 1826, 152
From Aberdeen to Ottawa in 1845: The
Diary of Alexander Muir, 270
From Bremen to America in 1850:
Fourteen Rare Emigrant Ship Lists,
49, 106
From Brig'o Balgownie to the Bullers
o'Buchan—A Travel Guide from the
1890s, 269
From Chantry to Oxfam: A Short His-
tory of Charities and Charity Legis-
lation, 218
From Generation to Generation: How to
Trace Your Jewish Genealogy and
Family History, 137
From Ireland to North America, 53, 282
From Lairds to Loons: Country and
Burgh Life in Aberdeen 1600-1800,
273
From Memories to Manuscript: The
Five-Step Method of Writing Your
Life Story, 178
From Slavery to Uncertain Freedom:
The Freedmen's Bureau in Arkansas,
1865-1869, 115
Further Undertakings of A Dead Rela-
tive Collector, 37
Fyvie Monumental Inscriptions, 260

Gabriel's Rebellion: The Virginia Slave
Conspiracies of 1800-1802, 115
Gazetteer (1824) of the State of New
York, 71, 113

Index to Advertisers